The *Revels*
History of Drama
in English

GENERAL EDITOR
Lois Potter

The *Revels* History of Drama in English

VOLUME IV 1613–1660
Philip Edwards,
Gerald Eades Bentley,
Kathleen McLuskie
& Lois Potter

Methuen
London and New York

First published in 1981 by
Methuen & Co. Ltd
11 New Fetter Lane, London EC4P 4EE
Published in the USA by
Methuen & Co.
in association with Methuen, Inc.
733 Third Avenue, New York, NY 10017

© *1981 Philip Edwards, Gerald Eades Bentley,*
Kathleen McLuskie, Lois Potter

Photoset by Servis Filmsetting Ltd, Manchester
Printed in Great Britain by
Fletcher & Son Ltd, Norwich

British Library Cataloguing in Publication Data

The Revels history of drama in English
   Vol. 4: 1613–1660
     1. English drama – History and criticism
     2. Theater – England – History
     I. Edwards, Philip
   822'.009   PR625

ISBN 0-416-13050-X

Contents

vi Contents

List of illustrations

Acknowledgements

The authors and publishers would like to thank the following for permission to reproduce the illustrations appearing in this book:

The Bibliography Society, Bodleian Library for Nos 26 and 27
The British Library for Nos 1, 7, 8, 28, 29 and 30
The Trustees of the Chatsworth Settlement and the Courtauld Institute of Art for Nos 3, 12, 13, 14, 15, 17, 18, 19, 21, 22, 23, 24 and the endpapers
The Governors of Dulwich Picture Gallery for Nos 6, 9 and 10
Emmanuel College Library, Cambridge for No. 11
The Folger Shakespeare Library for No. 2
Lord Harlech, Brogyntyn Library for No. 4
Her Gracious Majesty the Queen for No. 20
Malone Society Editions for No. 5
National Portrait Gallery for No. 25

Preface

This volume of the Revels History deals with English drama between Shakespeare's retirement from the stage and the reopening of the theatres under Charles II. Dryden, writing at the·end of the century, looked back to the pre-war dramatists as 'the Giant Race before the Flood'. To most modern readers, however, his comment on the Restoration – 'what we gained in skill we lost in strength' – is already true of the later Jacobean and Caroline period. It is easy to see it as one of moral and political, as well as theatrical, decline. Shakespeare's retirement, for example, coincided with the Essex divorce and Overbury murder, events which formed part of the process by which James I and his son lost their hold on popular affection. The new 'refinement' on which some writers prided themselves likewise represents a deliberate rejection of what was 'popular'. The contributors to this volume, though inevitably concerned with the intertwining of political and theatrical history, have tried to respond to the 'skill' of the playwrights who dominated the period, as well as to those who are more congenial to modern taste because they retain some of the earlier 'strength'.

The volume follows the same format as its predecessors, except where it has tried to avoid overlapping with Volume III (thus there is no section on the architecture of the playhouses, though some of the illustrations supplement those of the earlier volume). All the contributors have been very helpful in their suggestions for the chronological table and illustrations; the constant occurrence of Professor Bentley's name in the footnotes of all four contributors is a further indication of how much this volume owes to him. I should like to thank him and Professor Edwards for their patience during the long delay in publication of their part of this volume, which was due to the withdrawal of both the first and the second contributor commissioned to write the critical survey. It was on the recommendation of Professor R. A. Foakes of the University of Kent that I asked Dr Kathleen McLuskie to take on the enormous task of writing the greater part of this section: I am grateful to him for the suggestion, and to her for the energy and perseverance with which she has carried out the work. She has also supplied the bibliography on the theatres and actors; other sections of the bibliography are the work of the respective contributors.

My own editorial task has been made easier by the example of my predecessor, Professor T. W. Craik of Durham University, who seemed to me a model of what a general editor should be. I should also like to thank Professor W. P. Williams of Northern Illinois University for generously sharing with me his information about the Castle Ashby manuscripts and for commenting on some of my work at an earlier stage. Professor A. R. Braunmuller of the University of California at Los Angeles and Dr Richard Proudfoot of King's College, London, have also given helpful advice, and I have benefited from the expertise of the staffs of the Department of Manuscripts in the British Library and the Huntington Library, San Marino, California. In preparing the chronological table, I have drawn on Mr David Jeffreys of the University of Leicester for information about German drama of the period, and I am grateful to Dr John Pitcher, of St John's College, Oxford, for some corrections to the historical column. My greatest debt for advice and encouragement is to the late Ian Hilson, a colleague whose loss is irreparable.

Mrs Pat Taylor did a good deal of typing for me at a crucial stage, and it would be invidious not to mention also the other English department typists – Sylvia Garfield, Anne Sowter and Brenda Tracy – whose cheerfulness and cooperation was invaluable during the final weeks of preparing the typescript for the press.

Chronological table

This table draws freely on Douglas Bush's *English Literature in the Earlier Seventeenth Century* (Oxford, 1945), on Samuel Schoenbaum's revision of Alfred Harbage's *Annals of English Drama 975–1700* (London, 1964), and on the 'Annals of Jacobean and Caroline Theatrical Affairs' in G. E. Bentley's *Jacobean and Caroline Stage*, vol. VII (Oxford, 1968). For plays, the Harbage–Schoenbaum date is given, except where it has been decisively contradicted by more recent research.

Non-dramatic writings are listed under date of publication unless otherwise indicated, and plays under date of first performance (or, in the case of plays not performed, the date of composition). After 1642, dates of plays are those of composition unless otherwise stated.

A question mark before an entry indicates a doubt about the date; a question mark after an author's name indicates a doubt about the authorship.

Date	Historical events	Theatrical events	Non-dramatic literary events
1610	Petition of Right; plantation of Ulster; assassination of Henry IV; Hudson Bay discovered; Arminian views propounded in Holland by Olden Barneveldt and Grotius; Prince Henry created Prince of Wales		Donne, *Pseudo-Martyr*; Jourdain, *Discovery of the Bermudas*; Strachey, *True Reportory of the Wreck upon the Bermudas*; Honoré d'Urfé, *L'Astrée*, published (in five vols) between 1610 and 1627
1611	Abbot Archbishop of Canterbury; Carr made Viscount Rochester; sale of baronetcies		Byrd, *Psalms, Songs and Sonnets*; Coryate, *Coryate's Crudities*; Cotgrave, *Dictionary of the French and English Tongues*; Donne, *Anatomy of the World* and *Ignatius His Conclave*; King James (Authorized) version of Bible; first Folio of Spenser's works

Birth and death dates of non-dramatic writers	Dates of notable plays	Birth and death dates of playwrights	Continental theatrical events
(?) Falkland b.	Beaumont and Fletcher, *Philaster*; Fletcher (with Beaumont), *The Coxcomb*; Fletcher (?), Middleton (?), Rowley (?), *Wit at Several Weapons*; Field, *A Woman is a Weathercock*; Heywood and Rowley, *Fortune by Land and Sea*; Jonson, *Epicoene*; *The Masque of Queens*; Shakespeare, *Cymbeline*; Tourneur, *The Atheist's Tragedy*	Glapthorne b.	Hieronymo Giacobbi's opera *Andromeda* performed in Bologna; Paul Scarron b.; *Tisbe*, first Swedish comedy, acted in Arboga; English actors in Germany, Flanders and Holland throughout the period
Giles Fletcher, Sr, d. R. Mulcaster d.	Beaumont and Fletcher, *A King and No King*; Cooke, *Greene's Tu Quoque*; Dekker, *Match Me in London*; Dekker (with Daborne), *If It Be Not Good, The Devil is in It*; Field, *Amends for Ladies*; Fletcher, *The Night Walker*; *The Woman's Prize*; Heywood, *The Brazen Age*; *The Silver Age*; Jonson, *Catiline*; *Love Freed from Ignorance and Folly*; *Oberon*; Middleton, *A Chaste Maid in Cheapside*; Shakespeare, *The Tempest*; anon. (Middleton ?), *The Second Maiden's Tragedy*	Cartwright b.	Flaminio Scala's *Il Teatro delle favore*, containing forty-eight *commedia dell'arte* scenarios, published; Messenius' *Disa*, Sweden's first national history play, acted in Uppsala; first English translations of Sebastiano Serlio's *Second Book of Architecture* (1545); Jean de la Taille d.

Date	Historical events	Theatrical events	Non-dramatic literary events
1612	Prince Henry d.; Robert Cecil, Earl of Salisbury, d.; Lancashire witches hanged; first Baptist church established in England; last burning of heretics in England	T. Heywood, *Apology for Actors*	Bacon, *Essays* (enlarged); (?) Chapman (trans.), Homer's *Iliad*, I–XXIV; Donne, *Second Anniversary*; Drayton, *Polyolbion*, I–XVIII; Gibbons, *First Set of Madrigals and Motets*; Shelton (trans.), Cervantes' *Don Quixote*
1613	Princess Elizabeth marries the Elector Palatine; Coke Chief Justice of King's Bench; the Essex divorce: the Countess marries Robert Carr, now Earl of Somerset; death of Sir Thomas Overbury; Sarmiento (later Gondomar) Spanish ambassador; civil unrest in Russia (1605–13) ends with flight of Polish occupying forces and coronation of first Romanov Tsar	Amalgamation of Children of the Revels and the Lady Elizabeth's Men; the Globe burned	Browne, *Britannia's Pastorals*, I; (?) Campion, *Two Books of Airs*; Purchas, *Purchas His Pilgrimage*; Wither, *Abuses Stript and Whipt*; many elegies (in this and the following year) on Prince Henry

Birth and death dates of non-dramatic writers	Dates of notable plays	Birth and death dates of playwrights	Continental theatrical events
S. Butler b. (?) Crashaw b. Harington d.	Dekker, *Troia Nova Triumphans*; Fletcher (and Beaumont ?), *The Captain*; Fletcher (with Beaumont or Field ?), *Four Plays in One*; Heywood, *The Iron Age*, I and II; Jonson, *Love Restored*; Webster, *The White Devil*	T. Killigrew b.	Lope de Vega, *Los Pastores de Belen*
Sir Thomas Bodley d. J. Cleveland b. Constable d. Jeremy Taylor b.	Beaumont, *Masque of the Inner Temple and Gray's Inn*; Beaumont and Fletcher, *The Scornful Lady*; Campion, *The Lords' Masque*; Chapman, *Masque of the Middle Temple and Lincoln's Inn*; Fletcher, *Bonduca*; Fletcher (with others ?), *The Honest Man's Fortune*; Jonson, *A Challenge at Tilt*; *The Irish Masque*; Middleton, *No Wit, No Help, Like a Woman's*; Shakespeare (and Fletcher ?), *Henry VIII*; Shakespeare and Fletcher, *Cardenio* [lost]; *The Two Noble Kinsmen*: Tailor, *The Hog Hath Lost His Pearl*	H. Killigrew b.	Lope de Vega, *Fuente Ovejuna*

Date	Historical events	Theatrical events	Non-dramatic literary events
1614	'Addled' Parliament	The Hope built; the second Globe built	Bacon, *Charge Touching Duels*; Chapman (trans.), Homer's *Odyssey*, I–XII; Lodge (trans.), *Works of Seneca both Moral and Natural* (enlarg. 1620); Overbury, *Characters* (enlarg. 1614, 1615, 1616, etc., to 1638); Ralegh, *History of the World*
1615	Trial of Earl and Countess of Somerset for the murder of Overbury	(?) Cockpit theatre built	Breton, *Characters upon Essays Moral and Divine*; Chapman (trans.), Homer's *Odyssey* complete; Camden, *Annals*, I
1616	Ralegh's expedition to Guiana; Harvey's lectures on circulation of the blood; first Congregational Church founded in England	Jonson's *Works* published in Folio; he receives a life pension from the King; investiture of Prince Charles: masques, tilts, etc.	Browne, *Britannia's Pastorals*, II; Chapman (trans.), *Whole Works of Homer*; Drummond, *Poems*; James I, *Works*
1617	James's journey to Scotland; Louis XIII orders assassination of Concini, the favourite of Marie de Medici	Shrove Tuesday rioters damage Phoenix theatre	

Birth and death dates of non-dramatic writers	Dates of notable plays	Birth and death dates of playwrights	Continental theatrical events
H. More b.	Daniel, *Hymen's Triumph*; Fletcher, *Valentinian*; *Wit Without Money*; Jonson, *Bartholomew Fair*; Webster, *The Duchess of Malfi*		Cervantes, *Viaje del Parnaso*
R. Baxter b. J. Denham b. (?) J. Lilburne b.	Fletcher, *Monsieur Thomas*; Jonson, *The Golden Age Restored*; Middleton, *More Dissemblers Besides Women*; *The Witch*; Ruggle, *Ignoramus*; Tomkis, *Albumazar*; Webster, *The Guise* [lost]	R. Armin d.	
R. Hakluyt d.	Fletcher (with Beaumont ?), *Love's Pilgrimage*; (revised Middleton?), *The Nice Valour*; Jonson, *Christmas His Mask*; *The Devil is an Ass*; *Mercury Vindicated from the Alchemists at Court*; Middleton, *The Widow*	Beaumont d. Shakespeare d.	Cervantes d.; Andreas Gryphius b.; English actors in Poland and Moravia
T. Coryate d.	Daborne, *The Poor Man's Comfort*; Fletcher, *The Mad Lover*; (with Massinger? Field?), *The Queen of Corinth*; with Massinger (and Beaumont ?), *Thierry and Theodoret*; Jonson, *Lovers Made Men*; *The Vision of Delight*; Middleton and Rowley, *A Fair Quarrel*; Webster, *The Devil's Law Case*		Lope de Vega, *Comedias*, pt 1, pub.

Date	Historical events	Theatrical events	Non-dramatic literary events
1618	Execution of Ralegh; 'defenestration' of Prague; beginning of Thirty Years' War; Synod of Dort condemns Arminianism, and leading Dutch Arminians are arrested	Jonson's journey to Scotland and conversations with Drummond of Hawthornden; Lord Mayor's Show – Ralegh's execution deliberately arranged for same date (29 Oct.)	Breton, *The Court and the Country*; Chapman (trans.), Hesiod's *Georgics*; Stow, *Summary of English Chronicles* (final ed. of work begun in 1565)
1619	Death of Queen Anne; execution of Olden Barneveldt	Inigo Jones begins work on Banqueting House (completed 1622)	Jaggard's 'False Folio' (quartos of some Shakespeare plays); Purchas, *Purchas His Pilgrim*; *Microcosmus*; Sir A. Gorges, *Wisdom of the Ancients* (trans. of Bacon); Henry Lyle, *Decimall Arithmeticke*; Kepler, *Harmonice Mundi* and *De Cometis*

Birth and death dates of non-dramatic writers	*Dates of notable plays*	*Birth and death dates of playwrights*	*Continental theatrical events*
Davies of Hereford d. R. Lovelace b. J. Sylvester d.	Fletcher, *The Loyal Subject*; Jonson, *Pleasure Reconciled to Virtue* (rewritten and performed as *For the Honour of Wales*); Middleton, *Hengist, King of Kent, or The Mayor of Queenborough*; Middleton, Rowley and Massinger, *The Old Law*; H. Shirley (and T. Heywood?), *The Martyred Soldier*; anon., *Swetnam the Woman-Hater*	A. Cowley b.	Jakob Ayrer (1543–1605), *Opus Thaeatricum*, pub. (sixty-six plays, including many imitated from the repertoire of English actors in Germany); (?) Giacobbi's *Andromeda* performed in Salzburg: first opera produced outside Italy
S. Daniel d.	Field and Massinger, *The Fatal Dowry*; Fletcher, *The Humorous Lieutenant*; (with Massinger?, Jonson?, anon.?), *The Bloody Brother*; (with Massinger), *The Little French Lawyer* and *Sir John van Olden Barnavelt*; Ford, *The Laws of Candy*; Goffe (?), *The Careless Shepherdess*; Middleton, *The Inner-Temple Mask*; *The Triumphs of Love and Antiquity*; Rowley, *All's Lost by Lust*	(?) (or 1620) N. Field d.	

Date	Historical events	Theatrical events	Non-dramatic literary events
1620	Spanish invasion of the Palatinate; strong pro-war feeling in England; the Pilgrim Fathers found New Plymouth, Massachusetts		First complete trans. of Boccaccio's *Decameron*; Bacon, *Instauratio Magna*; *Horae Subsecivae*; Dekker, *Dekker His Dreame*; Quarles, *Feast for Worms*; Rowlands, *The Night Raven*; Sylvester, *Sacred Works* (in one vol.); Shelton (trans.), *Don Quixote*, II
1621	Parliament attacks patents and monopolies; Bacon convicted of taking bribes; hostility between King and Commons; Dutch war with Spain resumed	Fortune theatre burnt down	Burton, first ed. of *Anatomy of Melancholy*; Culpeper, *Tract Against Usury*; Hall, *Works*

Birth and death dates of non-dramatic writers	Dates of notable plays	Birth and death dates of playwrights	Continental theatrical events
T. Campion d. J. Evelyn b.	Dekker and Massinger, *The Virgin Martyr*; Fletcher, *Women Pleased*; (with Massinger), *The Custom of the Country*; *The Double Marriage*; *The False One*; Jonson, *The Entertainment at Blackfriars*; *News from the New World*; *Pan's Anniversary*; T. May, *The Heir*; Middleton, *The World Tossed at Tennis*	T. Jordan b.	*Englische Comödien und Tragödien* published in Germany (This book and its sequel (see 1630) contained eighteen dramas and some comic interludes)
A. Marvell b.	Dekker, Ford, Rowley, *The Witch of Edmonton*; Fletcher, *The Island Princess*; *The Pilgrim*; *The Wild Goose Chase*; Jonson, *The Gypsies Metamorphosed*; Massinger, *The Duke of Milan*; *The Maid of Honour*; *The Woman's Plot* [lost]; Middleton (and Webster?), *Anything for a Quiet Life*; *Honourable Entertainments* (ten short pieces); *Women Beware Women*; *The Sun in Aries*	R. Boyle b.	Guillen de Castro, *Comedias*, I; Lope de Vega, *Filomena*

Date	Historical events	Theatrical events	Non-dramatic literary events
1622			Weekly news-pamphlets ('The Corantos') begin; Bacon, *History of The Reign of Henry VII*; *Historia Naturalis*; Drayton, *Polyolbion*, II; Sir R. Hawkins, *Observations in His Voyage into the South Sea*; Peacham, *The Complete Gentleman*; Mabbe, *The Rogue*; Wither, *Juvenilia*
1623	Massacre at Amboyna; visit to Spain of Prince Charles and the Duke of Buckingham (they returned in Oct.)	Opening of new Fortune theatre	Daniel, *Whole Works*; Drummond, *Flowers of Sion*; Feltham, *Resolves*; Bacon, *De Augmentis Scientiarum*; Wither, *Hymns and Songs of the Church*; the Shakespeare First Folio

Birth and death dates of non-dramatic writers	Dates of notable plays	Birth and death dates of playwrights	Continental theatrical events
	Chapman, *Chabot, Admiral of France*; Fletcher (with Massinger?), *Beggar's Bush*; *The Prophetess*; *The Sea-Voyage*; *The Spanish Curate*; Jonson, *The Masque of Augurs*; G. Markham and W. Sampson, *Herod and Antipater*; Middleton, *The Triumphs of Honour and Virtue*; (with W. Rowley), *The Changeling*; W. Rowley (with Middleton?), *A Match at Midnight*	W. Gager d.	Molière b.
William Camden d. Giles Fletcher, Jr, d.	Dekker (and Ford?), *The Welsh Ambassador*; Fletcher (and Massinger?), *The Wandering Lovers*; Fletcher and Rowley, *The Maid in the Mill*; Jonson, *Time Vindicated*; Massinger, *The Bondman*; *The Parliament of Love*; Middleton, *The Triumphs of Integrity*; Middleton and Rowley, *The Spanish Gypsy*	(?) Duchess of Newcastle b.	

Date	Historical events	Theatrical events	Non-dramatic literary events
1624	War with Spain; Richelieu becomes First Minister of France	Performances of *A Game at Chess* at the Globe: author and actors called before Privy Council (Aug.)	Donne, *Devotions upon Emergent Occasions*; Quarles, *Sion's Elegies*; Capt. John Smith, *General History of Virginia*; Wotton, *Elements of Architecture*; Lord Herbert of Cherbury, *De Veritate* (published in Paris)
1625	Accession of Charles I and marriage to Henrietta Maria of France; plague in London	London theatres close at death of King James (27 Mar.) and probably remain closed because of plague until Nov./Dec.	Bacon, *Essays* (final form); Dekker, *A Rod for Runaways*; Purchas, *Purchas His Pilgrims*; *Mercurius Britannicus* (first English newspaper)

Birth and death dates of non-dramatic writers	Dates of notable plays	Birth and death dates of playwrights	Continental theatrical events
George Fox b.	Davenport, *The City Nightcap*; Dekker and Ford, *The Sun's Darling*; Fletcher, *Rule a Wife and Have a Wife*; *A Wife for a Month*; Heywood, *The Captives*; Jonson, *The Masque of Owls*; *Neptune's Triumph*; Massinger, *The Renegado*; *The Unnatural Combat*; Middleton, *A Game at Chess*; Webster, *Monuments of Honour*; *Appius and Virginia*; anon., *The Tragedy of Nero*	(?) W. Rowley d.	Alexandre Hardy, *Théâtre* (completed 1628); Tirso de Molina, *El Burlador de Sevilla*; Monteverdi, *Il Combattimento di Tancredi e Clorinda*; Martin Opitz, *Das Buch von der deutschen Poeterey*
	Davenport, *A New Trick to Cheat the Devil*; Fletcher, *The Chances*; *The Elder Brother* (revised Massinger?); Heywood, *The English Traveller*; Jonson, *The Fortunate Isles*; Massinger (revision of Beaumont and Fletcher?), *Love's Cure*; *A New Way to Pay Old Debts*; Rowley, *A New Wonder, a Woman Never Vexed*; Shirley, *Love's Tricks, or The School of Compliment*; Webster, Rowley (and Heywood?), *A Cure for a Cuckold*	Fletcher d. Lodge d.	First *opera ballo*: *La Liberazione di Ruggiero* by Francesca Caccini

Date	Historical events	Theatrical events	Non-dramatic literary events
1626	Opposition between King and Commons over the Forced Loan	Queen Henrietta Maria and her ladies perform in a French play at Somerset House; riot at Fortune theatre	Breton, *Fantasticks*; Donne, *Five Sermons*; J. Hall, *Contemplations*; W. Roper, *Life of Sir Thomas More* first published; Sandys (trans.), Ovid's *Metamorphoses*
1627	Siege of La Rochelle, 1627–8; Buckingham sends unsuccessful expedition to the Isle of Rhé.		Bacon, *Sylva Sylvarum*; Camden, *Annals*, II; Drayton, *Battle of Agincourt* and other poems; Phineas Fletcher, *Locustae*; T. May (trans.), Lucan's *Pharsalia*
1628	Petition of Right; murder of the Duke of Buckingham; La Rochelle expedition	Jonson appointed Chronologer to the City of London	Coke's *Institutes*, I; Earle, *Microcosmography* (enlarged 1629, 1629, 1633, 1638); Felltham, *Resolves* (complete ed.); Harvey, *Exercitio Anatomica de Motu Cordis et Sanguinis in Animalibus*; Wither, *Britain's Remembrance*
1629	Charles I dissolves his third Parliament and attempts to rule without one for the next eleven years; imprisonment of Sir John Eliot and other rebellious MPs; Rubens in England, 1629–30	Salisbury Court Playhouse opened; first public appearance of actresses in England (a visiting French troupe at Blackfriars) received with hostility; French company also performs at Red Bull and Fortune	Thomas Adams, *Sermons*; Launcelot Andrewes, *XCVI Sermons*; Hobbes (trans.), Thucydides, *Peloponnesian War*
1630	Role of French Parlements curtailed by Richelieu; death of Gustavus Adolphus at Lützen; Charles II born	Plague: theatres closed for seven months; Cockpit-in-Court opened	R. Braithwait, *The English Gentleman*; Drayton, *Muses Elizium*; John Taylor, *Works*

Birth and death dates of non-dramatic writers	*Dates of notable plays*	*Birth and death dates of playwrights*	*Continental theatrical events*
Bacon d. Sir John Davies d. Samuel Purchas d. (?) Nicholas Breton d. J. Aubrey b.	Fletcher (and others?), *The Noble Gentleman*; *The Fair Maid of the Inn*; Hemming, *The Jew's Tragedy*; Jonson, *The Staple of News*; Massinger, *The Roman Actor*; Shirley, *The Maid's Revenge*; *The Wedding*	Sir Robert Howard b. Tourneur d.	
Dorothy Osborne b.	Davenant, *The Cruel Brother*; Massinger, *The Great Duke of Florence*	Middleton d. J. Wilson b.	H. Schütz, *Daphne*, first German opera, performed at Torgau; Tirso de Molina, *Comedias*, published
Bunyan b. Sir William Temple b.	Davenant, *Albovine*; Ford, *The Lover's Melancholy*; Ford (?), *The Queen*; Shirley, *The Witty Fair One*	Fulke Greville d.	
	R. Brome, *The Northern Lass*; Davenant, *The Just Italian*; Ford, *The Broken Heart*; Jonson, *The New Inn*; Massinger, *The Picture*; Randolph, *The Drinking Academy*; Shirley, *The Grateful Servant*		Corneille's first play, *Mélite*, acted; Calderón, *El Principe Constante*
Isaac Barrow b. John Tillotson b. Charles Cotton b. Edward Phillips b. Gabriel Harvey d.	R. Brome, *The City Wit*; Randolph, *The Muses' Looking Glass*; *Amyntas*; A. Wilson, *The Inconstant Lady*		*Liebeskampff oder ander Theil der englischer Comödien und Tragödien* pub. (see 1620)

Date	Historical events	Theatrical events	Non-dramatic literary events
1631		Theatres probably closed because of plague in early part of the year	Braithwaite, *The English Gentlewoman*; Heywood, *England's Elizabeth*; James Mabbe, *The Spanish Bawd* (trans. of *La Celestina* by de Rojas); Stow's *Annals* (final ed.)
1632			Donne, *Death's Duel*; Quarles, *Divine Fancies*; Ralegh, *Instructions to His Son*; Reynolds, *Mythomystes*; Second Folio of Shakespeare; Galileo, *Dialogo sopra i due Massimi Sistemi*

Birth and death dates of non-dramatic writers	Dates of notable plays	Birth and death dates of playwrights	Continental theatrical events
Katherine Phillips ('the Matchless Orinda') b. Drayton d.	R. Brome, *The Queen's Exchange*; Davenport, *King John and Matilda*; Dekker (and Day?), *The Wonder of a Kingdom*; Heywood, *The Fair Maid of the West*, II; Jonson, *Chloridia*; *Love's Triumph through Callipolis*; Marmion, *Holland's Leaguer*; Massinger, *Believe as You List*; *The Emperor of the East*; Shirley, *The Humorous Courtier*; *Love's Cruelty*; *The Traitor*; A. Wilson, *The Swisser*	Dryden b.	
Locke b.	R. Brome, *The Novella*; *The Weeding of the Covent Garden*; Ford, *Love's Sacrifice*; *'Tis Pity She's a Whore*; Jonson, *The Magnetic Lady*; Massinger, *The City Madam*; Randolph, *The Jealous Lovers*; Shirley, *The Ball*; *Changes*; *Hyde Park*	Dekker d.	Calderón, *La Vida es Sueño* (completed 1635)

Date	Historical events	Theatrical events	Non-dramatic literary events
1633	Laud becomes Archbishop of Canterbury	Queen performs in *The Shepherd's Paradise* at Somerset House (Jan.)	Cowley, *Poetical Blossoms*; Donne, *Poems*; *Juvenilia, or Paradoxes and Problems*; Phineas Fletcher, *The Purple Island*; Greville, *Works*; Herbert, *The Temple*; Prynne, *Histrio-Mastix*; Quarles, *Divine Poems*
1634	Death of Wallenstein	Spanish actors perform at court (and in 1635); Prynne pilloried for *Histrio-Mastix* and imprisoned until 1637	Habington, *Castara*

Birth and death dates of non-dramatic writers	Dates of notable plays	Birth and death dates of playwrights	Continental theatrical events
G. Savile, Marquis of Halifax, b. S. Pepys b. G. Herbert d.	Cokain, *Trappolin Supposed a Prince*; Cowley, *Love's Riddle*; Drummond, *Entertainment at Edinburgh*; Ford (and Dekker?), *Perkin Warbeck*; Heywood, *A Maidenhead Well Lost*; Jonson, *The King's Entertainment at Welbeck*; *The Tale of a Tub* (revised version?); Marmion, *A Fine Companion*; Massinger, *The Guardian*; Milton, *Arcades*; Montague, *The Shepherd's Paradise*; Nabbes, *Covent Garden*; Shirley, *The Bird in a Cage*; *The Gamester*; *The Young Admiral*; Wilson, *The Corporal*		
Robert South b.	Brome, *The Late Lancashire Witches*; Carew, *Coelum Britannicum*; Davenant, *Love and Honour*; *The Wits*; Glapthorne, *Albertus Wallenstein*; Heywood, *Love's Mistress*; Jonson, *Love's Welcome at Bolsover*; Lovelace, *The Scholars* [lost]; Massinger, *A Very Woman*; Milton, *Comus*; Nabbes, *Tottenham Court*; Rutter, *The Shepherds' Holiday*; Shirley, *The Example*; *The Opportunity*; *The Triumph of Peace*	Chapman d. Etherege b. Marston d. Tomkis d. (?) J. Webster d. (or 1638)	First Oberammergau Passion Play acted

Date	Historical events	Theatrical events	Non-dramatic literary events
1635	Diplomatic relations established between Britain and the Vatican	French actors in London	Heywood, *Hierarchie of Blessed Angels*; Quarles, *Emblems*; Swan, *Speculum Mundi*; Wither, *Collection of Emblems*
1636	Charles I and Laud visit Oxford	Plague closes theatres from 12 May 1636 to 2 Oct. 1637, apart from a brief re-opening in Feb. 1637; many plays performed before the King in Oxford (Aug.–Sept.)	Hoylyn, *History of the Sabbath*; Sandys, *Paraphrase upon Psalms of David*; Prynne, *News from Ipswich*; Wither, *Nature of Man*

Birth and death dates of non-dramatic writers	Dates of notable plays	Birth and death dates of playwrights	Continental theatrical events
R. Stillingfleet b. T. Sprat b.	Bristowe, *King Free-Will* (trans. of Bassano); Brome, *The New Academy*; *Queen and Concubine*; *The Sparagus Garden*; Cartwright, *The Ordinary*; Davenant, *News from Plymouth*; *The Platonic Lovers*; *The Temple of Love*; K. Digby (trans.), Tasso's *Aminta*, and Guarini's *Pastor Fido* (both closet); Glapthorne, *The Lady Mother*; (Henrietta Maria?), *Florimène*; Heywood, *A Challenge for Beauty*; Jordan, *Money is an Ass*; T. Killigrew, *The Conspiracy*; *The Prisoners*; Marmion, *The Antiquary*; Shirley, *The Coronation*; *The Lady of Pleasure*	T. Randolph d.	Lope de Vega d.; Lohenstein b.; Académie Française founded; Calderón, *El Médico de su Honra*; final version of *La Vida es Sueño*; Corneille, *Médée*; Tirso, *Don Gil*; Vondel, *Josef*
J. Glanvill b.	Cartwright, *The Royal Slave*; Davenant, *The Prince d'Amour*; Glapthorne, *The Hollander*; T. Killigrew, *Claracilla*; *The Princess*; Massinger, *The Bashful Lover*; May, *The Old Couple*; Shirley, *The Duke's Mistress*; Strode, *The Floating Island*; Townshend, *Pastoral Mask*	T. Porter b.	Corneille, *L'Illusion Comique*, *Le Cid* (and subsequent critical controversy)

Date	Historical events	Theatrical events	Non-dramatic literary events
1637	Ship-money controversy; Charles I orders Scots to accept the English Prayer Book		Alexander, *Recreations with the Muses*; Heywood, *Pleasant Dialogues and Dramas*; Hobbes, *Art of Rhetoric* (trans. of Aristotle) Milton, *Comus* (published)
1638	Star Chamber ruling that 'Rex is lex'; Solemn League and Covenant	New Masking House at Whitehall	*Obsequies to the Memorie of Edward King* (including Milton's *Lycidas*); Chillingworth, *Religion of Protestants*; Quarles, *Hieroglyphicks of the Life of Man*; Shelton, *Tachygraphy*; Peacham, *The Truth of Our Times*

Birth and death dates of non-dramatic writers	Dates of notable plays	Birth and death dates of playwrights	Continental theatrical events
(?) T. Traherne b.	R. Brome, *The English Moor*; Carlell, *The Fool Would Be a Favourite*; *Osmond the Great Turk*; Cartwright, *The Lady Errant*; Glapthorne, *The Ladies' Privilege*; Jonson, *Mortimer His Fall*; *The Sad Shepherd* (both incomplete); Mayne, *The City Match*; Nabbes, *Microcosmus*; *The Spring's Glory*; Rutter (with E. and R. Sackville?), *The Cid*, I (trans. of Corneille); Suckling, *Aglaura*; *The Sad One* (incomplete)	Jonson d.	Vondel, *Gysbreght van Aemstel*; Calderon, *El Magico Prodigioso*; first public Opera House, in Venice, with a regular season of performances in Carnival time
	A. Brome, *The Cunning Lovers*; R. Brome, *The Antipodes*; *The Damoiselle*; Carlell, *The Passionate Lovers*, I and II; Cartwright, *The Siege*; Cowley, *Naufragium Joculare*; Davenant, *Britannia Triumphans*; *The Fair Favourite*; *Luminalia*; *The Unfortunate Lovers*; Ford, *The Lady's Trial*; *The Royal Combat*; Glapthorne, *Argalus and Parthenia*; *Wit in a Constable*; Heywood, *Porta Pietatis*; Mayne, *The Amorous War* (revised after 1642?); Nabbes, *The Bride*; *A* (cont. on p. xli)		

(cont. on p. xli)

Date	Historical events	Theatrical events	Non-dramatic literary events
1638 (cont.)			
1639	First Bishops' War; Strafford becomes King's chief counsellor; Dutch naval victory over Spain in Battle of the Downs: end of Spanish naval power	Red Bull players punished by Privy Council for acting a 'libellous' play, *The Whore New Vamped*; Lord Mayor's Show not held this year (nor until 1655)	
1640	The Short Parliament (13 Apr.–5 May); second Bishops' War; 'Long' Parliament summoned in Oct.; Laud and Strafford arrested; citizens bring 'Root and Branch' Petition to Commons, 11 Dec.	Beeston's Boys at the Cockpit act a play referring to King's 'journey' to Scotland; Beeston imprisoned and replaced by Davenant as governor of the company until 1641; plague: theatres closed Sept.–Nov.	Beaumont, *Poems*; Carew, *Poems*; Donne, *LXXX Sermons* with *Life* by Walton; Greville, Baron Brooke, *Nature of Truth*; Hall, *Episcopacy by Divine Right*; G. Herbert, *Wit's Recreations*; Jonson, *Works* (second vol. of First Folio, first vol. pub. 1616); Mabbe (trans.), Cervantes' *Exemplary Novels*; Sandys, *(cont. on p. xlii)*

Birth and death dates of non-dramatic writers	Dates of notable plays	Birth and death dates of playwrights	Continental theatrical events
	Presentation for the Prince; J. Rutter (and E. and R. Sackville?), The Cid, II (trans. of Desfontaines' La Vraie Suite du Cid); Shirley, The Constant Maid; The Doubtful Heir; Suckling, Aglaura (second) version); The Goblins		
Sir H. Wotton d. ? T. Carew d.	R. Brome, The Lovesick Court; A Mad Couple Well Matched; Cokain, The Obstinate Lady; 'J.D.', The Knave in Grain; 'T.D.', The Bloody Banquet; Davenant, The Spanish Lovers; Hemming, The Fatal Contract; Nabbes, The Unfortunate Mother; Sharpe, The Noble Stranger; Shirley, The Gentleman of Venice; The Politician; St Patrick for Ireland, I; Suckling, Brennoralt	(?) J. Ford d. (or 1640) Marmion d. Sedley b.	Bidermann b.; Racine b.; Mendoza d.; Vondel, Electra, De Maeghden; V. Mazzocchi and Marazzoli, Chi Soffre, Speri (first comic opera) possibly seen by Milton on his Italian journey
R. Burton d.	R. Brome, The Court Beggar; The Jewish Gentleman [lost]; Burnell, Landgartha; Cavendish and Shirley, The Country Captain; Davenant, Salamacida Spolia; Day, The Parliament of Bees; Mildmay Fane, Raguaillo d'Oceano; Glapthorne (?), (cont. on p. xliii)	W. Alexander d. Aphra Behn b. J. Crowne b. ? J. Day d. Massinger d. Wycherley b.	Avancini, Franciscus Xaverius; Calderón, Comedias, pub.; Corneille, Cinna and Horace

Date	Historical events	Theatrical events	Non-dramatic literary events
1640 (cont.)			*Christ's Passion*; Selden, *Discourse Concerning the Power of Peers*; Machiavelli, *The Prince* (first published trans. by Dacres)
1641	Execution of Strafford; Star Chamber and Court of High Commission abolished; Root and Branch Bill and Grand Remonstrance; Irish Rebellion	Plague: theatres closed Aug.–late Nov.; *The Stage-Player's Complaint*; Davenant, with Suckling and Jermyn, flees after being involved in the Army Plot	Habington, *Observations upon History*; Jonson, *Timber*; Sylvester, *Collected Works*; Wither, *Hallelujah*; Hall, *An Humble Remonstrance*; 'Smectymnuus', *Answer to An Humble Remonstrance*; Milton, *Of Reformation*; *Of Prelatical Episcopacy*; *Animadversions*
1642	Attempted arrest of the Five Members; Charles I flies to York; royal standard raised at Nottingham, 22 Aug.; battle of Edgehill, 23 Oct.; Turnham Green, 13 Nov.; royal headquarters at Oxford	In Feb. Parliament debates motion for suppression of plays; 2 Sept., Parliament orders closing of the theatres 'while these sad Causes and set times of Humiliation doe continue'	Denham, *Cooper's Hill* (first version); Fuller, *Holy State and Profane State*; Hartlib, *Reformation of Schools* (trans of Comenius); Hobbes, *De Cive*; Howell, *Instructions for Foreign Travel*; Milton, *Reason of Church Government Urged*; *Apology for Smectymnuus*; More, *Psychodia Platonica*; Ralegh, *The Prince*; Sir John Berkenhead edits *Mercurius Aulicus* from Oxford throughout the war

Birth and death dates of non-dramatic writers	Dates of notable plays	Birth and death dates of playwrights	Continental theatrical events
	Revenge for Honour; Habington, The Queen of Aragon; Sandys (trans.), Grotius's Christus Patiens; Shirley, The Imposture; The Arcadia		
	Braithwait, Mercurius Britannicus (in Latin and English); R. Brome, A Jovial Crew; W. Cavendish (and Shirley?), The Variety; Denham, The Sophy; Fane, Candy Restored; Jordan, The Walks of Islington and Hogsdon; T. Killigrew, The Parson's Wedding (revised later); Lovelace, The Soldier [lost]; anon., Canterbury His Change of Diet; Quarles, The Virgin Widow; Shirley, The Brothers; The Cardinal; Wild, The Benefice	T. Heywood d. T. Nabbes d. T. Rymer b. (?) T. Shadwell b. (or 1642)	
Isaac Newton b.	Cowley, The Guardian; Shirley, The Court Secret; The Sisters	J. Suckling d.	Corneille, Polyeucte; Christian Weise b.; Avancini, Fiducia in Deum; Monteverdi, L'Incoronazione di Poppea

Date	Historical events	Theatrical events	Non-dramatic literary events
1643	Parliament accepts Scottish alliance and Solemn League and Covenant; deaths of Hampden and Pym; death of Louis XIII	*The Actors' Remonstrance or Complaint*; plays continue at Oxford throughout the war, also masques; illicit performances in London (raid on the Fortune, 2 Oct.)	*Mercurius Civicus* (first illustrated London periodical); Baker, *Chronicle of the Kings of England*; Browne, *Religio Medici* (first authorized ed.); Milton, *Doctrine and Discipline of Divorce*
1644	Marston Moor (2 July); trial of Laud; Congress of Westphalia (1644–8) opens	Globe theatre 'pulled down' (i.e. interior dismantled)	Newcastle, after defeat at Marston Moor, goes abroad and remains until Restoration; Bunyan in militia (1644–7); Milton, *Of Education*; *Areopagitica*; Overton, *Man's Mortality*; Williams, *Bloody Tenet of Persecution*
1645	Prayer Book abolished; Laud executed; New Model Army: Cromwell and Fairfax replace Waller, Essex and Manchester; Battle of Naseby (14 June); scientists begin meeting at Gresham College (origins of Royal Society)	Masque House at Whitehall 'pulled down'	Milton, *Poems*, and divorce pamphlets; Waller, *Poems*; Wither, *Vox Pacifica*; T. Fuller, *Good Thoughts in Bad Times*; Lord Herbert, *De Causis Errorum*; Howell, *Epistolae Ho-Elianae*; J. Lilburne, *England's Birth-Right Justified*; Prynne, *Truth Triumphing*; A. Ross, *Medicus Medicatus* (attacks *Religio Medici*)

Birth and death dates of non-dramatic writers	Dates of notable plays	Birth and death dates of playwrights	Continental theatrical events
W. Browne d. Lord Falkland and S. Godolphin killed in battle	anon., *The Cruel War* (parody of *The Triumph of Peace*); *Tyrannical Government Anatomized, or a Discourse Concerning Evil Counsellors* (trans. of Buchanan's *Baptistes*), specially licensed by House of Commons; (T. Fuller ?), *Andronicus* (rev. by another hand for publication in 1661?)	W. Cartwright d. (?) H. Glapthorne d. E. Ravenscroft b.	Calderón, *El Alcade de Zalamea*; Corneille, *La Mort de Pompée*; *Le Menteur*
F. Quarles d. G. Sandys d.	Fane, *Virtue's Triumph* (closet drama? acted at Apthorpe?)		English actors at Hague, *c.* Nov. 1644–*c.* Feb. 1645
	H. Burkhead, *Cola's Fury* (on the Irish war [pub. 1646]); Fane, *Don Phoebo's Triumph* (acted at Apthorpe)	W. Strode d.	Corneille, *Théodore Vierge et Martyre*; Scarron, *Jodelet, ou le maître valet*; first Italian opera performed in Paris

Date	Historical events	Theatrical events	Non-dramatic literary events
1646	Presbyterianism made State religion; King takes refuge with Scots; Oxford surrenders	King's players petition House of Lords for pre-war arrears of salary, which are granted them; Davenant in Paris (1646–50)	Suckling, *Fragmenta Aurea*; Donne, *Biathanatos*; Browne, *Pseudoxia Epidemica*; Crashaw, *Steps to the Temple*; Shirley, *Poems*; H. Vaughan, *Poems*; E. Hyde begins writing *History of the Rebellion*
1647	King given up to Parliament by Scots, then (4 June) seized by army; army occupies London; King escapes to Isle of Wight; Putney debates between Levellers and army generals; Masaniello's uprising in Naples	Players return to London and act publicly at Salisbury Court, the Cockpit and the Fortune; further parliamentary orders against playing, 16 July and 22 Oct.; printing of Beaumont and Fletcher Folio	R. Corbet, *Poems*; L. Andrewes, *Private Devotions*; Cleveland, *Poems*; Howell, *Epistolae Ho-Elianae*, II; Cowley, *The Mistress*; H. More, *Philosophical Poems*; London royalist journals: *Mercurius Melancholicus* (1647–9), *Mercurius Pragmaticus* (1647–50), *Mercurius Elencticus* (1647–9) et al.
1648	Second Civil War; defeat of Scottish Royalist army at Preston; siege of Colchester; Pride's Purge, 6–7 Dec.; end of Thirty Years' War (Treaty of Westphalia); separate treaty frees Holland from Spanish rule; La Fronde, 1648–53	Players resume acting at Cockpit and Red Bull; new ordinance suppressing them passed 9 Feb.; players petition House of Lords for permission to go abroad, but are refused; further ordinances in June and July; surreptitious performances continue	Bacon, *Remains*; Herrick, *Hesperides*; *Noble Numbers*; Hooker, *Ecclesiastical Polity*, VI, VII

Birth and death dates of non-dramatic writers	Dates of notable plays	Birth and death dates of playwrights	Continental theatrical events
Anthony Hamilton b.	T. Killigrew, *The Pilgrim* (acted in Paris?); J. Shirley, *The Triumph of Beauty* (privately performed?); anon., *Ruff, Cuff and Band*, comic academic dialogue, acted at Oxford		Corneille, *Héraclius*; Vondel, *Maria Stuart*; Prince of Wales company of English actors in Paris dissolved for lack of money
J. Wilmot, Earl of Rochester, b.	Robert Baron, *The Cyprian Academy*, pub. (a romance, containing a pastoral, *Gripsius and Hegio*, and a masque, *Deorum Dona*, both heavily plagiarized from Shakespeare, Webster, Milton *et al.*); R. Fanshawe's trans. of Guarini's *Pastor Fido* pub.; short pamphlet-plays: S. Sheppard, *The Committee-Man Curried*, I and II; *The Scottish Politic Presbyter*; M. Nedham, *The Levellers Levelled*; anon., *News Out of the West*		Hooft d.; Gryphius, *Cardenio und Celinda*; Vondel, *De Leeuwendalers*
Lord Herbert of Cherbury d.	E. Sherburne, *Medea* (trans. of Seneca); pamphlet-plays: *Crafty Cromwell*, I and II, (by 'Mercurius Melancholicus' and 'Mercurius Pragmaticus' respectively); 'Mercurius Melancholicus', *Mistress Parliament* (*cont. on p. xlix*)	W. Percy d. E. Settle b.	Tirso de Molina d.; Vondel, *Salomon*; English actors move from France to the Hague (this may have been George Jolly's troop); an English company under Jolly continues to perform, in Holland, Germany and Austria, throughout the Interregnum

Date	Historical events	Theatrical events	Non-dramatic literary events
1648 (*cont.*)			
1649	King's trial and execution (30 Jan.); Rump Parliament abolishes House of Lords and monarchy, proclaims Commonwealth; Levellers captured at Burford; Cromwell crushes Irish rebellion; Diggers	*Mr William Prynne His Defence of Stage-Plays* (a mock recantation of *Histrio-Mastix*, by an anon. satirist), followed by Prynne's own disclaimer; interiors of Fortune, Cockpit and Salisbury Court 'pulled down'; Red Bull continues surreptitious performances	Donne's *Fifty Sermons*, first pub.; Lilburne, *England's New Chains Discovered*; Lovelace, *Lucasta*; Gauden (?), *Eikon Basilike*; Milton, *Tenure of Kings and Magistrates*; *Eikonoklastes*; Milton becomes Secretary for Foreign Tongues to Council of State
1650	Charles II in Scotland; accepts Covenant; Battle of Dunbar; execution of Montrose	'Humble Petition' of impoverished actors to Parliament; raid on the Red Bull; Beeston begins repairing the Cockpit and training a boys' company; Davenant in prison, 1650–2	Anne Bradstreet, *Tenth Muse*; Baxter, *Saints' Everlasting Rest*; Davenant, *Gondibert* (and Hobbes, *Discourse upon Gondibert*); Marvell's 'Horatian Ode' written; J. Taylor, *Holy Living*; Vaughan, *Silex Scintillans*, I; *Mercurius Politicus* (ed. M. Nedham) official government news-sheet until 1660

Birth and death dates of non-dramatic writers	Dates of notable plays	Birth and death dates of playwrights	Continental theatrical events
	Brought to Bed; *Ding-Dong, or Sir Pitiful Parliament on his Deathbed*; *Mistress Parliament Presented on her Bed*; *Mistress Parliament Her Gossiping*; *Mistress Parliament Her Invitation to Mrs London*; *The Cuckoo's Nest at Westminster*; anon., *The Devil and the Parliament*; *The Kentish Fair*; *Women Will Have Their Will*		
R. Crashaw d. W. Drummond d.	'T.B.', *The Rebellion of Naples*; C. Wase, *Electra* (trans. of Sophocles); anon., *The Famous Tragedy of Charles I*; pamphlet-plays: 'The Man in the Moon' (John Crouch?), *Newmarket Fair*, I and II; anon., *A New Bull-Baiting*; *The Disease of the House*; *A Bartholomew Fairing*		Gryphius, *Ermordete Majestät, oder Carolus Stuardus*
Jeremy Collier b. Phineas Fletcher d.	Mildmay Fane, *De Pugni Animi*; R. Flecknoe, *Love in Its Infancy* (lost); T. Killigrew, *Cicilia and Clorinda, or Love in Arms*, I and II; J. Tatham, *The Distracted State*; anon., *Love's Victory*; *The White Ethiopian*	J. Banks b. T. May d.	Avancini, *Pax Imperii*; Corneille, *Don Sancho d'Aragon*; first opera performed in Brussels; Corneille's *Andromède* performed with music and 'machines'

Date	Historical events	Theatrical events	Non-dramatic literary events
1651	Dutch War, 1651–4; Charles II crowned at Scone; Battle of Worcester and Charles's escape; royalist estates confiscated; Navigation Act	Printing of W. Cartwright's *Plays and Poems*	Cleveland, *Poems*; Hobbes, *Leviathan*; Milton, *Pro Populo Anglicano Defensio*; Stanley, *Poems*; J. Taylor, *Holy Dying*; H. Vaughan, *Olor Iscanus*
1652	End of Irish War; proposals for national church with toleration	Beeston buys lease of Salisbury Court playhouse	Crashaw, *Carmen Deo Nostro*; Donne, *Paradoxes, etc.*; G. Herbert, *Remains*; R. Filmer, *Original of Government*; H. Vaughan, *Mount of Olives*; G. Winstanley, *Law of Freedom*
1653	Parliament expelled by Cromwell; 'Barebones' Parliament July–Dec., then Instrument of Government establishes Protectorate; trial and acquittal of J. Lilburne	Robert Cox performing at the Red Bull; acting at Gibbons's Tennis Court, and raid on a performance of Killigrew's *Claracilla*; printing of R. Brome's *Five New Plays* and J. Shirley's *Six New Plays*; John Rowe, *Tragi-Comoedia*, describes accident at illicit provincial performance of *Mucedorus*	Duchess of Newcastle, *Poems and Fancies*; *Philosophical Fancies*; F.G., trans. of *Le Grand Cyrus* (Mlle de Scudéry); Urquhart, trans. of Rabelais, I, II; H. Lawes, *Airs and Dialogues*; Marvell writes 'Character of Holland'; Walton, *Compleat Angler*

Birth and death dates of non-dramatic writers	Dates of notable plays	Birth and death dates of playwrights	Continental theatrical events
(?) A. Townshend d.	W. Denny, *The Shepherd's Holiday*; L. Willan, *Astraea* (adapt. D'Urfé's romance); pamphlet-plays: S. Sheppard, *The Jovial Crew, or The Devil Turned Ranter*; 'J.S.', *The Prince of Priggs' Revels, or the Practices of that Grand Thief Capt. James Hind*	N. Lee b.	Corneille, *Nicomède*
Henry Parker d. Martin Parker d.	T. Killigrew, *Bellamira Her Dream, or, the Love of Shadows*, I and II; Cosmo Manuche, *The Just General*; *The Loyal Lovers*; John Tatham, *The Scots Figgaries, or a Knot of Knaves*; anon., *The Bastard*	R. Brome d. T. Otway b. N. Tate b. A. Wilson d.	Calderón, *Perseus*; Corneille, *Polyeucte*; Lohenstein, *Ibrahim Bassa*
Sir R. Filmer d. R. North b. J. Oldham b. John Taylor d.	Shirley, *Cupid and Death* (performed privately and at Whitehall); drolls written or (possibly) adapted by R. Cox: *Actaeon and Diana*; *John Swabber*; *Royal Sports, or The Birthday of the Nymph Oenone*; *Simpleton the Smith* (pub. 1656); *The Black Man*; *Diphilo and Granida*; *King Ahasuerus and Queen Esther*; *King Solomon's Wisdom*; *Philetis and* (cont. on p. liii)	T. D'Urfey b.	Calderón, *La Lija del aire*; Scarron, *Don Japhet d'Arménie*

(cont. on p. liii)

Date	Historical events	Theatrical events	Non-dramatic literary events
1653 (*cont.*)			
1654	Peace with Holland; treaties with Sweden, Portugal, Denmark; first Protectorate Parliament: reforms in law, education, etc.; royalist and Leveller plots; abdication of Queen Christina of Sweden	Further attempts to suppress plays ordered in Feb.; raid on a performance of *Wit Without Money* at Red Bull in Dec.	Hobbes, *Of Liberty and Necessity*; Milton, *Defensio Secunda*; E. Gayton, *Pleasant Notes upon Don Quixote*
1655	Proclamation on religious liberty; rule of the Major-Generals; massacre of Vaudois in Piedmont; Jamaica captured; war with Spain; treaty with France	Plays continue at Red Bull; a raid on 14 Sept.; Blackfriars Playhouse 'pulled down'; death of R. Cox; Cotgrave, *The English Treasury of Wit*, pub. (contains passages from at least 250 Elizabethan, Jacobean, Caroline plays); Lord Mayors' Shows resumed for first time since 1639	Trans. of Mlle de Scudéry's *Clélie* (by Davies and Hayers); Denham, *Cooper's Hill* (authorized ed.); Marvell, *First Anniversary of . . . Lord Protector*; Milton, *Pro Se Defensio*; J. Taylor, *Golden Grove*; suppression of seven independent newspapers
1656	Second Protectorate Parliament; end of Major-Generals' rule; naval victories against Spain	Davenant's use of theatres at Gibbons's Tennis Court, Cockpit and Apothecaries' Hall mentioned in ballad; performances at Rutland House begin 23 May; Hope Theatre 'pulled down'; public bear-baiting stops	Drummond, *Poems*; Cowley, *Poems*; Harrington, *Oceana*; Osborn, *Advice to a Son*, pt 1 (pt 2, 1658)

Birth and death dates of non-dramatic writers	Dates of notable plays	Birth and death dates of playwrights	Continental theatrical events
	Constantia; *Venus and Adonis, or The Maid's Philosophy* (all pub. 1673 in pt 2 of *The Wits, or Sport upon Sport*)		
W. Habington d.	R. Flecknoe, *Love's Dominion*; T. Jordan, *Cupid His Coronation* (masque performed at girls' school); T. Killigrew, *Thomaso, or The Wanderer*, I and II; pamphlet-play: *The New Brawl, or Turnmill Street Against Rosemary Lane*; F. Osborne, *The True Tragicomedy Lately Acted at Court*		Scarron, *L'Écolier de Salamanque*; Vondel, *Lucifer*; Jolly's company, now based in Frankfurt, includes actresses; *Le Nozze di Pele e di Theti* (F. Buti, music by Caproli) performed at Paris with members of English royal family taking part: first opera libretto to be translated (by James Howell) into English
Richard Blackmore b.	R. Baron, *Mirza*; W. Lower, trans. of Corneille's *Polyeucte*; anon., pamphlet-play: *The Gossips' Brawl, or The Women Wear the Breeches*	(?) S. Sheppard d.	J. F. Regnard b.; Molière, *L'Étourdi*; Scarron, *Le Marquis Ridicule*; *Le Triomphe d'Amour* (C. de Beys, music by La Guerre), first French opera
John Hales d. (?) Jacob Tonson b.	Davenant, *The Athenians' Reception of Phocion* [lost]; *The First Day's Entertainment at Rutland House*; *The Siege of Rhodes*, I (the first English opera); S. Holland, *Cupid and* (*cont. on p. lv*)		Molière, *Le Dépit Amoureux*; Gryphius's *Ermörderte Majestät* acted near Frankfurt by 'foreign comedians' (possibly George Jolly's company)

Date	Historical events	Theatrical events	Non-dramatic literary events
1656 *(cont.)*			
1657	Further naval successes against Spain; alliance with France; Cromwell declines kingship	Davenant sends memorandum to Secretary Thurloe, urging the usefulness of public entertainments	H. King, *Poems*
1658	Parliament dissolved; death of Cromwell (3 Sept.); Richard Cromwell Lord Protector	Davenant's performances at the Cockpit	Browne, *Hydriotaphia*; *Garden of Cyrus*

Birth and death dates of non-dramatic writers	Dates of notable plays	Birth and death dates of playwrights	Continental theatrical events
	Psyche; *The Enchanted Grove*; *Venus and Adonis* (burlesque masques); W. Lower, trans. of Corneille's *Horace*; anon., *The Hectors, or the False Challenge*		
R. Lovelace d.	G. Gerbier D'Ouvilley, *The False Favourite Disgraced*; T. Jordan, *Fancy's Festivals* (medley, incorporating *Cupid's Coronation*, privately performed)	J. Dennis b.	Calderón, *El Golfo de las Serenas*; Gryphius, *Catharina von Georgien*
J. Cleveland d.	Margaret Cavendish, Duchess of Newcastle, *Plays* (fifteen published in folio in 1662; Harbage/Schoenbaum assign them to the Interregnum); W. Cavendish, Duke of Newcastle, *A Pleasant and Merry Humour of a Rogue*; W. Chamberlaine, *Love's Victory*; W. Davenant, *The Cruelty of the Spaniards in Peru*; *Sir Francis Drake*, I; J. Shirley, *The Contention of Ajax and Ulysses*; *Honoria and Mammon*; L. Willan, *Orgula, or the Fatal Error*		Gryphius, *Absurda Comica, oder Herr Peter Squentz* (based on part of *Midsummer Night's Dream*) as translated by D. Schwenter (d. 1636); arrival of Molière in Paris

Date	Historical events	Theatrical events	Non-dramatic literary events
1659	End of Protectorate; Rump recalled; Monk leads army from Scotland; Rota club meetings (1659–60); Peace of the Pyrenees ends war between France and Spain	Performances at Red Bull; Davenant briefly imprisoned for involvement in royalist plot; *Siege of Rhodes* continues to be acted at Cockpit; actors arrested for performing at Red Bull; R. Brome, *Five New Plays*, pub.	
1660	Monk recalls MPs excluded since 1648, who vote for dissolution; Declaration of Breda; new Parliament recalls Charles II, who enters London 29 May; founding of Royal Society	Theatre patents granted by King to Killigrew (King's company) and Davenant (Duke of York's company)	Dryden, *Astraea Redux*; Milton, *Ready and Easy Way to Establish a Free Commonwealth*; Pepys begins diary; Bunyan in prison

Birth and death dates of non-dramatic writers	Dates of notable plays	Birth and death dates of playwrights	Continental theatrical events
	W. Davenant, *The Siege of Rhodes*, II; anon., *Lady Alimony*; *The London Chanticleers* (revisions of earlier plays?); pamphlet-play: *The World in a Maze, or Oliver's Ghost*		Corneille. *Œdipe*; Gryphius, *Grossmütiger Rechts-Gelehrter*; Molière, *Les Précieuses Ridicules*; Vondel, *Jephta*
D. Defoe b.	Thomas Jordan, *Bacchus' Festival*; *The Cheaters Cheated*; Cosmo Manuche, *The Banished Shepherdess*; John Tatham, *The Royal Oak*; *The Rump*; anon., pamphlet-plays: *The Life and Death of Mrs Rump*; *A Phanatique Play*; *The Tragical Actors, or The Martyrdom of the Late King Charles*	P. Motteux b. T. Southerne b.	Scarron d.; Molière, *Sganarelle*; Vondel, *Samson*; first Spanish opera, Hidalgo's *Celos aun del Ayre Matan*, performed in Madrid

I Society and the theatre
Philip Edwards

1 Introduction[1]

In the period 1613–60, conflict and change were as strong and violent as England has ever known, and the history of the English theatre at this time is tightly bound up with the history of the English people. As the challenge to the monarchy and the Church, and the reaction to that challenge, grew more intense until civil war broke out in 1642 between King and Parliament, theatrical life was immensely vigorous. Then for eighteen years, as the Civil War was followed by Commonwealth and Protectorate, there was hardly any theatrical life at all. The theatre fell with the monarchy, and it returned with it in 1660; without this simple fact of dependence there can be no understanding of what happened to drama in the later years of James, the reign of Charles and the Interregnum. The court and its followers adopted the theatre, and the players identified themselves with those who protected and financed them. By 1613 there were no officially recognized companies of actors which were not attached to the royal family, servants of the royal household.[2] Drama was part of the way of life of the court; the nobility

---

[1] Preliminary note: In quotations, original spelling has been preserved except for a few passages where understanding would have been seriously impeded; *u, v, i, j* have been normalized and contractions have generally been expanded.

[2] Some minor companies in the provinces retained their old allegiances. See p. 26.

needed the masques and entertainments which seemed to the austere mere dissolute frivolity. If one looks beneath the surface of the Puritan opposition to the extravagance, ostentation and impurity of plays, one can see that it is in fact the fundamental opposition of one way of life to another: that which finds it necessary to extend one's being and find one's image in the theatre, and that which permits a man to lose and to find himself only in a certain form of Christian worship.

In an age of disastrous divisions, the drama found its own forms of segregation, and the broad social base which existed in the best days of the Globe gradually disappeared. Theatre-going remained a popular pastime, but much of what went on at the Red Bull and the Fortune was special to the vulgar and is lost; what we know as the Caroline drama is primarily a drama for the gentry who frequented the indoor theatres, an educated, comparatively wealthy audience sympathetic to the court. The industrious inhabitants of Blackfriars were deeply offended by the blocking of the streets with the coaches of idle theatre-goers (see pp. 46–7). On Shrove Tuesday, 1617, a riotous crowd of apprentices, having attacked the brothels, went for the Phoenix Theatre; the players tried to drive the attack off with guns and killed three, but the apprentices got in and despoiled furniture, costumes and play-books. Was this popular animosity against the players inspired at all by resentment against the players' patrons? Probably it was, even though they were reported to have the Red Bull as well as the Phoenix on their list of targets in the following year.[1]

In looking at the theatrical life of James's and Charles's reigns, in which the stupendously lavish court masques are as important a feature as the plays which we study in our universities, and reflecting on what happened to it all, we may be excused if we sometimes feel that we are looking at the plumage of a dying bird. It is difficult to separate oneself entirely from Whig prejudice. A contemporary, Mrs Hutchinson, put it this way: 'To keep the people in their deplorable security, till vengeance overtook them, they were entertained with masks, stage-plays, and sorts of ruder sports.'[2] Two hundred years later, Charles Kingsley wrote this of Shirley's *The Gamester*:

If the cavaliers and damsels of Charles the First's day were in the habit of talking in that way to each other (and if they had not been, Shirley

[1] *Jacobean and Caroline Stage*, 1, 162–3.
[2] Lucy Hutchinson, *Memoirs of the Life of Colonel Hutchinson*, ed. C. H. Firth (London, 1906), 64. Quoted in H. J. C. Grierson, *Cross-Currents in English Literature of the Seventeenth Century* (London, 1929; Harmondsworth, 1966), 76.

would not have dared to represent them as doing so) one cannot much wonder that the fire of God was needed to burn up (though, alas! only for a while) such a state of society; and that when needed, the fire fell.[1]

Without adopting the millennial attitude of these two, we can still feel dismayed at the 'cavalier' tone of a fine play like *A New Way to Pay Old Debts*, in which that favourite theme of early seventeenth-century comedy, the mixed marriage between nobility and trade, is dealt with from a ludicrously superior position as regards the purity of aristocratic blood, whereas the sordid and mismanaged military ventures in the Low Countries are invested with a tatty halo of honour and *noblesse oblige*. Massinger was a man of strong moral and political convictions; he was also a very sharp observer of the shifting social scene: in this play he seems quite unaware of the gulf between his ideals and the world he was living in. He seems to partake of the self-delusion of histrionic characters such as Sir Kenelm Digby and the complacency of a court-entertainer like Carew (whose indifference to the alarms of war is described later in this chapter). It is very rash to make causal links between the moral condition of early Stuart society and the quality of the plays of that time, but plays and masques were the staple diet of a section of the gentry and nobility whose ethos does not appeal to us greatly and that ethos is sometimes shared by those who wrote the plays and masques; even when it is not shared, the manners and the fate of those who chose the entertainment give a certain colour to that entertainment.

[1] *Plays and Puritans* (London, 1873), 56.

2 Drama at court

The social context of drama in this period then is primarily the court: the world of the royal family, the greater nobility, the professional courtiers, the gentry on the fringes. The chief providers of dramatic entertainment at court were of course the professional acting companies of London; they brought with them the plays they were accustomed to perform in their own theatres. The acting season at court was late autumn to early spring: Allhallowtide to Shrovetide. Most of the performances came during the Christmas season, which could run as late as Candlemas (2 February). The King's company was the one most often seen at court, but it had no monopoly; in James's reign there were generally at least two other companies performing each season, and for some years in the early 1630s the Queen's company (managed by Christopher Beeston) challenged the predominance of the King's servants. Although the records of court performances are far from complete, it would seem that there were rarely fewer than twenty performances in a season and often more. In court records you can often hear the noise of hammering as the carpenters get the stage ready: in 1626–7 Richard Harris and eight assistants were paid for twenty-six days of work (October to March) making ready the Hall and the

Great Chamber at Whitehall for thirteen plays, as well as for six days' work preparing the Banqueting House for the Queen's masque.[1]

In the season 1630–1, the King's Men and the Queen's Men between them performed thirty-seven plays at court. We have the titles of the twenty-one plays given by the King's Men and the dates of performance; their first four contributions were at Hampton Court, the rest at the 'Cockpit-in-Court' at Whitehall. The company received a payment of £260 for the whole season.[2] The list (*see also plate 2*) is a valuable record of the court's dramatic fare. I have added the date of composition of each play.

30 Sept.	The Inconstant Lady	Wilson	c. 1630
3 Oct.	'Alfonso'	Chapman?	? 1604
17 Oct.	A Midsummer Night's Dream	Shakespeare	c. 1595
24 Oct.	The Custom of the Country	Fletcher and Massinger	c. 1620
5 Nov.	'An Induction for the Howse'	?	?
	The Mad Lover	Fletcher	c. 1616
7 Nov.	Rollo	Fletcher et al.	c. 1619
19 Nov.	Volpone	Jonson	1606
28 Nov.	Beauty in a Trance	Ford	?
30 Nov.	Beggars' Bush	Fletcher, Massinger, et al.	c. 1622
9 Dec.	The Maid's Tragedy	Beaumont and Fletcher	c. 1610
14 Dec.	Philaster	Beaumont and Fletcher	c. 1609
26 Dec.	The Duchess of Malfi	Webster	c. 1614
27 Dec.	The Scornful Lady	Beaumont and Fletcher	c. 1613
30 Dec.	The Chances	Fletcher	c. 1617
6 Jan.	Sir John Oldcastle	Drayton et al.	1599
3 Feb.	The Fatal Dowry	Massinger and Field	c. 1619

[1] *Jacobean and Caroline Stage*, VII, 63, and MSC, VI (1961), 122.
[2] ibid., I, 27–8, 96–7.

10 Feb.	*A King and No King*	Beaumont and Fletcher	1611
15 Feb.	*The Merry Devil of Edmonton*	?	*c.* 1602
17 Feb.	*Every Man in his Humour*	Jonson	1598
21 Feb.	*Rollo*	Fletcher *et al.*	*c.* 1619

These plays are old favourites indeed. Fifteen years earlier, John Chamberlain, not an enthusiastic supporter of the professional theatre, had remarked about court performances that 'our Poets braines and invention are growne very drie insomuch that of five new playes there is not one pleases, and therefore they are driven to forbish over theyre old, which stands them in best stead and bring them most profit.'[1] It would seem less the decay of invention than the pleasure of familiarity which causes old plays to be presented: the taste of the court is distinctly nostalgic. New plays were, however, occasionally performed. On 31 October 1614, the first performance of Jonson's *Bartholomew Fair* was given by the Lady Elizabeth's Men at the Hope Theatre. On the very next day, 1 November, the play was performed before the King at Whitehall.[2] Though Jonson has a special position, the ease of transfer of a play to the court from the Hope, which was used as much for the baiting of bulls and bears as for plays, is eloquent of the democracy of taste which existed at that time. Two of Massinger's plays, *The Bondman* (1623) and *The Guardian* (1633), were chosen for court soon after they had been licensed for public performance. Probably Fletcher's plays were often to be seen at court when still brand new, but evidence is lacking.

Foreign companies of actors were also welcomed at court. In February–March 1617, Antoine Cossart and his French company were paid half as much again as English players could expect (£15 a play instead of £10) for four performances at court – probably the plays of Alexandre Hardy, their speciality.[3] Charles Le Noir was paid at the same rate in September 1619 when his French players acted before the King.[4] In 1635, Josias Floridor and his French company acted at court over a period of almost a year. In February they were 'approved of by the queene at her house . . . and commended by her majesty to the kinge.' Among the plays they acted, mostly at the Cockpit-in-Court, were Du Rocher's *La Mélize*,

[1] J. Chamberlain, *Letters*, ed. N. E. McLure, 2 vols (Philadelphia, 1939), I, 567.
[2] MSC, VI (1961), 60.
[3] ibid., 62–4.
[4] ibid., 70–1.

Georges de Scudéry's *Le Trompeur puni* and Pierre du Ryer's *Alcimédon*.[1] This company got only £10 a play. There was also in England at this time Juan Navarro Oliver, with a Spanish company; they acted at court in October 1634 and December 1635.[2]

The showpiece of court entertainment was the masque. Perhaps its greatest days were already over in 1613, though it is no longer generally accepted that an increase in spectacle and in the use of the antimasque is a necessary sign of decadence in an art form in which music, dance and visual splendour are of the essence; Ben Jonson, insisting on the masque as philosophy and struggling against the dominance of Inigo Jones, still tries to govern us from the grave. In the season of 1630–1 which we have just been discussing as regards the contribution of the professional companies, there were two royal masques. The first, on 9 January 1631, was the King's masque, *Love's Triumph through Callipolis*, by Jonson and Inigo Jones, and Charles himself performed in it. The King paid £300 for his own costume and that of some of the other masquers 'on whom his Majestie is pleased to bestow their Attire.'[3] For Shrove Tuesday, 22 February, Jonson and Jones prepared *Chloridia* for the Queen and her ladies to take part in as a return gesture following the masculine *Love's Triumph*. As usual, the court letter-writers commented on the court's preoccupations with rehearsals. 'Everybody is busy about the performance of the Queen's mask on Shrovetide next. All the Court ladies are daily practitioners', wrote Sir Thomas Colepeper a week beforehand.[4]

The question of who was entitled to attend and who did attend these court performances of plays and masques is one not easily settled at this distance of time. How many of the gentry and nobility were qualified? Sir Humphrey Mildmay attended; he was no courtier, but he was a knight and the son of a courtier, and two of his younger brothers held posts in the royal household. His invaluable diary and account book has such entries as: '. . . att nighte to the Courte with a freinde to see Catteline Acted' (*9 November 1634*); 'To White hall I wente Supped with Mr Secretary Cooke and Came home durty and weary the playe beinge full' (*3 February 1638*); 'This nighte I was att Whitehall att the dauncinge and playe, and laye all nighte with Bor Anth: [brother Anthony]' (*?6 February 1634*).[5]

[1] Adams, *Herbert*, 60–1.
[2] J. P. Feil, 'Dramatic References from the Scudamore Papers', *Shakespeare Survey*, 11 (1958), 110; MSC, VI (1961), 88.
[3] Herford and Simpson, X (1950), 677.
[4] *Jacobean and Caroline Stage*, IV, 637.
[5] Printed in *Jacobean and Caroline Stage*, II, 673–81.

Thomas Knyvett of Norfolk wrote to his wife (February 1635?): 'I am this night for the Queens maske at court, And though a country Gentleman, yet am I graced with a Tickett of her ma[ist], but to tell thee true, if I doe not like my waye of going in, I doubt I shall let it alone.'[1] Jonson talks of citizens' wives sneaking in (*Love Restored*, l. 116), and among the ambitions of the merchant's daughter in Massinger's *The City Madam* (II.ii.117) is 'A friend at Court to place me at a Mask'. It was part of the folklore of the righteous that courtiers invited citizens' wives to court masques and plays and then had sexual intercourse with them in some private corner.[2]

Whatever the entitlement to attendance was, often more people tried to get in than there was room for. In the great festivities for the marriage of Princess Elizabeth with the Elector Palatine in 1613, the masque provided by the Inner Temple and Gray's Inn was postponed at the very last minute, not only because the King was tired out, but also because the room was so crowded that 'a very great number of principal ladies and other noble persons' could not get in – in spite of the decree that farthingales should not be worn. When the masque was performed a few days later, the larger banqueting house took the place of the great hall.[3] The Lord Chamberlain in person, or the Controller of the Household, would apparently try to control the crowd with his white staff of office. In 1617, we are told, 'Sir Thomas Edmonds was made controller, and had the white staffe delivered him. . . . They say he doth somewhat too much flourish and fence with his staves, whereof he hath broken two alredy (not at tilt) but stickling at the playes this Christmas.'[4] (To stickle is to act as umpire or to regulate.) At the famous performance of Montague's pastoral by the Queen and her ladies in 1633 (see below, p. 13), we are told of 'the difficulty of getting in on Wednesday being such or so apprehended, that there was a scarcitie of spectators and room for many more than were present'. The novelty of the occasion had made the Lord Chamberlain restrict admission. Commentators found the arrangements a joke. John Pory wrote: 'My lord chamberlain saith that no chambermaid shall enter, unless she will sit cross-legged on the top of a bulk.'[5] Since no 'great lady' was to be kept out, it

[1] *The Knyvett Letters*, ed. B. Schofield (London, 1949), 88.
[2] See Colin Gibson's quotation from Sir Edward Peyton (1652) in P. Edwards and C. Gibson (eds), *The Plays and Poems of Philip Massinger*, 5 vols (Oxford, 1976), V, 147; and the same author's 'Behind the Arras', *Notes and Queries*, 114 (1969), 296–7.
[3] *A Book of Masques in Honour of Allardyce Nicoll*, ed. T. J. B. Spencer and S. W. Wells (Cambridge, 1967), 129–30, 133.
[4] Chamberlain, *Letters*, II, 47.
[5] *Jacobean and Caroline Stage*, IV, 918.

seems that priorities were according to rank.

At the performance of the court masque of Shrovetide 1634 (Shirley's *Triumph of Peace*), the Lord Chamberlain, then Philip Earl of Pembroke and Montgomery, was in some kind of collision with Thomas May, gentleman, poet and pensioner of the King. 'He broke his Staff over his Shoulders, not knowing who he was.' On the King's telling him what he had done, he apologized to May and paid him the huge sum of £50.[1] Special precautions were taken a week later for Carew's *Coelum Britannicum*: 'They have found a new way of letting them in by a turning chair, besides they let in none but such as have tickets sent them beforehand, so that now the keeping of the door is no trouble.'[2] A revealing comment was made in 1642 in a pamphlet lamenting the emptiness of the deserted court; of 'the Cockpit and Revelling Roomes' it says: 'Now you may goe in without a Ticket, or the danger of a broken pate.'[3]

Foreign visitors and court letter-writers are generous recorders of the goings-on at court revels, not only of the splendours but also of the snags and difficulties, like the frequent wranglings for precedence among ambassadors. Orazio Busino wrote about the performance of Jonson's *Pleasure Reconciled to Virtue* on Twelfth Night, 1618. The audience had to wait two hours for the King in a very crowded hall: 'although they profess to admit only the favoured ones who are invited, yet every stand [*palco*] was full, particularly with very noble and richly arrayed ladies, in number some 600 and more'. The King arrived at ten, and the masque began; towards the end, in the small hours, James was dissatisfied with the dancing which is the heart of the masque. 'Why don't they dance? What did they make me come here for? Devil take you all, dance!' After the masque there was a supper, and Busino describes as others do on similar occasions the wolfish way the food was devoured. 'The story ended at half past two in the morning, and half-disgusted and weary we returned home.'[1]

There were many other revels, pageants and entertainments at court besides the main masques and the command performances of the public players. Such chivalric exercises as tilts and barriers are only marginally

---

[1] ibid., v. 1158.
[2] Letter from Garrard to Strafford, quoted by Rhodes Dunlap (ed.), *The Poems of Thomas Carew* (Oxford, 1949), 274.
[3] *Jacobean and Caroline Stage*, VI, 283–4.
[4] Quoted in A. M. Nagler, *A Source Book in Theatrical History* (New York, 1952), 148–54; also Herford and Simpson, x, 580, 584.

theatrical:[1] James I kept the anniversary of his accession (24 March) with a tilt. How these joustings could be used for beautiful emblematic exercises may be seen from Jonson's 'A Challenge at Tilt' (1613) for the wedding of the Earl of Somerset and Lady Frances Howard. The symbolic resolution of strife between Eros and Anteros ends with a prayer for concord between the wife and husband, the tilters, and the whole court. Jonson later suppressed the details of the occasion of the masque – as well he might, for Frances Howard, having lied her way into a divorce from the Earl of Essex, was, as she came to the altar with her hair flowing over her shoulders in the way customary for virgins, an adultress and a murderess. The strange bringing together in this ritual of the tilt of sentimentally preserved chivalry, delicate Renaissance mythology, and such an unsavoury couple as the bride and groom, is characteristic of the flawed beauty of early Stuart culture.

Masques or plays to celebrate noble weddings were not infrequent: Daniel's *Hymen's Triumph* was given by the Queen at Somerset House (at a cost of £3000 it was said) to celebrate the marriage of Lord Roxborough to Jean Drummond in 1614. Noblemen for various reasons might present a masque or a play at court. On 12 December 1618, Chamberlain reported that 'the last weeke the Lord Digbie made a great supper and a play at Whitehall to the best part of the great Lords and Ladies about this towne'.[2] In May 1619 there was a performance of Shakespeare's *Pericles* as part of the entertainment given at court by the Duke of Lennox for the departing French ambassador. Sir Gerard Herbert wrote to Sir Dudley Carleton about it:

> The Marquise Trenell . . . that night was feasted at white hall by the duke of Lenox in the Queenes greate chamber: where many great Lordes weare to keep them Company but no ladyes. . . . The supper was greate and the banquett curious, served in 24 greate Chynay worcke platters or voyders. . . . After supper they weare carried to the queenes pryvy chamber, where french singinge was by the Queenes Musitians: after in the Queenes bedd chamber, they hearde the Irish harpp, a violl, and mr Lanyer, excellently singinge and playinge on the lute. In the kinges great Chamber they went to see the play of Pirrocles, Prince of Tyre, which lasted till 2 aclocke; after two actes, the players ceased till

---

[1] See Glynne Wickham, *Early English Stages* (1959–   ), I (London, 1959), 13–50, and II, pt I (London, 1963), 229–36.
[2] Chamberlain, *Letters*, II, 193.

the french all refreshed them with sweetmeats brought on Chynay voiders, and wine and ale in bottels; after, the players begann anewe.[1]

A number of these examples of festivities are from King James's time; his court was more flamboyant, more public in its revelry, than that of his son. Yet the link between court and theatre in the new reign was stronger, and that is because of the passion of Queen Henrietta Maria for drama and theatricals. Under the Queen's influence, courtiers became actors and dramatists. In her first season at court she startled everyone by rehearsing her French ladies-in-waiting in the Marquis de Racan's pastoral *L'Arténice*, in which she herself took the principal part. Court ladies who appeared in masques were normally silent and decorative: they were to be admired and to dance. But now they were to speak and, worse still, to take male parts. Chamberlain is fairly tolerant:

> On Shrovetuisday the Quene and her women had a maske or pastorall play at Somerset House, wherin herself acted a part, and some of the rest were disguised like men with beards. I have knowne the time when this wold have seemed a straunge sight, to see a Quene act in a play but *tempora mutantur et nos*.[2]

Eight years later (1633), the Queen acted in *The Shepherd's Paradise*, a tedious pastoral by Walter Montague, second son of the Earl of Manchester. Rehearsals started months beforehand: in September 1632, John Pory wrote that 'the Queens Majesty with some of her ladies, and maides of honour is daylie practizing upon a Pastorall penned by Mr Walter Montague'. Pory adds the interesting note that 'Taylour the prime actor at the Globe goes every day to teach them action'.[3] For his work as a coach, it was said that Taylor had 'the making of a knight' given him. The favour is a peculiar one for an actor and peculiar at this time when, with Buckingham dead, Charles had temporarily abandoned the sale of honours. The meaning of the gift was that Taylor should receive the fee offered by an aspirant to knighthood; he would be unlikely to make a full £100 out of it.[4] More valuable, probably, was the Queen's gift of the costumes worn in the play: they were used by Taylor for the King's company production of Fletcher's *The Faithful*

---

[1] J. Munro, *Shakespeare Allusion Book*, 2 vols (London, 1932), I, 276–7 (punctuation slightly altered).

[2] Chamberlain, *Letters*, II, 630.

[3] Feil, 'Dramatic References', 109, 115.

[4] Laurence Stone, *The Crisis of the Aristocracy 1558–1641* (Oxford, 1965), 76–82.

Shepherdess at court in the following year.[1] Walter Montague naturally got a good deal more, according to Pory – £2000 from the King (out of the Queen's portion-money!) and £500 from the Queen's own purse.[2]

Apart from learning action, the ladies had to learn excessively long parts: Pory said that the Marquess of Hamilton's part alone 'is as long as an ordinary play'. When the play was eventually given, on 9 January 1633, the performance lasted 'seven or eight hours'.[3]

By a great misfortune for its author, William Prynne's *Histrio-Mastix*, *The Players' Scourge*, with its vicious attack on 'Women-Actors, notorious whores', had just been published.[4] Prynne could hardly have had the Queen's participation in Montague's pastoral in mind unless he knew of the early rehearsals. According to him, his bulky diatribe was 'finished at the press about ten weeks before her Majesty's Pastoral';[5] certainly it had been a very long time in the writing and a very long time in the printing. The immediate and particular cause of his wrath against actresses was their appearance on stages in London during the visit of a French company in 1629. In Prynne's words, 'some French-women, or Monsters rather, on Michaelmas Terme 1629, attempted to act a French Play, at the Play-house in Black-friers: an impudent, shamefull, unwomanish, gracelesse, if not more than whorish attempt'.[6]

Yet whether or not Prynne had the Queen in mind when he attacked actresses is not really material. The coincidence of the book's being published about the same time as the Queen was on the stage gave a special sharpness to the obvious fact that the book was a prolonged and determined attack on an institution and an activity associated with and indispensable to the royal way of life. It seemed to the establishment a confrontation and they met it as a confrontation. In the immediately preceding months, religious antagonism to the monarchy had chosen as its battleground matters of entertainment and revelry. The Sabbatarians of Somerset had attempted to suppress the wakes, or Sunday saint's-day festivals, at local churches. The Lord Chief Justice had been complaisant enough to back up local justices with an order suppressing all 'ales and revels' in the county. At this, Laud

[1] Adams, *Herbert*, 53.
[2] Feil, 'Dramatic References', 110.
[3] *Jacobean and Caroline Stage*, IV, 918.
[4] *Histrio-Mastix* is dated 1633. At Prynne's trial it was stated that the book was bound 'about Christmas'; copies probably became available at the very end of December or the beginning of January – ten days or so before the court performance.
[5] S. R. Gardiner, *History of England . . . 1603–1642*, 10 vols (London, 1883–4), VII, 328–9.
[6] Quoted in *Jacobean and Caroline Stage*, VI, 226.

stepped in, countermanded the Lord Chief Justice's edict, demanded that 'the Feasts themselves . . . be kept, for the Neighbourly meeting, and Recreation of the People', and made it clear that he saw the suppression of the people's revels as a matter not of inhibiting disorder but of advancing Puritan practice.[1] Laud's letter was reinforced by Charles's reissue of his father's *Declaration Concerning Lawful Sports*. 'For when shall the Common-people have leave to exercise, if not upon the Sundays and Holy-days, seeing they must apply their labour and win their Living in all Working-days?' Although 'Interludes' were forbidden on Sundays, 'harm-less Recreation' such as 'May-Games, Whitson-Ales, and Morice-Dances' was encouraged.[2]

And now it seemed that the attack was upon the recreations of the court. Prynne was arrested and sent to the Tower; the ecclesiastical Court of High Commission charged him with offence against the clergy, and a prosecution for libel was commenced against him in the Court of Star Chamber. The man who was charged with writing 'that Plays are the chief delight of the Devil; that they that frequent Plays are damned' could hardly hope to be acquitted of libel of the King and Queen. But the extreme severity of the punishment was unexpected. Prynne was sentenced to be imprisoned for life, to be fined £5000, to be expelled from Lincoln's Inn, to be barred from the practice of his profession (law), to be degraded from his Oxford degree, to stand in the pillory in both Westminster and Cheapside, and *to have an ear cut off in each place*. The book itself was to be burned by the hangman. There are social niceties in old punishments which may escape a later age – such as the class distinction between being hanged and having one's head chopped off – and the barbarous sentence on Prynne was the more barbarous in that it was passed on a gentleman and a member of one of the learned professions. 'Most men were affrighted to see that neither his academical nor barrister's gown could free him from the infamous loss of his ears,' wrote Simonds D'Ewes.[3]

A few days before Prynne's trial began (7 February 1634), one of the most magnificent of all the Stuart masques was staged at Whitehall – Shirley's *Triumph of Peace*, done by the members of the Inns of Court at the King's request. As Prynne was a lawyer, a member of Lincoln's Inn, and had dedicated his work in part to the 'young gentleman-students of the four

[1] J. Rushworth, *Historical Collections*, 8 vols (London, 1659–1701), II (1680), 192.
[2] ibid., 194–5.
[3] Gardiner, *History of England*, VII, 334.

famous inns-of-court', the preparation of a masque, with the great expense of money and time which it necessitated, was a demonstration of loyalty to the Crown, as Bulstrode Whitelocke, one of those responsible for it, made clear.[1] As was usual with Inns of Court masques, a special feature was the splendid procession to Whitehall. The occasion as a whole was so spectacular that both the procession and the performance were repeated in the City some days later (Merchant Taylors' Hall) in the presence once again of the King and Queen.

A dazzling masque requested by the King, presented and paid for by the gentlemen of the Inns of Court, paraded twice through the London streets, given in splendour both at Westminster and London, published in an edition of 3000 copies, is a public rite, a public assertion of the unity of all who prepare it, perform it and witness it, and a public pronouncement of a belief in theatrical show and ceremony. Undoubtedly theatrical spectacle was not only the means by which the court enjoyed itself but also the means by which it expressed itself. It is more than a matter of affirming every event with a play or show of some kind (wedding, visit, diplomatic encounter); it is more than a matter of the didactic and propagandist content of the masque:[2] it approaches a belief in the magical power of what is displayed and enacted. Hidden beneath the extravagance of luxurious costume, ingenious machines and unending rehearsals, there is perhaps something of the notion of a sacrament, the idea that the rite may enshrine a mystical truth and confer benefits on those who share in it. 'As a substitute for effective government', remarked Miss C. V. Wedgwood, 'it was useless.'[3]

Contemporaries too thought that to be so absorbed in ritual was evidence not of the splendour of monarchy but of its weakening hold. *Coelum Britannicum* by Carew and Inigo Jones was given in this same season of 1634. Garrard wrote to Strafford on 9 January:

> There are two Masques in hand, the first of the Inns of Court, which is to be presented on *Candlemas-day*; the other the King presents the Queen with on *Shrove-Tuesday* at Night: High Expences, they speak of 20000 *l.* that it will cost the Men of the Law. Oh that they would once give over these Things, or lay them aside for a Time, and bend all their Endeavours to make the King Rich![4]

[1] *Jacobean and Caroline Stage*, v, 1160–1.
[2] See C. V. Wedgwood, *Poetry and Politics under the Stuarts* (Cambridge, 1961), 15–16.
[3] ibid., 49.
[4] *Strafford's Letters and Dispatches* (1739), I, 177; quoted in Dunlap, *Poems of Carew*, 273.

Coelum Britannicum, ordered by the King, and with the King and Queen taking part, opens with Mercury speaking to Charles and his consort:

> From the high Senate of the gods, to You
> Bright glorious Twins of Love and Majesty,
> Before whose Throne three warlike Nations bend
> Their willing knees, on whose Imperiall browes
> The Regall Circle prints no awfull frownes
> To fright your Subjects, but whose calmer eyes
> Shed joy and safety on their melting hearts
> That flow with cheerfull loyall reverence,
> Come I *Cyllenius, Joves* Ambassador. . . .[1]

The King, acting as a personage representing himself, is brought to the Queen:

> *We bring Prince* Arthur, *or the brave*
>   St George *himselfe (great Queene) to you. . . .*

Over the 'Royall Turtles' blessings and benedictions are pronounced as they are stellified amidst Religion, Truth, Wisdom, Concord, Government and Reputation.

It is interesting that the author of *Coelum Britannicum* is also the author of a classic *locus* on the blindness of the court to the seriousness of the national situation. Replying to Aurelian Townshend's request (probably 1633) to write in commemoration of Gustavus Adolphus, Carew replied:

> Let us that in myrtle bowers sit
> Under secure shades, use the benefit
> Of peace and plenty, which the blessed hand
> Of our good King gives this obdurate Land,
> Let us of Revels sing. . . .
>
>   these are subjects proper to our clyme.
> Tourneyes, Masques, Theaters, better become
> Our *Halcyon* dayes; what though the German Drum
> Bellow for freedome and revenge, the noyse
> Concernes not us, nor should divert our joyes.[2]

Carew's editor quotes the remark of W. J. Courthope: 'Such lines are

[1] Dunlap, *Poems of Carew*, 154.
[2] ibid., 75, 77.

sufficient in themselves to explain the overthrow of the Cavaliers within twelve years at Marston Moor.'[1]

In the famous 'last masque' of 1640, Davenant and Jones's *Salmacida Spolia*, some of the masquers held political views which made them inappropriate emblems of monarchical infallibility.[2] In spite of its ironies – and its futility – this extraordinary gesture, designed to avert danger and consolidate a threatened society, has earned itself a special place in the history of English culture as the final and culminating rite of its kind. The King and Queen are again centrally on stage and the argument is as follows:

> Discord, a malicious Fury, appears in a storm and by the invocation of malignant spirits . . . having already put most of the world into disorder, endeavours to disturb these parts, envying the blessings and tranquillity we have long enjoyed.
>
> These incantations . . . are surprised and stopped in their motion by a secret power . . . and depart as foreknowing that wisdom will change all their malicious hope of these disorders into a sudden calm. . . .
>
> This secret wisdom, in the person of the King attended by his Nobles and under the name of Philogenes or Lover of his People, hath his appearance prepared by a Chorus, representing his beloved people. . . .
>
> Then the Queen personating the chief heroine . . . is sent down from Heaven by Pallas as a reward of his prudence for reducing the threatening storm into the following calm.[3]

Dis aliter visum.

[1] Dunlap, *Poems of Carew*, 253.
[2] C. V. Wedgwood, *Truth and Opinion: Historical Essays* (London, 1960), 139–56.
[3] *A Book of Masques in Honour of Allardyce Nicoll*, 347. See also plate 3.

3 Royal visits

Wherever royalty went, there were theatrical entertainments of one kind or another. In 1613, as Anne of Denmark progressed towards Bath, there was an entertainment by Lord Knolles at Cawsome, near Reading, in which Campion helped, and on Salisbury Plain the vicar of Bishop's Cannings 'made a pleasant pastorall, and gave her an entertaynment with his fellow songsters in shepherds' weeds and bagpipes, he himself like an old bard'.[1] At Bristol, the mayor, sheriffs and aldermen received the Queen with 'Triumphs, Water-combats and other Showes' (thus the title-page of the 'Relation of the Royal Magnificent and Sumptuous Entertainment', a naïve versification by Robert Naile).[2] James's pleasure in progresses and in dramatic entertainment (whether he attended to it or not) shows up strongly in the records of his reign when they are compared with those for Charles's. But Charles's journey to Scotland in 1633 was marked by the very splendid entertainment prepared for him by William Cavendish, Earl of Newcastle, at Welbeck (Ben Jonson was enlisted for it). This entertainment, and others provided on the same journey, were the occasion of a curiously sour

[1] John Aubrey, *Brief Lives*, ed. A. Clark, 2 vols (Oxford, 1898), I, 251; quoted by E. K. Chambers, *The Elizabethan Stage*, 4 vols (Oxford, 1923), III, 312.
[2] J. Nichols, *The Progresses . . . of King James I* (London, 1828), II, 648.

comment from Clarendon, who (twenty-four years old at the time) would not remember the lavish entertainment which the peerage were accustomed to offer in the previous reign!

> This whole Progress was made from the first setting out, to the end of it, with the greatest Magnificence imaginable; and the highest excess of Feasting was then introduced, or at least, Feasting was then carried to a height it never had attain'd before, from whence it hardly declined afterwards, to the great damage and mischief of the Nation in their Estates, and Manners. All Persons of Quality and Condition who liv'd within distance of the Northern Road, receiv'd the great persons of the Nobility with that Hospitality which became them; in which all cost was employ'd to make their Entertainments splendid, and their Houses capable of those entertainments. The King himself met with many entertainments of that nature, at the charge of particular Men, who desired the honour of his Presence, which had been rarely practised till then by the Persons of the best Condition, though it hath since grown into a very inconvenient custom. But when he pass'd through *Nottinghamshire*, both King and Court were receiv'd and entertain'd by the Earl of *Newcastle*, and at his own proper expence, in such a wonderful manner, and in such an excess of Feasting, as had scarce ever before been known in *England*; and would be still thought very prodigious, if the same noble Person had not, within a year or two afterwards, made the King and Queen a more stupendious Entertainment; which (God be thanked) though possibly it might too much whet the appetite of others to Excess, no man ever after in those days imitated.[1]'

The 'more stupendious Entertainment' was apparently at the request of Charles himself at the end of July 1634. The Duchess of Newcastle tells how Ben Jonson was again 'employed in fitting such scenes and speeches as he could best devise'.[2] The Earl 'sent for all the gentry of the country to come and wait on their Majesties' and 'it cost him in all between fourteen and fifteen thousand pounds'.[3] The entertainment at Welbeck in the previous year had cost 'between four and five thousand pounds'.

The universities as well as the great houses gave theatrical welcomes to

---

[1] *History of the Rebellion and Civil Wars in England*, 3 vols (Oxford, 1704), I, 61.
[2] *Love's Welcome at Bolsover*, Herford and Simpson, VII, 806–14.
[3] *Life of William Cavendish, Duke of Newcastle . . . by Margaret, Duchess of Newcastle*, ed. C. H. Firth (London, 1886), 192.

royal visitors; two occasions (one from each reign) are worth describing. On 16 March 1615, John Chamberlain wrote to Sir Dudley Carleton at Turin of the visit by King James and Prince Charles to Cambridge. Their entry to the city was made on 7 March 'with as much solemnitie . . . as the hard weather and extreme fowle wayes wold permit':

> The Kinge and Prince lay at Trinitie College where the playes were represented, and the hall so well ordered for roome that above 2000 persons were conveniently placed. The first nights entertainment was a comedie made and acted by St Johns men [*Æmilia* by T. Cecil, not extant]. . . . Though yt were larded with pretty shewes at the beginning and end, and with somwhat too brode speach for such a presence, yet yt was still drie.
>
> The second night was a comedie of Clare Hall [*Ignoramus*, by George Ruggle, published 1630]. . . . The thing was full of mirth and varietie, with many excellent actors, (among whom the Lord Comptons sonne though least yet was not worst) but more then halfe marred with extreme length.
>
> The third night was an English comedie called Albumazer [by Thomas Tomkis, published 1615], of Trinitie Colleges action and invention, but there was no great matter in yt more then one goode clownes part. The last night was a Latin pastorall of the same houses [*Melanthe* by S. Brooke, published 1615] excellently written and as well acted, which gave great contentment as well to the King as to all the rest.[1]

The King's pleasure was evidently real. In his next letter, Chamberlain reported that the King kept on talking of going to Cambridge privately to see two of the plays, and then decided 'to have the actors come hither, which wilbe a difficult thing to perswade, some of them beeing preachers and bachelors of Divinitie to become players any where but in the universitie, which was incongruitie enough, and wherto the Oxford men tooke exception'. Next year, when the King stopped at Royston on his way from Newmarket, Chamberlain said that he sent for 'some of the younger sort of Cantabrigians' to act their play which he had heard commended, and bore their charges.[2]

At the end of the summer progress in 1636, Charles, Henrietta Maria, Prince Charles, the Elector Palatine and Prince Rupert visited Oxford. As

[1] J. Chamberlain, *Letters*, 1, 587.
[2] ibid., 1, 618.

Chancellor of the University, Archbishop Laud took great personal pains in the theatrical side of their entertainment. On the first day, in Christ Church Hall, there was *The Floating Island*, by the University Orator, William Strode; it was found too grave and moral, 'fitter for scholars than a court'.[1] The next day it was Laud's own college, St John's, and the expense was borne entirely by Laud. The Archbishop took a Laudian interest in the arrangements, to make sure that all went off 'without any the least disturbance' and that the hall was 'fresh and cool'. For the play, Laud had chosen *Love's Hospital*, by George Wilde, who later became his chaplain. Laud thought that 'the plot was very good, and the action. It was merry, and without offence, and so gave a great deal of content.'[2] After supper, the royal party saw another play, Cartwright's *The Royal Slave*. It was elaborately staged and elaborately costumed – 'the strangeness of the Persian habits gave great content', said Laud. The play was an enormous success: the King gave Cartwright £40, and the Queen was so impressed that she wanted to have the play performed at Hampton Court by 'her own players'. She later wrote to the Chancellor asking to borrow the costumes and scenery; he dispatched 'the clothes and the perspectives of the stage' with the proviso that nothing should come into the general use of the common players.[3]

The Queen's passion for drama took her several times to the public theatre – four visits to Blackfriars are on record. Sir Henry Herbert noted: 'The 13 May, 1634, the Queene was at Blackfryers, to see Messengers play.'[4] A year or two later, the Queen saw Lodowick Carlell's *Arviragus and Philicia* at Blackfriars. There was another visit in May 1636 (*Alphonsus*) and in the season of 1638–9 a fourth visit to see Davenant's *The Unfortunate Lovers*. G. E. Bentley, pointing out that the company was paid court fees for the last two of these performances, remarks: 'The performances attended by the Queen were almost certainly special night productions for the court, not the regular afternoon performances.'[5] The visit of the King and Queen to the Phoenix to see Heywood's masque, *Love's Mistress*, in 1634, was obviously a private occasion, perhaps to see a dress rehearsal before the production at Denmark House.[6]

[1] George Garrard, quoted in *Jacobean and Caroline Stage*, V, 1190.
[2] *Autobiography* (London, 1839), 207; quoted in *Jacobean and Caroline Stage*, V, 1263–4. Laud notes that, at the time, the college was 'so well furnished, as that they did not borrow any one actor from any College in town.'
[3] *Jacobean and Caroline Stage*, III, 137.
[4] Probably, as Malone suggested, the lost *Cleander*, a new play recently licensed. Adams, *Herbert*, 65, quoted in *Jacobean and Caroline Stage*, IV, 774.
[5] *Jacobean and Caroline Stage*, VI, 34–6.
[6] ibid., I, 232–3.

4 The nobility
   and the drama

How firmly drama had become established as an indispensable element of Caroline court life can be seen from the activities of Wentworth (later Earl of Strafford) in Dublin where he was Lord Deputy from 1633. Wentworth added greatly to the stateliness of Dublin Castle and to the ceremony within its walls, and from the beginning he encouraged plays by the gentlemen of his own train.[1] By 1636 he had brought over the resourceful Scotsman John Ogilby to organize a professional company of players, who were to be the Irish equivalent of the King's Men. Ogilby had been a professional dancer at court masques, and had taken boy-actors as his apprentices; he must have been closely in touch with the London theatres. In Dublin he undertook, he said, 'great preparations and disbursements in building a new theatre, stocking and bringing over a Company of Actors and Musicians, and settling them in Dublin'.[2] He built his theatre in Werburgh Street hard by the castle and brought James Shirley over as resident dramatist. In 1638 Strafford grandly appointed the dancing-master as 'Master of the Revells in and through our said Kingdome of Ireland'.[3] Though Shirley always

[1] W. S. Clark, *The Early Irish Stage: The Beginning to 1720* (Oxford, 1955), 26–7.
[2] ibid., 27.
[3] ibid., 31.

abused his Irish audience for their resistance to good theatrical literature (see his prologue to *St Patrick for Ireland*), it is fair to say that for a year or two before the outbreak of violence in Ireland in 1641 there was a vigorous theatre-life associated with the viceregal court in Dublin.

In our period the great nobility had lost to royalty their traditional role of founding and providing for companies of actors, but the nobility as a whole continued to encourage drama in all sorts of ways. Aristocratic dramatists were no new thing, but the fashion for the courtier to try his hand at playwriting was new, and derived directly from the Queen's enthusiasms and her recollection of the courtly contributors to drama in France. Cartwright said: 'He's scarce a courtier now, that hath not writ/His brace of plays.'[1] Montague's work we have already mentioned. Sir John Suckling's *Aglaura* was probably the most famous, produced in 1637 with great expense and ostentation. Suckling – soldier, courtier, gambler, philanderer, wit and poet – probably comes as near as anyone to the common definition of the Caroline courtier. *Aglaura* was not acted by courtiers but by the King's Men, for whom Suckling bought costumes of legendary richness.

A few other courtier-dramatists may be worth listing. Sir William Berkeley was a Gentleman of the Privy Chamber and he tried his hand at the platonic play with *The Lost Lady* of 1637; it was well soaked in the conventions of D'Urfé's *Astrée*. Acted by the King's Men at court, it was then taken to Blackfriars for a wider audience. Lodowick Carlell, son of a Scottish peer, became huntsman to Charles I and keeper of the royal park at Richmond; he was considerably more than the nonce-dramatist that Berkeley was, with seven plays to his credit, some of them written for the public theatre. William Cavendish, Earl of Newcastle, who fostered drama by acting as patron of Jonson, Davenant, Shirley and Shadwell, wrote *The Country Captain* (*c.* 1640) – or most of it – and had it performed possibly at court, certainly at Blackfriars. He survived his own eccentric and comic style of warfare to become a dramatist again at the Restoration.

Sir John Denham, author of *Cooper's Hill* and a very rich courtier (and gambler), in 1641 wrote *The Sophy*, which was acted at Blackfriars by the King's Men. William Habington, a member of the higher Catholic gentry and a kingsman by marriage of the mighty Herberts, wrote *The Queen of Aragon* for the Lord Chamberlain (the Earl of Pembroke) to present as a gift

---

[1] *The Siege*, quoted in A. Harbage, *Cavalier Drama* (New York, 1936), 23. See this book for a full account of courtly drama.

to the King and Queen. The Master of the Revels said: 'It was performd by my lords servants out of his own family, and [at] his charge in the cloathes and sceanes, which were very riche and curious.'[1] The play was given a second time at court, played at Blackfriars and revived at the Restoration. Thomas Killigrew seems altogether too much a professional to include in a list of amateur courtier-dramatists, but he was a career courtier who had started as a page and become a member of the Queen's household. His plays really belong to the history of the public theatre.

Dramatic entertainment in the great houses of the land did not depend on the approach of royalty and it was not snuffed out during the Interregnum, although with so many estates sequestrated and their owners forlorn in France it became much more limited. Masques and plays to celebrate special occasions in London are often hard to separate from the life of the court: the performance of Henry Killigrew's *The Conspiracy* at York House in 1635, to celebrate the marriage of Buckingham's daughter to the Lord Chamberlain's son, took place in the presence of the King and Queen and perhaps belongs with the royal occasions we have been considering. But the initiative is with the noblemen: Lord Hay commissions a masque from Jonson (*Lovers Made Men*) to feast the French ambassador (1617). 'A supper and a play' seems to have been the usual way for the great ones about the court to mark an occasion or to create notice. Here are a few examples from Chamberlain's letters showing the strategic uses to which entertainment could be put. 'The Lord Digbie made a great supper and a play at White-hall to the best part of the great Lords and Ladies about this towne' (1618). 'The Lady Hatton made a great supper with a play the last weeke, where were all the gallants and great ones about the court, but specially the Howards, whom she would faine soder [solder] and lincke fast again with the Marquis Buckingham and that side' (1619). Buckingham gave his own gentlemen £100 'to make them a supper and a play the next night at the Miter in Fleet-street' (1618). The year before, Buckingham had himself been given 'a supper and a maske' by the Middle Templars, either because 'he was of theyre societie, or that they would preoccupate his favor'.[2]

Two dramatic entertainments in the country are famous because of their author. About the year 1632, John Milton was asked to provide the words for an entertainment (*Arcades*) which her family presented to the Dowager

[1] Adams, *Herbert*, 58.
[2] J. Chamberlain, *Letters*, ed. N. E. McClure, 2 vols (Philadelphia, 1939), II, 193, 199–200, 159, 49.

Countess of Derby at Harefield (in Middlesex, twenty miles north-west of London). 'A Masque presented at Ludlow Castle' (*Comus*) is much more ambitious. In a way, it is court entertainment. The Earl of Bridgwater had taken up his official residence at Ludlow Castle as Lord President of Wales some months before, and *Comus*, given on Michaelmas night 1634, was no doubt part of the solemnities and celebrations required to establish the new 'reign'. The part of the Lady was taken by the Earl's youngest daughter, Lady Alice Egerton (aged 14 or 15), and the brothers were her own younger brothers, Viscount Brackley and Thomas Egerton. Henry Lawes, who had been music tutor to the Egerton children, composed the music and acted the part of the Attendant Spirit.

The traditional visits of the public companies of actors to the great houses of the land continued in our period. Lawrence Stone has published the records of the reception of touring companies of professional players by the Earl of Cumberland either at Londesborough or Hazelwood, and by his son Lord Clifford at Skipton Castle in Yorkshire.[1] Many companies came to offer their service: the Children of the Revels, Lord Dudley's players, Prince Charles's Men, the King's Men, the Lady Elizabeth's servants, Lord Shrewsbury's players, and so on. The offer to play was not always accepted and the players would sometimes be sent away with ten shillings or so. But often they stayed for more than a single performance. In February 1620 at Londesborough, Lord Derby's Men stayed three nights and performed five plays; they were followed by the King's Men, fourteen actors, who 'stayed here . . . from Tewsday till fryday and played v playes'. The Skipton Castle records give us two conspicuous entries for 1636: 'To a certeyne company of Roguish players whoe represented A new way to pay old debtes', and 'To Adam Gerdler whome my lord sent for frome Yorke to act a part in the Kt of the burning pestell'. (The roguish players got the usual pound, and Gerdler five shillings.)

Often enough, one hears of some dramatic activity which would in normal times be too ordinary to comment on only because of some unusual consequence. In or about 1631, the Bishop of Lincoln arranged a performance of a play, possibly *A Midsummer Night's Dream*, in his own house, before 'divers Knights and Ladyes, with many other householders servants'. The performance was not by professional players, but unfortunately it was on a Sunday night and scandal was caused.[2]

[1] MSC, v (1960), 17–28.
[2] E. K. Chambers, *William Shakespeare*, 2 vols (Oxford, 1930), II, 348–52.

The custom of private theatricals is illustrated by the minor playwright Arthur Wilson (1595–1652), describing his life in the service of the Earl of Essex. From 1620, he spent the summers of three years campaigning in the Palatinate:

> The winters wee spent in England. Either at Draiton, my Lord's grandmother's; Chartley, his owne house; or some of his brother, the Earl of Hertford's, houses. Our private sports abroad, hunting; at home, chesse or catastrophe. Our publique sports (and sometimes with great charge and expence) were masks or playes. Wherein I was a contriver both of words and matter. For as long as the good old Countess of Leicester lived (the grandmother to theise noble families,) her hospitable entertainment was garnisht with such, then, harmeles recreations.[1]

The most ambitious theatricals in great private houses (apart from special masques) were those arranged by Mildmay Fane, Earl of Westmorland, in his house at Apthorpe, Northamptonshire. Fane wrote half a dozen plays between 1640 and 1650, and three or four of them were presented, with elaborate staging and with actors from his own household, in his private theatre.[2] Although it is unlikely that Fane's ambitions would have been in the direction of the public theatre if times had been different, the giving of plays in private houses was one way of circumventing the prohibitions of Parliament. James Wright noted in *Historia Histrionica* that 'in *Oliver's* time, they [the professional players] used to Act privately, three or four Miles, or more, out of Town, now here, now there, sometimes in Noblemens Houses, in particular *Holland-house* at *Kensington*, where the Nobility and Gentry who met (but in no great Numbers) used to make a Sum for them'.[3] At a time near the outbreak of the troubles, Francis Quarles had his play *The Virgin Widow* privately acted at Chelsea 'by a company of young Gentlemen'.[4] In 1654, at the house of Sir Thomas Peyton in Kent, Dorothy Osborne wrote that 'we go abroad all day and play all night and say our prayers when we have time'. They were rehearsing *The Lost Lady* by Sir William Berkeley.[5]

---

[1] Quoted in *Jacobean and Caroline Stage*, V, 1268.
[2] See Clifford Leech, *Mildmay Fane's Raguaillo d'Oceano 1640 and Candy Restored 1641*, Materials for the Study of Old English Drama, NS 15 (Louvain, 1938), 23–60.
[3] *Jacobean and Caroline Stage*, II, 695.
[4] ibid., IV, 957.
[5] Harbage, *Cavalier Drama*, 202–3.

5 The managers of the public theatres

Philip Henslowe, whose purse controlled so much of English drama and so many English dramatists, died in January 1616. He, like Edward Alleyn who inherited his theatrical interests, belongs to an earlier period of the drama. Alleyn did not have much to do with the direct control of the Fortune, but gave it over to a syndicate of players. It is not an unimportant item in the social history of the theatre at this period that Alleyn, the actor who had married Henslowe's daughter, took as his second wife in 1623 the daughter of the Dean of St Paul's, Dr John Donne. Alleyn completed the purchase of the manor of Dulwich in 1614 for nearly £10,000, and then founded his school and hospital. He died in 1626.

Richard Gunnell (a Roman Catholic) came to the fore as the manager of the Fortune in the 1620s. He had been an actor and he became a dramatist, though his plays are lost. He probably managed the Salisbury Court theatre, which he and William Blagrave built in 1629. He is a shadowy figure. We know nothing about his birth and education, though an elegy referred to him as '*Mr*. Richard Gunnell, *Gent*.'.

We have more information about a more important theatre-manager, Christopher Beeston. Like Alleyn and Gunnell, he was an actor. He was a leading man in Queen Anne's company when in 1619 he converted the old cockpit in Drury Lane into a new private theatre (the Phoenix) to cash in on the select audience being attracted to Blackfriars. During his long reign at the Phoenix, he formed and re-formed companies of actors, negotiated with every leading dramatist of his day, and kept on good terms with the Master of the Revels. Whether he fired dramatists as well as hiring them is not known, because no records of his contracts exist (see pp. 38–9). His blandishments of the censor were carefully recorded by Sir Henry Herbert. For example:

> A Newyeres gift this 10 March 1623 – Received as a newyeres gift from the Cockpitt company Sir Walter Rawleys booke worth 1ˡⁱ.

> [? 15 August 1633] Meetinge with him [Beeston] at the ould exchange, he gave my wife a payre of gloves, that cost him at least twenty shillings. [1]

In view of presents like these, it is not surprising that Beeston was able on at least one occasion to change Herbert's mind about banning a play (see the episode of *The Ball* quoted on pp. 101–2). A man of Beeston's power and energy is not likely to have been popular, and records of court-cases preserve the grumblings of the players about his authority – in 1619, 'there was great variance and strife between the said defendants and the said Beeston'. [2]

We should like to know more than we do about Beeston: we may well feel we know more than enough about William Davenant, great impresario in the final days of the Protectorate and in the Restoration, who was beginning to emerge as a theatre-manager just before the Civil War. If his family were not gentry, they were very respectable. His father had been to Merchant Taylors' school and was host of the Crown Tavern at Oxford; he became Mayor just before his death in 1622. A cousin of his father became Bishop of Salisbury. His brother was ordained and two sisters married into the Church. All the same, it is surprising to find the 16-year-old orphan entering the service of the Duchess of Richmond, then becoming a page to Fulke Greville, Lord Brooke. In his early twenties he started to write plays and he followed Buckingham to the wars as an Ancient. No doubt his kinsman the bishop helped him to advance, though it is still difficult to see how he became a member of the Middle Temple and a friend of Edward Hyde. Davenant evidently worked very hard indeed at his entrance into noble

[1] Adams, *Herbert*, 19, 67; *Jacobean and Caroline Stage*, VI, 59.
[2] *Jacobean and Caroline Stage*, II, 367 (modernized).

society. He won Endymion Porter and Henry Jermyn as patrons, both of them courtiers in close touch with the King and Queen. His verse-epistles from the pre-war years are voluminous; anyone who cares to plough through these poetic exercises in servility will learn a great deal about patronage, about Davenant, and about the English court. 'Ambition', he said in the Preface to *Gondibert* (1650), is 'no more then an extraordinary lifting of the feet in the rough ways of Honor over the impediments of Fortune', and it is 'necessary for every vertuous breast'. 'Good men are guilty of too little appetite to greatness.'[1] All rising, Davenant knew, was by a winding stair:

> And as in Ships, so in a Palace all
> Proceed by Aids that are collateral.
> The way to highest Pow'r is still oblique;
> Which when we strive to move, we, Seamen-like,
> Must hand a lesser string, untill it stir
> A distant cord which does our force prefer.[2]

Davenant courted favour so successfully that he survived both the loss of his nose through syphilis and the murder of a waiter in an Essex tavern in 1633. Charles reduced the sentence for the murder to transportation to America, but it is certain that Davenant didn't go. His use of his patron to intervene with the King against Herbert's banning of *The Wits* will be described in a later section (see p. 58). He succeeded Aurelian Townshend as Jones's collaborator in the court masques and (rather informally?) became Poet Laureate. It is quite fitting that he should have written the text of *Salmacida Spolia*, because he had come to take the identification of art and monarchy as seriously as he took anything outside his own advancement.[3]

In 1639 Davenant began his managerial ventures with elaborate proposals for a big new theatre in Fleet Street; he got a patent but the project was suppressed. But, ever at hand, he received the control of the Phoenix in Drury Lane in June 1640, after the disgrace and imprisonment of William Beeston (son of Christopher Beeston) for producing an unlicensed play. His reign was very short, for in 1641 he had left London. In the Civil War, the playwright and court-poet put to the test his beliefs in the alliance of arts and arms. The Earl of Newcastle gave him a major military post and the King knighted him. He was a very active man and much hated by

[1] J. E. Spingarn, *Critical Essays of the Seventeenth Century*, 3 vols (Oxford, 1909), II, 14.
[2] 'To the Duke of Richmond, in the year 1639', *Works* (1673), 293.
[3] See e.g. 'To the Earl of Orrery' and 'To him who Prophecy'd a Successles end of the Parliament, in the year 1630', in *Works* (1673), 275–88.

Parliament. He continued to write *Gondibert* when he was in prison, and his luck held when the Commons (just) voted against trying him for high treason. He eventually persuaded Cromwell to grant him complete freedom, and the question became one of survival. He tried his hand at the old trade of congratulatory verses, to Cromwell's children, and at a newer one of wedding widows. But his best and most resourceful enterprise was circumventing the ban on public playing with his famous 'operas'. These 'moral representations' with music, declamation and elaborate scenery began in 1656. After cultivating Bulstrode Whitelocke and Secretary Thurloe, Davenant moved from the semi-private location of Rutland House to the Cockpit. At the Restoration he was excellently placed to battle with his rivals and obtain with Killigrew the monopoly of the London stage. It is in 1660 that his real career as theatre-manager begins, but his career to this point throws a great deal of light on the social history of the theatre between Shakespeare and the Restoration.[1]

---

[1] To be fair to Davenant, I should add that it has been persuasively argued that the murder mentioned above was the act of another man of the same name. See J. P. Feil, 'Davenant Exonerated', *MLR* 58 (1963), 335–42.

6 The dramatists

The most important professional writers for the stage who were still in mid-career when Shakespeare stopped writing in 1613 were Ben Jonson (41), Thomas Dekker (41?), Thomas Heywood (39), John Fletcher (34), Thomas Middleton (33), John Webster (33?). Of those who had their careers in front of them, the best known are Philip Massinger (30), John Ford (27), Richard Brome (23?) and James Shirley (17).

In asking who these men were and how they lived, we ought to treat Jonson as unique. He was the established court-poet and the most famous man of letters in England – and as near to security as a writer could be. He had many patrons: the Countess of Bedford, the Countess of Rutland, Sir Robert and Lady Wroth, Sir Kenelm Digby, the Earl of Pembroke, Sir Robert Sidney, Sir Henry Goodyere and others. Aubrey said of one Sylvanus Scory: ''Tis a good testimoniall of his worth, that Mr Benjamin Johnson (who ever scorned an unworthy Patrone) dedicated to him.'[1] Jonson was on terms of friendship with many of his patrons and indeed he claimed equality with them.[2] Dekker strongly objected to this hobnobbing with the great:

---

[1] *Aubrey's Brief Lives*, ed. O. L. Dick (London, 1949), 269.
[2] See what he said to Drummond about his non-dinner with Salisbury: Herford and Simpson, I, 141.

'Horace did not screw and wriggle himself into great men's familiarity, impudently, as thou dost: nor wear the badge of gentlemen's company, as thou dost.'[1]

Claims to equality do not remove the need for constant supplication: there was prodigious work to be done with epistles of request, thanks and sheer flattery. That we study some of these in our universities is a measure of the superiority of Jonson's rhetoric over Davenant's. Jonson's later years were years of sickness and of poverty. He was deeply in debt,[2] and one comes across begging letters like this to Newcastle in 1631: 'I make a most humble petition to your Lordships bounty, to succour my present necessities this good time of Easter, and it shall conclude all begging requests hereafter.'[3] From the Crown, Jonson received, first, payments for court masques and entertainments. Then, in 1616, James awarded him an annual pension of 100 marks. Chamberlain says that in 1621 this was increased to £200, but this must be a mistake, for, after a plea from Jonson, Charles raised the fee from 100 marks to £100 (an increase of $33\frac{1}{3}$ per cent).[4] There were presents as well. In 1621, Jonson 'escaped narrowly' from being knighted, and he was granted the reversion of the Mastership of the Revels, but this was unfortunately the second reversion and Jonson never obtained the post. (It is perhaps just as well; a man of Jonson's scornful temperament as licenser of plays is hard to imagine.)

In an age of amateurs, Jonson asserted professionalism. To his protégé Brome (who shared his contempt for the courtier-playwrights) he wrote:

> You . . . serv'd your time
> A Prentise-ship: which few doe now a dayes.
> Now each Court-Hobby-horse will wince in rime;
> Both learned, and unlearned, all write *Playes*.
> It was not so of old. . . .[5]

It galled Jonson that, while the professional scraped for his living, the amateur (who wasn't working for profit) found that dabbling in literature was a useful aid to promotion:

> *Poetry*, in this latter Age, hath prov'd but a meane Mistresse, to such as

[1] *Satiro-Mastix* (1601), v. ii. 254–8.
[2] See e.g. MSC, II, 411.
[3] Herford and Simpson, I, 211–12.
[4] J. Chamberlain, *Letters*, II, 104; Herford and Simpson, I, 245–7
[5] Herford and Simpson, VIII, 410.

have wholly addicted themselves to her. . . . They who have but saluted her on the by, and now and then tendred their visits, shee hath done much for, and advanced in the way of their owne professions (both the *Law*, and the *Gospel*) beyond all they could have hoped, or done for themselves, without her favour.[1]

As the drama allies itself more closely with the pleasures of the court and the metropolitan gentry, questions of the social rank which the dramatists were born into and the social rank which they achieved become very interesting. Was the fellow-feeling of the dramatists with their patrons a matter of birth and breeding, or was it (as with Davenant) acquired? Or was it simply pretended? It is important to remember that the gentry and the nobility were a very tiny fraction of the English population. To be a gentleman meant, essentially, that one's family owned land and that one did not need to work at a trade for one's living. Jonson was not a gentleman and nor was his one-time servant Richard Brome; and neither of them acquired honorary gentility by getting to the university. Dekker's origin is mysterious: he may have been a gentleman down on his luck, but absence of information is often an argument against gentility. It does not seem that he went to either university. Heywood was a clergyman's son, but clerics were a lowly enough class at this time, and he is not for that reason alone sealed of the gentry. Field was a clergyman's son too – his father was an extreme Puritan. One of his brothers was a well-known printer, the other became Bishop of Llandaff. Webster, it has recently been learned, was the son and brother of coachmakers with a sideline in 'pageants'.[2] Middleton looks like a repetition of Marlowe: the boy from rather humble surroundings who wins his way to the university and suffers a sense of social dislocation which fundamentally affects his art. Davenant is a rarity in being of the merchant class. Perhaps Shirley was, too: he went to Merchant Taylors' school and on to Cambridge.

The main gentlemen-dramatists were Fletcher, Massinger and Ford. (By 1613, Francis Beaumont was probably writing very little for the stage – he had married an heiress and no longer needed the money.) To these should be added less important dramatists like Thomas May, Thomas Randolph, Henry Glapthorne, Shackerley Marmion, Henry Shirley. Robert Daborne *said* he was a gentleman. There is a romantic figure, John Clavell, who was

[1] ibid., VIII, 583.
[2] See Mary Edmond, 'In Search of John Webster', *TLS* (24 December 1976), 1621–2, and her further letter, *TLS* (24 October 1980), 1201.

not only a knight's son but a highwayman, but he wrote only one play.

Fletcher's father was a senior fellow of Bene't College, Cambridge, who became vicar of Rye and chaplain to the Queen, then held three bishoprics, including that of London. But he died in 1596, when John Fletcher was 17, and left nothing but debts to be divided among his nine children. Massinger's father also had been a fellow of a college, Merton College, Oxford. Massinger senior married the daughter of a substantial merchant and then made his career in the household of the Earl of Pembroke. He was a man of considerable importance, managing the Earl's affairs in London, Member of Parliament, Examiner to the Council of the Welsh Marches. Philip Massinger was 19 years old and at Oxford when his father died. He left without taking a degree and it may well be that the only patrimony he received was the somewhat unfortunate recollection of his father's familiarity with one of the greatest lords in the land.

John Ford belonged to an old Devonshire family. He was perhaps at Oxford, certainly at the Middle Temple, from which he was expelled for two years for failing to pay his buttery bill. In 1610, Ford's father died and the dramatist (aged 24) received as his total inheritance £10. Thomas May's family had acquired the land necessary to gentility as recently as the sixteenth century. May grew up in surroundings of wealth and influence, and went to Cambridge and Gray's Inn. But in 1616, when he was 21, his father died and it was discovered that he had dissipated his whole estate, and mortgaged all the property except one house which May was forced to sell. May emerged from this disaster with only a small annuity. Shackerley Marmion's father was lord of the manor of Aynho (Northamptonshire) but Anthony à Wood says that the father 'profusely wasted much of his estate', and much of the family's land had been sold while the future dramatist was only a boy. Marmion nevertheless went to Oxford and obtained his degree. He thereafter tried soldiering before turning to the pen.

There is an extraordinary similarity in these lives. In each case a gentleman's son is bred to gentility and then is left poor by the death of his father when he is at the start of his career. It is hard to resist the conclusion that many dramatists in this period were dramatists *faute de mieux*; that they wrote plays because they needed the money; and that they published plays because they hoped that a cunningly lodged dedication would free them from the necessity of writing plays. Ford seems to have turned to the theatre when other things failed: he was 40 when he launched out as a playwright on his own, after doing journeyman-collaboration with Dekker. Massinger was 30 when he surfaced in theatrical history as a hack-dramatist in a debtors' prison. The dedication of his first printed play in 1623 spoke of 'my misfortunes having cast me on this course'. In an early poem which he sent to the Earl of Pembroke appealing for patronage on the grounds of his father's post, he asked the earl 'to cast an eye/Of favour on my trodd down povertie'.[1] If he had a patron, he remarked, he would be able to attempt greater kinds of literature, but he is not servile enough to enjoy cringing and flattering: 'let me rather/Live poorely on those toyes I would not father'.

'Live poorely': one feels they all did. Massinger complained of poverty for the greater part of his life. Dekker spent six years and more in prison for debt and he died in debt.[2] 'The first step to beggary, is to write for the stage', says the wife to her poet-husband in *Divers Crab-tree Lectures* (1639). 'The players . . . have the wit to keep you poor, that they themselves may prank it in plush.'[3] The lowly position of dramatist as compared with successful actor is revealed in Dekker's appeal from prison for financial help to Edward Alleyn, using the suitor's traditional approach, the eulogistic poem.[4] G. E. Bentley's close analysis of the earnings of playwrights in *The Profession of Dramatist in Shakespeare's Time* (1971) concluded (p. 110) that the early seventeenth-century dramatists 'may have complained of their poverty, but they were not ill-paid for the plays they wrote. . . . The professional playwrights made more money than other literary men of their time, and more than they could have made as schoolmasters or curates.' From the inside of a debtors' prison it may not have been possible to look on the situation so philosophically. Poverty is relative to one's expectations, and for the gentlemen-dramatists, at least, writing plays provided neither the social status nor the style of living they were born to.

[1] 'The Copie of a Letter', MS. G.2.21, Trinity College, Dublin, reprinted in *The Plays and Poems of Philip Massinger*, ed. P. Edwards and C. Gibson, 5 vols (Oxford, 1976), IV, 386–91.
[2] M. T. Jones-Davies, *Un Peintre de la Vie Londinienne: Thomas Dekker*, 2 vols (Paris, 1958), 71.
[3] Quoted by A. M. Clark in *Thomas Heywood* (Oxford, 1931), 41.
[4] *Henslowe Papers*, ed. W. W. Greg (London, 1907), 91–2.

7 The economics of playwriting

The position of the dramatist who has struck a bargain with a manager to write a play for a company of players for a certain fee is richly illustrated in the series of letters from Robert Daborne to Philip Henslowe in 1613. On 17 April, Daborne agreed to deliver *Machiavel and the Devil* to Henslowe before the end of the Easter term. He was to receive £20. He got £6 in advance and was to have £4 when the first three acts were delivered and a final payment of £10 on completion of 'ye last scean'.[1] Unfortunately, Daborne was at this time bedevilled by his creditors. A week after the initial contract, he wanted a further pound, and another on 3 May with the first three acts still undelivered. The comedy of the uncompleted tragedy and Daborne's exigencies dragged on for many months. A single letter will give the flavour of the situation (for the sake of legibility I have modernized the spelling):

> Mr Hinchlow,
> Your tried courtesy hath so far engaged me that howsoever this term hath much hindered my business, you shall see on Tuesday night I have

[1] *Henslowe Papers*, ed. W. W. Greg (London, 1907), 67.

not been idle. I thank God most of my troubles are ended, upon clearing whereof I have taken home my wife again, so that I will now after Monday intend your business carefully, that the company shall acknowledge themselves bound to you. I doubt not on Tuesday night, if you will appoint, I will meet you and Mr Alleyn and read some, for I am unwilling to read to the general company till all be finished; which, upon my credit, shall be to play it this next term with the first.

Sir, my occasions of expense have been so great and so many I am ashamed to think how much I am forced to press you, wherein I pray let me find your favourablest construction, and add one 20-shillings more to the money I have received, which makes eleven pounds, and you shall on Tuesday see I will deserve to my best ability your love, which I value more in itself than the best company's in the town.

So, myself and labours resting at your service, I commit you to God.

Yours to command,

16 May 1613   Rob. Daborne[1]

Twice in his letters Daborne threatens to transfer his plays to another company. For a new play he is offered the same terms as for the still-unfinished *Machiavel*: 'My necessity is such I must use other means to be furnished upon it. Before God, I can have £25 for it as some of the company know.'[2] He later wrote to Henslowe asking 'to know your determination for the company whether you purpose they shall have the play or no; they rail upon me I hear, because the King's men have given out they shall have it.'[3] These comments at once raise the extremely difficult question of contracts between a company (or a theatre-manager) and a dramatist for lengthy periods instead of for individual plays. When the dramatist is a sharer in the company, as Shakespeare was, the question of contract does not arise, but the role of actor-sharer-playwright is rare at this time (Nathan Field and Richard Gunnell are examples). The only evidence we have of a contract relates to Richard Brome. In 1635, Brome, who had previously been writing for the company at the Red Bull, signed a contract by which he undertook to write three plays a year for three years for the Salisbury Court theatre. He was to get fifteen shillings a week, plus one day's profit from each new play (estimated at not less than £5). In 1638 the contract was to be renewed,

giving Brome £1 a week for seven years. But the Cockpit enticed him away –
he had in fact already broken his contract by writing for it.[1] Contracts
similar to Brome's must have existed. The King's Men must have had a
contract with Fletcher, who wrote for no other company after 1613. They
probably had one with Massinger after 1627; before that date he wrote plays
for both Beeston's companies at the Cockpit and for the King's Men. James
Shirley wrote about two plays a year for Beeston for eleven years, and one
infers that he was under contract. Ogilby must have offered him terms of
employment when he invited him to Ireland. When he returned to England
in 1640, he may, as Bentley suggests, have taken the place of Massinger, who
had recently died, and worked under contract for the King's Men until the
theatres were closed.[2]

The necessity to bring a play out quickly and the existence of needy
dramatists combined to make collaboration a quite normal feature of
dramaturgy. In a letter to Alleyn, Daborne remarks very casually: 'I have
not only laboured my own play, which shall be ready before they come over,
but given Cyril Tourneur an act of *The Arraignment of London* to write, that
we may have that likewise ready for them.'[3] A great deal of Dekker's work
was collaborative, and there is a good account of what collaboration might
involve in a court case discovered by C. J. Sisson concerning a play of 1624,
Keep the Widow Waking (now lost), which was a dramatization of a recent
murder. Dekker, Ford, Webster and Rowley 'were privy, consenting and
acquainted with the making and contriving of the said play *Keep the Widow
Waking* and did make and contrive the same upon the instructions given
them by one Raph Savage'. Dekker 'wrote two sheets of paper containing
the first act . . . and a speech . . . in the last act of the boy who had killed his
mother'.[4] Fletcher wrote plays on his own, of course, but his normal method
of composition was to work with a team. The whole nature of drama at this
time is profoundly affected by the practice of sharing work in playwriting,
and to approach a collaborative play as though it were the same kind of work
of art as a play for which the author would never dream of sharing the
responsibility would be to make a fundamental critical error. Perhaps the

[1] See *Jacobean and Caroline Stage*, III, 52–3. C. W. Wallace reported the discovery of the
contract without either printing the documents or giving a reference to their source. The
documents have only recently been rediscovered.
[2] *Jacobean and Caroline Stage*, V, 1070.
[3] *Henslowe Papers*, 72.
[4] *The Library*, 4th series, 8 (1927); reprinted in *Lost Plays of Shakespeare's Age* (Cambridge,
1936). See also M. T. Jones-Davies, *Thomas Dekker*, I, 64–5 (spelling modernized).

initial impetus towards collaboration was a certain indifference to the final shape of the finished work of art, but it is as likely that the conditions of the playhouse bred that indifference.

It is very improbable that a man could live on what he earned from writing for the public stage. For the penurious dramatist, the main source of additional income was the patron. The system of patronage was (of course) inadequate as a means of support for the vast army of writers who looked hopefully towards it, but it is a mistake to think of patronage as a relic of a former age: it was a deep-rooted and indispensable feature of the seventeenth-century literary scene, and there was considerable enthusiasm for the office of patron. Not only the great families of Herbert, Sackville and Cavendish, but also gentlemen at court, country gentlemen and merchants are found dispensing financial favours.

I have already mentioned the widespread patronage of Jonson (and its failure in the end to keep him from want) and the victims of Davenant's charms. Fletcher seems to have had a fairly secure relationship with a single patron, the Earl of Huntingdon. Massinger's efforts to interest the Pembrokes in his poverty seem eventually to have won him a pension of twenty or thirty pounds a year. He consistently used the dedications of his plays as bids for patronage and for acknowledgement of favours received. He will have a shot in the dark, as with the dedication of *The Renegado* to Lord Berkeley, in which he refers to himself as 'the writer, your countryman, never yet made happy in your notice and favour'. In a quite different tone he addresses *The Roman Actor* (1629) to his 'much honoured and most true friends', Sir Philip Knyvet, Sir Thomas Jay and Mr Thomas Bellingham, and acknowledges himself bound to them for their 'many and extraordinary favours'. In dedicating *The Great Duke of Florence* (1636) to Sir Robert Wiseman, he writes that 'for many years I had but faintly subsisted, if I had not often tasted of your bounty'. *The Maid of Honour* (1631) is dedicated to Sir Francis Foljambe and Sir Thomas Bland, and thanks them for being 'patrons to me and my despised studies' for many years. 'I had not to this time subsisted, but that I was supported by your frequent courtesies and favours.'

James Shirley, who had taken orders and then become a schoolmaster before turning to the stage, was fortunate enough – no doubt his conversion to Catholicism helped – to obtain court preferment. In his lucky years in the mid-1630s he became a valet of the chamber in the Queen's household. Shirley prospered more than all his fellows. In the Interregnum he taught school again and did well. He was a family man and at his death there was a 'sizeable estate for a poet' to be divided among his widow and children.[1]

On the whole, professional dramatists do not seem to have combined playwriting with 'other employment'. Ford's legal work we know nothing of; Daborne's unlikely transformation into a clergyman – he became Dean of Lismore – ended his dramatic career. Middleton was fortunate to hold the post of Chronologer to the City of London, for which he received gifts and rewards, as well as a stipend reaching £10 a year. He worked as historian and pageant-writer. For him, as for Dekker and Heywood, the preparation of city-pageants and Lord Mayors' Shows was an extremely important source of income, and as these shows were also an important part of the festive life of London, as important to the city, perhaps, as the masques were at court, they are worth pausing for. D. M. Bergeron writes:

> The lord mayor's show had its beginning as an institution in the mid-sixteenth century, but it reached its apogee in the first several decades of the seventeenth. Each October 29, the new mayor would leave the Guildhall in London, go to Westminster via the Thames, take his oath, return to the city, and make his way again to Guildhall. On his return, the sponsoring guild would offer entertainment along the route to honor him and their company. The more elaborate shows also included entertainment on the river.[2]

The Lord Mayors' Shows stopped in 1639 and were not resumed until 1655.

Middleton took over as main librettist from Anthony Munday in 1617 and ruled until 1626, except for the years 1620 (Squire) and 1624 (Webster). Dekker was the poet in 1627, 1628 and 1629; Heywood took over in 1631, and was the poet for all pageants, except in 1634, until they ended in 1639. It is hard to tell just how much a poet made out of one of these shows, because the companies gave him an overall payment for devising, organizing and writing the pageant, for costuming it, and often for the carpentry and painting.[3] In 1613, for example, when the show was put on by the Grocers for Sir Thomas Middleton, and prepared by Munday and Middleton, Munday got £149 for 'the devyse of the Pageant and other shewes (excepting the Pageant) and alsoe for the Portage and Carryage both by land and by water'; Middleton got £40 for 'the ordering overseeing and wrytinge of the whole Devyse and alsoe for the appareling the personage in the

[1] *Jacobean and Caroline Stage*, v, 1071.
[2] 'Anthony Munday: Pageant-Poet to the City of London', *HLQ*, 30 (1967), 345–68.
[3] Glynne Wickham, *Early English Stages* (1959–   ), II, pt 1 (1963), 242–3.

Pageant'.[1] Middleton got £282 from the Grocers in 1617 but had to make huge disbursements out of that, including 'Dyvells and fyer workes'. A customary fee to a poet seems to have been £180. In 1626, the Drapers tried to get out of paying Middleton and Garrett Christmas the agreed fee 'in regarde of the ill performance'.[2]

The office of pageant-poet was sometimes competitive. Webster succeeded in 1624 partly because he was a member of the Merchant Tailors, who were the sponsoring company. In 1619, three poets were suitors to the Skinners' company: 'Anthonie Mondaie, Thomas Middleton and Richard Grimston poettes, all shewed to the table their severall plottes for devices for the shewes and pagente against Symon and Judes tide and each desired to searve the Companie.'[3] Middleton won.

The Grocers in 1617 (when Middleton was again successful) were generous enough to pay fees to the disappointed suitors, Munday (£5) and Dekker (£4), the latter 'for his paines in drawing a project for this busynes which was offered to the Comyttees'. Dekker got £1 from the Merchant Tailors in 1630 merely for offering his services. The Ironmongers' accounts of 1619 show Dekker and Christmas bargaining with the company. That year Dekker had been invited to furnish the pageant. The two men 'presented them with a plott wherein was contayned 6 severall Pageants . . . ffor the accomplishing whereof they demaunded 200li, which theis present conceived to be an over-value, and thereupon offerred them 180li which they accepted'. In 1635, Robert Norman and John Taylor (the Water Poet) presented a scheme to the Ironmongers for £190, 'and under that price they would not undertake it', but the more experienced Heywood, with Garrett Christmas's sons, offered their 'invention of 5 pageants' for £180 and got the contract. Christmas's sons took matters completely into their own hands in 1639, and for £196 promised to undertake the pageants and shows 'and to dischardge Mr Thomas Heyward the Poett for writing the booke'.[4] D. J. Gordon and J. Robertson comment that 'we seem to have a situation exactly parallel to what was happening at Court in connexion with the Masque: to the uneasy relationship that existed between Inigo Jones and the poets'.[5] The texts of the pageants were customarily printed at the sponsoring company's cost.

[1] MSC, III (1954), 87.
[2] ibid., 110.
[3] ibid., 99.
[4] ibid., 93, 113, 115, 129.
[5] ibid., xliii.

8 The audience

Most of the references to playgoing relate to the gentry and nobility and to the private theatres: these are the classes which are noticed, and these are the theatres they go to. The private theatres made themselves exclusive by a simple price-differential; the audience at the cheaper public theatres tended naturally to be lower in the social and economic hierarchy, and such people do not frequently appear in letters of court gossip and so on. James Wright in his *Historia Histrionica* said that the Fortune and the Red Bull 'were mostly frequented by Citizens, and the meaner sort of People'.[1] Between 1613 and 1642 the social status of the old public theatres declined rapidly as the new indoor theatres were opened. References to gentry going to the open theatres tend to come early in the period. Chamberlain called on Elizabeth Williams in June 1614 but discovered that 'she was gon to the new Globe to a play'. In 1621 he reported to Gondomar, the Spanish ambassador, that 'with his whole traine he went to a common play at the Fortune in Golding-Lane, and the players (not to be overcome with curtesie) made him a banket when the play

---

[1] *Jacobean and Caroline Stage*, II, 693. Although James Wright, born in 1643, was not an eye-witness of the pre-war theatre, his father, Abraham, was a keen and critical theatre-goer, and presumably is the source of his son's priceless information. See J. G. McManaway, *Studies in Shakespeare* (New York, 1969), 279–80.

was don in the garden adjoyning'.[1] Dr Lambe, the associate of Buckingham, was set on by the mob as he left the Fortune in 1626, and it was at the Globe that the Duke of Buckingham himself saw *Henry VIII* shortly before his murder. (In the same week he went to *The Rape of Lucrece* at the Cockpit.)[2] The Fortune always seems to have had a very mixed audience. In 1612 there were 'divers cutt-purses and other lewde and ill disposed persons in great multitudes' who resorted to the Fortune 'at th'end of everye playe', 'by reason of certayne lewde Jigges songes and daunces used and accustomed'. Sailors were involved in riots there in 1626, and in 1632 there is a scornful mention of the 'prentizes and apell-wyfes' at the theatre.[3]

One cannot do much more than present the fragments of the playgoing life as they are preserved in records in the hope that put together they make some kind of a picture – there being no hope of finding enough material for statistics of any kind. Much of what follows is culled from *The Jacobean and Caroline Stage*.

The Duchess of Newcastle, writing of her brothers, Sir John, Sir Charles and Sir Thomas Lucas, before the troubles that cost two of them their lives, said that they usually lived in London for half the year.

> But to rehearse their recreations. Their customs were in winter time to go sometimes to plays, or to ride in their coaches about the streets to see the concourse and recourse of people; and in the spring time to visit the Spring Garden, Hyde Park, and the like places; and sometimes they would have music and sup in barges upon the water.[4]

John Greene, a student at Lincoln's Inn and a regular theatre-goer, recorded in his diary a wedding party when his sister got married in 1635. They were all together for two days, during which 'wee were at a play, some at cockpit, some at blackfriers'.[5] Sir Humphrey Mildmay was a middle-aged enthusiast for the theatre, though he was often conscience-stricken at the waste of his time. Here are a few extracts from his records of visits to the public theatres:

> *8 December 1635* . . . dined with Rob: Dowgill, wente to the La[dy] of

[1] J. Chamberlain, *Letters*, II, 391.
[2] *Jacobean and Caroline Stage*, I, 266 and 22–3.
[3] ibid., VI, 146, 160–1; I, 268.
[4] *Life of William Cavendish, Duke of Newcastle . . . by Margaret, Duchess of Newcastle*, ed. C. H. Furth (London, 1886), 284–5.
[5] E. M. Symonds, 'The Diary of John Greene (1635–59)', *English Historical Review*, 43 (1928), 386, 389.

pleasure and saw that rare playe, came home late, Supped. . . .

11 December 1635 To dynner came Sir Chr: Abdy and wente to the Newe playe with my wife, I wente abroade by myselfe to worse places alone.

12 February 1639 To a play with Mrs James, and to supper with Dr Doriela and Tho: Chichley and home.

18 February 1639 . . . dined with Mrs James and wente to a playe with her. . . .

15 May 1640 . . . to dynner and then to the Newe play att Bl[ack]fryers with my Company [including his wife this time] where I loste the whole day.

9 November 1640 Came home to dynner and founde good Company there, after Noone to a playe . . . .

16 November 1640 . . . after Noone with my wife and Pretty Cozen to a playe and home late. . . .[1]

Bulstrode Whitelocke, the great lawyer and parliamentarian who took a leading part in the impeachment of Strafford, was such a familiar visitor at Blackfriars that the musicians would play his own piece, 'Whitelocke's Coranto', when he entered.[2] Whitelocke, who was in charge of the music of *The Triumph of Peace*, was another of those, like the Lord Chamberlain himself (Philip, Earl of Pembroke), who could combine a great enthusiasm for plays and masques with a decision for Parliament rather than King in 1642.

A good deal of information about playgoers comes from reports of quarrels among the nobility. Sir John Suckling waylaid the younger brother of Sir Kenelm Digby as he was coming from a play at Blackfriars and started an affray (1634). In 1632, Captain Charles Essex was sitting by his patron's wife, the second Countess of Essex, in a box on the Blackfriars stage, when Lord Thurles stood in front of them and obscured their view. Words and worse passed until the lord drew his sword 'and ran full butt at him, though hee missed him'. Lord Thurles, who was then 21 years of age, later became the Duke of Ormonde. His biographer, Thomas Carte, said that he was 'a great admirer of plays, and acquainted with all the good actors of the stage. He took such delight in the theatre that it scarce ever wanted his presence.'[3] In 1635 there is news of a 'Quarrell that lately broke out betwixt my Lord *Digby* and *Will Crofts* in the *Black-Fryars* at a play'. In 1636, 'a little Pique

---

[1] *Jacobean and Caroline Stage*, II, 673–81; contractions expanded and light punctuation supplied.
[2] ibid., I, 40 and VI, 32.
[3] H. Berry, 'The Stage and Boxes at Blackfriars', *SP*, 63 (1966), 163–86.

happened betwixt the Duke of *Lenox* and the Lord Chamberlain about a Box at a new Play in the *Black Fryars*, of which the Duke had got the Key. . . . His Majesty hearing of it, sent the Earl of *Holland* to commend them not to dispute it, but before him, so he heard it and made them Friends.' After a quarrel at a play in 1625, Will Murray of the Prince's Bedchamber fought a duel with Sir Humphrey Tufton.[1]

Some other visitors to the theatres we hear of incidentally are Lord Falkland, Sir Richard (later Viscount) Wenman, Tobie Mathew, the Duke of Brunswick (on a visit). The inconstant Lady Newport 'went one evening as she came from a Play in *Drury-Lane* to *Somerset-House*, where one of the Capuchins reconciled her to the *Popish* Church, of which she is now a weak Member'.[2] A list of theatre-lovers could be drawn up from the names of those who wrote the execrable verse-epistles printed in editions of plays in commendation of the author. Inns of Court students, said to have numbered about 700,[3] are traditionally considered to have been pillars of the private-theatre audience. It is a fair guess that Puritan merchants were not likely to be found in the theatre. Documents in the Folger Library give details of an extraordinary Roman Catholic controversy of 1618 about the desirability of English secular priests attending plays by common players upon common stages. It is astonishing that there were enough priests about to warrant the discussion. Apparently a number were actually in prison, but had liberty to 'goe from prison to play-house'. A prohibition against attendance, by the Arch-priest of England, was soon lifted.[4]

The popularity of the private theatres created special problems, demonstrated in the vivid petitions of the parishioners of St Anne's, Blackfriars, to the Lord Mayor and Corporation of London (late 1618?):

> There is daily such resort of people, and such multitudes of coaches (whereof many are hackney-coaches, bringing people of all sorts) that sometimes all our streets cannot contain them, but that they clog up Ludgate also . . . and the inhabitants there cannot come to their houses, nor bring in their necessary provisions of beer, wood, coal or hay, nor the tradesmen or shopkeepers utter their wares, nor the passenger go to the common water-stairs without danger of their lives and limbs. . . .

[1] *Jacobean and Caroline Stage*, I, 42, 47, 48; VII, 58.
[2] ibid., IV, 693; Chamberlain, *Letters*, II, 181 and 137; *Jacobean and Caroline Stage*, I, 16; VI, 4 and 69.
[3] A. Harbage, *Shakespeare's Audience* (New York, 1941), 80.
[4] I. J. Semper, 'The Jacobean Theater through the Eyes of Catholic Clerics', *Shakespeare Quarterly*, 3 (1952), 45–51.

These inconveniences falling out almost every day in the winter-time (not forbearing the time of Lent) from one or two of the clock till six at night, which being the time also most usual for christenings and burials and afternoons service, we cannot have passage to the church for performance of these necessary duties.[1]

A further petition said that 'such is the unruliness of some of the resorters to that house, and of coaches, horses and people of all sorts gathered together by that occasion, in those narrow and crooked streets, that many hurts have heretofore been thereby done'.[2] The Corporation of London actually gave orders for the playhouse to be suppressed (January 1619)[3] but it was the King's Men they were dealing with and it was too early to oppose the royal prerogative.

[1] MSC, I, pt I (1907 [1908]), 91–2 (modernized).
[2] ibid., I, 93–4.
[3] *Jacobean and Caroline Stage*, VI, 19.

9 Plays performed and plays published

To satisfy a large regular audience, a company had to keep many plays in repertory. Consecutive performances of a play for even a week at a time were no more good business in the theatres in the thirties of the seventeenth century than were long runs of films in suburban cinemas in the thirties of the twentieth. The nine-days run of *A Game at Chess* in 1624 was one of the unusual features of this theatrical 'sensation'. Thousands saw the play, and it was reckoned that the King's Men were making £100 a day.[1] Even John Chamberlain thought of going, 'but I could not sit so long, for we must have ben there before one a clocke at farthest to find any roome'.[2]

The constantly changing programme of a theatre is achieved by blending old favourites and new plays. Some guesses can be made at the number of new plays available in London in a year. *Annals of English Drama*, arranged by Alfred Harbage and revised by S. Schoenbaum, prints the titles of 396 new plays known to have been performed in the London theatres between 1613 and 1642. Of these plays, 148 are lost. Without doubt there are many more lost plays of which we have no record of any kind – I should not be

---

[1] *Jacobean and Caroline Stage*, IV, 873.
[2] J. Chamberlain, *Letters*, II, 578.

surprised if the number of plays which have not survived exceeded the number of those which are now extant.[1] If to the 248 extant plays we add the figure 252 for those which are lost, we get a convenient total of 500 new plays in a period of 30 years. Not all of these years were full playing years: 1625 and 1636–7 were ruined by the plague, for example, and there were less severe interruptions in other years. So a figure of 18 new plays in a full year would come near to our 500 for 1613–42. Malone said that he got from Sir Henry Herbert's office-book (now lost) the fact that the King's Men produced at least 4 new plays every year between 1622 and 1641.[2] With four companies normally operating in London, our figure of 18 new plays a year seems not to be far out, although in fact the writing of new plays is not at a steady production rate. Bentley notes that when the King of Bohemia's company opened their new theatre in 1623 after the disastrous loss by fire of the old Fortune with all their play-books, no fewer than 14 new plays were licensed in a period of fifteen months.[3]

Figures for the performance of new plays are obviously very dubious; we are on much more certain ground with the question of publication. In this period the publication of plays becomes respectable. The old-timer Heywood, who had 'either an entire hand, or at least a maine finger' in 220 plays, was not much interested in appearing in print – 'it never was any great ambition in me, to be in this kind voluminously read'.[4] But Ben Jonson had printed his 'workes' in 1616, and although the great collection of Shakespeare's 'Comedies, Histories, and Tragedies' in 1623 is posthumous, its publication both witnessed and encouraged the growing feeling that a play was a worthy literary as well as theatrical object.[5]

Non-publication of a play may be a sign not of the author's indifference nor of a play's badness but that it had a strong popular appeal. The desire to prevent plays from being published because they were the capital and stock-in-trade of a theatre-company was still strong late in this period. There are Lord Chamberlain's edicts of 1627 and 1641 protecting the plays of the King's Men from being printed: the latter contains a list of 60 plays.[6] There may seem something of a paradox here: on the one hand no bookseller will

---

[1] Of the plays which Massinger is known to have written, about half are extant.
[2] Adams, *Herbert*, 66.
[3] *Jacobean and Caroline Stage*, I, 149–51.
[4] Address to the reader in *The English Traveller* (1633); quoted in *Jacobean and Caroline Stage*, IV, 555.
[5] Cf. E. M. Albright, *Dramatic Publication in England* (New York, 1927), 215–16.
[6] *Jacobean and Caroline Stage*, I, 54, 65–6.

bother to publish a play unless he thinks it will appeal to the public; on the other, a company which has paid money for a play, finds that it is successful and continues to get profit from the exclusive playing of it is simply not going to lose its monopoly by permitting publication. The paradox is not real. Although publication of plays by the author grew very much more fashionable in Charles's reign, it was still very exceptional for a play to be published within a year or so of its first performance. The procedure must have been for a dramatist to approach a company to seek permission to publish once his play had lost the appeal of freshness. Richard Brome's contract had a clause that Brome could not publish his plays without the consent of the company. Unless this permission was sought and granted, a good play remained in the repertory, unpublished (except by stealth). The publication of Shakespeare's plays was a sacrifice for the King's Men. A collection of the Fletcher plays was not made until well after the closing of the theatres.

Since the dates of the original performances of seventeenth-century plays are often hard to ascertain, figures for the lapse of time between first performance and publication are anything but firm. What follows uses Harbage's *Annals* as a basis for dating with a few private corrections; all academic, court and private plays are excluded. Of the 248 extant plays first produced on the public stage from 1613 to 1642, 70 were printed within three years of first performance (28.6 per cent), 58 were printed between three and ten years after first performance, and 101 were printed later in the seventeenth century, mostly before 1660. Nineteen plays remained in manuscript until modern times.

The figures of 1613–24 are worth comparing with those of 1625–42. The total of *known* plays of the first period is 162. Of these, 84 are lost (over half). Of the surviving 78, 13 were printed within three years of first performance (16.5 per cent) and a further 9 between three and ten years. In the second period, 234 plays are known and of these only 64 are lost (just over a quarter). Of the surviving 170 plays, no fewer than 57 were printed within three years of first performance (33.5 per cent) and a further 49 between three and ten years.

Period	Known plays	Lost	Extant	Published in 3 yrs	Published 3–10 yrs	Published later 17c.	Remained in MS.
1613–24	162	84	78	13	9	49	7
1625–42	234	64	170	57	49	52	12
1613–42	396	148	248	70	58	101	19

The difference in the volume of publication can best be seen by percentages. In the first period, the percentage of known plays to be published within ten years of first performance is 13.6 per cent; in the second period it is 45.3 per cent.

The attitude of individual dramatists to publication varied a great deal.[1] Heywood's indifference we have seen. On the other hand when Shirley was in Ireland he had sixteen of his plays or revisions published by the London booksellers, William Cooke and Andrew Crooke.[2] Massinger took a personal interest in the printing of his plays, providing dedications and securing commendatory epistles. A volume of eight of his most important publications up to 1633 (now in the Folger Library) contains many corrections in his own hand and was intended either as a gift to a patron or as a move towards publishing his 'Works'.[3] He sent a copy of *The Duke of Milan* to his friend and patron Sir Francis Foljambe with a verse epistle in his own hand. This use of the printed object as a substitute for the traditional gift of a manuscript was quite common; indeed, the old pretence continues, that a work has been published only in order to supply friends with copies. Randolph remarks in the address to the reader in *The Jealous Lovers* (1632): 'If I could by mine own industry have furnished the desires of my Friends, I had not troubled the Press.' And the practice of presenting manuscript copies still survived. Ralph Crane the scrivener provided copies of *A Game at Chess* for Middleton to present to William Hammond and Thomas Holmes.[4] Crane would also make presentations of manuscripts of plays on his own account for what he could get out of them. The manuscript of Fletcher's *Demetrius and Enanthe* (*The Humorous Lieutenant*), dedicated by Crane to the 22-year-old Sir Kenelm Digby towards the end of the terrifying year of plague 1625, mentions 'a Season so sad', but does not comment on the fact that the 'John Fletcher gent.' whose name is encircled with flourishes on the title-page had died of the plague three months earlier (*see plate 4*). Richard Brome sent a manuscript of *The English Moor* to the Earl of Hertford. The manuscript of Suckling's *Aglaura* in the British Museum is probably the copy presented to the King after the first court performance.

[1] For a fuller account, see Albright, *Dramatic Publication*, 204–17.
[2] A. Stevenson, 'Shirley's Publishers', *The Library*, 4th series, 25 (1944–5), 140–61.
[3] The volume is described by W. W. Greg in *Collected Papers*, ed. J. C. Maxwell (Oxford, 1966), 120–48.
[4] F. P. Wilson, 'Ralph Grane, Scrivener to the King's Players', *The Library*, 4th Series, 7 (1927), 194–215.

10 Provincial playing

Our knowledge of theatrical life in the provinces of England in the seventeenth century is very sketchy. J. T. Murray's book, *English Dramatic Companies 1558–1642* (2 vols, New York, 1910), is the standard work on the subject, but a notable collection made by Giles E. Dawson of the records of plays and players in Kent from 1450 to 1642 in the Malone Society Collections, VII (1965), shows how incomplete had been our previous knowledge of provincial playing in that county, and suggests how incomplete our knowledge is for other counties. Even this new research does not provide a complete record: Mr Dawson suspects that the visits of players to towns are recorded only if they have cost the authorities money, or (we can add) caused them trouble. Because our knowledge of provincial performances is a cloth with more holes than fabric in it, the results of the interesting attempts by L. G. Salingar (with G. Harrison and B. Cochrane) to establish statistical trends must be provisional.[1]

The little town of Maldon on the Blackwater in Essex is quite unrecognized as a seventeenth-century venue for players: in fact it was

---

[1] L. G. Salingar, 'Les Comédiens et leur public en Angleterre de 1520 à 1640', in *Dramaturgie et Société aux XVIe et XVIIe Siècles*, ed. J. Jacquot (Paris, 1968), 525–76. For work in progress in this important field see Bibliography (p. 313).

regularly visited by the touring companies. W. A. Mepham collected all the references from the local records and published a few of them (unfortunately not all) in the *Essex Review* for 1948. Here is an entry for 1619 referring to a visit of the Lady Elizabeth's players which gives a glimpse of what still awaits collection:

> The Jury presented —— Moore gent. and others of the company of Princess Elizabeth's players because when they prolonged ther playes until XI of the clocke in the Blue Boore in Maldon, Mr Baylyff coming and requesting them to breake off ther play so that the company might departe they called Bayliff Francis 'foole' to the great disparagement of the government of the borough.[1]

Dogberry lives again! '—— Moore gent.' is Joseph Moore, well known as a leader of the Lady Elizabeth's company. The visit to Maldon was presumably on the same itinerary of 1619 which included visits to Ipswich and Norwich.[2]

It was Moore's colleague Francis Wambus who was involved in a serious brush with the Norwich authorities which highlights the worsening relation in our period between city authorities and the professional companies. The actors came armed with their royal licence giving them the right to play in any city or town, and it is clear that many municipal authorities wanted nothing to do with them and were glad to buy them off with a gratuity. Salingar notes in his study a peak in provincial playing in the years 1615–19 and then a steady decline in the number of recorded visits, with a steady increase in the refusals of permission to perform. The Norwich authorities, who were traditionally very guarded about admitting players, became adamant against them in the early 1620s. Between May 1620 and May 1623, only a bearward is recorded as being allowed to give shows. In that latter month, the Mayor and the Justices got from the Privy Council letters giving them special authority to refuse players altogether. When in April 1624 Francis Wambus showed the court his licence to act, they exhibited the Privy Council's letter in return. He 'peremptorily affirmed that he would play in this city, and would lay in prison here this twelvemonth but he would try whether the king's command or the council's be the greater'. Wambus

---

[1] *Essex Review*, LVII, 208. No reference is given; in his typescript, deposited in the Essex Record Office, Dr Mepham says 'Maldon Court Rolls'. These documents are now in the Essex Record Office, but I have not found the quoted entry.

[2] J. T. Murray, *English Dramatic Companies 1558–1642*, 2 vols (New York, 1910), II, 345; and MSC, II, 283.

wrote out a playbill and exhibited it outside the White Horse inn. 'Here within this place, at one of the clock, shall be acted an excellent new comedy, called THE SPANISH CONTRACT by the Princess' Servants. VIVAT REX!' He was arrested and 'accused the Mayor to his face that he contemned the king's authority'. He refused to find sureties for good behaviour, and so gave the city no alternative but to commit him to prison. No doubt Wambus, whose career depended on defeating the machinations of city authorities to override the royal patent, considered this a test case. But he does not seem to have won; he was released a month later, before a letter arrived from Sir Henry Herbert purporting that it was the Lord Chamberlain's pleasure that he should be set at liberty. He lost his case against the city for the cost of his imprisonment.[1]

What is the reason for the increasing antagonism of the cities? Norwich gives its reasons very clearly. The authorities got the Privy Council injunction on the grounds that actors were 'a sort of vagrant and licentious rabble by whose means and devices the purses of poor servants and apprentices and the meaner sort of people are drained and emptied and which pinches the more in these times of scarcity and dearth'. The 'cause of the poor' is advanced in many of the entries of the Mayors' Court Books. Their work 'cannot be wanted' – that is, they cannot afford to forgo work. 'Denied to play by reason of the want [that is, the need] of work for the poor'; 'they having now stayed fifteen days to the great hurt of the poor'.[2] This concern for the welfare of the poor seems to me to be crocodile's tears. The mayor and aldermen of the city of Norwich must have been employers of labour themselves and it is very hard to think that if an apprentice or journeyman took the afternoon off it was the employee's loss of earnings that was worrying the employer. At the same time Salingar and his colleagues may well be right in saying that Puritan objections to the whole business of playing had little to do with the matter.[3] It was the certain knowledge that the arrival of the players meant a general disruption of work and public order that moved the authorities. Would not this knowledge always have existed? And would not the authorities always have wished that they might flout the royal writs which countenanced playing in every shire and city? And would they not, as Charles's reign progressed, have begun to dare to oppose the writs, or at least grow bolder in denying entrance?[4] The players

[1] Murray, *English Dramatic Companies*, II, 346, 360, 348 (spellings have been modernized).
[2] ibid., II, 360, 347, 355.
[3] Salingar, 'Les Comédiens et leur public', 40–9.
[4] Cf. Glynne Wickham, *Early English Stages* (1959–   ), II, pt I, 106.

found their occupation disappearing before their eyes. In 1635, Dr Mepham noted, the Maldon records of players' visits end. This is the last record:

> And vi^s viii^d by m^r: Bailiffes appointment given to players this yeere not to shewe their playes in this towne.[1]

The town of Maldon, whether it knew it or not, was following a national trend. Dawson gives the theatrical records of thirteen towns in Kent. Between 1635 and 1642 there are exactly three records of payments to players among all these towns. A table by Salingar (using information chiefly from Murray) shows that the total of 153 visits of players in the provinces in the years 1615–19 dwindles to 43 visits in the years 1635–9. Glynne Wickham notes that Coventry, a city with a long and distinguished theatrical tradition, was exceptional in welcoming players as late as 1640.[2]

---

[1] Essex Record Office, D/B 3/3/80; Maldon Chamberlain's Accounts for the year 1635. See Mepham, *Essex Review*, 208.
[2] Wickham, *Early English Stages*, II, pt 1, 147.

11 Regulation and licensing

The control of the drama includes the inhibition of playing and the closing of the theatres for reasons of public health, as in time of plague,[1] for national mourning, as at the death of a monarch, or for punitive reasons. Inhibitions as punishment were much more frequent as the Civil War drew nearer. Beeston was imprisoned, and playing at the Phoenix was suspended for the acting of an unlicensed play in 1640 touching on the King's expedition to force the prayer-book on the Scots. The Fortune company suffered severe fines and prohibitions of playing in 1639 for appearing to touch on the arcana of religion and statecraft in two successive plays.[2]

The regulation of playing was entirely a matter for the Crown and not the City of London, nor (before 1642) Parliament. The Crown, that is to say the King in Council, acted through the Master of the Revels.[3] Suspension of playing was his ultimate weapon; the day-to-day control of the drama was by the licensing of plays. An extraordinary fact about an office as important as that of Master of the Revels is that it could be bought, and that it could be manipulated by its possessor for personal enrichment. Queen Elizabeth's

[1] A full account of plague-closures 1616–42 is in *Jacobean and Caroline Stage*, II, 652–72.
[2] L. Hotson, *The Commonwealth and Restoration Stage* (Cambridge, Mass., 1928), 3–4.
[3] Glynne Wickham, *Early English Stages* (1959–   ), II, pt 1, 91.

Master of the Revels secured the reversion of the post for his nephew George Buc, who held it from 1610 until he went mad and was made to resign in 1622. In 1612, King James had granted the reversion of the office to Sir John Astley; then in 1621 he granted a second reversion to Ben Jonson, giving him the right to succeed Astley. In 1621 there was therefore a queue of two for this lucrative post. Astley succeeded Buc in 1622, but after a few months along came the 28-year-old Henry Herbert, kinsman of the Earl of Pembroke (the Lord Chamberlain), brother of Lord Herbert of Cherbury and George Herbert, and bought the office off Astley for £150 a year! Legally, Astley remained Master of the Revels and Herbert undertook to do all the work for him.

Sir Henry Herbert's office-book has vanished (it may simply have disintegrated) but many extracts were made from it by Malone and Chalmers; most of these were collected by Joseph Quincy Adams in 1917 as *The Dramatic Records of Sir Henry Herbert* and they give an illuminating picture of Herbert's work.

For the first ten years of his reign (he doubled his charges in 1632) Herbert charged £1 for licensing a new play, and the fee had to be brought with the manuscript. If there were any problems about the play, if there was matter requiring censorship or alteration, then the fee was doubled, £2. Herbert recorded that he burned one play brought to him for a licence by the Red Bull company 'for the ribaldry and offense that was in it' and he still charged them the £2. For an old play previously licensed and newly revived without alteration there might be no charge; if there had been alterations or additions a *pro rata* charge was made. There were higher fees at Christmas and Lent.[1]

These fees were only the beginning of Herbert's income. Most of our information about his perks comes from documents which Herbert prepared at the time of the Restoration when he was battling for his right to continue his office against the irresistible Davenant and Killigrew; he may have remembered his winnings too indulgently. He had an annual payment from each company, which in some cases was actually the equivalent of a single share in the company. He claimed that his earnings from this source were £400 a year. He also took the profits of a single play from the King's Men twice each year; in 1633 this was commuted into a £10 fee twice a year, at Christmas and Midsummer. He took, besides, endless fees and grants: in 1662 he remembered them as 'severall occasionall gratuityes'. There was £3

[1] Adams, *Herbert*, 17–18; *Jacobean and Caroline Stage*, III, 265.

from Heminges in 1626 'for a courtesie done him about their Blackfriers hous'. He got £5 from Heminges for stopping the Red Bull players from acting Shakespeare's plays (1627). Also from the King's Men in 1631 came £3.10s. for giving them permission to start playing again after the cessation of the plague.[1]

From the Treasury, Herbert got £1 a day for lodging out of court in 1627; when he was trying to recover the sum of £2025.12s.10d. owed him for his 'wages and board wages' from before the Civil War, he was claiming £230 a year for 'dyet and boardinges'.[2] It is not surprising to hear Lord Herbert say that his brother 'attained to a great fortune' and became 'dexterous in the ways of the court, as having gotten much by it'.[3]

Herbert's terms of reference were wide: he could make objections to plays, or parts of them, on political, religious and moral grounds. An anonymous document of 1663 put it thus: 'The designe is, that all prophaneness, oathes, ribaldry, and matters reflecting upon piety, and the present government may bee obliterated, before there bee any action in a publique Theatre.'[4] Two important additions to the improprieties are reflections on other governments and the impersonation (or fancied impersonation) of people powerful enough to object.

Profanity includes oaths, and Herbert's scruples in this matter led to a brush with Davenant and the King which shows extraordinarily well the relations between poet and patron and between the theatre and the Crown. In 1633 Herbert read Davenant's *The Wits* and marked many passages which were to be deleted or altered before he would license it. Davenant angrily went to his patron Endymion Porter and Porter went to the King. Charles refused to accept the manuscript from Porter and told him to give it to Herbert. He then sent for Herbert and went over the play with him. Herbert says that he allowed *faith* and *slight* 'to be asseverations only, and no oathes', 'but in the greater part allowed of my reformations'. Herbert added in his office-book, under his breath as it were:

> The kinge is pleased to take *faith, death, slight*, for asseverations, and no oaths, to which I doe humbly submit as my masters judgment; but, under favour, conceive them to be oaths, and enter them here, to declare my opinion and submission.[5]

[1] Adams, *Herbert*, 121, 44, 64.
[2] ibid., 74.
[3] ibid., 9.
[4] ibid., 125.
[5] ibid., 22.

On impersonations, we note Herbert's objections to Shirley's *The Ball* (1632) because 'lords and others of the court' were 'personated so naturally', and to Jonson's *Tale of a Tub* (1633).[1]

Herbert's best-known political censorings both concerned plays of Massinger:

> This day being the 11 of Janu. 1630 [1631], I did refuse to allow of a play of Messinger's because itt did contain dangerous matter, as the deposing of Sebastian king of Portugal, by Philip the [Second], and ther being a peace sworen twixte the kings of England and Spayne. I had my fee notwithstandinge, which belongs to me for reading itt over, and ought to be brought always with the booke.[2]

It can be shown that one of the most famous of English play-manuscripts, the 'book' of Massinger's *Believe as You List*, is his reworking of the censored play, the risky realm of recent history being exchanged for the safety of an ancient Roman story.[3] The second occasion shows once again the King's personal control of the drama. Here, Charles is moved not by an understandable desire to avoid offending foreign powers, but by an exaggerated sensitivity to personal affront. The date is 1638. Herbert quotes some lines from a lost play of Massinger's, once called *The King and the Subject*, which the King had marked as 'too insolent, and to bee changed'.[4] But the King was willing for it to be acted if changes were made and under an altered title (not recorded) Herbert licensed the play.

Even after a play had been licensed, the players were not safe. In 1619 *Sir John van Olden Barnavelt*, a play by Fletcher and Massinger on the downfall of the Dutch Protestant patriot, had been allowed by Sir George Buc after amendment, but its political and religious tone offended the Bishop of London, or someone who moved the Bishop of London to act, and the play was prohibited (it was not published until 1883). Middleton's *Game at Chess* in 1624 had been allowed by the unfortunate Herbert, and when the storm broke over this anti-Spanish political allegory Herbert came in for some of the wrath. Gondomar's fury caused James to order the Privy Council to examine both players and dramatist. Middleton made himself scarce. The Privy Council reported that they had demanded of the players by what

---

[1] See pp. 101–2.
[2] Adams, *Herbert*, 19.
[3] See C. J. Sisson's introduction to the Malone Society Reprint of 1928, *and plate 5*.
[4] Adams, *Herbert*, 23. See also below, pp. 112–13.

licence and authority they had presumed to act the play. The players produced their trump card:

> They produced a Booke being an Orriginall and perfect Coppie thereof (as they affirmed) seene and allowed by Sir Henry Herbert knight Master of the Revells under his owne hand, and subscribed in the last page of the said Booke.

The Privy Council asked that Herbert be summoned before the Secretary of State. The players were reprimanded and the play was prohibited. They were stopped from playing altogether, but the King quickly released them from the injunction. Middleton seems to have got off lightly and there is no record of what was said to Herbert.[1]

The Privy Council seems to have stepped in over Herbert's head in refusing to allow a play on the massacre at Amboyna in 1625.[2] In 1632–3 it was the Archbishop of Canterbury and the Court of High Commission who made an objection to an allowance of Herbert's, Jonson's *Magnetic Lady*. The leading players of the King's Men were summoned before the court on 17 November;[3] they blamed Jonson for writing and Herbert for allowing the matter which was alleged to be abusive of the Scriptures. There was clearly a prolonged suit, for nearly a year later Herbert recorded that the Archbishop of Canterbury absolved him and laid the fault on the players' heads. I imagine considerable pressure was exerted by Herbert on the King's Men to clear him; at any rate, they altered their earlier plea and, says Herbert, 'did me right in my care to purge their plays of all offense'. There was a complaint in 1639 that a play being acted at the Red Bull called *The Whore New Vamped* was libelling aldermen and proctors. The King in Council ordered the Attorney-General to call before him the poet, the players, *and* 'the person that licensed it'.[4] The consequences are not known.

[1] *A Game at Chesse*, ed. R. C. Bald (Cambridge, 1929), 20–3, 162–3.
[2] J. Chamberlain, *Letters*, II, 602.
[3] J. P. Feil, 'Dramatic References from the Scudamore Papers', *Shakespeare Survey*, II (1958), 109.
[4] *Jacobean and Caroline Stage*, V, 1441–2.

12 The closing of the theatres

At the outbreak of civil war in the summer of 1642, Parliament arrogated from the Crown the work of regulating the theatre; it decided that in a time of national calamity play-acting and theatre-going were altogether too frivolous, and on Friday, 2 September 1642, a House of Commons in which few royalists remained passed an order forbidding stage-plays. In the Journal of the House of Lords the order is entered as follows:[1]

Order for Stage-plays to cease.
Die Veneris, 2° Septembris, 1642.

Whereas the distressed Estate of *Ireland*, steeped in her own Blood, and the distracted Estate of *England*, threatened with a Cloud of Blood by a Civil War, call for all possible Means to appease and avert the Wrath of GOD, appearing in these Judgements; among which, Fasting and Prayer having been often tried to be very effectual, have been lately and are still enjoined; and whereas Public Sports do not well agree with Public Calamities, nor Public Stage-plays with the Seasons of Humiliation, this being an Exercise of sad and pious Solemnity, and the other

---

[1] There are slight variations from the proclamation which is printed, from Downes's *Roscius Anglicanus*, in *Jacobean and Caroline Stage*, II, 690.

being Spectacles of Pleasure, too commonly expressing lascivious Mirth and Levity: It is therefore thought fit, and Ordained, by the Lords and Commons in this Parliament assembled, That, while these sad Causes and set Times of Humiliation do continue, Public Stage Plays shall cease, and bee forborn, instead of which are recommended to the People of this Land the profitable and seasonable Considerations of Repentance, Reconciliation and Peace with GOD, which probably may produce outward Peace and Prosperity, and bring again Times of Joy and Gladness to these Nations.

The closing of the theatres (strictly it is the forbidding of stage-plays) is a subject which needs more light. In the first place, it is wrong to write, as H. J. C. Grierson carelessly did, of 'a continuous storm of protest against drama and the stage, gathering in strength till when the Long Parliament meets one of its earliest acts is to close the public theatres'.[1] The Long Parliament met on 3 November 1640; it was almost two years before they banned stage-plays. Secondly, is it certain that the 1642 proclamation is the culmination of decades of Puritan attack on the theatre? One of the few people to question the usual assumption, L. G. Salingar, has suggested that the closure is to be seen as a suspension of playing quite normal in times of difficulty which has little to do with Puritan sentiments.[2] It is quite true that in a time of national crisis the King in Council might have suspended playing. The wording of the Privy Council's declaration after the death of Prince Henry in 1612 is not far removed from that of Parliament thirty years later: 'These tymes doe not suite with such playes and idle shewes, as are daily to be seene in and neere the cittie of London, to the scandall of order and good government at all occasions when they are most tollerable.'[3] In addition, the character of the third ordinance against plays (1647) is quite different in moral tone from that of 1642. The 1642 order has indeed moral objections to the levity and lasciviousness of plays, but its justification for action is that frivolous entertainment is inappropriate in a time of war. The ordinance of 1647 is really a Puritan tract, and it says in the first sentence that stage-plays are not to be tolerated among professors of the Christian religion.[4]

It is probable that part of the motivation for closing the theatres in 1642

---

[1] H. J. C. Grierson, *Cross-Currents in English Literature* (London, 1929; Harmondsworth, 1966), 76.
[2] L. G. Salingar, 'Les Comédiens et leur public', 49.
[3] Quoted in E. K. Chambers, *The Elizabethan Stage*, 4 vols (Oxford, 1923), I, 304.
[4] W. C. Hazlitt, *English Drama and Stage* (London, 1869), 67.

was the traditional conviction that plays are out of place when times are grave, although it would be perverse to deny that religious scruple played its part. It seems possible, however, that the central motivation (in which religion certainly has a share) was antagonism to the monarchy and all its works. The players themselves, or some of them, foresaw that their identification with the court would become so complete that they would suffer along with the other appurtenances of Charles's personal rule. The anonymous *Stage-Players' Complaint* of 1641 contains this farsighted remark:

> For Monopolers are downe, Projectors are downe, the High Commission Court is downe, the Starre-Chamber is down, and (some think) Bishops will downe, and why should we then that are farre inferior to any of those not justly feare, least we should be downe too? [1]

The players were the King's puppets: the municipalities of the country had given a lead in resisting them; wartime provided the occasion for suppressing them; religion was later to provide the justification for imprisoning them.

To argue that there were mixed motives in the 1642 ban is not to underestimate the force of Puritan opposition to the drama in the years before the theatres closed. It is true that the only major diatribe against the stage in our period is Prynne's *Histrio-Mastix*: it is quite sufficient. The great days of invective and controversy were over; the work had been done. The proof is in the maintenance of Parliament's ban for eighteen years.

Although we do not know fully what went on at the Red Bull, in the jigs and dances and so on, the strength and bitterness of the opposition to the theatre seem very much in excess of the provocation given. As Grierson remarked: 'Prynne's attack is not directed against the abuses of the stage but against the drama as such.'[2] The purpose of *Histrio-Mastix* is not to belittle and to pour scorn on the theatre but fiercely and tediously to insist on its importance as an enemy and a rival to religion. Theatres are 'devil's chapels'. The origin of plays was in religion, says Prynne, but the religions which the first plays served were idolatrous; to continue with plays in the days of the true worship of the true God is to continue paganism and idolatry. 'What have Christians any more to doe with Idoles? what with the Devill? . . . yea, what with Stage-Playes?' (p. 54).

---

[1] Hazlitt, *English Drama and Stage*, 256.
[2] Grierson, *Cross-Currents in English Literature*, 76.

Prynne's belief that drama was a satanic form of worship is well shown in the following passage:

> He who serves Satan all the weeke in the Stage or Play-house, can never worship Christ upon the Lords day in the Temple. . . . Now Stage-playes are the very Devils owne peculiar pompes, Play-houses his Synagogues: Players his professed Masse-priests and Choristers: Play-haunters his devoted servants. . . . No man can drinke the Cup of the Lord, and the cup of the Devils; nor yet partake of the Lords Table, and of the table of Devils. (fo. 528 v)

Grierson was puzzled by Prynne's tendency to hammer away at Caroline drama with the weapons which the early Church used against 'the paganism and obscenities of the later Roman theatre'. The theatre of Prynne's day, said Grierson, 'was as ignorant and innocent of pagan beliefs and cults as Prynne himself'.[1] The late 1920s, when Grierson was writing, was perhaps a period when an academic might not know from experience the full power of the theatre. Prynne attacks theatre-going as satanic because it is an involvement and an engagement which at the very least diverts man from the only true way of finding and expressing himself. The absence of overt idolatry is immaterial. The point of Prynne's attack is not revealed, however, until we look at what he says about the ceremony of the Catholic Church (pp. 108–19). The papists 'have turned the Sacraments of Christ's body and blood into a Masse-play'. He quotes triumphantly from Honorius Augustodunensis, *De Antiquo Ritu Missarum*, to prove that 'the Popish Masse is now no other but a *Tragicke Play*'. His author explains how the priest 'acteth or expresseth Christ'; for example, 'by the stretching out of his hands, he denotes the extension of Christ upon the Crosse'. 'Loe here', explodes Prynne, 'a Roman Masse-priest becomes a *Player*, and in stead of preaching, of reading, acts Christs Passion in the Masse.'

Not only do they make the Mass a drama, but they make plays out of the holy events of Christianity: 'A sufficient testimony how little Papists really esteem the bitter passion of our blessed Saviour since they make a common play or pastime of it.'

All acting, Prynne constantly reminds us, is a lie. We can try expressing this in gentler and fuller terms. When he is acting, a man stands outside of himself and takes on another identity. In the theatre and in the formal ceremony of the Roman liturgy, the roles which an actor or a priest adopts

[1] ibid., 77.

are contrived and studied roles. They might seem in Puritan eyes a deliberate perversion of man's true nature, a perversion which becomes monstrous when a boy dresses up as a woman and becomes unspeakable blasphemy when a priest pretends to be Christ. In his own worship, the Puritan eschews the dressing-up and the acting which all formal ceremony and ritual require in some degree. But it would be an oversimplification to say that the Puritan opposed the stage because it showed a deceitfulness and insincerity which he hated also in church. Puritan worship, especially the preaching, is recognized by its 'enthusiasm', which is a standing outside of oneself kindled by an inner light which is from God, spontaneous and not contrived. This ecstasy (it might have been argued) is the only true one; others are worked-up impositions and denials of the true self. It can only be a false worship when the true God is mocked by the mimicry and antics of the Catholics and the Laudians; they can only be false gods who are worshipped in the rites of the secular theatre. To understand why Prynne pays the theatre the enormous tribute of his block of a book one must posit that drama for him was worse than an immoral entertainment. Whether he is on the stage or in the audience, the man of the theatre is drawn by the play into another life. In the chapels of the godly, men are so deeply moved by the word that they also are drawn into another life (the unsympathetic say that their behaviour looks like play-acting). The nerve of the passage from Prynne quoted above is that a man cannot have it both ways – he cannot live in the contradiction of the double service of the theatre and the Church: 'No man can drink the Cup of the Lord, and the cup of the Devils.' Prynne recognized what we recognize, that there are innumerable points of overlap between drama and religion, and with *Histrio-Mastix*, a scourge for the players, he tried to drive away the invading *Doppelgänger*.[1]

It proved impossible to put down playing altogether. Leslie Hotson, in *The Commonwealth and Restoration Stage* (1928), gave a full account of the twenty-year twilight of the theatre (twenty years because the years before the Civil War were bad ones for drama). When war broke out and the theatres were closed, many of the players joined the King's forces, and James Wright (in *Historia Histrionica*) had heard of only one player 'that sided with the other Party', Swanston, who 'professed himself a Presbyterian'.[2] For those who did not or could not find employment with the King, or who returned as total defeat drew nearer, the loss of occupation was

[1] See Marion Jones, 'The Court and the Dramatists', *Elizabethan Theatre*, ed. J. R. Brown and Bernard Harris (London, 1966), 193–4.
[2] *Jacobean and Caroline Stage*, II, 695.

extremely serious. As late as 1650 the players were complaining to Parliament of the complete loss of their livelihood.

The extent of the clandestine playing in the late 1640s at the old theatres and elsewhere can be judged by the reports of raids and by the need to repeat the injunctions against playing. In 1648, after severe penalties for acting had been passed by Parliament, performances were actually being advertised by handbills.[1] In the spring of 1649, after the trial and execution of the King, the soldiers began to carry out the ordinances previously published, and dismantled the Salisbury Court, the Cockpit and the Fortune. But there was acting in private houses near London and there was the institution of the 'drolls', scenes extracted from established plays and acted at the Red Bull in spite of constant raids. Francis Kirkman wrote:

> All that we could divert ourselves with were these humours and pieces of Plays . . . and that but by stealth too, and under pretence of Rope-dancing, or the like. . . . I have seen the Red Bull Play-House, which was a large one, so full, that as many went back for want of room as had entred; and as meanly as you may think of these Drols, they were then Acted by the best Comedians then and now in being.[2]

In 1656, Davenant began his 'operas' or musical entertainments, first at Rutland House and then at the Cockpit. *The Siege of Rhodes* was followed by *The Cruelty of the Spaniards in Peru* and *The History of Sir Francis Drake*. Hotson describes *The Cruelty of the Spaniards* as 'merely a series of pictures with illustrative songs, dances and intercalated acrobatic feats'. The fact that these new dramas were musical and patriotic did not lessen the indignation of the fundamentalists: 'It is thought the Opera will speedily go down; the godly party are so much discontented with it.'[3] The Council of State set up an enquiry into 'the *Opera* shewed at the *Cockpit* in Drury-lane', 'to examine by what authority the same is exposed to public view'.[4] This was at the end of 1658. Nothing happened. Another committee was set up in February 1659, but still the opera seems to have continued unmolested. Actors of other kinds of drama were still being tried and fined in the months immediately preceding the restoration of the monarchy. Thomas Lilleston, for example, was before the Middlesex Sessions 'charged by Gervis Jones to act a publique stage-play this present 4th of February in

[1] L. Hotson, *The Commonwealth and Restoration Stage*, 34.
[2] Quoted by Hotson, in ibid., 48.
[3] From a letter quoted by Hotson, in ibid., 159.
[4] ibid., 160.

the Cock-Pitt in Drury Lane . . . contrary to the law'.[1] On 23 April 1660,
General Monk and his Council found time during preparations for the new
Parliament and the negotiations for the King's return to prohibit stage-plays
once again.

Charles II entered London on 29 May 1660. On 9 July, Thomas
Killigrew obtained from the King a grant to establish a company of players
and Davenant moved rapidly to obtain a half-monopoly with him – to the
great annoyance of Sir Henry Herbert. The players had come right out into
the open at the Restoration without waiting for permission: the order for
Killigrew speaks of 'the Extraordinary Licence that hath bin lately used in
things of this nature'.[2] The theatre had never been totally suppressed.

[1] ibid., 197.
[2] ibid., 400.

11 The theatres and the actors

Gerald Eades Bentley

1 Introduction

Play-acting in London during the years 1613–60 was broken into four periods by three catastrophic events which suppressed the actors and playwrights and extinguished the dramatic entertainment of the audience for long stretches of time. The first break came in 1625 when all theatres were closed for most of the year, first by the usual period of Lenten restrictions during the first four weeks of March, then by the period of mourning following the death of King James on 27 March, and finally by the terrible plague of that year which protracted the closing until about the last week of November. Such a long starvation period made bankrupt all the London acting troupes except the King's Men, and a group of reorganized companies appeared in the reign of the new king, Charles I.

In 1636 and 1637 another bad plague, somewhat less severe, but more protracted, caused the closing of the theatres on 12 May 1636, and kept them closed except for about a week until 2 October 1637. Again demoralized companies broke and were reorganized.

The third and fatal break came on 2 September 1642 when the Puritan-dominated Parliament ordered all theatres and similar places of entertainment, such as the bear-garden, to be closed indefinitely. There was no significant reopening until the restoration of Charles II was imminent. All regular dramatic companies disbanded; there was no viable profession of acting and no professional playwriting, only sporadic and profitless performances of old plays for nearly eighteen years. The ensuing account will therefore present the environment of London playgoers in four periods: 1613–25; 1626–36; 1637–42; 1642–60.

2 The period 1613–25

In the year 1613 there were four chartered dramatic companies performing with some regularity at five London theatres, and the town was offered dramatic fare of a distinction and copiousness seldom available in any city before or since. Each of these companies was a repertory troupe performing by right of a royal charter, before a paying audience, in a theatre which they owned or leased. Each company owned a stock of play manuscripts which they had bought, usually from the authors, and which they cherished as a principal and exclusive asset. Most of the plays presented by any company in any season were old ones which the company had owned from one to as many as twenty-five years, but each season they bought new plays which were expected to be special attractions, and for whose early performances they doubled the admission prices. Ordinarily the same play was not presented on consecutive days, but three to five different plays might be performed in a single week. A company's selection for the day was announced on cheap playbills tacked up about the town, but it is likely that a good many members of any audience had simply decided to go to a play that afternoon with no advance knowledge of what the play would be.

All four London companies were similar in make-up, however much individual members may have differed in talent. All companies were made up of three groups of men and boys.[1] Most important was the group of senior actors who had contributed capital to the enterprise, who took the principal roles, and who participated in management. These senior men were sometimes called 'sharers' because they held shares of stock in the company and participated in the profits; sometimes they were called the 'fellows' of the company. This group varied in size according to the prosperity of the company, from five to as many as fourteen in the later, most prosperous days of the King's company. In the eyes of the law these sharers were the company; their names commonly appeared in the patent, hence their occasional designation as the 'patented members'.

The second group was made up of lesser adult actors commonly called the 'hired men'. They assumed minor roles and miscellaneous functions in the theatre. They had invested no capital and did not share in the profits but were paid weekly wages.

The third group was made up of boys who took the roles of women and children in the plays, since women did not appear on the English commercial stage of the time. This group was small; they were in the status of apprentices to the senior actors, and in any period several of them would have been new and not yet well trained. Hence the comparatively small number of women's roles in all plays of the time.

These groups of actors seldom added up to the number of roles in any play. As a consequence, the doubling of parts was a standard practice. Professional dramatists were careful to construct their plays so that doubling was easy and no revision would be necessary to enable twelve or fifteen actors to present a play with twice that many characters.[2]

(i) Private and public theatres

Private theatres were comparatively small, completely enclosed from the weather, and lighted by candles. Their admission prices were much higher than those of the public theatres; they gave more time and emphasis to music; and their audiences tended to be more socially sophisticated and

[1] At some periods of the sixteenth and seventeenth centuries there were companies in London in which all the actors were boys, but no such company was performing in London during the period 1613–25.

[2] See William A. Ringler, Jr, 'The Number of Actors in Shakespeare's Early Plays', in *The Seventeenth Century Stage*, ed. G. E. Bentley (Chicago, Ill., 1968), 110–34.

well-to-do than those at the public theatres. The private theatres operating
at one time or another in London in the years 1613–42 were the Blackfriars
(1613–42); the Phoenix or Cockpit in Drury Lane (1617–42); the Salisbury
Court (1629–42); and for a very brief period the theatre variously called
Porters' Hall or Rosseter's Blackfriars or Puddle Wharf (1615–16).

Public theatres were large structures with roofed galleries running
around the house but open to the sky in the centre above the pit where the
poorer spectators stood through the performance. General admission to
public theatres was cheap, and consequently their audiences were less
exclusive than those of the private theatres. Public theatres were large, with
a greater capacity than most twentieth-century theatres. There are three
contemporary estimates of their size: in 1596 a visiting Dutchman said that
the Swan theatre, whose interior he sketched, could hold 3000 spectators;
and in 1624 the Spanish ambassador in London reported back to Madrid
that more than 3000 people attended a performance of *A Game at Chess* at
the Globe, and later in the same letter he said that a total of more than 12,000
people had attended the play at the Globe in four days.

The public theatres were more numerous than the private ones. During
most of the period 1613–42 seven were still standing: the Globe (1613–42);
the Hope (1613/1614–42, but after 1617 used only sporadically for plays);
the Fortune (1613–42); the Red Bull (1613–42); the Swan (generally
superseded by 1613 and used for plays only occasionally until 1621, after
which it was seldom used for anything except fencing exhibitions); the
Curtain, an old theatre built in 1577 and little used in the reign of James I,
though Prince Charles's Men played there for a few years in the early 1620s;
the Rose, built by Henslowe in 1587 but not known to have been used by
players in this period.

(ii) The King's company

The dominant troupe throughout this period was King James's Men, or the
King's company, which had already been performing in London with great
success since the accession of James I, and for a decade before that under
their Elizabethan name, the Lord Chamberlain's company. Their letters
patent as the new royal troupe were issued at the very beginning of the new
reign. This patent, dated 19 May 1603, extended royal protection to the
patented members of the old Lord Chamberlain's Men: Lawrence Fletcher,

William Shakespeare, Richard Burbage, Augustine Philips, John Heminges, Henry Condell, William Sly, Robert Armin, Richard Cowley, 'and the
rest of their associates'. They were the only London company which owned
and operated two different theatres: in the winter months they played at
Blackfriars, a private theatre in the precincts of the former Dominican
monastery between St Paul's Cathedral and the river, and near to the
Middle Temple and the Inner Temple whose students were notorious
patrons of plays and playhouses. In the warmer months they played at the
Globe, a large public theatre on the south bank of the river a short distance
west of London Bridge, the only easy crossing of the Thames for many
miles. Ordinarily the King's Men moved from the Globe to the Blackfriars
about October and back to the Globe about May.

The majority of the shares in both theatres were owned by a group of the
actors themselves. The King's Men were thus more fortunate, or more
provident, than other companies which were at the mercy of landlords with
alien interests. This financial advantage was one of the sources of the
company's strength, which enabled it to survive the blows that sooner or
later destroyed every other London troupe. In 1613 the owners of the
Globe, or the housekeepers as they were called, were Richard Burbage,
William Shakespeare, William Ostler, John Heminges, Cuthbert Burbage,
Henry Condell and John Underwood. Six of them were patented members
of the company; Cuthbert Burbage was the brother of Richard. The
householders of the Blackfriars in 1613 were Richard Burbage, Cuthbert
Burbage, John Heminges, William Shakespeare, Henry Condell, William
Ostler and Thomas Evans. The Blackfriars syndicate was thus made up of
five of the same actors who owned the Globe, plus Richard Burbage's
brother Cuthbert, and Thomas Evans, the representative of the former
lessor of the theatre when it had been used by boy companies.

The repertory of the King's Men was by far the most distinguished in
London. In 1613 they owned all, or nearly all, the plays of Shakespeare;
many of the early plays of Beaumont and Fletcher, such as *Philaster, A King
and No King, Bonduca, The Captain, The Maid's Tragedy* and *Valentinian*;
much of the early Jonson – *Every Man in His Humour, Every Man Out of
His Humour, Sejanus, Volpone, The Alchemist* and *Catiline*; and odd plays by
other well-known dramatists – Marston's *Malcontent*, Dekker's *Satiro-
Mastix*, Webster's *Duchess of Malfi*, and the popular anonymous *Merry Devil
of Edmonton*.

In the next twelve years, up to his death in August 1625, the majority of
the company's new plays were composed by John Fletcher. Several of his

earlier plays, written during Shakespeare's incumbency when Beaumont and Fletcher were working in collaboration for the boy companies, had been prepared for the King's Men too, but about 1609 Fletcher evidently succeeded Shakespeare as the company's principal dramatist, probably under contract, and all the rest of his plays – about fifty of them – were written for the royal troupe and brought out at Blackfriars or the Globe.[1] Other dramatists, such as Jonson and Middleton, wrote occasional plays for them, and Massinger and Field (generally in collaboration with Fletcher) wrote several, but the bulk of their new plays from 1613 to 1625 were prepared for the exclusive use of the King's company by the popular John Fletcher.

In the middle of 1613 the company suffered a heavy loss when the 15-year-old Globe burned to the ground on the afternoon of 29 June during a performance of one of their newest plays, Shakespeare and Fletcher's *Henry VIII*. The fire was a London sensation recorded by half a dozen contemporaries. The best account was written four days after the catastrophe by Sir Henry Wotton in a letter to his nephew, Sir Edmund Bacon:

> Now, to let matters of state sleep, I will entertain you at the present with what hath happened this week at the Bank's side. The King's players had a new play called *All is True*, representing some principal pieces of the reign of *Henry* VIII which was set forth with many extraordinary circumstances of pomp and majesty, even to the matting of the stage; the Knights of the Order with their Georges and Garter, the Guards with their embroidered coats, and the like: sufficient in truth within a while to make greatness very familiar, if not ridiculous. Now, King *Henry* making a masque at the Cardinal *Wolsey's* house, and certain chambers being shot off at his entry [1.iv] some of the paper, or other stuff, wherewith one of them was stopped, did light on the thatch, where being thought at first but an idle smoke, and their eyes more attentive to the show, it kindled inwardly, and ran round like a train, consuming within less than an hour the whole house to the very grounds.
>
> This was the fatal period of that virtuous fabric, wherein yet nothing did perish but wood and straw, and a few forsaken cloaks; only one man

---

[1] On the subject of professional dramatists and their exclusive contracted work for particular companies, see G. E. Bentley, *The Profession of Dramatist in Shakespeare's Time, 1590–1642* (Princeton, N.J., 1971), 111–44.

had his breeches set on fire, that would perhaps have broiled him, if he
had not by the benefit of a provident wit put it out with bottle ale.[1]

This disaster brought into play the reserve strength of the King's company.
Shortly after the fire the housekeepers must have laid plans for a new theatre
to be built on the site of the old, for the second Globe, which was said to have
cost £1400, was in operation less than a year after the first was burned. On
30 June 1614, John Chamberlain wrote of the 'new Globe': 'Indeed I heare
much speach of this new play-house, which is said to be the fayrest that ever
was in England'.[2]

While the new theatre was under construction the company presumably
presented all their plays at Blackfriars; afterwards they renewed their
alternation between the two houses. The popularity of their productions at
Blackfriars is suggested by a petition of early 1619, in which the constables,
officers and inhabitants of the precinct complained of the 'multitudes of
Coaches' which the theatre attracted.[3] One can see that the petitioners had
some grievances, however important an underlying Puritan anti-theatre
motive may have been. But the Lord Chamberlain, under the Privy Council
and the King, exercised final control over players and playhouses, and their
approval of Blackfriars is indicated by the issuance of a new royal patent for
the company a few weeks later, on 27 March 1619, specifically authorizing
the King's Men to play 'within their two now usual houses called the Globe
within our county of Surrey and their private house scituate in the precincts
of the Blackfriars within our city of London. . . .'[4] This new patent for the
company names twelve sharers as compared with the nine of 1603.

Just before the new patent was issued, the company suffered a heavy loss
in the death of Richard Burbage, for he was not only the most important
man in the company but the most famous actor of his time. Thomas
Middleton said that to the people 'Dick Burbage was their mortal God on
earth' and that there was more mourning for him than for Queen Anne, who
died about the same time.[5] Few actors in the history of the English stage
have created as many famous roles as Richard Burbage (*plate 6*).

[1] *Letters of Sir Henry Wotton to Sir Edmund Bacon* (London, 1661), 30–1. The letter is
    reprinted by Logan Pearsall Smith in *The Life and Letters of Sir Henry Wotton*, 2 vols
    (Oxford, 1907), II, 32.
[2] J. Chamberlain, *Letters*, ed. N. E. McClure, 2 vols (Philadelphia, 1939), I, p. 544.
[3] MSC, I, pt 1 (1907) 91. See above, pp. 46–7.
[4] MSC, I, pt 3, 281–2 (text slightly modernized).
[5] Quoted in C. C. Stopes, *Burbage and Shakespeare's Stage* (London, 1913), 117.

The publication of the Shakespeare Folio in 1623 was an event in the affairs of the company. In the universal acclaim of Shakespeare the poet it is often forgotten that this principal edition of his plays is an integral part of the history of his company: it is very much a King's Men's book. The plays were 'collected & publish'd' by the two senior members of the company, John Heminges and Henry Condell, as they say in their signed address to the 'great majority of readers'. The two leaders of the company also sign the dedication to the Earl of Pembroke, Lord Chamberlain, the most important government official in the lives of players, and to his brother, the Earl of Montgomery, who succeeded him in that office. Probably all the plays in the book belonged to the company, and nearly all had been written for them. The texts for almost half the plays evidently came from their archives. Most striking in the volume is an unique feature of the front matter, a list headed 'The Names of the Principal Actors in all these Plays'. Listed are the names of twenty-six actors, all of whom were or had been members of the company. More than half of them were dead at the time of the publication of the Folio, and it is doubtful that their names could have been collected without the memories of Heminges and Condell, and the archives of the Globe and Blackfriars.

In 1624 the King's Men were involved in the most sensational performances of the early seventeenth century. On 6 August 1624, Middleton's play *A Game at Chess* opened at the Globe and had a spectacular run of nine days, a record for the time. The run was terminated by order of the Privy Council, which called the players before them, ordered the theatre closed, put the company under bond, issued a warrant for the arrest of Middleton, called in the Master of the Revels for questioning, and generally created a great stir.

The clue to both the success of this mediocre play and to the punitive measures of the Privy Council was the strictly illegal political propaganda which was the essence of *A Game at Chess*. At this time the overwhelming majority of Londoners were strongly – sometimes violently – anti-Spanish and anti-Catholic. For three or four years there had been widespread uneasiness at the pro-Spanish policies of the King, and the influence of the Spanish ambassador, Count Gondomar. Seven or eight months before the play was written Prince Charles had returned from Madrid without the threatened Spanish bride, and there had been general rejoicing even to the extent of bonfires in the streets of London. Middleton exploited this popular hatred in the play he wrote for the King's company. How the manuscript got past the censor, the Master of the Revels, is still a mystery, but this official did license the play for performance on 12 June. The company cannily held off their opening for two months until the King and most of the members of the Privy Council were out of town, hence the delay in official action until the players had reaped the profits from nine sold-out performances. Contemporary gossip said that they took £1500 in admissions, and though this is probably an exaggeration, the play was certainly the talk of the town.[1]

The suppression of acting at the Globe lasted for about ten days and there is no record of further punishment for either the players or the Master of the Revels. Middleton evidently went into hiding, but the Privy Council took indemnities from his son, Edward, and ordered him to appear again for questioning. The punishments seem very slight for such a grave offence – evidently powerful influences were brought to bear on behalf of the King's Men and their dramatist.

By 1624, the last year of acting before the devastating plague of 1625, the King's Men had attained a size, prosperity and prestige unprecedented in English theatrical affairs. The company supported thirty-five adult members and employees, and an unrecorded number of boy actors. These figures derive from two lists: a protection against arrest granted by the Master of the Revels in December 1624 for twenty-one hired men, musicians, book-keepers and 'other necessary attendants' of the company; and a list of patented members who were issued royal livery for the funeral of King James three or four months later (there is one duplication). Only a very profitable enterprise could have supported so many men.

Evidence of prestige as well as profit is exhibited in the number of command performances given at court by these players. Some of the records of court performances have probably disappeared, but we still have evidence of more than 150 occasions in the years 1613–25 (twelve or thirteen a year) when the King's company was selected to go to the court at Whitehall or Denmark House or Hampton Court to present one of the plays of their repertory before royalty. No other London company was given this distinction so frequently; indeed, all the other London companies together did not present so many royal performances.

Most of the records of dramatic activities at the court give simply the number of performances paid for in a given season, but for about forty occasions the accounts give the name of the play the King saw. Three-fourths of the plays selected by the Master of the Revels for court performance had been written by Fletcher, Shakespeare and Jonson, in that

---

[1] See *Jacobean and Caroline Stage*, IV, 870–7, for contemporary allusions to this play.

order. Those plays which had sufficient royal appeal to be selected more than once in these years were *Rule a Wife and Have a Wife*, *The Maid in the Mill* (three times in one season), *The Pilgrim*, *Twelfth Night*, *The Winter's Tale*, 'Sir John Falstaff', *The Alchemist* and *The Merry Devil of Edmonton*.[1]

(iii) The Palsgrave's company

In 1613 and for a few years thereafter the principal rival of the King's company was the Palsgrave's. This troupe had received a patent under its new name on 11 January 1612/13. At that time the Elector Palatine was about to marry Elizabeth, daughter of James I, an unusually popular princess, and the name had drawing power.

Only the name was new, however, for the organization had been in existence for at least twenty years. From 1603 to 1612 it had been the company of Prince Henry, heir to the English throne, and only after his death in 1612 were Prince Henry's Men transferred to the sponsorship of the Palsgrave. In the reign of Queen Elizabeth they had been the Lord Admiral's Men, and under the leadership of the great actor Edward Alleyn and financed by his father-in-law, Philip Henslowe, they had been the chief competitor of the Lord Chamberlain's company. The rivalry of these troupes in the closing years of the old queen's reign was expressed, among other ways, in the building of their two theatres. In 1599 the Lord Chamberlain's Men built the Globe, the finest playhouse in town for about a year after it was built. In 1600 Henslowe and Alleyn built, on the other side of town in the parish of St Giles-without-Cripplegate, the Fortune for the Lord Admiral's Men. The rivalry which prompted this action is apparent in the contract which Henslowe and Alleyn drew up with their builder, Peter Streete. At least three times in this document he is directed to build some feature of the new theatre like the comparable one at the Globe, and once he agrees to make the scantlings (small wooden beams) of the new Fortune 'lardger and bigger in assize' than those at the Globe. Apparently Alleyn and Henslowe succeeded in surpassing the playhouse of their rivals, for when the Fortune burned twenty-one years later John Chamberlain called it 'the fayrest play-house in this towne'.[2]

[1] See E. K. Chambers, *The Elizabethan Stage*, 4 vols (Oxford, 1923), IV, 180–2; and *Jacobean and Caroline Stage*, I, 94–6, 173, 194, 213.
[2] Chamberlain, *Letters*, II, 415.

The repertory of the Palsgrave's Men in 1613 seems to us distinctly inferior to that of King James's company, but they had plays of known appeal in London. They still performed *Doctor Faustus*, *The Spanish Tragedy* and *Friar Bacon and Friar Bungay*. Probably others of the more than one hundred plays which Henslowe is known to have bought for the Lord Admiral's Men in the 1590s were still in their repertory, though we have no evidence of Jacobean revivals, and most of them were never printed and are now lost.

In spite of the success of the Lord Admiral's – Prince Henry's – Palsgrave's company and the superiority of their theatre, by 1613 the Fortune had acquired a reputation for vulgar fare and uncultivated audiences. It seems to have been the London theatre most popularly associated with the jig, a simple song–dance afterpiece, always vulgar and frequently bawdy.[1] This reputation is clearly indicated in an order issued by the General Sessions of the Peace at Westminster on 1 October 1612:

> Whereas complaint has been made at this last General Session that by reason of certain lewd jigs, songs and dances used and accustomed at the playhouse called the Fortune in Golding Lane, divers cut purses and other lewd and ill disposed persons in great multitude do resort thither at the end of every play, many times causing tumults and outrages whereby His Majesty's peace is often broken and much mischief like to ensue thereby. . . .[2]

Because of this situation the General Sessions ordered all London theatres to stop performing 'jigs, Rymes, and dances' at the end of their plays.

Another suggestion of the sort of appeal the Fortune was making in these years is to be seen in the affairs of Moll Frith. Moll was a notorious London female roysterer who was an *habituée* of the theatre of the Palsgrave's Men; she is said to have appeared on the Fortune stage in men's clothes and there to have sung, played the lute and made bawdy remarks. Indeed the actors of the company exploited the popular interest in this local character by performing (and presumably ordering the writing of) *The Roaring Girl, or Moll Cut-purse*, by Thomas Dekker and Thomas Middleton. Moll appears as a sentimentalized character in the play; when the piece was printed in 1611, a picture of her, dressed in men's clothes, smoking a pipe and carrying

---

[1] See Charles Read Baskervill, *The Elizabethan Jig and Related Song Drama* (Chicago, Ill., 1929).

[2] John Cordy Jeaffreson, *Middlesex County Records*, 3 vols (London, 1886–92), III, 83.

a sword, appeared on the title page (*plate 7*).

Though the King's company was the only London troupe which controlled its own theatres throughout the reign of James I, Edward Alleyn, after the death of Philip Henslowe in 1616, arranged a similar independence for the Palsgrave's: he leased his theatre to ten of the patented members of the company. According to their lease of 31 October 1618, they were to hold the theatre for a period of thirty-one years at an annual rent of £200. Probably this new self-sufficiency increased the stability of the Palsgrave's Men at the Fortune, but it did not last for long.

In the middle of the night of 9 December 1621, the Fortune burned to the ground. The loss was disastrous, much more serious than the burning of the Globe had been for King James's Men. In the first place, the time of the fire meant that the building was deserted, not full of actors and friends to save manuscripts and costumes, as at the Globe. Apparently the Fortune fire destroyed both, and their costumes and repertory were the most costly assets of any troupe. In the second place, the Palsgrave's Men had no second theatre like the Blackfriars to fall back upon. Alleyn did build them a new playhouse, but after 1621 the company was never prominent again.

The new Fortune, probably opened in the spring of 1623, was also leased out by Alleyn who had built it, but most of the actors apparently had no capital, for the new theatre was leased to thirteen men, only three of whom were players, and the company was no longer in control of the house. One of the actor-lessors was Richard Gunnell who had some prominence for several years as manager, first of the Fortune and later of the Salisbury Court theatre.

The struggles of the Palsgrave's company to replace their burned-up repertory are apparent in the years 1623 and 1624. A prosperous company with a full repertory, like the King's Men, needed to have three or four new plays a year at this time. In the fifteen months from late July 1623 to early November 1624, the Palsgrave's Men are known to have submitted to the Master of the Revels for licensing at least fourteen new play manuscripts, all but one probably inferior productions since they never got into print. Most of them would never have been heard of had not Edmond Malone copied Sir Henry Herbert's office-book entries licensing them.

Such a struggling company was in no position to withstand further disasters, and the prohibition of all theatrical performances in London for eight or nine months in 1625 evidently destroyed them. After 1625 they are not heard of in the city again.

(iv) Queen Anne's company

The third of the old Elizabethan dramatic companies of the 1590s which was still performing in London in 1613 was Queen Anne's Men. In the last decade of the old queen's reign they had been the Earl of Worcester's company, and in the early years of the seventeenth century they had been financed by Philip Henslowe. When the Stuarts came to the throne, Worcester's company was transferred to the patronage of Queen Anne, a distinction which they enjoyed until the Queen's death in 1619.

In the first five or six years of the seventeenth century the company had performed at Henslowe's Rose theatre, at the Curtain, and at the theatre in the Boar's Head inn in Whitechapel, but, probably in 1606, they transferred to the new Red Bull theatre, which may have been built for them,[1] and in this theatre they played until 1617.

There are several lists of the actor-sharers of Queen Anne's company. In 1612 the most prominent were Thomas Greene, Thomas Heywood, Christopher Beeston and Richard Perkins. Thomas Greene, evidently their leading actor, was widely praised in his time. John Cooke's play, probably originally called *The City Gallant*, came to be known from the performances of this comedian as *Greene's Tu Quoque*, under which title it was printed with a woodcut of Greene in his popular role on the title page (*plate 8*). For this edition Greene's fellow sharer Thomas Heywood wrote an address to the reader:

> To gratulate the love and memory of my worthy friend the Author, and my entirely beloved Fellow, the Actor, I could not chuse . . . but to prefix some token of my affection to either in the frontispire [frontispiece] of the Booke. . . . As for Master *Greene*, all that I will speake of him (and that without flattery) is this (if I were worthy to censure) there was not an Actor of his nature, in his time, of better ability in performance of what he undertooke, more applauded by the Audience, of greater grace at the Court, or of more general love in the Citty. . . .

When Greene died in 1612, leaving a bequest to 'my fellowes of the redd Bull', the blow to his company was a heavy one. Not only was he their best-known actor, but his ties to the company must have been close: besides his general bequest to all the members of Queen Anne's, he left a special

---

[1] See *Jacobean and Caroline Stage*, VI, 214–18.

bequest to another member of the company, John Cumber; he made two others, Christopher Beeston and Richard Perkins, his executors; and a fourth, Thomas Heywood, was a witness. The protracted lawsuits of his widow to recover from the company the value of his shares and the money he had loaned them was one of the causes of the decline of Queen Anne's company as well as the source of a good deal of our knowledge of the operation of the organization.[1]

Thomas Heywood, the dramatist, was a leading sharer of the company, apparently from the beginning. His value to them was primarily as a playwright, not as an actor; for nearly twenty years he appears to have written almost all his known plays for them. It is likely that he had some sort of exclusive agreement with the Queen's Men as Shakespeare, Fletcher, Massinger and Shirley had successively with the King's. Several poems, prologues or prefaces of Heywood express his affection for his fellows in the company.

Heywood's friend and fellow-sharer, Christopher Beeston, was active in London theatrical affairs for nearly forty years. In the last few years of Elizabeth's reign he had been a colleague of Shakespeare in the Lord Chamberlain's company, and he was apparently the source of the story his son relayed to John Aubrey that Shakespeare had been a schoolmaster for a time. In 1613, and for at least four years thereafter, he was handling the business affairs of Queen Anne's Men in much the same way, it would appear, as John Heminges and Henry Condell handled such affairs for the King's. Beeston built the Phoenix or Cockpit in Drury Lane in 1617, and he managed whatever company was there until his death in 1638, when his theatre and his function passed to his son William, who, Richard Flecknoe said in 1654, had 'brought up most of the actors extant' and who became one of the leading managers in the early Restoration period.

A fourth sharer in this company was a leading London actor for many years. At the end of the 1612 quarto of *The White Devil*, John Webster appended a note praising the performance by Queen Anne's Men and concluding, 'whereof as I make a general acknowledgment, so in particular I must remember the well approved industry of my friend *Maister Perkins*, and confess the worth of his action did crown both the beginning and the end'.

Many years later Thomas Heywood in both the prologue and the epilogue of the 1633 quarto of Marlowe's *Jew of Malta* praised Perkins in the title

[1] See F. G. Fleay, *A Chronicle History of the London Stage* (London, 1890), 192–4 and 270–97.

role. Perkins along with two other members of the company, Christopher Beeston and Robert Pallant, had written commendatory verses for the 1612 edition of Heywood's *Apology for Actors*. There is a contemporary portrait of Richard Perkins in the picture gallery at Dulwich College (*plate 9*).

In 1613 the archives of Queen Anne's Men at the Red Bull probably still included several of the manuscripts Henslowe had loaned them money to buy in the early years of the century, such plays as *The Black Dog of Newgate, Marshall Osric, Lady Jane* and *A Woman Killed with Kindness*. A few others can be identified from title pages as having been performed by Queen Anne's company: Dekker and Webster's *Sir Thomas Wyatt* (probably the same as *Lady Jane*); *The Travels of Three English Brothers* by Day, Wilkins and Rowley; *Greene's Tu Quoque*; Webster's *White Devil* and *The Devil's Law Case*; Dekker's *If it be not Good the Devil is in It*; Marlowe's *Edward II*; and the anonymous plays *The Honest Lawyer* and *Swetnam the Woman Hater*. But the backbone of the repertory was made up of the plays of a leading member of the company, Thomas Heywood. The company is known to have performed his *Four Prentices of London, The Royal King and the Loyal Subject, A Woman Killed with Kindness, If You Know Not Me You Know Nobody, Fortune by Land and Sea, The Rape of Lucrece, The Golden Age, The Silver Age, The Brazen Age* and *The Iron Age*. It is most likely that they also produced his *Wise Woman of Hogsdon* and *The Fair Maid of the West*, pt I. Since so many of Heywood's plays are lost (he said in 1633 that he had had a hand in 220) and since his attachment to this company was so close and so affectionate, it is likely that there were in the repertory of Queen Anne's company a good many of Thomas Heywood's plays which are now totally unknown, or at least not known to have been written by Heywood.

From 1613 until well after the death of Queen Anne, the members of the company were in financial difficulties. To repay their debt of £113 to Greene's widow, Susan Baskerville, they made various agreements and borrowed more money from her until in 1615 they agreed to pay to Susan or her son Francis Brown eight pence a day, six days a week, in every week the company played in London for so long as either should live. They repeatedly defaulted and she repeatedly sued. In 1617 Christopher Beeston moved the company into his newly completed theatre, the Phoenix. But their occupancy was cut short on 4 March 1616/17 by a destructive riot which gutted the theatre. The best account of the disaster appears in a letter written from London four days after the event by John Chamberlain to his regular correspondent, Sir Dudley Carleton:

On the 4th of this present beeing our Shrove Tewsday the prentises or rather the unruly people of the suburbs played theyr parts, in divers places, as Finsburie feilds, about Wapping by St Katherines, and in Lincolns Ynne fields, in which places being assembled in great numbers they fell to great disorders in pulling downe of houses and beating the guards that were set to kepe rule, specially at a new play house (somtime a cockpit) in Drurie Lane, where the Quenes players used to play. Though the fellowes defended themselves as well as they could and slew three of them with shot and hurt divers, yet they entered the house and defaced yt, cutting the players apparell all in pieces, and all other theyre furniture and burnt theyre play bookes and did what other mischeife they could: in Finsburie they brake the prison and let out all the prisoners, spoyled the house by untiling and breaking downe the roofe and all the windowes and at Wapping they pulled downe seven or eight houses and defaced five times as many, besides many other outrages as beating the sheriffe from his horse with stones and dooing much other hurt too long to write. There be divers of them taken since and clapt up, and I make no question but we shall see some of them hangd this next weeke, as yt is more then time they were. . . .[1]

Chamberlain's zeal to hang the rioters is easy to understand, but it is not clear what punishment, if any, was meted out to them, and certainly the rioters were not required to recompense Queen Anne's Men for their costumes and playbooks, i.e. prompt manuscripts, a loss which must have been comparable to that of the Palsgrave's Men in the Fortune fire.

   Though, in June following, the company was expected to return to the repaired Phoenix from the Red Bull, this vandalism surely accelerated their decline, and no prosperity or great reputation is associated with their next two years at the Phoenix. Indeed the contrary is indicated in some lines which Thomas Middleton wrote for his masque performed for the lawyers of the Inner Temple in January 1618/19. In this piece several characters are personifications of seasons of the year, and before the first antimasque Doctor Almanac delivers a charge to the masquers, Candlemas, Shrove Tuesday, Ill Mayday, etc.:

   Stand forth Shrove Tuesday, one a the silenced bricklayers.
   'Tis in your charge to pull down bawdy-houses,

[1] Chamberlain, *Letters*, II, 59–60.

To set your tribe a-work, cause spoil in Shoreditch,
And make a dangerous leak there; deface Turnbull
And tickle Codpiece Row; ruin the Cockpit;
The poor players never thriv'd in't; a' my conscience
Some quean pissed upon the first brick.

On 2 March 1618/19 Queen Anne died, and the last record of her troupe of players is the list of seventeen men who were granted livery allowances to march in her funeral procession on 13 May. Evidently the company never recovered from this loss. Beeston evicted them from his theatre and brought in Prince Charles's company, which he joined. A remnant of Queen Anne's company joined a road troupe which played in the provinces under the name of the deceased Queen; others returned to the Red Bull and acted there under the name of the Company of the Revels, performing such plays as *The Two Merry Milkmaids*, *The Costly Whore*, Thomas May's *The Heir*, *The Tragedy of Herod and Antipater*, *The Two Noble Lords*, *The Welsh Traveller*, and *The Virgin Martyr* by Massinger and Dekker. The company was evidently in a precarious state: they were still harrassed by Susan Baskerville, and in 1622 the Middlesex County Sessions proceeded against them because they refused to repair the footways around the Red Bull theatre. By the middle of 1623 the Players of the Revels had been replaced at the Red Bull by Prince Charles's company.

(v) The Lady Elizabeth's company

The players of Lady Elizabeth, daughter of James I and, after 14 February 1612/13, wife of the Elector Palatine, or the Palsgrave, came into existence in 1611. For several years the company was financed by Philip Henslowe, and a number of documents preserved at Dulwich College show something of their troubled relations with Henslowe and of their complex arrangements about theatre rents, the payment of hired men, and the purchase of plays and costumes. Early in 1613 Henslowe seems to have brought about some sort of amalgamation of the Lady Elizabeth's Men with Philip Rosseter's Queen's Revels, the most distinguished of the disappearing boy companies, though the name Queen's Revels continues to appear in occasional documents. The new arrangement, whatever it was, added to the repertory of the Lady Elizabeth's a number of plays and several actors who became prominent, notably the actor-dramatist Nathan Field (*plate 10*).

Before 1614 the theatres used by the company are uncertain – probably the Swan, the Rose and Whitefriars – and the troupe seems to have been spending more time touring in the provinces than the King's Men or Queen Anne's company did. By the autumn of 1614 they were installed in the new playhouse called the Hope. This theatre, owned by Philip Henslowe and Jacob Meade, was built with a demountable stage so that the house could be used for bull-baiting and bear-baiting as well as for playing. Here, on 31 October 1614, the company presented Ben Jonson's *Bartholomew Fair*, whose induction contains comments on the theatre. In the dialogue Jonson praises his protégé, Nathan Field, by making one of the characters inquire: 'Which is your Burbage now? . . . Your best Actor? Your Field?'

Other well-known players in the troupe during its early years were Joseph Taylor and Robert Benfield, who later became important members of the King's company; less famous were Robert Hamlen, Robert Pallant and William Barksted.

The repertory of the Lady Elizabeth's company was rather distinguished. In the years before 1625 they are known to have acted Beaumont and Fletcher's *Cupid's Revenge, The Coxcomb* and *The Honest Man's Fortune*; Marston's *The Dutch Courtezan*; Marston, Chapman and Jonson's *Eastward Ho*; Jonson's *Bartholomew Fair*; Middleton's *A Chaste Maid in Cheapside*; Middleton and Rowley's *The Changeling* and *The Spanish Gypsy*; Field's *Amends for Ladies*; Massinger's *The Bondman, The Parliament of Love* and *The Renegado*.

In 1613, 1614 and 1615, Robert Daborne, who had been one of the patentees of the Queen's Revels Boys before the amalgamation, was writing plays for the Lady Elizabeth's Men through the agency of Philip Henslowe. Among Henslowe's papers preserved at Dulwich College are more than thirty letters, bonds and receipts by or concerning Daborne and his writing for the company. At least five plays are involved, some of them collaborations with Nathan Field, Philip Massinger, John Fletcher or Cyril Tourneur. Generally the letters do not give the titles of the plays but there are references to *Machiavel and the Devil, The Owl*, and *The Bellman of London* or *The Arraignment of London*. For such plays Daborne was being paid from £12 to £20 apiece. In the letters he asks for advances; sometimes he threatens to take his manuscript to the King's company; sometimes he refers to the custom of reading the play to the acting company as part of the composition process; sometimes he asks to be bailed out of gaol with other dramatists who are working with him. The whole series of letters illuminates the process of getting a play manuscript prepared for production in the middle of the reign of James I.[1]

During these years 1613–15 there were various disagreements between members of the company and Henslowe, and in 1615 certain of the actors drew up a list of their grievances. Unfortunately no reply from Henslowe is extant, and as usual in such disagreements one can assume that at least some of the charges are distortions or misunderstandings. Most of the accusations derive from the fact that Henslowe dispensed the cash and kept the accounts, and the actors assert that they do not have all the costumes which they have paid for; that they have expended £200 for the plays Henslowe bought for them, but that he keeps the manuscripts; that he has bonds from the hired men to work for whatever company he selects and that he can therefore withdraw them all at will; that he has juggled the company accounts and his private accounts with some of the actors; and that he has not paid them the full sum agreed upon when their theatre was used for bear-baiting instead of play performances.[2]

In 1615 some sort of co-operative agreement was worked out between the Lady Elizabeth's Men and Prince Charles's Men were to play. This company received payment for plays presented by the other; the 1618 title page of Field's *Amends for Ladies* says that it was performed by 'both the Princes Seruants and the Lady Elizabeths'; on 3 June 1615 Philip Rosseter was authorized to build a new theatre in which the Children of the Revels, Lady Elizabeth's Men and Prince Charles's Men were to play. This scattered evidence is confused, but at least it does indicate some sort of agreement by which the company of the Lady Elizabeth was no longer completely distinct.

In January 1615/16 Philip Henslowe died and his theatrical interests were taken over by his son-in-law, the retired actor Edward Alleyn. Under Alleyn's direction, four of the leading actors of the company – Joseph Taylor, Robert Hamlen, Robert Pallant and William Barksted – joined with six of Prince Charles's Men to agree to play at the Hope and to give Alleyn one quarter of the takings from the galleries until their indebtedness to him had been discharged. Since Nathan Field and Robert Benfield had recently deserted the Lady Elizabeth's company for the King's, the old troupe was sadly reduced and has left records only in the provinces for the next six years.

[1] *Henslowe Papers*, ed. W. W. Greg (London, 1907), 67–85. See above, pp. 37–9.
[2] ibid., 86–90.

In 1621 or 1622 a revived Lady Elizabeth's company was formed and began playing at the Phoenix under Christopher Beeston. In 1622 the new Master of the Revels, Sir Henry Herbert, listed the chief actors at the Phoenix as Christopher Beeston, Joseph Moore, Eyllaerdt Swanston, Andrew Cane, Curtis Greville, William Sherlock and Anthony Turner.

For a few years, until the great plague of 1625, this new Lady Elizabeth's company, now frequently called the Queen of Bohemia's Men, was quite successful. In their epistle for the First Folio, Heminges and Condell coupled the theatre of the Lady Elizabeth's Men with that of the King's as haunts of sophisticated Londoners – 'And though you be a Magistrate of wit and sit on the stage at *Black-Friers*, or the *Cock-pit* to arraigne plays dailie. . . .'

The company repertory was receiving distinguished additions in these years: in the thirty-three months between May 1622 and February 1624/5 Sir Henry Herbert is known to have licensed twelve new plays and one old one for them. Nine of the thirteen were written by notable dramatists of the time: Thomas Middleton, William Rowley, Philip Massinger, John Ford, Thomas Dekker, Thomas Heywood and (with his first extant play) the new dramatist, James Shirley. At court in the same period they performed *The Spanish Gypsy*, *The Bondman*, *The Changeling*, *Cupid's Revenge* and *Greene's Tu Quoque*.

But their days of prosperity were numbered; the protracted and deadly plague of 1625 finished off the Lady Elizabeth's Men as a London company. After 1625 Queen Henrietta's Men occupied their theatre, performed a number of their plays and absorbed several of their actors.

(vi) Prince Charles's (I) company

In 1610, when Charles, the second son of King James I, was still the 9-year-old Duke of York, and two and a half years before the death of his elder brother, 'the' Prince, a company was licensed under Charles's patronage to play in London and in the provinces. But for the next four years there is no evidence that it ever did perform in London except occasionally at court before the younger members of the royal family. In these years there are, however, a number of records of the company's presence in such provincial towns as Barnstaple, Dover, Coventry, Oxford, Leicester and Nottingham.

The repertory of Prince Charles's company included very few plays of any distinction. Of the plays which belonged to them between 1613 and 1625 about twenty are known by title, but three-quarters never achieved print, presumably because no publisher thought them worth the investment. Their four extant plays are all compositions or collaborations of their leading member, William Rowley: *All's Lost by Lust* and *The Witch of Edmonton* with Ford and Dekker, *A Fair Quarrel* and *The World Tossed at Tennis* with Thomas Middleton. Some of their lost plays had fairly distinguished authorship – *A Fault in Friendship* by Richard Brome and 'Young' Johnson, *The Bellman of Paris* by Thomas Dekker and John Day, and *The Late Murder of the Son upon the Mother, or Keep the Widow Waking* by Rowley, Webster, Ford and Dekker – but the others are by slightly known writers such as Barnes (whose first name is unknown) and William Sampson, or of wholly unknown authorship.

The best-known actor of the organization throughout its existence was the actor-dramatist William Rowley. Others – Joseph Taylor, Thomas Hobbs, John Newton, Gilbert Reason and Anthony Smith – were either little known or were members for short periods. Rowley, like the other actor-dramatists – Nathan Field, William Shakespeare and Thomas Heywood – both wrote and acted for his company: in his play *All's Lost by Lust* he is known to have played 'a simple clownish Gentleman'.

Prince Charles's company does not appear as a settled London troupe until their co-operative arrangement with the Lady Elizabeth's company in 1615, as noted in the discussion of Lady Elizabeth's. After Henslowe's death in January 1615/16, his successor, Edward Alleyn, made of the two troupes one company under the patronage of Prince Charles. This augmented Prince Charles's company played at the dual-purpose Hope for a year or two, and they made an agreement with Alleyn and Meade (owners of the theatre) about the old debts of the Elizabeth–Prince's group. But there was trouble about the apportionment of days for playing and bear-baiting, and they left the Hope and settled, probably in the Red Bull, early in 1617.

For the next two years little is known of the affairs of the company at the Red Bull. On 3 October 1617, Edward Alleyn recorded in his diary that he had gone to the Red Bull and 'received for *The Younger Brother* but £3.6s.4d.'. Presumably this payment to Alleyn was made by Prince Charles's Men from their receipts at a performance of the lost anonymous play *The Younger Brother*.

About the time of the death of Queen Anne in March 1618/19, which deprived her players of a patroness, Christopher Beeston deserted her company and became a member of Prince Charles's. He then moved them from the Red Bull to his theatre, the Phoenix, and apparently succeeded in keeping some of the plays and costumes of the disintegrating Queen Anne's company for the use of Prince Charles's Men at his theatre.

The Phoenix was not only a private theatre, and the newest playhouse in London, but the best located, for it was within easy walking distance of all the four major Inns of Court and of Prince Charles's residence at Denmark House, and nearer than any other commercial theatre to the principal residence of the King and his court at Whitehall palace. Such an environment was a far cry from the customary noise and vulgarity of the Red Bull, but there is no evidence that Prince Charles's Men were ever notably successful in exploiting it. Certainly they had a try at this audience when they participated in Middleton's *Inner Temple Masque, or Masque of Heroes*, performed in January 1618/19. Of course the masquers were Templars, but the quarto of 1619 records that the speaking parts were taken by five men and a boy from Prince Charles's company: Joseph Taylor, William Rowley, John Newton, Hugh Attewell, William Carpenter and the unnamed boy.

Middleton says in his preliminary verses for the Quarto that this masque pleased the ladies, but the company was less successful in its next appeal to an exclusive audience. In January 1619/20 they presented an unnamed play at court. The only known account of the event comes from a letter sent by the Venetian ambassador back to the Doge and Senate in Venice. He wrote:

> The comedians of the prince, in the presence of the king his father, played a drama the other day in which a king with his two sons has one of them put to death, simply upon suspicion that he wished to deprive him of his crown, and the other son actually did deprive him of it afterwards. This moved the king in an extraordinary manner, both inwardly and outwardly. In this country however the comedians have absolute liberty to say whatever they wish against any one soever, so the only demonstration against them will be the words spoken by the king. [1]

Though the Venetian ambassador probably saw this performance at

[1] *Catalogue of State Papers and Manuscripts, Relating to English, Affairs Existing in the Archives and Collections of Venice, and in Other Libraries of Northern Italy (1202–1668)*, ed. Rawdon Brown, G. C. Bentick, H. F. Brown and A. B. Hinds, 35 vols (London, 1864–1935), vol. 1619–21, p. 111. King James's sensitivity derived from the fact that after the death of his popular elder son, Henry, seven years before, there had been rumours that the death of the prince had not been a natural one. The surviving son, Charles, patron of this company, did, of course, succeed his father six years later.

court, as was usual for the principal ambassadors in London, he knew very little about English censorship, for plays were normally censored and offending actors often punished,[1] though perhaps not so severely as they might have been for similar offences in Venice. There is, however, no extant record of punishment of the Prince's Men for this performance at court.

Some time during the winter of 1619–20 Prince Charles's Men had a curious masque prepared for them by their leading actor, William Rowley, in collaboration with Thomas Middleton. It was entitled *The World Tossed at Tennis* and was originally intended for performance in the prince's palace, Denmark House, before Charles and his father. But for reasons unknown it was not presented there but in the company's theatre. Obviously the usual type of spectacular court masque could not be mounted in a regular theatre, and this piece has been modified by the elimination of much of the spectacle and of the elaborate presentation of masquers, though it still includes more songs and dances than were usual in commercial theatres.

By the middle of 1622 the company had left the Phoenix and gone to the old and little-frequented theatre, the Curtain. For the next three years the career of the Prince's Men is very obscure, but they seem to have been playing part of the time at the Red Bull, and they licensed several plays which have been lost, pieces like *The Bellman of Paris, The Peaceable King or the Lord Mendall, A Fault in Friendship*, and probably *The Late Murder of the Son upon the Mother, or Keep the Widow Waking*. The last, acted in the autumn of 1624, was the dramatization of a contemporary murder with a subplot involving the debauching of Ann Elsden. Her son-in-law brought suit against the players and the dramatists, William Rowley, John Ford, Thomas Dekker and John Webster. The outcome of the suit is not known, but the Bill, the Answer and the depositions give a good deal of information about the preparation of a sensational play.[2]

The last notice of Prince Charles's Men is the list of the members of the company granted livery allowances to march in the funeral procession of King James. When their master succeeded to his father's throne, he took over the King's company and added to it three of the leading members of his former company, Thomas Hobbs, William Penn and Anthony Smith; William Rowley had joined the King's Men a year or two before. After the death of King James the company was never revived.

[1] See Bentley, *The Profession of Dramatist in Shakespeare's Time*, ch. IX, 145–96.
[2] See *Jacobean and Caroline Stage*, I, 208–9; III, 252–6; and C. J. Sisson, *Lost Plays of Shakespeare's Age* (Cambridge, 1936), 80–124.

3 The period 1625–36

(i) Introduction

The terrible plague of 1625 which claimed more than 35,000 lives in London and the suburbs was, of course, ruinous to the players. Several actors, numerous members of their households, and at least one dramatist, John Fletcher, were carried off by the epidemic. For eight or nine months no theatre in London was in operation, and bankruptcy was the fate of most London theatrical organizations.

The death of King James in March 1625, the accession of his son, and the arrival of the new queen, Henrietta Maria of France, in June, also led to changes in theatrical patronage during the plague period. King James's company became King Charles's company, with the addition of three or four players who had been part of his old troupe when he had been Prince of Wales. Thus by the time of the reopening of the theatres in late November or early December 1625 four of the old companies had disappeared from London: Prince Charles's (I) company, the Palsgrave's company, Queen Anne's company and the Lady Elizabeth's company.

Christopher Beeston organized a new troupe for the patronage of the new queen and set them up in his theatre, the Phoenix or Cockpit in Drury Lane, from which he had evicted the remnant of the old Lady Elizabeth's company, taking several of their leading actors and one or two of the old Queen Anne's company, as well as a number of plays from their old repertories, for the newly organized Queen Henrietta's Men. Three or four years later, another new company was organized for the new Salisbury Court theatre erected in 1629. This troupe was called the King's Revels company. The other new companies of the period 1625–36 performing at the Fortune and the Red Bull were less prominent and less successful.

King Charles and Queen Henrietta Maria took a more active interest in theatrical affairs than their predecessors had done. They ordered more performances at court; on several occasions the King secured the manuscripts of special court plays for commercial performance by his London company; he sometimes suggested a plot for a comedy or went over a censored manuscript himself. The Queen gave the elaborate costumes of a private production by her court ladies to the King's company; she established a precedent by visiting the Blackfriars herself.

One result of this royal interest was that, in the reign of Charles I, the Blackfriars and the Phoenix theatres were more extensively patronized by courtiers and nobility than they had been in the reign of James I.

(ii) The King's company

In the years 1625–36 the King's company dominated the London theatrical world even more completely than it had done before the plague closing. They still moved from the Blackfriars to the Globe in the late spring and back to the Blackfriars in the autumn, and Blackfriars continued to be the premier London theatre. The company was still selected more frequently than any other to entertain the distinguished audience of courtiers, noblemen, ambassadors and the royal family at court – more than 160 times in these eleven years.[1]

One of the many losses suffered by the company during the long plague closing was that of their regular dramatist, John Fletcher, who succumbed to the epidemic at the age of 46. He was replaced as regular dramatist for the company by Philip Massinger, who wrote at least fourteen of his assignable

[1] See *Jacobean and Caroline Stage*, 1, 96–8.

and dated plays and probably four or five of his unassignable and undated ones for King Charles's Men during this period. In addition he revised their older plays, including several of Fletcher's, for revival.

Though Philip Massinger prepared about two new compositions a year for the King's Men, they needed more new plays than that, and during these eleven years about twenty-three others are known to have been written for them by other well-known playwrights: Richard Brome, *The Lovesick Court* and *The Novella*; William Davenant, *The Cruel Brother*, *The Just Italian*, *Love and Honour*, *News from Plymouth*, *The Platonic Lovers* and *The Wits*; John Ford, *Beauty in a Trance* and *The Lover's Melancholy*; Thomas Heywood, *A Challenge for Beauty* and (with Richard Brome) *The Late Lancashire Witches*; Ben Jonson, *The Staple of News*, *The Magnetic Lady* and *The New Inn*. Of their other new plays several were written by amateurs, some of them, like Lodowick Carlell and John Suckling, courtiers who wrote plays primarily for private production at court but on several occasions gave their manuscripts to the King's Men for later performance at Blackfriars.[1]

John Heminges and Henry Condell, who had managed most of the company's affairs in the earlier period, began tapering off their managerial activities after the reopening. Condell does not appear as payee for the company after 1625; he died in 1627. Heminges, after 1625, was generally joined by Joseph Taylor as payee, and after 1627 by Taylor and John Lowin; he died in 1630. From 1630 to 1642 Taylor and Lowin are the usual representatives of the company.

One set of figures which has come down to us gives a rough idea of the amount of money the King's Men were taking in during these years at an average performance in their theatres. All companies in London paid regularly to the Master of the Revels company fees, in addition to the allowance fees paid for each new play produced. In May 1628 the King's Men agreed with the Master to give him the receipts from two specified performances instead of set, semi-annual fees – that is, the total admission receipts, minus daily charges, for one performance in winter and one in the summer. It was agreed that Herbert could select the play from their repertory himself, but not a new play and not the first day of the revival of an old play. Thus the agreement eliminated the two occasions which normally brought the greatest profit. Herbert's record of his receipts under this agreement shows that his average take at summer (Globe) performances was

[1] See Alfred Harbage, *Cavalier Drama* (New York, 1936), *passim*.

£6.13s.8d. and at winter (Blackfriars) performances was £15.15s. The plays Herbert selected for his benefit performances reveal his educated guesses as to which old plays in the King's repertory would draw the largest crowds. He chose three Fletcher plays, two Shakespeare plays and two Jonson ones. His three other choices are not named, though the receipts are noted. The largest sums came from the receipts at *The Custom of the Country* and *The Wild Goose Chase*; the next largest at *The Alchemist* and *Every Man in His Humour*; the smallest at *Othello*, *The Prophetess* and *Richard II*.[1] There is no way to tell how much the weather or other non-dramatic factors influenced attendance at these performances, but, considering the agreed limitations on his choice of plays, Sir Henry's receipts are likely to have been less than the company's returns on their best days but more than those on their worst.

The great prosperity of this troupe in the 1630s is also reflected in a set of statements made by three leading actors in 1635.[2] It will be remembered that, from their first occupancies by the company in 1599 and 1609, the Globe and the Blackfriars had been owned by groups of fellows of the company plus an outsider or two. In the succeeding years, deaths and purchases had altered this group of proprietors and by 1635 the owners of the Globe were Cuthbert Burbage, Mrs Richard Burbage Robinson, Mrs Henry Condell, and the actors John Shank, Joseph Taylor and John Lowin. The owners of the Blackfriars were the same group plus the heirs of the actor John Underwood, who had died in 1624 or 1625. In 1635 three other leading patented members of the company – Robert Benfield, Eyllaerdt Swanston and Thomas Pollard – presented a petition to the Lord Chamberlain (the final arbiter of theatrical and dramatic affairs in the kingdom) requesting that these owners of the two theatres be required to sell some of their shares to the petitioners. In these petitions and answers there are several assertions about incomes, rents and theatrical expenses made by men who were certainly in a position to know the facts, though it may have been to their advantage to shade them somewhat.

John Shanks asserted in his answer that each of the petitioners had received in the past year, as his share of the company profits, £180. Obviously John Shanks, Joseph Taylor and John Lowin must have received the same sum plus their profits from theatre rents, which the petitioners assert were even more. The prosperity of the enterprise of the King's Men at the Globe and Blackfriars can be inferred by a comparison of these annual earnings of £180 by one group and more than £360 by the other, with the

[1] *Jacobean and Caroline Stage*, I, 23–4.
[2] See MSC, II (1914), 362–73, and the summaries in *Jacobean and Caroline Stage*, I, 43–7.

£10 per annum plus diet which Robert Burton says was the normal stipend of a schoolmaster or curate, or the approximately £26 or £27 per annum which James Shirley received in 1621–3 as schoolmaster at St Albans, or the £52 per year which the proprietors of the Salisbury Court theatre hopefully agreed to pay Richard Brome as the regular poet for that house in 1638.[1]

The enterprise of the King's company was not only profitable in these years but their private theatre in the Blackfriars had become a favourite resort of nobility and gentry. In 1633 the crowding of the coaches of the well-to-do for performances at this theatre created a traffic problem necessitating the issuance of an order by the Privy Council regulating parking. As has been shown elsewhere, the theatre was also the setting for a number of notorious quarrels among aristocrats.[2] Even more sensational, Queen Henrietta herself visited Blackfriars in May 1634 and again in 1635 or 1636. No previous king or queen is known to have visited a commercial theatre in London.[3]

This period of great success was brought to a close by the protracted plague of 1636–7. The closing order was sent to all companies by the Master of the Revels on 12 May 1636; except for a respite of about a week in February 1636/7, all theatres were shut for nearly seventeen months. The prestige of the company brought some alleviation to their distress – £240 for performances at court; a special allowance of £20 per month to help them in the winter of 1636/7; and a special command from the Lord Chamberlain to the Stationers' Company that all play manuscripts offered to London printers should be denied publication until they had been submitted to John Lowin and Joseph Taylor to see if they belonged to the King's Men's repertory, and that those which did should not be published without the express permission of Lowin and Taylor. These were extraordinary benefits, but they were not enough to compensate for seventeen months of dark theatres.

(iii) Queen Henrietta's company

The chief rival of the King's company in the years 1625–36 was Queen Henrietta's Men, a new troupe apparently assembled during the long plague

[1] See G. E. Bentley, *The Profession of Dramatist in Shakespeare's Time, 1590–1642* (Princeton, N.J., 1971), ch. V, 'Dramatists' Pay', esp. 89–97.
[2] See pp. 45–6.
[3] *Jacobean and Caroline Stage*, 1, 33–4, 39, 42, 47, 48.

closing of 1625. Throughout the decade, their managing director or 'Master' was Christopher Beeston, and their playhouse was always his Phoenix or Cockpit in Drury Lane, which was until 1629 the newest playhouse in town and second only to Blackfriars in prestige. The distinction of Queen Henrietta's Men is further indicated by the fact that in these years they were the only company besides King Charles's Men allowed to wear royal livery. Every other year at Michaelmas, the manager and thirteen of the actors of the company were granted livery allowances as Grooms of the Chamber in ordinary, four yards of bastard scarlet cloth for a cloak and a quarter of a yard for a cape.

Queen Henrietta's patronage was a distinct asset in the first half of the reign of Charles I. The new king was very popular in the early years after his accession, and his marriage by proxy, six weeks after his father's death, with Henrietta Maria, sister of Louis XIII of France, was followed by her arrival, on 16 June 1625, in London, where the new king and queen were enthusiastically received. The time was auspicious for the organization of a new dramatic troupe to bear the name of the new queen. Beeston saw his opportunity and recruited several actors from companies to which he had formerly belonged and which had acted at his theatre, Queen Anne's Men and the Lady Elizabeth's Men. But for the majority of the actors in the new company the previous affiliations cannot now be determined. The leading players of the troupe throughout these years were Richard Perkins, Michael Bowyer, John Sumner, William Sherlock, Anthony Turner, William Allen, William Robbins and Hugh Clarke, always under the management of Christopher Beeston, who is not known to have acted in their plays but devoted his energies to managing their affairs.

Very early in their history – probably at the beginning – the company, or Beeston, secured as their regular dramatist James Shirley, newly arrived from his teaching career at St Albans. In the following years 1625–35/6 he appears to have written all but one of his twenty-three plays for this company, approximately the two-a-year average which was usual for regular attached dramatists of the leading companies.[1] The best known of his plays prepared for performance by Queen Henrietta's Men at the Phoenix are *The Bird in a Cage*, *The Gamester*, *Hyde Park*, *The Lady of Pleasure*, *The Maid's Revenge*, *The Traitor*, *The Wedding* and *The Young Admiral*. Other writers whose plays the company bought now and then were Robert Davenport, John Ford, Thomas Heywood, Ben Jonson, Richard Lovelace and Thomas

[1] See Bentley, *The Profession of Dramatist in Shakespeare's Time*, 'Dramatists' central obligations'.

Nabbes. But a good part of their known repertory was made up of older plays which Beeston had evidently retained in the archives of the Phoenix from the days of Queen Anne's Men, Prince Charles's Men and the Lady Elizabeth's Men: *The Knight of the Burning Pestle, The Night Walker, The Honest Whore, The Witch of Edmonton, The Fair Maid of the West*, I, *If You Know Not Me You Know Nobody, The Rape of Lucrece, The Jew of Malta, A Mad World My Masters, The Changeling, The Spanish Gypsy* and *All's Lost by Lust*.

Like all London theatres, the Phoenix was closed by order of the Privy Council on 14 April 1630 until the plague deaths in London were reduced. Though this epidemic was much less severe than the one in 1625 (the largest number of plague deaths in any week in 1630 was 77, in the last week in July, whereas the number had been 4463 in the third week in August in 1625) the theatres were closed for thirty weeks until 12 November. The company survived the strain, and when the epidemic had abated continued at their theatre in Drury Lane.

Timely plays appear to have been a feature of the repertory of Queen Henrietta's company. Though satirization of individuals of rank or position was forbidden by the Master of the Revels, the temptation to indulge in such satire was always strong for actors who knew its audience appeal. Shirley's London comedies, like *Hyde Park, The Ball, The Example, The Gamester* and *The Lady of Pleasure*, provided ideal vehicles for titillating the fashionable audience at the Phoenix with impersonations of their contemporaries, and we know of at least two occasions when the company and their dramatists succumbed. On 18 November 1632, two days after he had licensed the play, Sir Henry Herbert made a revealing entry in his official record of the Revels Office:

> In the play of *The Ball*, written by Sherley, and acted by the Queens players, there were divers personated so naturally, both of lords and others of the court, that I took it ill, and would have forbidden the play, but that Biston [Beeston] promiste many things which I found faulte withall should be left out, and that he would not suffer it to be done by the poett any more, who deserves to be punisht; and the first that offends in this kind, of poets or players, shall be sure of publique punishment.[1]

The tenses Herbert uses and such phrases as 'personated so naturally' imply

---

[1] Adams, *Herbert*, 19.

that he is speaking of a performance involving mimicry, rather than of a text – presumably he had had complaints from the victims or their friends. In any case, the fact that Shirley and the actors escaped punishment through Christopher Beeston's promise of reform suggests the manager's persuasiveness and competence.

But the players at the Cockpit were again dabbling in personal satire less than a year later when they produced a play by Ben Jonson, who for nearly twenty years had been giving all his new plays to the King's Men. In this case the order to reform the comedy came from a higher authority than the Master of the Revels. On 7 May 1635 Sir Henry noted:

> R[eceived] for allowing *The Tale of the Tubb*, Vitru[vius] Hoop's part wholly strucke out, and the motion of the tubb, by commande from my lorde chamberlin; exceptions being taken against it by Inigo Jones, surveyor of the Kings workes, as a personal injury unto him. . . .[1]

Jonson's enmity for Inigo Jones was of long standing and had been frequently expressed, but not in the commercial theatres. Queen Henrietta's Men performed the expurgated play in their theatre and acted it at court in the following January, but it was not liked there.

But the company was not always unsuccessful at court: they performed more plays there than any other troupe except the King's Men, and in the following year they had a notable success with the courtly audience. Thomas Heywood, an old friend of Beeston's, had written two or three plays for Queen Henrietta's Men before he composed *Love's Mistress* for them late in 1634. The success of this piece, a sort of simplified allegorical masque, is recorded on the title page of the 1636 edition:

> Loves Maistresse: Or, The Queens Masque. As it was three times presented before their two Excellent Maiesties, within the space of eight dayes; In the presence of sundry Forraigne Ambassadors. *Publikely Acted by the* Queens Comoedians, *At the* Phoenix *in* Drury-lane. Written by Thomas Heywood.

From remarks in the several prologues and epilogues, and in Heywood's address to the reader in his edition, it is apparent that the King and Queen saw the first performance at the Phoenix and that Inigo Jones created sets for the two subsequent performances at court. Such triumphs were generally confined to the King's company, but in the wake of Prynne's

---

[1] Adams, *Herbert*, 34.

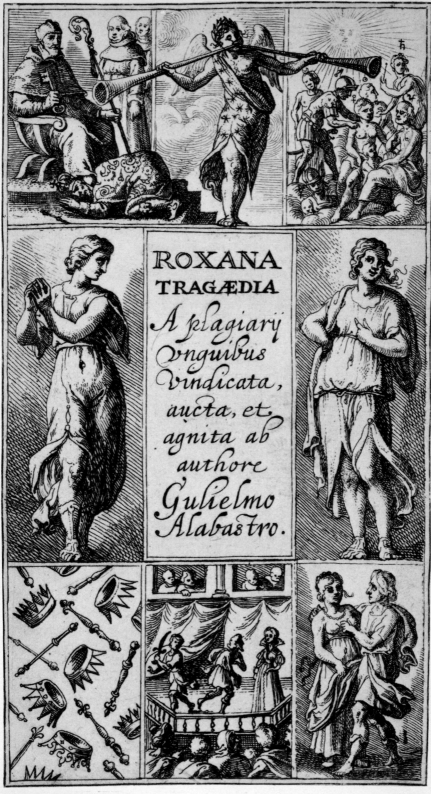

ROXANA
TRAGÆDIA
A plagiarij
vnguibus
vindicata,
aucta, et
agnita ab
authore
Gulielmo
Alabastro.

1 *Roxana*, frontispiece, 1632

X.d.
110
(2)

Playes for the Kinge this present
yeare of oᵘ Lord God 1630

At
Hampton Court

The 30ᵗʰ of September, The Inconstant Ladye
The 3 of October : Alfonso
The 17 of October Midsomers Nights Dreame
The 24 of October : The Custome of the Contrie

The 5 of November, An Induction for the Howse; And
the Madd Lover
The 7 of November . Rollo
The 19 of November . The Fox
The 28 of November . Beauty in a Traunce
The 30 of November . Beggers Bushe
The 9 of December . The Maides Tragedy
The 14 of December . Philaster

At the
Cock-pitt

The 26 of December The Duches of Malfy
The 27 of December The Scornfull Lady
The 30 of December . Chaunces
The 6 of Januarie . Ilde Castle .
The 3 of Februarie . The Fatall Dowrie
The 10 of Februarie . The Kinge and No Kinge
The 15 of Februarie . The merry Devill of Edmonton
The 17 of Februarie . Everie man in his Humor
The 21 of Februarie . Rollo, and
the Dance at Ly Howse, Loskie . 20

first & yᵉ last double .

2 The bill of the King's men, 1630–1

3 *Salmacida Spolia*, scenery design by Inigo Jones, 1640

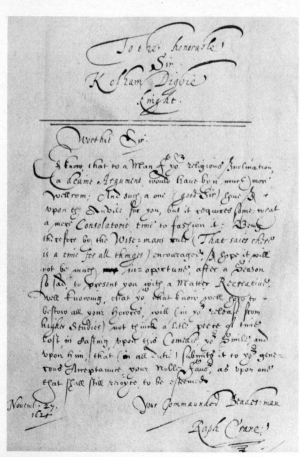

4 *Demetrius and Enanthe*, dedication, 1625

al in the Affran marchaunts.

Enter the 2 marchaunts
& a garde

... ow to bee punyshd
... hym that protecte thee.

sir & will proue that you tooke bribes
of the carthaginian marchaunts to detaine
their lawfull prize, & for youre sordid endes
abusde the trust comitted by the state
to wright their vassalls. the wise senate, as
they will rewarde youre good, and faithfull seruice
cannot in iustice without punishment
passe ore youre ill. guiltinesse makes you dumbe
but till that shame beshrine, and you finde
your tongue, to prison with hym.

Flaminius: I proue to late
 as heauen is mercifull, many crueltie
neuer escapes longnum vide.

[Exeunt with flaminius]

Antiochus: how a smile
labours to breake forth from mee. but what is
heauens pleasure shall bes donne with mee.

Marcellus: pray you Antioch: s~
a roman not your constant frende that tells you
you are confinde vnto the Gyaræ

Ent: Garde — with a stronge garde vpon you.
Antiochus: thou tis easie
to prophiecie I haue not longe to liue
though the manner how I shall dye is vncertaine.
nay weepe not still, tis not in you to helpe mee
theis showers of teares are fruitlesse. may my storie
teach potentates humilitie, and instructe
prowde monarchs, though they gouerne humeaund things,
a greater power doth rayse or pull down noe things.

Florish

THE ENDE

This Play, called Beleue
as you liste, may bee acted, this
6. of May. 1631.

Henry Herbert.

6 Richard Burbage

7 *The Roaring Girle*, title page, 1611

8 *Greene's Tu quoque*, title page, 1614

9 Richard Perkins

10 Nathan Field

11 *A Game at Chess*, title page, *c.* 1624–5

Histrio-Mastix, Heywood's praise of the Queen and his attack on her slanderers was particularly timely.[1]

Shortly after this triumph, a distinguished acting troupe of Queen Henrietta's countrymen visited London from Paris. Their performances at court were well received, and the King commanded that the French company be allowed to act at the theatre of the company of the Queen on the two 'sermon days' each week and for the entire week before Easter, occasions when performances by the London players were ordinarily forbidden. The season of the French troupe at the Phoenix was probably confined to Lent, for in April the Parisian company was authorized to set up temporary acting quarters in le Fevre's riding school in Drury Lane. Probably the Queen's Men derived no financial reward from the sojourn of the French company in their theatre, but the generosity of the local company cannot have hurt their standing in the eyes of their French queen.

In 1636 the scourge of the plague descended upon London again, and on 12 May the Master of the Revels sent out his closing order to the theatres; they remained closed, except for about a week at the end of February, for nearly seventeen months, until 2 October 1637. In this period Christopher Beeston broke the company and evicted them from his theatre.[2]

(iv) The King and Queen of Bohemia's company

The King and Queen of Bohemia's company is the most obscure of all London troupes in the reign of Charles I. It appears to have been formed during or shortly after the long plague closing of 1625 by combining remnants of the companies of the Lady Elizabeth (Queen of Bohemia) and of the Palsgrave (King of Bohemia). The actors known to have been members of the organization are former Palsgrave's Men: Richard Gunnell, William Cartwright, Richard Fowler, Richard Price and Mathew Smith. They played at the Fortune theatre, and one would guess that their repertory consisted largely of plays in the archives of that theatre formerly used by the Palsgrave's Men, but the name of the company appears on no title pages and it is not found in the extant licences for performances in the records of the Master of the Revels.

[1] *Jacobean and Caroline Stage*, IV, 580–2.
[2] ibid., I, 236–9 and II, 661–5, 669–70.

Presumably the King and Queen of Bohemia's company was playing at the Fortune theatre when a mob, mostly sailors, staged a riot there in May 1626, but though there are a number of accounts in the Middlesex County Records concerning the punishment of the rioters at the Fortune none mentions the name of the company performing there at the time.

Again presumably, it was the King and Queen of Bohemia's players who were acting the play at the Fortune performance attended by Dr John Lambe, the associate of the Duke of Buckingham and a reputed conjurer, just before he was lynched. Contemporary accounts say that as he was leaving the theatre he was set upon by a mob, and the assault resulted in his death the next day.

In 1629 Richard Gunnell, the apparent leader of the company, joined with William Blagrave to construct the new Salisbury Court theatre for a new company. After this nothing more is heard of the King and Queen of Bohemia's company. Apparently the organization was broken up when Gunnell took over the Salisbury Court.[1]

(v) The Red Bull–King's company

This is another very obscure troupe: their name is uncertain, appearing on no title pages nor in any performance licence. They are found most often in the provinces where they are generally called the King's company, or His Majesty's Servants of the City of York, though they are clearly not the troupe which played at the Blackfriars and the Globe. In London what appears to be the same company is most often called the company at the Red Bull, hence the compound name.

On 11 April 1627 the Master of the Revels noted that he had accepted £5 from John Heminges 'in their company's name to forbid the playing of Shakespeare's plays to the Red Bull'. After 1623 the First Folio was available to any company which had the price of a copy, but in London there is no record that any other company presumed to take advantage of the availability. It is not easy to see how the Red Bull–King's company could have imagined that they had any special right to perform these plays which were the property of a rival organization.

There are no plays which can be assigned with assurance to the repertory

[1] *Jacobean and Caroline Stage*, I, 260–9.

of this company, but evidence of performance at the Red Bull theatre during the years they appear to have been there suggest that the Red Bull–King's company may have owned *The Knave in Grain New Vampt*, by J. D., *The Valiant Scot* by J.W., and the lost, anonymous play *The Cardinal's Conspiracy*.

By July 1634 the Red Bull–King's company had been succeeded at their theatre by Prince Charles's (II) Men and themselves had transferred to the Fortune where they seem to have played until the plague closing of 12 May 1636. That is, when they were in London, for there are actually more records of the presence of this obscure troupe in provincial towns such as Reading, Ludlow, Doncaster, Worcester, Bristol, Leicester and Coventry than there are in London.

(vi) The King's Revels company

This company, sometimes called 'The Children of the Revels', was organized in 1629 by Richard Gunnell, actor, minor playwright, friend of Edward Alleyn and manager of the Fortune theatre, in collaboration with William Blagrave, deputy to Sir Henry Herbert, Master of the Revels. It was planned:

> to train and bring up certain boys in the quality of playing not only with intent to be a supply of able actors to his Majesty's servants of Blackfriars when there should be occasion . . . but the solace of his Royal Majesty when his Majesty should please to see them, and also for the recreation of his Majesty's loving subjects.[1]

For their new company Gunnell and Blagrave leased from the Earl of Dorset a plot of ground containing a large barn, which they made over into the Salisbury Court theatre to house their troupe of boys. The new playhouse was close to St Bride's church, between Fleet Street and the Thames, comfortably close to the Inner Temple and the Middle Temple, whose younger members were notorious theatre-lovers. It was a few hundred yards west of Shakespeare's Blackfriars theatre, the principal house of the King's company for which Gunnell and Blagrave planned to train boy actors.

The number of boys at the beginning in 1629 is not known, but by July

---

[1] Statement of Richard Gunnell in his answer to the bill of Christopher Babham, Court of Requests, 2 October 1632, as quoted by G. E. Bentley, 'The Salisbury Court Theatre and its Boy Players', *HLQ* 40 (1976–7), 137.

1630 the troupe consisted of at least fourteen boys, who were housed and fed by Richard Gunnell. How soon the boys had begun to perform at Salisbury Court is uncertain because there is no evidence as to how many months were required to remodel the barn. Construction cannot have begun before the signing of the ground lease on 6 July 1629, and unless the structure was completed before 17 April 1630 the opening was long delayed, for on that date all theatres were closed because of plague and remained so until 12 November.

The long plague closing was a severe, almost fatal, strain on the new organization. Even if they opened in their new theatre before the plague closing, they can have received admission fees for no more than a few months, not enough to pay the heavy charges entailed in the setting up of a new theatre and a new company. There is ample evidence of their financial difficulties. On 11 September 1630 Richard Gunnell was forced to sell his interests to Christopher Babham, a man with no known theatre connections, for £550, to be paid in stated instalments. This new money did not save the situation, for after 11 September there were still two months without receipts from dark theatres in London before the plague restrictions were lifted on 12 November. Babham was forced to default on his payments, and Gunnell took back his share of the theatre and company in March 1631, though later arrangements apparently allowed Babham to pay more money and take back part of Gunnell's shares.

In the attempt to keep the enterprise solvent, the boys were taken on the road in the summer of 1630. On this tour they performed Thomas Randolph's play, *The Muses' Looking Glass*, though they did not get it licensed by the Master of the Revels until 25 November 1630. Apparently the company acquired Thomas Randolph as their attached poet about this time, for his *Amyntas, or The Impossible Dowry* was licensed to them just the day after *The Muses' Looking Glass*. He also wrote his *Praeludium*, an occasional induction, for them to use at the opening of the Salisbury Court, presumably on or very shortly after 12 November.[1] It is not unlikely that other presently unassigned plays of Randolph were performed by the boys of the King's Revels.

After Gunnell took back from Babham his share of the theatre and the boy company, their activities and location are obscure for a year or so. Though neither Gunnell nor Babham alludes to the fact, the boys must have left the

[1] See G. E. Bentley, 'Randolph's *Praeludium* and the Salisbury Court Theatre', *Joseph Quincy Adams Memorial Studies* (1948), 775–83.

Salisbury Court for a time in the autumn of 1631 and played at Gunnell's other theatre, the Fortune. A new company, Prince Charles's (II) troupe was at the Salisbury Court on 7 December 1631, and they seem to have been there for a few weeks before.[1] Presumably the boys were back at the Salisbury Court before 3 November 1632, when Gunnell said that Babham 'doth stil inioy one equall pte' of the profits in the theatre and company.

Between this date and July 1634 the character of the company changed. When the troupe visited Oxford in the summer of 1634, Thomas Crosfield, Fellow of Queen's, entered in his diary a long note of what Richard Kendall, one of the two 'close keepers' (wardrobe masters) for the Salisbury Court, told him about the company. Kendall listed nine adult actors in the company, beginning with Richard Gunnell, and he said that seven of them were 'sharers, i.e. such as pay wages to y^c servants & equally share in the overplus'. Obviously the troupe at the Salisbury Court was no longer a boy company, though it seems to have continued to make use of an abnormally large number of boys.

It is not clear just how long before July 1634 this transformation took place, but there is a suggestion that it was about January 1633/4. Richard Brome, the dramatist, says in his answer to a complaint of members of the company in the Court of Requests that 'eighteene monthes or thereabboutes' before he signed a contract on 20 July 1635, he was approached by 'Richard Gunnell and others . . . being the company knowne by the name of Salisbury Court Actors . . . their company beinge in the Infancie of theire setting vpp and first playing at Salisbury Court aforesaid'.

Brome also says in his answer that in the period January 1633/4 to July 1635 he wrote for these actors several plays which brought them 'esteem and fame' and that one of these plays, *The Sparagus Garden*, brought them in an estimated £1000. However exaggerated this estimate may have been, the company certainly valued Brome enough to offer him a contract to write three plays a year for three years, or at least to write exclusively for them, for which they agreed to pay him fifteen shillings a week plus a benefit performance of each new play.[2]

By the time this contract was signed Richard Gunnell had died (in October 1634) and the Salisbury Court playhouse had passed into the hands of Richard Heton, John Robinson and Nathaniel Speed, the first of whom

[1] See *Jacobean and Caroline Stage*, i, 303–7.
[2] *Heton* v. *Brome*, Court of Requests, 12 February and 6 March 1639/40, as transcribed by Ann Haaker, 'The Plague, the Theatre, and the Poet', *Renaissance Drama*, NS 1 (1968), 296–306.

became manager of the dramatic company. This troupe must have produced several of Brome's plays before their dissolution, but only *The Sparagus Garden* and *The Queen and the Concubine* can now be identified. Other plays known to have been in this repertory are Glapthorne's *The Lady Mother*, Randolph's *Amyntas* and *The Muses' Looking Glass*, Thomas Rawlins's *The Rebellion*, Nathaniel Richards's *Messalina*, and the anonymous plays *Doctor Lambe and the Witches*, *Sir Giles Goosecap* and *The Proxy, or Love's Aftergame*.

Some play in the Salisbury Court repertory got the actors into trouble in February 1634/5 when they produced it with 'a Flamen, a priest of the heathens' dressed in 'a church-robe with the name of JESUS upon it'. The Master of the Revels committed the broker who had loaned the robe to the actors to the Marshalsea for his indiscretion. Surely the acting company would also have been in difficulties with the Master, but there is no record of their punishment.

In the winter season of 1635–1635/6 the Salisbury Court players performed three times at Hampton Court and at St James's, but this is the last known record of them. They did not survive the long plague closing of May 1636 to November 1637. Several of their members reappear as actors in Queen Henrietta's company at the Salisbury Court after the theatres were released from the plague restrictions. The Master of the Revels made an entry in his office-book during the plague closing: 'I disposed of Perkins, Sumner, Sherlock and Turner [veterans of Queen Henrietta's company] to Salisbury Court, and joynd them with the best of that company.'[1]

This amalgamation played under the sponsorship of Queen Henrietta until all theatres were closed at the outbreak of the Civil War, and the King's Revels appear no more in London.

(vii) Prince Charles's (II) company

The dramatic company under the patronage of the infant Prince Charles (b. 29 May 1630; later King Charles II) appears to have been organized late in 1631, certainly before 7 December of that year, the date of their licence which says that they were then playing at the Salisbury Court theatre.

Though the records of this company are spotty, we have five documents

[1] Adams, *Herbert*, 66.

of 1631 and 1632 which together provide an unusually full list of the personnel – twenty-one names, six of whom were boys who played female roles in Shackerley Marmion's comedy *Holland's Leaguer*, performed at Salisbury Court in December 1631. The leading members of the troupe were Ellis Worth, Mathew Smith and Andrew Cane, who became one of the prominent comedians of the 1630s and 1640s.

Some time before 1634, the company left the Salisbury Court and for reasons unknown moved to the Red Bull. Certain records suggest that their Salisbury Court sojourn had not been very profitable.[1] The prologue and epilogue to Shirley's *Changes* and the prologue to *Holland's Leaguer* comment on the struggles of the company. The same ill success is implied in a note made by Sir Henry Herbert that for six performances at the Salisbury Court in December 1631 his one-ninth share of the profits came to only £1.19s. This figure should be compared with others from Herbert's office book. At about the same time, i.e. 1628–33, he recorded the profits at five performances of old plays at the nearby Blackfriars, £67.10s. The smallest day's profit for a single day was £9.19s. and the largest £17. No wonder that Shirley and Marmion had found the situation discouraging.

But the standing of the company must have improved, for they were taken with the royal household on the progress of the summer of 1634, and they are known to have put on three royal performances at Hampton Court in the summer of 1634 and four more at Whitehall in the late winter and spring of 1635. What plays they presented on these court occasions is unknown, but their repertory included, besides *Holland's Leaguer* and *Changes*, Marmion's *A Fine Companion*, the anonymous *Edmond Ironsides*, and perhaps John Day's *The Blind Beggar of Bethnal Green*.

The repertory must have also included one or more plays by Richard Brome, for he asserted in a law suit that before he became the dramatist under contract for the Salisbury Court theatre in 1635 he had been writing plays for the company at the Red Bull. None of his known plays afford evidence that they were written for this troupe, but three of his lost plays, *The Apprentice's Prize*, *Christianetta* and *The Life and Death of Sir Martin Skink*, might have been, since they seemed to fall within the proper dates and cannot be assigned to any other company.

In Lent of 1636, when playing at all London theatres was severely restricted, Prince Charles's were on tour and in the second week of March

[1] See G. E. Bentley, 'The Troubles of a Caroline Acting Troupe: Prince Charles's Company', *HLQ* 41 (1977–8).

appeared at Norwich. The Mayor's Court Book records their presence, and Anthony Mingay of Norwich wrote to his friend Framlingham Gaudy in Norfolk: 'I pray you tell your sons that the Red Bull company of players are now in town, and have acted one play with good applause and are well clad and act by candlelight.'[1]

If the company returned to London at the end of Lent, they had less than a month of playing before all theatres were closed again because of the plague, a prohibition which lasted (with one week of intermission) for more than a year.

---

[1] From *Historical Manuscripts Commission*, Report X, Appendix 2, p. 157 (Gawdy MSS), quoted in *Jacobean and Caroline Stage*, 1, 312.

4 The period 1637–42

(i) Introduction

Though the death rate was not so high in 1636–7 as it had been in the plague
of 1625, the epidemic lasted longer, and the London theatres were closed for
fifteen months except for one short intermission of a week or so. Again the
players and dramatists were in dire straits: James Shirley deserted the
London scene and went to serve as playwright for the Werburgh Street
theatre in Dublin; most London acting troupes, except the King's Men,
disbanded or had to be reorganized. Queen Henrietta's company broke up
and was forced out of the Phoenix by Christopher Beeston, who retained
much of their repertory and several of their leading actors to form a new
troupe called the King and Queen's Young Company, or sometimes
Beeston's Boys. The remnants of Queen Henrietta's Men and the remnants
of the King's Revels company were reorganized by Richard Heton, manager
of the Salisbury Court, to play at his theatre under their old name but
without several of their leading actors and without a good part of their old
repertory. Prince Charles's (II) company apparently managed to hold
together, but their later career at the Red Bull and the Fortune was
undistinguished. And so with the obscure Red Bull–King's troupe which

seems more or less to have alternated with Prince Charles's at these two theatres notable for noise and vulgar appeal.

This final lustrum of the 'Elizabethan' theatre was not a glorious one. The drift of civil dissension into civil war was accelerating; the Puritan animosity towards the theatres was increasing; there were plague visitations during the summer and autumn of 1640 and again during the summer and autumn of 1641; audiences were distracted by riots and by the Bishops' Wars. Playwrights frequently complained of reduced attendance at the theatres. The final closing order in September 1642 struck down an institution which had been rather feebly struggling for two or three years.

(ii) The King's Men

As in the previous periods, the London theatre was dominated through the years 1637–42 by the King's Men. They continued to perform at court more frequently than any other troupe; plays specially prepared for court production by amateurs like Sir John Suckling, William Cartwright, Sir William Berkeley, William Habington, Lodowick Carlell and Jasper Mayne generally passed into their repertory after court openings, sometimes, as in the case of Sucklings *Aglaura*, with sumptuous costumes paid for by the dramatist. They secured the best actors from other companies, men like Michael Bowyer, Theophilus Bird and the comedian William Robbins from Queen Henrietta's company. In August of 1641 the Lord Chamberlain, the Earl of Essex, ordered the Master and Wardens of the Stationers' Company to forbid all their members to print any play belonging to the King's Men without the company's explicit permission. The Earl listed sixty-one plays so protected, but this is only about one third of the known repertory of the company. Omitted are all previously printed plays, notably Shakespeare's and Jonson's, and also a number of others, probably because they were no longer considered viable.

Until his death in the spring of 1639, Philip Massinger continued as the attached dramatist for the company, revising old pieces in their repertory, preparing new prologues and epilogues, and composing about two new plays each year.

One of Massinger's new plays for the company got them into censorship troubles again. In the spring of 1638 he delivered to the company a piece now lost called *The King and the Subject*, in which he foolishly glanced at

current political strains. At this time there had been a good deal of protest
against some of the devices employed by the King in raising money for his
depleted treasury. Only one passage from Massinger's play is known, one
the King himself marked in the manuscript. Sir Henry Herbert recorded the
affair in his office-book:

> The name of *The King and the Subject* is altered, and I allowed the play
> to bee acted, the reformations most strictly observed, and not otherwise,
> the 5th of June, 1638.
>
> At Greenwich the 4 of June, Mr. W. Murray, gave mee power from
> the king to allowe of the play, and tould me that hee would warrant it.
>
> 'Monys? Wee'le rayse supplies what ways we please,
> 'And force you to subscribe to blanks, in which
> 'We'le mulct you as wee shall thinke fitt. The Caesars
> 'In Rome were wise, acknowledginge no lawes
> 'But what their swords did ratifye, the wives
> 'And daughters of the senators bowinge to
> 'Their wills, as deities,' &c
>
> This is a peece taken out of Phillip Messingers play, called *The King and
> the Subject*, and entered here forever to bee remembered by my son and
> those that cast their eyes on it, in honour of Kinge Charles, my master,
> who readinge over the play at Newmarket, set his marke upon the place
> with his owne hande, and in thes words:
>
> 'This is too insolent, and to bee changed.'
>
> Note that the poett makes it the speech of a king, Don Pedro, king of
> Spayne, and spoken to his subjects.[1]

This passage is interesting as an example of the preferential treatment
accorded to the King's Men and their dramatists, for Herbert is known on
occasion to have burned the manuscript of a play he disapproved. That
Massinger's script passed through the hands of the King himself is also most
unusual. So far as is known, the only penalty incurred by the company
which proposed to speak these 'insolent' lines from their stage is the pound
fee which they paid to Sir Henry for his revisions.

After Massinger's death the company lured James Shirley back from
Dublin to replace him. Shirley prepared a new spring play and a new
autumn play for them in 1640, 1641 and 1642. In addition to these plays by
their attached playwrights and special court pieces given to them by the

---

[1] Adams, *Herbert*, 22–3.

King, the company bought occasional plays from William Davenant, Thomas Killigrew and Sir John Denham.

But in spite of all these new plays the theatre was fading. In the prologue for *The Sisters*, his spring play of 1642 (licensed for acting on 26 April), the company's regular dramatist, James Shirley, complained that the old standbys of the King's repertory, Shakespeare, Fletcher and Jonson, would no longer draw custom,

> and a play
> Though ne'r so new will starve the second day.

(iii) The King and Queen's Young Company, or Beeston's Boys

This troupe was a new and different one, formed during the plague closing by Christopher Beeston to play at his theatre, the Phoenix or Cockpit in Drury Lane, from which he had evicted Queen Henrietta's Men. In spite of its name, this organization was not an old-fashioned children's company in which all, or nearly all, the roles were played by young boys. The King and Queen's Young Company included at least half a dozen adults, and it appears that the performances utilized a large number of children, but not an overwhelming majority as in the Elizabethan boy companies of the Children of the Chapel or Paul's Boys.

The company had explicit royal patronage, indicated not only by the name but by the note entered by the Master of the Revels in his office-book that 'Mr Beeston was *commanded* to make a company of boyes' (italics mine),[1] and by the fact that the first dated record of their existence indicates their performance of two plays at court on 7 and 14 February 1636/7 during the brief intermission from the plague.

Beeston evidently managed to retain in the archives of his theatre for the use of his new troupe most of the plays which had belonged to Queen Henrietta's Men. In August 1639, the Lord Chamberlain warned all other London companies that they must not presume to act any of the plays belonging to Beeston and the King and Queen's Young Company of Players. The forty-five plays listed in the official order had mostly been written for Queen Henrietta's Men or the Lady Elizabeth's company, when those troupes had been performing at Beeston's theatre – plays by

[1] Adams, *Herbert*, 66.

Massinger, Middleton, Rowley, Ford, and fourteen by James Shirley. Shortly after this list was made, apparently, Richard Brome broke away from the Salisbury Court company, Queen Henrietta's Men, to whom he had been contracted as their regular theatre poet, and began writing for Beeston's Boys at the Phoenix. At least three of his plays, *The Court Beggar*, *A Mad Couple Well Matched* and *The Jovial Crew*, were performed by the King and Queen's Young Company.

In the spring of 1640 the company, by that time managed by William Beeston, son and heir of the deceased Christopher, got into serious trouble by presuming to produce a play which indulged in political comment. The play is not named, but the Master of the Revels said that it had relation to the King's journey into the north, presumably meaning Charles's complete failure at Berwick the year before to intimidate the Scots Presbyterians. Herbert says that the play was complained of by the King himself with command to punish the players. The manuscript of the play was confiscated, the company suppressed, and the manager and two leading members were imprisoned in the Marshalsea. The company was restrained from acting for only three or four days, but William Beeston was more severely punished. How long he languished in the Marshalsea is unknown, but a month later, in June 1640, the Lord Chamberlain had him supplanted as manager and director of the company. In his place the Lord Chamberlain appointed the dramatist William Davenant, recently made Poet Laureate after the death of Ben Jonson.

Presumably it was intended that Davenant should be the permanent manager and director of the company at the Phoenix, but in the following May he fled when he was exposed as heavily involved in the Army Plot against Parliament.

There are no later records of the King and Queen's Young Company. Like all others they were suppressed by Parliament in the order of September 1642.

(iv) Queen Henrietta's company

We have seen that a new Queen Henrietta's company was formed from the remnants of the old. According to Richard Heton, manager of the Salisbury Court theatre:

> When Her Majesty's servants were at the Cockpit, being all at liberty
> [i.e. disbanded] they dispersed themselves to several companies, so that
> had not my lord of Dorset [landlord of the Salisbury Court and Lord
> Chamberlain to Queen Henrietta Maria] taken care to make up a new
> company for the Queen, she had not had any at all.[1]

Though the name of the company remained the same as before, the
personnel was more than half made up of the former King's Revels
company, and the new troupe performed at the Salisbury Court under the
management of Richard Heton. At their new theatre, the company took over
the contract of the Salisbury Court theatre poet, Richard Brome. His
services were sorely needed, since Beeston had kept most of the old
repertory at the Phoenix, where the plays were now performed by the King
and Queen's Young Company.

Under this contract, which had been drawn up in 1635, Brome agreed to
write plays exclusively for the company at the Salisbury Court, to write
prologues and songs for them, and to revise old plays. For this work he was
to receive the profits at a benefit performance of each of his new plays and a
salary of fifteen shillings a week. In 1638 this contract was renewed with an
increased salary of a pound each week. Brome wrote for Queen Henrietta's
company for about two years until he broke his contract, with mutual
recriminations, and went to write for William Beeston and his company at
the Phoenix. Though Brome wrote for Queen Henrietta's Men for about two
years, the only plays of his authorship which can now be identified as part of
his commitment to them are *The English Moor, or the Mock Marriage* and
The Antipodes. Other plays which became part of their new repertory at
Salisbury Court are Richard Lovelace's lost play *The Scholars*, Thomas
Nabbes's *Microcosmus* and Shirley's *The Gentleman of Venice*, written for
them before Shirley became the regular dramatist for the King's company in
1640.[2]

Though Queen Henrietta's Men never attained the prominence at the
Salisbury Court which they had had before the plague closing at the
Phoenix, they continued to receive livery every other year as servants to the
Queen, and in 1638 and 1639 they performed seven times at court. Like all
the other London companies they were forced by the plague to close for two
months in 1639 and three in 1640. There are no known records of their
activities in the last two years before the theatres were closed.

[1] *Jacobean and Caroline Stage*, II, 684.
[2] See Ann Haaker, 'The Plague, the Theatre and the Poet', *Renaissance Drama*, NS I (1968).

(v) Prince Charles's (II) company

It is surprising that a company no stronger than this one was able to keep together during the long plague closing, or at any rate to reassemble after the restrictions were lifted in 1637. But they did, for the troupe is known to have performed three plays at court in November and December of that year. Their court performances are oddly contrasted with the repeated records of disturbances at their theatre, the Red Bull, where violent disorders in 1638 and 1639 led to the indictment of the perpetrators.

In September 1639 Prince Charles's players were having some success at the Red Bull with a lost play called *The Whore New Vamped*, in which various officials were libelled and the popular comedian of the company, Andrew Cane, slandered one of the London aldermen. The Privy Council ordered the Attorney General to investigate and to punish the dramatist and the players, but no further records of the affair have been found. In these troubled times, when the audiences were dwindling at all London theatres, the temptation for playwrights and players to attract custom by ridiculing unpopular local figures must have been very strong. Punishments may have been meted out to Prince Charles's Men, but if the company was suppressed it was not for long; they were performing at court again two months later.

At the following Easter, Prince Charles's Men left the Red Bull for the Fortune. The transfer is noted by the Master of the Revels. The removal to the Fortune did not bring any extended prosperity to the company, for that autumn all London theatres suffered a plague closing for two months and the following autumn for three.

Nevertheless the company was not obscure; they had a clientele, and their comedian and dancer, Andrew Cane, had a growing reputation, as did their 'heavy', Richard Fowler. As late as 1664 a character in *Knavery in all Trades*, often attributed to Tatham, recalls his delight at the Fortune more than twenty years before and tells a story about '*Fowler* at the Fortune ... [who] you know was appointed for the Conquering parts ... [and] drew much Company'.[1]

(vi) The Red Bull–King's company

Prince Charles's Men's chief rival for the patronage of the vulgar audience in

[1] See *Jacobean and Caroline Stage*, II, 440.

the last three years of theatrical activities was the troupe called the Red Bull–King's Men.

For eighteen months after the long plague restrictions were revived, there are no extant records of this company, but they were playing at the Fortune in May 1639. A letter of 8 May in this year notes that members of the company were fined and imprisoned for performing a play which ridiculed Anglican ritual, a subject of bitter debate in the years of preparation for the Puritan revolution. A much delayed account, not published until 1641 in *Vox Borealis*, says that the suppressed play was the lost *Cardinal's Conspiracy*, and that when the company got their liberty again they put on *The Valiant Scot*. It may be so, but the delay, the contemporary applicability of the titles – *The Cardinal's Conspiracy* to Archbishop Laud's alleged plot to be made a Roman Catholic cardinal, and *The Valiant Scot* to the humiliating defeat of the King's forces in the Bishops' Wars – and the strongly anti-Anglican bias of *Vox Borealis* make one suspicious.

The mysterious relationship of the Red Bull–King's players to King Charles's company at the Blackfriars and Globe is faintly implied again in the Lord Chamberlain's records of a warrant obtained by the King's Men in October 1639 against 'Iohn Rodes of yᵉ fortune Playhouse . . . for selling their Playes'. Presumably Rhodes is accused of selling the plays to his company at the Fortune, i.e. the Red Bull–King's players. The company had been similarly indicted by King Charles's company in 1627 for performing Shakespeare's plays. Apparently there was some unknown claim which twice led this company to steal from the repertory of the richest and most powerful troupe of the time.

In the following year the previously mentioned exchange of theatres with Prince Charles's company took the Red Bull–King's company away from the Fortune and back to their old house, the Red Bull in St John's Street. Though a prologue by John Tatham sneers at the customary violence and rant of these rivals of the Red Bull–King's company who had forced them to move, contemporary reference suggests that there was not much to choose between them. Typical is Edmund Gayton's remark: 'I have heard that the Poets of the Fortune and red Bull, had alwaye a mouth-measure for their Actors (who were terrible teare-throats) and made their lines proportionable to their compasse, which were *sesquipedales*, a foot and a halfe.'[1]

No records have been found of the last two years of this company at the

---

[1] *Pleasant Notes upon Don Quixote* (1654), p. 24; quoted in *Jacobean and Caroline Stage*, II, 690–1.

Red Bull. Presumably their violence and rant continued until September 1642, when Parliament closed all theatres without distinguishing between the 'terrible teare-throats' at the Red Bull and the performers of the plays of Shakespeare, Jonson and Fletcher at Blackfriars.

5 The period 1642–60

Unlike the three previous periods in the history of the London theatre, these years 1642–60 were a time of only surreptitious dramatic activity. In the earlier periods there had been occasional illegal performances when some company acted a play which had not been licensed by the Master of the Revels or inserted unallowed lines or mimicry into an allowed play script. But the vast majority of performances were presentations of officially allowed plays in officially allowed theatres by troupes of professional actors which had been granted royal charters.

All this came to an end with the order of the Lords and Commons on 2 September 1642 that 'publike Stage-Playes shall cease, and bee forborne'. And this order was generally enforced. Such records of dramatic activity as exist show only sporadic and usually hasty play-acting in an extremely hostile environment.

After all playhouses had been suppressed at the beginning of the wars, there were no officially allowed theatres or acting companies in London until the return of Charles II to his throne. The lamentable plight of the profession is set out in an anonymous pamphlet called *The Actors' Remonstrance, or Complaint, for the silencing of their Profession and banishment from their several playhouses*. The pamphlet, which is dated 24

January 1643/4, sets forth the plight of the theatre people after more than a year of suppression and incidentally reflects the former elaborateness of the organizations at the private theatres, the Blackfriars, the Phoenix and the Salisbury Court:

First, our House-keepers, that grew wealthy by our endevours, complaine that they are enforced to pay the grand Land-lords rents, during this long Vacation out of their former gettings; instead of ten, twenty, nay thirty shillings shares, which used nightly to adorne and comfort with their harmonious musique, their large and well-stuffed pockets, they have shares in nothing with us now but our mis-fortunes; living meerely out of the stock, out of the interest and principall of their former gotten moneyes, which daily is exhausted by the maintenance of themselves and families.

For our selves, such as were sharers, are so impoverished, that were it not for some slender helps afforded us in this time of calamitie by our former providence, we might be enforced to act our Tragedies; our Hired-men are disperst, some turned Souldiers and Trumpetters, others destin'd to meaner courses, or depending upon us, whom in courtesie wee cannot see want, for old acquaintance sakes. . . . Our Fooles who had wont to allure and excite laughter with their very countenances, at their first appearance on the stage (hard shifts are better than none) are enforced, some of them at least, to maintaine themselves, by vertue of their bables. Our boyes, ere wee shall have libertie to act againe, will be growne out of use, like crackt organ-pipes, and have faces as old as our flags.

Nay, our very Doore-Keepers, men and women, most grievously complains that by this cessation they are robbed of the privilege of stealing from us with licence; they cannot now, as in King *Agamemnons* dayes, seeme to scratch their heads where they itch not, and drop shillings and half Crowne-pieces in at their collars. Our Musike that was held so delectable and precious, that they scorned to come to a Taverne under twentie shillings salary for two houres, now wander with their Instruments under their cloaks, I meane such as have any, into all houses of good fellowship, saluting every roome where there is company, with *Will you have any musike Gentlemen?* For our Tiremen, and others that belonged formerly to our ward-robe, with the rest, they are out of service: our stock of cloaths, such as are not in tribulation for the generall use, being a sacrifice to moths. The Tobacco-men, that used to walk up and downe, selling for a penny pipe, that which was not worth twelve-pence an horse-load; Being now under Tapsters in Inns and Tippling houses. Nay such a terrible distresse and dissolution hath befallen us, and all those that had dependance on the stage, that it hath quite unmade our hopes of future recoverie. For some of our ablest ordinarie Poets instead of their annuall stipends and beneficiall second-dayes, being for meere necessitie compelled to get a living by writing contemptible penny-pamphlets in which they have not so much as poetical licence to use any attribution of their profession; but that of *Quid libet audendi?* and faining miraculous stories, and relations of unheard of battels. Nay, it is to be feared, that shortly some of them; (if they have not been enforced to do it already) will be encited to enter themselves into *Martin Parkers* societie, and write ballads. . . .

But this sad state of affairs, which the author of *The Actors' Remonstrance* hoped would soon be altered, continued for many years. Not until the Restoration was it again possible for a man to make a living from the theatre as actor, poet, entrepreneur or attendant. And only a few London printers – notably Humphrey Moseley – could make a reasonable living out of the dead past by publishing old plays. As a viable profession the theatre was dead.

But there were a good many attempts to collect a few shillings by producing some of the old plays surreptitiously. Such illegal performances are known mostly from the accounts of the raids made to suppress them as recounted in public records or in weekly journals. In the newsbook called *The Weekly Account* of 4 October 1643 there is a paragraph about a raid by the soldiers during a performance at the Fortune in which the actors were despoiled of their costumes. As usual, the account names neither the play nor the players. Again on 4 September 1647 *Mercurius Melancholicus* records a raid on the Fortune in which the actors were carried off to gaol. In the second week of October 1647 *Mercurius Pragmaticus, Perfect Occurrences* and *Mercurius Melancholicus* all carry brief stories of a raid on the Salisbury Court, where actors were putting on a performance of Beaumont and Fletcher's *A King and No King*. At least one of the players was arrested and taken to gaol.

In this autumn and winter of 1647–8, after the end of the first Civil War, there seems to have been a mild, disorganized renewal of activities in a few London theatres, but there is no evidence of new plays, of regular dramatists or of fully organized dramatic companies. On 9 February 1647/8 a new and severe ordinance was issued directing the arrest of players, the demolition of theatres, the seizure of admissions collected, and the fining of every member of the audience. This ordinance, though only casually enforced at first, eventually led to the demolition, or at least the wrecking of the interiors, of most of the Caroline theatres. The Red Bull must have been some sort of exception, for raids on performances at that theatre are several times noted in the 1650s.

These scattered dramatic activities during the Civil Wars and the Commonwealth were unauthorized, generally sporadic, often disastrous for the players. Accepted dramatic activity had a timid harbinger in 1656.

The resuscitator of English drama was Sir William Davenant, an experienced man of the theatre who in the 1620s and 1630s had had ten or eleven plays produced by the King's Men at Blackfriars and five masques staged at court; who had, in 1639, secured a patent for a huge new London theatre which had never been built; and who had been manager and director of the King and Queen's Young Company at the Phoenix in 1640 and early 1641. After a number of very discreet preliminary steps, Sir William issued, in May 1656, bills for *The First Day's Entertainment at Rutland House*, 'The Entertainment by Musicke and Declamations after the Manner of the Ancients'. The piece was presented on a stage in the back part of the author's home, Rutland House by Charterhouse Yard. The performance consisted of music, songs and declamations, and was really a preparation for his next venture. Davenant had been careful to incorporate into his 'Entertainment' anti-French propaganda and songs in praise of Cromwell, the Lord Protector.

Later in 1656 Davenant wrote *The Siege of Rhodes Made a Representation by the Art of Perspective in Scenes and the Story Sung in Recitative Musick*, which he caused to be printed in the summer of that year and later, in September, produced on the tiny stage in his house. Neither of these shows was a professional production, for the readers and singers were all amateur not professional actors, and the place of production was the private house of the author and producer. In the cast of *The Siege of Rhodes* there appeared for the first time in England the name of a woman, Mrs Edward Coleman, who read and sang the role of Ianthe. She was not a professional, and so far as is known never continued on the professional stage.

Davenant's next step in the gradual reintroduction of drama was a crucial one, prepared for by a letter to Secretary Thurloe, by a flattering epithalamium on the marriage of Cromwell's daughter, and by the selection of a subject which was excellent propaganda for Cromwell's government in its developing campaign against Spain. The piece, produced in the summer of 1658, was called *The Cruelty of the Spaniards in Peru, Exprest by Instrumental and Vocall Musick, and by the Art of Perspective in Scenes, &c*. But the most daring and important step in the preparation for the return of professional drama was the performance of the show not in Davenant's house but in a repaired and refurbished theatre, the old Phoenix or Cockpit in Drury Lane, where there were not only more stage and audience facilities but all the old associations of a regular playhouse.

What Sir William presented was, however, still not really a play: it had neither plot nor dialogue. It was a sort of variety show with monologues, songs, instrumental music, scenery displays, tight-rope walkers, tumblers, and dances of various kinds. But it was staged in a public theatre 'at Three in the after noone punctually' and the audience was charged admission.

The Lord Protector, Oliver Cromwell, whom Davenant had cultivated so successfully, died on 3 September 1658, and under his weak son, Richard, Davenant, like many others, was apparently uncertain as to where he stood. Nevertheless he prepared a sort of sequel to *The Cruelty of the Spaniards in Peru* which he called *The History of Sir Francis Drake*. Though the new piece was still operatic, it had more of the elements of a play than its predecessors – dialogue, more action, and conflict. Davenant was then encouraged to prepare a sequel for his first tentative piece, *The Siege of Rhodes*. It was called *The Second Part of the Siege of Rhodes* and it moved even closer to the standard dramatic form, with act and scene divisions rather than the operatic entries and more fully developed characters.

After General Monk marched down to London with his army from Scotland in February 1659/60, it became clear to many people that the return of Charles II to his father's throne would sooner or later follow. The old professional actors about London began to reorganize and to present plays at the Phoenix, the Red Bull and the Salisbury Court. Though the situation of players and theatres was quite confused for a time, the return of the King in May 1660 set up a recognized authority favourable to the professional production of plays. An authorized and regulated theatre was again organized in London in the first year of his reign.

III The plays and the playwrights: 1613–42

Kathleen McLuskie

1 The laurel and the crown

(i) Plays and politics

A history of drama invites analogies with other kinds of historical writing. It implies a model of cause and effect, of influences and continuities, and of significant connections between different aspects of a culture. It is tempting, for example, to see Stuart drama as a long decline from the eminence of Shakespeare, to designate certain themes and forms as decadent and place them in the historical scheme accordingly. In seventeenth-century history, analogies between decadence in art and decadence in society impose themselves with overwhelming force, since the closing of the theatres in 1642 directly implicated the drama in the other great upheavals of the age:

> They that would have no KING, would have no Play:
> The *Laurel* and the *Crown* together went,
> Had the same *Foes*, and the same *Banishment*.[1]

Such connections must, however, be considered with care. The Laurel and the Crown fell together because they were part of the same establishment;

---

[1] 'The Prologue to his Majesty' (1660), in *The Poetical Works of Sir John Denham*, ed. T. H. Banks, Jr (New Haven, Conn., and London, 1928), 94.

the theatrical profession were entertainers to the court and the court fostered its own theatricals, both in the masque and in Henrietta Maria's excursions into amateur acting. Yet an attack on the theatre was not in itself tantamount to an attack on the court, as even the case of Prynne shows.[1] Despite the tactlessness of his reference to 'women actors, notorious whores', one observer could write, 'I do not conceive this to be the cause why he is called in question, but some exorbitant passages concerning ecclesiastical government'.[2] The theatres, moreover, were closed as much in the interests of public order as from any disapproval of a decadent drama. The cultural role of the plays themselves is similarly difficult to assess, but the sheer variety of drama produced for the Stuart theatre suggests that dramatists were neither hidebound by official propaganda nor driven by the demands of a covert opposition.

Isolated statements within the plays sometimes provide tantalizing evidence of the political culture of Stuart drama; official reactions to them show how hard it is, in retrospect, to assess their contemporary impact. Charles I himself objected to a speech on forced loans in Massinger's lost play *The King and the Subject* (1638), and yet Shirley had already depicted a comic steward in *The Grateful Servant* (1626) planning to imitate his betters: 'I will oppress the Subject, flatter the Prince, take bribes a both sides, doe right to neither, serve heaven as farre as my profit will give me leave, and tremble only at the summons of a Parliament (II.i).[3]

At times the censorship seems to have been impervious to the topical application of themes and speeches in plays. Massinger's *The Maid of Honour* (1621) deals with the refusal of Roberto, King of Sicily, to help Urbino in his campaign against the Duchess of Siena, just as James I, against a good deal of opposition, had refused to aid his son-in-law, Frederick of Bohemia, in the Thirty Years War. Roberto's policy is opposed by a speech from Bertoldo in which he argues not only the claims of honour but also the defects of peace, urging Roberto to 'looke on *England*':

> When did she flourish so, as when she was
> The Mistress of the Ocean, her navies
> Putting a girdle round about the world;
> When the *Iberian* quak'd, her worthies nam'd;

[1] See pp. 14–15.
[2] Letter from Pagitt to Harrington in S. R. Gardiner, *Documents Relating to Proceedings Against William Prynne*, Camden Society Publications, NS xviii, quoted in William Lamont, *Marginall Prynne* (London, 1963), 31.
[3] For editions and texts see Bibliography.

And the faire flowre Deluce grew pale, set by
The red Rose and the white? (1.i.224–9)

Comparison with the great days of Elizabeth was a common vehicle for disparaging James I's court and foreign policy, yet the play aroused no official comment. The commonplace theme of the conflict between peace and honour, 'city valour/And service in the field', may have been enough to disguise the play's particular implications.

This interaction between topical material and dramatic form poses interesting critical problems in assessing the political significance of particular plays. For instance, Henry Herbert did require *Believe as You List* (1631) to be rewritten, its setting changed from contemporary Portugal to a vague classical period. And yet, despite this official attention, *Believe as You List* cannot really be described as a political play. Its theme is Antiochus' attempt to reclaim Carthage from its Roman oppressors, but the conflict is dealt with in entirely personal, moral terms. Flaminius, the Roman governor, is an unsympathetic figure not because he violates Carthaginian sovereignty but because he is tyrannical, arrogantly mistreating the local populace and murdering the slaves who recognize Antiochus on his return. The political theme, moreover, is essentially at odds with the romantic dramaturgy, which proceeds by startling revelations – '*Enter . . . Antiochus (Habited like a kinge)* (II.ii. 119 S.D.) – or by tirades of passion and demonstrations of stoic fortitude. When the Romans capture Antiochus, they try to make him renounce his claims by tricking him into a seduction scene with a courtesan. His stoic rejection of her passionately displayed wiles has a theatrical appeal quite unrelated to the intellectual issues at stake. In the tragi-comic conclusion, brought about by the devices of both a recognition scene and a sudden reversal, Antiochus regains his rights. He then draws the moral of his story. It will:

> teach potentates humilitie, and instructe
> prowde monarchs, though they governe humane thinges
> A greater power does rayse, or pull downe kinges. (v.ii.241–3)

The play demonstrates no such thing, but it is a more comfortable conclusion than any analysis of the real source of a ruler's power could provide.

A more complicated case is presented by Massinger's collaboration with Fletcher on *Sir John van Olden Barnaveldt* (1619), which touched on recent events in the Low Countries. In the conflict between Prince Maurice and

Olden Barnaveldt, James had supported the Calvinist ruler for theological as well as political reasons,[1] and the authorities refused a licence for the play until it had been rewritten. The rewritten version is full of political and dramatic ambiguity. Rebellion in the name of religion is at least discussed (1.ii) and in allowing Barnaveldt to assert that his Prince 'is but as *Barnauelt*, a Servant to/yo[r] Lordships, and the State' (1.ii. 305–6) the authors touched on dangerous ground indeed. However, at no point are the particular theological tenets of Arminianism canvassed, and in the course of the play the heresy is associated with such diverse subversions as insubordinate feminism (11.ii) and the totally unsympathetic Roman Catholic conspirators:

> that hatchd in England
> that bloody Powder-Plot, and thought like meteors
> to have flashd their Cuntryes peace out in a Moment. (v.iii.2943–5)

The play could not have appealed to popular opposition. Official nervousness may have been caused simply by the treatment of a contemporary conjunction of religion and politics.

The presentation of Barnaveldt himself is similarly ambiguous. His initial political isolation grants him a certain dramatic power but his grievance is presented as unrewarded heroism rather than more specifically political ambition. His arrogant treatment of the Prince of Orange undermines his hold on the audience's sympathy and it is not until his conspiracy is safely overthrown that he is allowed to re-emerge as a popular hero (iv.iv). This ambiguity is partly a result of political confusion. It is also inherent in the form of the play, which deals in the theatrical counters of pathos and heroism rather than the more complex concepts of Realpolitik. After he is captured, Barnaveldt indulges in an inventive tirade which draws an extended analogy between the ungrateful state and an insatiable seducer. It is a wonderful theatrical moment but completely irrelevant to the stated ideological concerns of the play. The same is true of the manipulation of pathos in the scene of Leidenberch's suicide and the mindless tenacity of Barnaveldt's last stand at his trial. The form in which Massinger worked and the demands of theatrical fashion neutralized the full political impact of his plays; it is none the less interesting that so many of them deal with contemporary issues and attracted official attention.[1]

[1] See Nicholas Tyacke, 'Puritanism, Arminianism and Counter-Revolution', in Conrad Russell (ed.), *The Origins of the English Civil War* (London, 1973).

Even when plays did not deal with topical issues they were sometimes felt to have dangerous implications.[2] This was particularly true of the history play. The crisis of Prince Henry's death in 1612 coincided with the revival of a number of old history plays written by the 'bourgeois' dramatists of the Elizabethan adult companies and based on the 'elect nation' theme central to Puritan politics.[3] The following year saw a curious history play, *The Hector of Germany*, written by Wentworth Smith and performed by apprentices at the Red Bull theatre. It was written to celebrate the marriage of Princess Elizabeth to the Elector Palatine, an important event for those committed to specifically Protestant alliances, and deals with a mythologized fourteenth-century Palsgrave. The denials of the prologue make the implied connections plain:

> What Pen dares be so bold in this strict age,
> To bring him while he liues vpon the stage?
> And though he would, Authorities sterne brow
> Such a presumtuous deede will not allow:
> And he must not offend Authoritie. (Prologue, ll.5–9)

The play does not make a firm statement about anything, since it combines the political conflict between the Palsgrave and the Bastard with a romantic plot of eloping lovers, but there are incidental passages which make its affiliations clear. The play is dedicated to the Lord Mayor and explicitly directed to citizen taste. Spaniards are denounced in simple-minded terms; and when the King of England arrives at the wedding feast, he chides the old men for quarrelling over the lovers' escape, suggesting that they go instead and help the Palsgrave against the Bastard. At the end of the play, moreover, there is a brief satiric scene between an Englishman and a Frenchman. In place of the usual chauvinistic mockery of the French, it depicts the two men as united in their complaints against lords who do not pay their bills and wanton court ladies who set a bad example to industrious citizens' wives.

Wentworth Smith's play seems to have passed without comment from the censor since it violated no contemporary sensibilities. By 1623/4, however,

---

[1] See Allen Gross, 'Contemporary Politics in Massinger', *SEL*, 6 (1960). It would be instructive to study Massinger's political connections in a context such as the one Margot Heinemann has constructed for Middleton (see p. 137, n. 2).

[2] See W. Reavley Gair, 'The Politics of Scholarship: A Dramatic Comment on the Autocracy of Charles I', in *Elizabethan Theatre*, III, ed. David Galloway (London and Toronto, 1973).

[3] Judith Doolin Spikes, 'The Elect Nation and the English History Play', *Renaissance Drama*, NS 8 (1977).

another historical play, Thomas Drue's *Duchess of Suffolk*, was found to be 'full of dangerous matter' and in need of reform by Henry Herbert. Drue's subject matter, though less apparently topical, was much more threatening, since the Duchess's story was taken from Foxe's *Acts and Monuments*, a record of Antichrist's persecution, regarded by Puritans as second in importance only to the Bible. The play offers no direct political or personal parallel with contemporary events and a good deal of its dramatic life comes from its sentimental presentation of the Duchess's resolute courage in the face of continued persecution. Its episodic structure, however, gives scope for the presentation of a number of Puritan heroes, from the martyrs Ridley and Latimer to the good constable and the kind merchant who helps the Duchess to escape.

A similar mixture of political history and sentimental romance is found in Davenport's *King John and Matilda* (1631), which fails to weld the emotional with the political action. The most affecting scenes in the play are those where the King's wicked gaoler, Brand, starves the captured Lady Bruce and her son to death, while throughout the action Matilda's heroic chastity provides an emotional centre from which to denounce the King's cruelty and lust. The figure of King John himself is, however, treated in a more interesting manner. Instead of presenting him in his traditional role of the prototype Protestant monarch, the play deals with the more dangerous subject of conflict with the barons over their ancient rights enshrined in Magna Carta. In a central episode of the play the barons confront the King with their demands, making it clear that they are not merely rebellious but ask only their rights and prerogatives established in law. Davenport's play seems to have escaped the attentions of the censor; the figure of the lustful king may have seemed such a stereotype that it masked the more subversive implications of the story.

For the history play, despite its potentially subversive subject matter, is constantly affected by the tension between statement and style. The cautious authorities may have objected to particular statements, but the political argument of individual plays was dissipated by their focus on the personal and the sentimental. Ford, for example, was conscious of reviving an old-fashioned form in his *Perkin Warbeck* (1622–32). The prologue's praise of older 'wise Industrie' in contrast to 'The antick follyes of the Times' could be seen as a political statement, but it is a statement about politics in terms of personal style, even as the action of the play reflects on the personal style appropriate to a king. The play is patterned to avoid the simplicities of military confrontation, and the conflicting claims of king and pretender are tested in the characters' responses to the situation which confronts them. Historically Henry is the rightful king of England; the ceremonial opening of the action reinforces his determination not to become

> a mockery King in state,
> Onely ordaind to lauish sweat and bloud
> In scorne and laughter to the ghosts of *Yorke*. (i.i. 4–6)

He confronts the Cornish rebellion with great resolution:

> Rage shall not fright
> The bosome of our confidence . . .
> now if *Black heath*
> Must be reserv'd the fatall tombe to swallow
> Such stifneckt Abjects, as with wearie Marches,
> Have travaild from their homes, their wives and children,
> To pay instead of *Subsidies* their lives,
> Wee may continue sovereign. (iii.i.17–18, 23–8)

Moreover, he is no tyrant, for in opposing the rebels he is only demanding 'what in *Parliament*/Hath freely beene contributed'.

The structure of the play alternates this view of Henry with Perkin's presentation of himself. The pretender's claims are neither questioned nor confirmed; the audience is left to judge who is the more kingly actor. Perkin is first introduced in an elaborate ceremony in which he is greeted by the King of Scotland in dumb show before rehearsing the story of his birth and lineage in a set speech played to an audience on stage as well as off (ii.i). Having no power, he has no scope for the diplomacy which shows Henry's nobility but he takes over the Scottish court, displaying a sense of *noblesse oblige* in the masque presented at his marriage to Katherine Huntley. Moreover he is granted a characteristically Fordian moment of sympathy in the poetic and emotional resonances of the parting duet with his bride before he leaves to fight for his claim.

Perkin loses the political and military conflict but that conflict is the least significant in the play. At the end of Act iv he is proclaimed king by the Cornish rebels, whereas his ultimate defeat is merely reported at the beginning of Act v. In the remainder of the play he is allowed a dramatic and emotional triumph. When he and Henry eventually meet, the rightful king taunts him with the frivolity of his attempt on the throne:

> What revells in combustion through our Kingdome,
> A frenzie of aspiring youth hath daunc'd,

> Till wanting breath, thy feete of pride haue slipt
> To breake thy necke.

Perkin replies with characteristic commitment to his role:

> But not my heart; my heart
> Will mount, till every drop of bloud be frozen
> By deaths perpetuall Winter. If the *Sunne*
> Of *Majestie* be darkned, let the *Sunne*
> Of *Life* be hid from mee, in an eclipse
> Lasting, and universall. (v.ii.50–8)

Henry dismisses Perkin's resolution as 'anticke Pageantrie' – 'The player's on the stage still'. Yet the whole action is but a play and in those terms Perkin is triumphant. In a heavily ironic final scene Perkin is placed in the stocks but even in that ignominious position he can behave with dignity. He is also granted the dramatic justification of Katherine's love. She stands by him both literally and metaphorically as he speaks the words illustrating the emblematic meaning of the stage image:

> Harrie Richmond!
> A womans faith, hath robd thy fame of triumph. (v.iii.101–2)

The ironic tension between the words and the physical image on stage continues to the end as he leads his followers 'with halters about their necks' to the gallows, crying,

> Be men of spirit!
> Spurne coward passion! so illustrious mention,
> Shall blaze *our names*, and stile us KINGS O'RE DEATH. (v.iii.205–7)

Henry's superior handling of diplomacy is inevitably less dramatically powerful than this resounding heroism. But he is not presented merely as the politic machiavel. The crucial political manoeuvre separating Perkin Warbeck from James of Scotland is left to a Spanish diplomat. In the episode of Stanley's treachery, likewise, Henry expresses his regret at both the act and the need for the execution, on which his advisers insist; there seems no irony in Surrey's assertion, ''Tis a King composed of gentlenesse' (ll.48–9). It is Henry's personal qualities that are at issue: the play involves no consideration of the dialectic between policy and morals which gives such bite to Shakespeare's political plays. *Perkin Warbeck* has been associated with 'a deep current of hostility to Charles',[1] but such a specific political position is blurred by the romance values in the play, which indicate a sentimental (and reactionary) preference for grand gesture and individual integrity over statecraft and the thoughtful exercise of power. They were values which would rebound in Charles's favour when his turn came to play the royal martyr.

The only clear opposition to establishment policy in a contemporary play is found in Middleton's *A Game at Chess* (1624), though its wide success might indicate that there was an audience for plays on topical themes. Margot Heinemann suggests that Middleton's courtly patron, the Earl of Pembroke, had Puritan sympathies and that *A Game at Chess*, with its savage attack on Spain and the Spanish ambassador in particular, was able to reach the London stage with an official licence because of a split between the pro- and anti-Spanish factions at court.[2] *A Game at Chess* itself, however, is as interesting theatrically as politically. The satire on Gondomar and the other black figures provides no subtle analysis of Renaissance diplomacy: it is personal and abusive in the broadest comic fashion. As the outraged Don Carlos Coloma protested in a letter to Olivares:

> The second act was directed against the Archbishop of Spalato, at that time a white piece, but afterwards won over to the black side by the Count of Gondomar, who, brought on to the stage in his litter almost to the life, and seated on his chair with a hole in it . . . confessed all the treacherous actions with which he had deceived and soothed the king of the whites, and, when he discussed the matter of confessions with the Jesuits, the actor disguised as the Count took out a book in which were rated all the prices for which henceforward, sins were to be forgiven.[3]

The play's satire exploits familiar Protestant myths about Roman Catholic abuses, from the sale of indulgences to the exploitation of the confessional, and presents the Jesuits as crude intriguers. Its structure ingeniously combines the old-fashioned psychomachia, in which the losing figures are hustled into a hell mouth (here the bag in which the pieces are kept), with the tragi-comic plot of the Black Bishop's Pawn's sexual attempts on the naïvely chaste White Queen's Pawn. The hostility between the black and the white faction is conveyed partly by the action of the game

---

[1] Philip Edwards, *Threshold of a Nation* (London, 1980), 186.

[2] Margot Heinemann, *Puritanism and Theatre* (London, 1980), *passim*, and 'Middleton's *Game at Chess*: Parliamentary Puritans and Opposition Drama', *ELR*, 5 (1975).

[3] Quoted in *Jacobean and Caroline Stage*, IV, 871–2.

in which attempts are made to 'take' particular pieces, but more interestingly in set-piece scenes of verbal antagonism and flytings where the language of insult provides its own dramatic energy. The most interesting and the most politically pointed sequence comes near the end of the play where the White Knight (Buckingham) and the White Duke (Prince Charles) politicly feign interest in joining the Black Kingdom. In order to make the Black Kingdom attractive to its potential converts, the Black Knight describes in detail the full extent of its vices, intrigues and power:

> In the large Feast of our Vast Ambition
> Wee count but the White Kingdome whence you came from
> The garden for our Cooke to pick his Salletts;
> The Foode's leane France larded wth Germanie,
> Before wch comes the Graue-Chast Seigniorie
> Of Venice, serude in Capon-like in whitebroath;
> From our cheif Ouen, Italie, the Bake-meates
> Sauoye, the Salt, Geneua, the Chipt Manchet. . . . (v.iii.92–9)

The scene ends in a crescendo of energy as the White Knight overcomes the Black in 'Checkmate by Discouerye, . . . the Noblest Mate of all' (V.iii. 177–8) (see plate 11).

The specific political import of A Game at Chess cannot be denied. Middleton was evidently less tied to establishment interests than other major dramatists of the period. Despite his mockery of factious Puritans in The Family of Love (1602) and A Chaste Maid in Cheapside (1612), we are told that:

> Middleton they seemd much to Adore
> fors [for his] learned Exercise gaynst Gundomore.[1]

Apart from A Game at Chess, however, Middleton's explicit political statements are much more circumspect, as in the final dance of The World Tossed at Tennis (1620), a masque-like entertainment produced at the Phoenix theatre. The entertainment ends with a contest between Simplicity and Deceit for control of the world. Deceit loses:

> the Diuell and Deceit ayming at the World, but the World remaining now in the Lawyers possession, expressing his reuerend and noble acknowledge-

---

[1] William Hemming, 'Elegy on Randolph's Finger', ed. G. C. Moore Smith (London, 1923), quoted in Jacobean and Caroline Stage, IV, 877.

*ment to the absolute power of Maiesty resignes it loyally to it's royal
government: Maiesty, to Valour; Valour, to Law agen; Law to Religion;
Religion, to Soueraignty; where it firmely and fairly settles; The Law
confounding Deceit, and the Church, the Diuell.*

Relations between Religion, Law and Sovereignty were of course to prove a
contentious issue in the 1630s,[1] but in 1618, in the context of a courtly
entertainment, Middleton was content to beg the question of their relative
legitimacy and power.

(ii) Masques and ideology

Political statement in drama is constantly modified by context and form.
Even in the court masque, most explicitly devoted to the presentation of
courtly ideology, the interplay between statement and form creates a
complex image of Stuart culture. Individual masques, particularly at the
court of Charles, may have referred to court policies, but the form of the
masque as developed by Ben Jonson and Inigo Jones established a dialectic
between masque and antimasque. The masque's finale was designed to
demonstrate the absolute perfection of royal power and authority but the
theatrical process by which it came about often reflected on the precarious-
ness of absolute rule.

In Jonson's *The Golden Age Restored* (1615) the power of absolute rule is
enacted in a clear and schematic way. Pallas enters, heralding the Golden
Age. She is prevented from establishing it by the 'tumult and clashing of
arms' of the Iron Age calling forth evils who present an antimasque dance of
'two drums, trumpets, and a confusion of martial music'. The Iron Age is,
however, easily overcome by the power of Pallas' shield, and the Golden Age
achieved in a scene change. Astraea and the Golden Age are then brought in;
while rejoicing that they are 'to live again with men', they wonder how they
can survive on earth without any followers. These are provided by the poet-
masquers, James's own courtiers, who perform the main dance while
Astraea, Pallas and the Golden Age sing the praises of a new, pastoral,

---

[1] As is shown in detail in, e.g., Christopher Hill, *The Century of Revolution* (Edinburgh, 1961),
64–8, and below, 141–3.

golden age. This vision of perfection is explicitly extended to the court by having the courtier-masquers dance with court ladies, while a song articulates the symbolic significance of their action:

> The male and female us'd to ioyne
> And into all delight did coyne
> That pure simplicitie.
> Then feature did to forme advance,
> And youth call'd beautie forth to dance,
> And everie grace was by. (ll. 181 ff.)

James's personal power to bring on the golden age is made further explicit by Astraea's final decision to remain at his court:

> This, this and onely such as this,
> The bright *Astraea's* region is,
> Where she would pray to live,
> And in the midd'st of so much gold
> Unbought with grace or feare unsold,
> The law to mortals give. (ll. 234–9)

In using the figure of Astraea, more usually connected with Elizabeth, Jonson creates politic connections with the previous reign. However, the movement of the masque shows his characteristic concern with absolute moral virtues rather than particular political strategy. It is unexceptionable to insist that Envy, Slander, Ignorance and Corruption, the vices of the Iron Age, must be banished, and the power of Pallas' shield is a suitably vague image for absolute authority.

In *Pleasure Reconciled to Virtue* (1618), on the other hand, the vices of the antimasque have rather more pointed reference to the particular circumstances of James's court. Vicious pleasure and over-indulgence in the form of Comus, the belly god, are banished by Hercules who makes his contempt for them explicit. Hercules himself, however, must be taught that the ideal court can be virtuous without being ascetic. Pleasure and Virtue can be harmonized in the dance by Daedalus the wise, who, like the word explaining the picture of an emblem, enunciates its symbolism:

> Come on, come on; and where you goe,
> So enter-weave the curious knot,
> As ev'n th'observer scarce may know
> Which lines are Pleasures and which not . . .

For Dauncing is an exercise
Not only shows the movers wit,
But maketh the beholder wise,
As he hath powre to rise to it. (ll. 253–6; 269–72)

Under the control of Jonson's imagination the masque had a unity and coherence which imposed the rightness of its view, combining didacticism with flattery. Contemporary observers were all too aware of the gap between his idealized courtly world and the excesses of James's drunken, vulgar and mysogynist court, but the antimasque allowed Jonson to absorb those criticisms and make them part of the moral lesson.

Chapman, too, made use of the opposition to masquing in his *Masque of the Middle Temple*, performed for the marriage of Princess Elizabeth to the Elector Palatine in 1613, in which the antimasque turns on a discussion of the proper use of riches. In this case, the masque is more politically pointed. When Capriccio in the antimasque argues that riches are damnable, Plutus replies:

Sinfull? and damnable? what, a Puritane? . . . a Religion-forger I see you are, and presume of inspiration from these Bellowes; with which yee study to blow vp the setled gouernments of kingdomes. (ll. 82–6)

Opposition to masquing is seen even at this early date as parallel to opposition to lawful government. The masque further connects bad politics with bad aesthetics. Capriccio's contribution to courtly entertainment is an antimasque of baboons, which Plutus rejects, calling on the main masque:

Eunomia (or the sacred power of Lawe)
Daughter of *Jove*, and Goddesse *Honors* Priest;
Appeare to *Plutus*, and his love assist. (ll. 194–6)

The appearance of Eunomia (Law) as an equal presiding deity with Love at this feast gives the main masque a further political point. The barristers of the Middle Temple and Lincoln's Inn who financed this masque are reminding James that, despite his announced views about the divine right of kings, he still has to rule within the prerogative of law. Moreover, although the theme of the main masque is an elegant conceit, appropriate to a wedding, about the marriage of Love and Beauty, Honour and Riches, the physical image which introduces the main masquers refers more specifically to James's policy. In the centre of the scene was presented a gold-mine in front of which the Phoebades, who had previously adored the setting sun, are converted by Eunomia to the worship of

> our Britan *Phoebus,* whose bright skie
> (Enlightned with a Christian Piety)
> Is neuer subiect to black Errors night. (ll. 330–2)

The speeches keep the masque within the symbolic framework of an abstract debate about the right way to Honour. But the Templars used the method of the masque to remind James of the importance of the mercantile activity and colonial policy, which they financed, in maintaining the riches which brought Fortune to live with him for ever.[1]

An even more pointed reminder of the importance of law was seen in a later Inns of Court masque, Shirley's magnificent *Triumph of Peace* (1634). The masque was the lawyers' expensive apology for the affair of Prynne, Burton and Bastwick. Yet it presents no servile acquiescence to the power of monarchy. Once again Eunomia figures in the main masque, and the antimasques make explicit reference to controversial abuses of the day. The magnificent masque procession through the streets was led by Fancy, Opinion and Confidence followed by Jollity and Laughter, while the main antimasque consisted of six projectors, parodies of the various money-making and improvement schemes financed by Charles's courtiers. Bulstrode Whitelock noted in his *Memorials* that

> it pleased the spectators the more, because by it an information was covertly given to the King of the unfairness and ridiculousness of these projects against the law: and Attorney Noy, who had most knowledge of them, had a great hand in this Antimasque of Projectors.[2]

In performance the masque followed the usual opposition between antimasque and masque, presenting the false attributes of peace in the escapades of Fancy and the followers of Opinion, while the main masque demonstrated the true values of Peace established by the monarchy. However, the King's peace (Irene) cannot rule alone. She confesses that she is 'lost with them/that know not how to order me'. At this call, Law (Eunomia) descends from the opposite side on a matching cloud and they sing a duet of mutual congratulation:

> The world shall give prerogative to neyther
> We cannot flourish but together.

[1] Theodore K. Rabb, *Enterprise and Empire* (Cambridge, Mass., 1967), 102, n., remarks 'the close attachment of members of the Middle Temple to overseas enterprise'.
[2] Quoted in *The Dramatic Works and Poems of James Shirley*, ed. W. Gifford and A. Dyce, 6 vols (London, 1833), VI, 258.

Only then can Justice join them to make up the symmetry of the scene, and the three of them turn to the State, which holds the King and Queen 'whose smile/Doth scatter blessings through this Ile [isle]'.

In the Jonsonian form of the masque, the entertainment would have ended on this positive note: the glory of the monarchy, in collaboration with the law, had been defined and reasserted; the purposes of propaganda had been met; the expression of loyalty was complete. However, Shirley disrupted this harmonious vision by a belated intrusion of low-life characters demanding to see the masque and reminding the audiences that they, the craftsmen and their wives, were in the truest sense responsible for its production. Their comic insistence is frozen out by the patient contempt of the masquers who simply stop the action until the discomfited artisans conclude, ''tis our best course to dance a figary our selves . . . let us goe off cleanely, and some body will thinke, this was meant for an Antimasque.'

The antimasque for Jonson always stood before the main masque, by which it was either banished or absorbed, and the proliferation of comic and grotesque antimasques which became fashionable as a way of varying the limited themes of main masques met with his particular contempt. His objection was to a loss of the organic form of the masque, where the dramatic coherence signified a moral coherence clearly enunciated in the poetic themes of dialogue and songs. The variety of later antimasques (*plates 12–15*), and, most significantly, their creation of comic character as opposed to symbolic vice, served to subvert and undermine the certainties of the main masque, however glorious its scenic presentation. In Shirley's *Triumph of Peace* it is as hard to despise the figures of Confidence, Jollity, Laughter and their friends, who dance and get drunk, as it is to object to the low-life figures of city comedy. Opinion may attack them as the effects of Corruption rather than Peace, but it is harder to place them in the straightforward symbolic opposition which banished the pygmies of *Pleasure Reconciled to Virtue* or the evils of the Iron Age.

It would be absurd to assert that the form of the masque always subverted its expressly stated ideological position. Nevertheless, as the styles of masques and antimasques became increasingly distinct, the tension between them became potentially disruptive of a coherent effect. In their account of the politics of spectacle, Orgel and Strong make the point that in his masques Inigo Jones 'celebrates the power of the rational mind in controlling the physical world',[1] but, compared with the comic power of the

[1] Stephen Orgel and Roy Strong, *Splendour at Court, Renaissance Spectacle and Illusion* (London, 1973), 219.

antimasque, Inigo Jones's final visions all too often display a sterile architecture, empty of human life. The final scene of Jones's and Carew's *Coelum Britannicum* (1634), for example, presents the acme of classical control:

> *a delicious garden with severall walkes and perterra's set round with low trees, and on the sides against these walkes, were fountaines and grots, and in the furthest part a Palace, from whence went high walkes upon Arches, and above them open Tarraces planted with Cypresse trees, and all this together was composed of such Ornaments as might expresse a Princely Villa.* (ll. 1014–20)

The conceit behind the masque was that Jove had purged the heavens of their original constellations and remodelled them on the lines of Charles's London, as designed by Inigo Jones. Though this idea makes perfect sense, the antimasque vignettes of the unruly elements banished by Jove take up much more time than the ultimate consoling vision of architectural perfection.

These vignettes are presented by Momus, whose iconoclastic and colloquial prose suggests that he is modelled on the satirist figures of drama. He subverts the force of the main masque by suggesting that Jove's reforms are the result 'of a consideration of the decay of his natural abilities' and he further suggests dangerous analogies between Jove's and Charles's reforms: 'Monopolies are called in, sophistication of wares punished, and rates imposed on Commodities. . . . Edicts are made for the restoring of decayed housekeeping, prohibiting the repayre of Families to the Metropolis. . . .' (ll. 236–7, 241–3), and so on. Charles's clearing up of court and city was both necessary and beneficial, but Momus deals it the crushing blow of ridicule. Even the Queen's celebrated cult of pure and platonic love is reduced to silly prudery: '*Cupid* must goe no more so scandalously naked, but is enjoyned to make him breeches though of his mothers petticotes. *Ganimede* is forbidden the Bedchamber, and must onely minister in publique' (ll. 248–51).

By mocking the whole idea of the masque, Momus makes it impossible to regard the deviant figures as anything but comic. Some of them are neither vicious nor deformed: for instance, Poenia, presenting the delights of the simple life and the joys of divine contemplation, introduces a jolly antimasque of gypsies. Carew seems to be wrenching the action when a censorious speech from Mercury denounces her 'lazie or Pedantique virtue'. There is no symbolic reason why riches and poverty, battles and pleasure, should all be banished from the new heaven. The muddled clearing out of people and variety suggests that the parterres and palaces of the final image will be peopled by a Caroline court whose particular virtue is defined as a dull absence of vice.

Such close analysis of the arguments and ethical implications of the speeches is perhaps inappropriate to such a transitory form as the masque. The gap between conception and achievement was certainly not apparent to its original audience; Sir Henry Herbert found that 'The kinge and queene were very well pleased with my service, and the Q was pleased to tell me before the king "Pour les habits elle n'avoit jamais rien vue de si brave".'[1] As the Queen's remarks show, the masque had become a spectator sport. The integration of masquers and audience which characterized the early forms of the masque had been replaced by spectacle, increasingly confined behind a proscenium arch. The finale of Davenant's and Jones' *Britannia Triumphans* (1638) presented a sea scene with Galatea on a dolphin's back and a wonderful mechanical device revealed '*a great fleet . . . which passing by with a side wind, tacked about, and with a prosperous gale entered into the haven*'.

Charles's plans for an expensive navy may be figured here, but more important for the form was the fact that the scene was merely 'to entertain the sight while the dancing lasted'. The physical involvement of the court was no longer necessary or even implied. The visions of the masque embodied the specific aspirations of absolute rule as statement (*plates 16–17*).

Such aspirations did not of themselves produce bad art. Inigo Jones's masques were an ingenious combination of architectural innovation, derived ultimately from Palladio, with ideals of kingship derived likewise from European models. Even the proliferation of antimasques which dissipated the unity of the classic Jonsonian masque owed as much to the European traditions of the intermedii as to any decadence of courtly taste.[2] Court culture was innovative and European; this trend, as much as any prefiguring of later conflict, separated it from the mainstream of English art.

(iii) Platonic masques

The so-called cult of platonic love at the court of Charles I was a further

[1] Adams, *Herbert*, 55.
[2] See Jean Jacquot, 'La Reine Henriette Marie et l'influence française dans les spectacles à la cour de Charles Ier', *Cahiers de l'Association Internationale des Études Françaises*, 9 (1957).

manifestation of its European outlook. To say that it 'directly drew Puritan fire and hastened Marston Moor and Naseby,'[1] is, however, to overrate its political significance. In fact, the cult provided the subject matter for a variety of entertainments, both at court and in the professional theatre. Even in the court masque, the common theme of a contrast between passionate love and pure love can take on interestingly different shades of meaning according to the form chosen by the author.

The theme is treated most simply in Davenant's *Temple of Love* (1634), where all the inventiveness goes into the exotic settings. The action of the masque is based on the thesis that Divine Poesy leads to the temple of chaste love, but the antimasque of magicians provides an all too coherent attack on the affectation of platonic lovers who 'practise generation not/Of Bodies but of Soules':

> Beleeve me, my Magicall friends,
> They must bring bodies with 'em that worship
> In our pleasant Temple: I have an odde
> Fantasticke faith perswades me there will be
> Little pastime upon earth without Bodies.
> Your Spirit's a cold companion at midnight.

In the context of the masque, the magicians and their spirits are easily subdued but even the platonic love is expressed in poetry whose sensuality denies its particular qualities:

> —Come melt thy soule in mine, that when unite
> We may become one virtuous appetite
> —First breath[e] thine into me, thine is the part
> More heavenly, and doth more adorne the heart.

The precise application of the ideas of platonic love to Charles's court is more carefully expressed in Aurelian Townshend's *Tempe Restored* (1632). It explicitly acknowledges a European inspiration in that it is based on Beaujolyeux's *Balet Comique de La Royne*, presented at the French court in 1582. A courtier who has escaped from the lustful world of Circe begs refuge from the King; this situation gives rise to a scene in Circe's palace with '*All the Antimasques, consisting of Indians, and Barbarians, who naturally are bestiall, and others which are voluntaries, and but halfe transformed into*

---

[1] G. F. Sensabaugh, 'Platonic Love and the Puritan Rebellion', *SP*, 37 (1940), 457.

beastes', as well as succeeding scenes of spheres and stars and the sun rising. At the high point in the masque, eight spheres seated on a cloud are let down 'as in a chain' and are then followed by two groups of eight stars and six stars. At this point the text comments that the scene:

> *Was for the difficulty of the Ingining and number of the persons the greatest that hath beene seene here in our time. For the apparitions of such as came down in the ayre, and the Chorus standing beneath arrived to the number of fifty persons all richly attired, shewing the magnificence of the court of England.*

The magnificence of the court of England and its basis in lust-free love could now be presented by 'Ingining', while the moral message of the masque was appended to the printed text in the form of an Allegory or outlined in the moral debates between Circe and Pallas. The various scenes are conceived as intermedii and the traditional revels are a sequel to rather than a culmination of the action of the masque. It is not until 'the last Intermedium' that 'the Queene and her Ladies began the Revels with the King and his Lords, which continued all night'. The physical connection between the world of the masque and the world of the court is no longer possible or necessary, and the masque's theme is simply the basis for scenic inventiveness.

Ben Jonson had scorned such 'Mythology there painted on slit deale', and in *Love's Triumph through Callipolis* (1631) he constructed an entertainment which enacted the differences between true and perverted love, and through poetry and design connected the values of the masque to the world of the court. He acquiesced in the taste for a variety of antimasques but used each of them to present a demonstration of perverted love:

> The glorious, whining, the adventurous foole,
> Phantastique, bribing, and the jealous asse,
> The sordid, scornefull, and the angry mule,
> The melancholique, dull and envious masse,
> With all the rest, that in the sensuall schoole
> Of lust, for their degree of brute may passe. (ll. 88–93)

The main masque '*consisteth of fifteene Lovers, and as many Cupids, who ranke themselves seaven and seaven on a side, with each a Cupid before him, with a lighted torch, and the middle person (which is his Majesty,) placed in the center*' (ll. 103–6). By placing the King in the centre opposite the Queen, Jonson, using the old-fashioned device of dancers with cupids as torchbearers, dramatizes the point of the masque and makes it explicit in the poetry:

> AMPHITRITE.   To you, best Iudge then, of perfection!
> EUPHEMUS.   The Queene of what is wonder, in the place!
> AMPHITRITE.   Pure object, of Heroique Love, alone!
> EUPHEMUS.   The center of proportion —
> AMPHITRITE.   Sweetnesse—
> EUPHEMUS.   Grace!
> AMPHITRITE.   Daigne to receive all lines of love in one.
> EUPHEMUS.   And by reflecting of them fill this space.
> CHO[RUS]   Till it a circle of these glories prove
>   Fit to be sought in *Beauty*, found by *Love*. (ll. 124 ff.)

Although the scenery and the visual effects remain on the horizontal axis, a scene for spectators, the 'lines of love' are carried by the poetry from the King at the centre of the masque into the centre of the audience, the Queen in her state.

The most interesting treatment of pure and passionate love was produced outside the aegis of the court altogether. The flattering assumption that wise and true love existed in the persons of Charles and Henrietta Maria (*see plates 18 and 19*), 'whose lives have brought/Virtue in fashion',[1] was a necessary prerequisite for courtly treatments of the theme, but in *Comus* (1634) Milton could express the connections between masque and audience with telling ambiguity. His entertainment was not responding directly to the cult of platonic love – the theme has a more ancient heritage in Renaissance debate – but it takes up the argument about chastity and pleasure which had informed Beaujolyeux's *Balet Comique* and Jonson's *Pleasure Reconciled to Virtue*, and which lay behind the new court philosophy. The form of Milton's masque also deviated from courtly practice since he used argument rather than revelation to make his moral points. The work dramatizes a narrative about the loss of a Lady and her escape from Comus and his beast-headed crew, but the action is not purely dramatic: it is moved forward by the superior power of virtue over vice and produces a slightly uneasy combination of the dramatic and the revelatory.

Comus's vice is visible in the presence of his beast-headed crew but at the same time he is allowed to argue his case against the Lady with some poetic power:

[1] Court prologue to Joseph Rutter, *The Shepherd's Holiday* (1633–4).

Beauty is natures coyn, must not be hoorded,
But must be currant, and the good therof
Consists in mutual and partak'n bliss,
Unsavoury in th'injoyment of it self. (ll. 739–42)

His arguments against chastity are familiar from Renaissance debates and he himself informs us that they are merely 'well-plac't words of glozing courtesie' (l. 161). However, it creates a dramatic imbalance to place on him the onus not only of presenting evil but also of asserting the superior power of good in his recognition of the Lady's virtue. For her part, she does not have to argue at all, since Comus has 'nor Ear nor Soul to apprehend . . . the sage / And serious doctrine of Virginity'. In dramatic terms, moreover, the Lady is freed not by the superiority of her arguments but by the magical power of the moly which the Elder Brother brings to her rescue, and by the chaste Sabrina.

The argument becomes more complex when Milton tries to assert the nice distinction between different kings of festivity. The Lady fastidiously disapproves of

                    the sound
Of riot and ill managed merriment
Such as the jocund flute or gamesom pipe
Stirs up amongst the loose unletter'd hinds, . . . (ll. 171–4)

but in the country to which the travellers return with the aid of Sabrina,

All the swains that there abide,
With Jiggs and rural dance resort. (ll. 951–2)

The distinction between the two kinds of merriment is understandable in argument, but it is most difficult to dramatize without the resources of scenery which will demonstrate the point by a change in style. However, it is precisely the instant change of the masque which Milton is seeking to avoid. He is not presenting the transformation by *fiat*, appropriate to the ideology of the absolute court, but seeking to dramatize the process of moral learning which will produce true virtue in the young Egertons, the subject of the masque. At the end of the masque these young people are presented to their parents and the point of the action becomes clear:

Heer behold so goodly grown
Three fair branches of your own.
Heav'n hath timely tri'd thir youth,

Thir faith, thir patience, and thir truth.
And sent them heer through hard assays
With a crown of deathless praise,
    To triumph in victorious dance
O're sensual folly, and intemperance. (ll. 967–74)

This speech clearly demonstrates the difference between Milton's scheme and the usual method of the masque. In the court masque, the masquers are embodiments of virtue with no need to prove it. The Hercules who overcomes the pygmies, the Heroic Virtue who overthrows the witches or the Iron Age, is never a masquer. The courtly masquers are merely the attendants of such figures, reflecting their moral power but in no way involved in enforcing it.

The theme of platonic love was not of itself politically significant. However, the different artistic expressions it received indicate the potential ideological implications of form. Jonson's characteristic aim was to dramatize moral distinctions, to make celebration a vehicle for didacticism. Townshend was content with a spectacular restatement of a familiar and acceptable ideal. Milton's stress on the process of learning carried with it political as well as theological ideas about individual freedom and responsibility, which burst the boundaries of the masque.

(iv) Academic drama

The stress on refinement was much more a feature of Charles's court than James's and this is reflected in the plays written specially for each court at the universities. In James's time, the academic dramatists showed themselves aware of the professional London theatres as setters of standards and trends. In the induction to George Ruggle's *Ignoramus*, acted in Latin before James I in 1615, Davus Dromo, a pantomime horse, has this conversation with his keeper:

KEEPER.   But what will they say of the play it self?
HORSE.   Why, they will say there are every day better playes to be seen for mony at *London*, and that the Comedies are here spoyled by the two [too] strict observance of the laws of Comedy.
KEEPER.   What will be their censure of the Actors?
HORSE.   That *Academicians* are pitiful Actors.

KEEPER.   But who amongst all the Actors will be most commended?
HORSE.   Who but *Davus Dromo* the most noble, and most famous
Horse in all the Universe. (1.i)

In the second prologue the horse is put on trial and arraigned with the
humorous malapropisms of typical comic policemen. The main plot of the
play is an adaptation of Plautus' *Menaechmi* but its subplot proceeds by
familiar comic set-pieces and comic routines such as Ignoramus' visit to a
bawd or the dialogue between a deaf dwarf and a clever fool. *Ignoramus* was a
great favourite with the King, but not, presumably, because it appealed to
the taste for the classics which he had learned from George Buchanan.

During the same visit to Trinity College, Cambridge, James was also
entertained by an English comedy, *Albumazar* by Thomas Tomkis. The
play is a close adaptation of a contemporary Venetian comedy, and both its
humour and staging are more reminiscent of Italian *commedia erudita* than
native comedy. The clown sequences, however, derive from memories of
English plays: Trinculo parodies *The Spanish Tragedy* and woos his
mistress 'with compliments drawn from the plaies I see at the Fortune and
the Red Bull'.

In the Caroline period the courtiers who visited the universities
demanded more explicit attention to their newly developed tastes. Peter
Hausted's *The Rival Friends* (1631–2) 'gave much offense' to the courtly
audience, a fact which he attributes to the low bearing of his women who
'plaid as *Chackstones*, when it may be some of our butterfly judgements
expected a set at *Maw* or *Primivista*'. It should be said that some of Hausted's
low life characters are pretty low, including a midwife called Placenta and
her daughter Merda, and the satire on ecclesiastical pluralism, though
directed more at the aspirant parsons than at the abuse itself, takes much of
the attention away from the high-flown dilemma of the rivals in love.

The visit of Charles and Henrietta Maria to Oxford in 1636 saw the most
courtly of academic productions in Strode's *The Floating Island* and
Cartwright's *The Royal Slave*. The visit and its entertainments were
arranged by Laud, and both politically and aesthetically they reflected
courtly ideals. Strode's play was too scholarly to please most of the court,
but it contains the clearest political allegory in the passions' rebellion against
their king, Prudentius. The action takes the form of a psychomachia in
which Prudence leaves the passions to their will and they elect Fancy as their
queen. The morality action is made explicitly political in the characterization of Malevolo, whose connection with Prynne is seen not only in his

discontented opposition to the King but also in references to his mutilated ears and his scourge of the stage. In spite of this topical note, the play does not deal with the detail of political unrest or dramatize specific opposition to the King. The morality action ensures an acceptable conclusion, and at the end the King can demonstrate that all of the passions belong under his rightful rule.

Flattery of the court was further manifest in the imitation of masque staging. The stage was equipped with a mechanical Floating Island and the setting of the different scenes involved changes of landscape by moving flats. The scenes are only used for variety of spectacle: the morality is not adapted to the resolutions of the masque and the entertainments provided for Lady Fancy are old-fashioned spectacular shows rather than the appropriate emblems of absolute rule.

Cartwright's *The Royal Slave* (1636) was altogether more suited to courtly taste. The story of Queen Atossa's platonic love for the royal slave is one of the most eloquent and appropriate treatments of the theme, since it provides the necessary elevated passion without the disturbing suggestion that a queen might be moved by adulterous feeling. Crantander for his part displays his superiority by understanding the finer points of platonic love and the necessary self-denial, in his willingness to be sacrificed at the end of his three-day rule. As well as its appeal to fashionable sentiment, the play also provided glamorous spectacle, and Laud noted that 'the strangeness of the Persian habits gave great content'. The scenes were designed by Inigo Jones and provided a variety of settings for the action as well as the visual climax of the play when Cratander is delivered up for sacrifice and, after the full formality of the ritual, '*Whiles the last Chorus is singing, the Sunne appeares eclipsed and a showre of raine dashing out the fire*' (ll. 1575–6 S.D.).

The play was an immense success. It was repeated during the following season (1637) at Hampton Court with the same costumes and stage sets which had enlivened it at Oxford, though on this occasion it was acted by the King's Men. Laud and the university authorities were most insistent 'that neither the Play, nor clothes, nor stage, might come into the hands and use of the common players abroad'.[1]

Laud's comments show clearly how far the university theatre's point of reference had moved from the London theatres to the world of the court. If any general trend in court drama can be discerned, it is this growing sense of exclusiveness: the creation of a court culture which was self-consciously separate from the cultural life of the rest of the nation, in intention if not in fact.

[1] *Jacobean and Caroline Stage*, III, 147.

2 Tradition, revival, innovation

(i) Introduction

In the two-way traffic between the Stuart court and the professional theatre, the court was not always the dominant partner. After the accession of James I, the major London companies were nominally the court's servants and all plays had to be licensed for performance by the Master of the Revels, a court officer. Courtly approval accorded high status and financial stability to those companies which attained it. Nevertheless the court was as much the consumer as the instigator of important trends in Stuart drama. A more complex triangular relationship between the playwright, the employing company and theatrical tradition must be taken into account in assessing the theatrical culture of the age. The tension between tradition and innovation found in other areas of seventeenth-century life had its counterpart in the drama. Revivals of old plays and the continued influence of a rich theatrical past combined with the effect of new work to provide a wide variety of entertainment for any theatre-goer, courtly or plebeian, between 1613 and 1642.

In the absence of complete repertory lists, it is impossible to achieve a comprehensive view of the changing fortunes of older plays. Often an old play would be revived simply because it was available in a company's repertory. In 1634 such different plays as *Richard III* and *Cymbeline* were revived for the same court season and apparently both 'likte'.[1] It may be that the preponderance of revivals, like those of *Dr Faustus* and *Edward II* in 1622 at the Red Bull, occurred because the companies who used the theatres did not have the financial resources to commission new plays. Old plays were certainly a valuable commodity, whatever their topical appeal, as we can deduce from the King's Men's payment to prevent the Red Bull company from illegally performing the works of Shakespeare in 1627.[2]

The connection between revivals and changing taste is correspondingly difficult to assess. Sometimes, as with Fletcher's *Faithful Shepherdess* or Rowley's *Hymen's Holiday*, the revivals (both in 1633) respond to the latest fashion; others are a self-conscious return to the excellencies of the past, as Heywood stresses in his only slightly apologetic prologue to the revival of Marlowe's *Jew of Malta* in 1633. Contemporary comments on revivals reflect a lively preoccupation with the theatrical past and a sense of its cultural significance. In 1612, Webster's Preface to *The White Devil* scornfully denounced the search for novelty among 'those ignorant asses who visiting stationers shops their use is not to inquire for good books, but new books'. In 1629 Joseph Taylor made the opposite complaint, defending Massinger's *The Roman Actor* against

> some sowre censurer who's apt to say
> No one in these times can produce a Play
> Worthy his reading since of late, 'tis true
> The old accepted are more than the new. (1.i)

The status of the implied audience for revivals is not always obvious. This is particularly true in the case of complex satire like *The Knight of The Burning Pestle* (1607). The play's lack of success on its first production at the Blackfriars theatre has puzzled many theatre historians. In his dedicatory epistle to Robert Keysar, Beaumont blamed the wide world's 'want of judgement, or not understanding the privy mark of irony about it'; subsequent commentators have disagreed about whether the mockery of the citizen participants was too severe or not severe enough. The play was revived at the Phoenix theatre in 1632 and again at court in the Christmas season of 1635/6. Its appeal to a coterie audience of the 1630s can be seen as

[1] Adams, *Herbert*, 53.
[2] *Jacobean and Caroline Stage*, I, 270.

evidence of the specialized tastes of a fashionable town literati who would appreciate the parody of Spanish romance and laugh wholeheartedly at the naïve, if courageous, interventions of Ralph the apprentice. However, even in 1635 the play held a double appeal. The energy with which the citizen couple insist on altering the play, and the success of Ralph's heroic adventures as the knight of the burning pestle, exalt citizen aspirations as much as they mock them, so that Rebecca Brittleware, the citizen's wife in Brome's *Sparagus Garden* (1635), regards the play as 'the play of all playes', comparable among London sights to the Great Bed of Ware and the new steeple of Paul's.

(ii) Pastoral plays

A similar breadth of appeal can be seen even in the most apparently courtly of genres. True, it is inconceivable that such courtly pastorals as Montague's seven-hour marathon *The Shepherd's Paradise* (1632/3) or Carlell's ten-act *Arviragus and Philicia* (1635) could have been popular. The refined abstractions of their debates, and the distant and inaccessible lands of their setting, established a kind of exclusiveness which provided an attractive self-image for the court. The troubling satiric element of earlier pastoral, its implicit condemnation of courtly and city ways, had disappeared: 'The idea of pastoral current among the playwrights . . . was largely derived from novels such as the Arcadia . . . the tradition of these works was one rather of polite chivalry and courtly adventure than of pastoralism proper.'[1]

But the bulk of the drama produced at court was put on by professional companies whose work constantly shows interaction between new styles and the resilient native traditions. Fletcher's *Faithful Shepherdess* (1608), for example, had failed in its first production, according to him, because it lacked 'Whitsun-ales, cream wassail, and morris dances', yet it was successfully revived in 1633 as a means of reusing Inigo Jones's costumes and designs for Montague's play (*see plate 22*). In the complicated emotional encounters between Fletcher's shepherds, both silly and sullen, is to be found the pattern of later courtly pastoral. His characters mark points along the spectrum from chaste to passionate love and the action of the play consists of encounters, avowals and denials which express rather than explore these

[1] W. W. Greg, *Pastoral Poetry and Pastoral Drama* (London, 1906), 337–8.

principles. However, despite Fletcher's denials, his play is animated by elements from more popular comedy and romance. His characters are certainly not 'country hired shepherds in gray cloaks, with curtailed dogs in strings', but the lively characterization, particularly of Cloe and the Sullen Shepherd, the anti-romantic figures, together with the magical well of life and the enchanted transformations, owe as much to the traditions of Peele and Lyly as to D'Urfé.

The real courtly innovation, then, was not the subject matter of pastoral plays but their use of movable scenery (*plates 21, 23 and 24*). We have already (p. 152) noted Laud's insistence that the scenery from Cartwright's play should not fall into the hands of common players. Conversely, the performances of common players could be brought up to courtly standard, however English and old-fashioned their form, by the addition of scenery. In 1632 the Queen's Men under Beeston produced Thomas Heywood's *Love's Mistress, or The Queen's Masque*. None of its dramatic effects demands more scenic resource than was available in the public theatre where it was first performed. For the court performance, however, Inigo Jones added scenic effects which 'to every Act, nay almost to every Sceane, by his excellent Inuentions gave such an extraordinary Luster'.[1] The location of the action in Vulcan's forge or the Court of Hell gave ample scope for architectural invention and these scenic effects are the most likely explanation of why this play was the choice for three separate court entertainments 'In the presence of sundry Forraigne Ambassadors'.[2] Heywood's own contribution was much more old-fashioned, looking back to the allegorical entertainments at the court of Elizabeth I. It consists of interlocking stories dealing with Cupid and Psyche, and the contention between Apuleius and Midas. A good deal of its charm derives from the mock-heroic domestication of the gods in passages such as Cupid's description (1.i) of Ceres

> binding garlands for God Pan
> Of Blew-bottles, and yellow pissabeds

or the presentation of Vulcan as a grumbling tradesman with the Cyclopes as his journeymen. Set pieces like the banquet with its echo effect, the dances of the entr'actes or the song contest of Act III, create a charming world of mythology quite different from the chivalric pastoral of Montague and Carlell.

[1] Heywood's dedication, quoted in *Jacobean and Caroline Stage*, I, 233.
[2] As the title page of one early edition proudly states.

The most successful and pleasing courtly pastorals are those which followed Fletcher's model of simple oppositions, clear-cut dramatic situations and elegant verse. In Joseph Rutter's *The Shepherd's Holiday* (1633–4), the only connection between the shepherds and sheep is the anthropomorphism expressed in Thyrsis' lament in the prologue:

> All as the shepheard is, such be his flocks,
> So pine and languish, they, as in despaire
> He pines and languishes. (1.i)

The pastoral setting provides the complication of the main plot, in which a princess has fled the court to live in the pastoral world. The courtly ethos is elegantly endorsed when her shepherd lover turns out to be a prince; his union with Sylvia not only vindicates his elevated passion but also fulfils the oracle. In the subplot of the play, the three-way complication of love rejected and love pursued provides Rutter with his only dramatic device. Dorinda loves Daphnis, who loves Nerina. When they meet, the following lament charmingly evokes both the themes and the action of the play:

> DORINDA.   Will you then slight my love, because 'tis offer'd?
> DAPHNIS.   Will you then slight my love, because 'tis offer'd?
> NERINA.   Somebody else may love you, I cannot.
> DAPHNIS.   Somebody else may love you, I cannot.
> DORINDA.   O cruell words, how they do peirce my heart!
> DAPHNIS.   O cruell words, how they do peirce my heart! (11.v)

The patterning on the stage and the musical effects of the echoed lines give a dramatic life to the simple situation, as do the songs and refined poetic dialogues elsewhere in the play.

When the taste for courtly pastoral was extended to the professional stage, it was presented as a refinement of existing dramatic practice, a view not shared by all the professional dramatists. Rutter's play was performed at court by Queen Henrietta's Men, a professional company, and the prologue to the Stage suggests that there was at least one performance before the public.[1] In that prologue, Rutter explicitly rejects existing dramatic traditions:

> All bitter straines, that suit a Satyr Muse:
> And that which so much takes the Vulgar Eare,
> Loosenes of speech, which they for jests do heare.

[1] *Jacobean and Caroline Stage*, v, 1033.

Such exclusiveness, however, was rare. Ben Jonson, who had defended Fletcher's pastoral at the time of its first performance, toyed with the form himself twenty years later in his incomplete *Sad Shepherd* (1637). He explicitly chooses an English setting, asserting that it will match 'those of *Sicily* or *Greece*', and his tale of Robin and Marion is more energetic than the effete platonism of contemporary pastoral. The wit and gaiety of their meeting in Act I establishes their mutual love as a significant value in the play, a contrast to both the more lyrical devotion of Aeglamour (the Sad Shepherd) to his lost love Earine, and the baser attractions of Lorel the swineherd. Jonson avoids the *longueurs* of other plays on love by presenting the passion in these more recognizable forms and by a lively plot moved along by the energetic hatred of Maudlin the witch and her magical demon, Puck Hairy. It is an altogether more traditional treatment of both form and theme, and amply justifies Jonson's contention that pastoral can transcend 'what is stamp'd with *Ah*, and *O*'.

(iii) Platonic love

In order to provide something more than 'Ah!' and 'Oh!', the plays on platonic love often contrasted it with passionate love, thus placing the courtly ideal in a different perspective. But a feature of the courtier plays on this subject was their lack of dynamic form or moral ambiguity. Discussions and arguments they contained in plenty, but the terms of those arguments were as predetermined as the shape of the plots and the status of the characters who engaged in them. When more skilled dramatists turned their hand to the theme, however, they produced interesting variations on the courtly paradigm.

Davenant's *Platonic Lovers* (1635) sought to adapt the new theme to a romance of love and friendship. Because the distinction between platonic and passionate love is abstract rather than dramatic, he embodies it in the patterned relationship of two pairs of lovers, each of which acts out the kind of love they represent. The first meeting of the two pairs is described by onlookers to make the schematic opposition clear. They address one another in patterned and almost euphuistic dialogue, in which, paradoxically, the platonic lovers can be more free with one another than the pair who recognize the demands of passion. Davenant continues the patterning in a set of parallel sequences where each lover visits his mistress at night. The passionate lovers give him more scope for his theatrical sense and their midnight visit includes the sensationalism of a threatened rape. The suppressed violence of Phylomont's frustration is then contrasted with the following scene where Eurithea, the platonic mistress, '*is found sleeping on a Couch, a vaile on, with her Lute*' (Act II S.D.). The sensual impact of the scene is sublimated in the charming, if static, image of the lovers as a rose entwined with 'wanton Woodbine' and 'Intangled with chast courtesies of love'.

A reminder of the original pastoral impulse behind the cult occurs in Act III where the lovers dress up as shepherds to enact a set piece of platonic wooing. They see themselves as figures out of Ovid fit to be apotheosed in needlework. The static nature of platonic love cannot, however, provide sufficient movement for drama. Consequently, in the midst of his artificial wooing, the platonic Theander finds himself overcome with passion. The consequences of this lapse create the entanglements which provide action for the play. The ostensible theme is thus undermined, and all the lovers find themselves married in the end in order to ensure the comic conclusion.

The play also clearly expresses the exclusive, aristocratic context of platonic love. When Phylomont, perfectly honourably, asks to marry his mistress,

and then

As Lords and Princes use, that love their wives,
Ly with her

Theander retorts furiously:

You are too Masculine! . . .
    Poor Ruffians in their drinke, that dwell
In Suburbe Allies, and in smoaky Lanes,
Are not so rude. (III.i)

When Theander himself succumbs to passion and marries his platonic mistress, she is in her turn outraged by the prospect of sexual love, and in a marriage-night sequence reminiscent of Fletcher's *The Maid's Tragedy* (1608–11) angrily repels his advances. She is particularly appalled 'That we should sleep together in one bed'. Her aristocratic sense of privacy is as much violated as her chaste sensibilities.

In Suckling's *Aglaura* (1637), one of the most successful of the courtly amateur plays, the same theme recurs. The strictly platonic parts of this love story are restricted to a series of set-piece dialogues. In one of these, Orithie, asserting the higher pleasures of 'soules refin'd', asks her opponent:

Will you then place the happinesse, but there
Where the dull plow-man and the plow-mans horse
Can finde it out? (I.v. 16–18)

The commonplace analogy between love and food is given a further twist
when Semanthe argues that truly refined love would live on air – 'starving is
his food'. This notion is countered with an account of Love's epicureanism
that reads like a parody of the decadent feasting of James's court:

>   Harts newly slaine
> Serv'd up intire, and stucke with little Arrowes
> In stead of Cloves . . .
>   Sometimes a cheeke plumpt up
> With broth, with creame and clarret mingled
> For sauce, and round about the dish
> Pomegranate kernells, strew'd on leaves of Lillies. (I.v.27–32)

The tongue-in-cheek wit of this dialogue suggests that Suckling is less than
totally committed to an analysis of platonic love; indeed, he avoids the
dramatic restrictions of the theme by linking it to a plot which also involves
politics and courtly intrigue, so that the one animates the other. His
idealized lovers are threatened, not by an opposite kind of love, but by the
more theatrically immediate danger of a lustful king. The result is a well-
plotted play using techniques from the professional stage rather than the
posturing of courtly drama. This professionalism includes the tendency to
over-complicate the plot to the point of farce, but every turn of the action
provides opportunity for virtuoso demonstrations of highmindedness.

   Suckling's skilled and easy handling of the theatrical forms which he took
over is shown by his ability to write both a tragic and a tragi-comic ending
for the play. In the tragic version of the play, the king is murdered by
mistake. Aglaura then plans to murder him in order to preserve her chastity
and kills her lover instead, dying of grief as a consequence. Each character is
given a moment of death with appropriately passionate speeches, and the
timing and pacing of the death-scenes shows a masterly control of the
medium. The tragi-comic finale, on the other hand, is contrived by
repentance and skilled doctoring, and Suckling's own amusement at his skill
is clear from his prologue to this version of the play. A courtier himself, he
could afford to patronize his courtly audience. In the prologue to the court
he advises:

> Gentlemen be thriftie, save your doomes
> For the next man, or the next Play that comes;
> For smiles are nothing, where men do not care,
> And frownes as little, where they need not feare. (ll. 13–16)

The play was performed at court with scenery by Inigo Jones, though none of the action requires scenic effects beyond the resources of the Blackfriars stage, where it was also performed by the King's Men.

Suckling's easy movement between the courtly and the professional theatre particularly enraged Richard Brome, whose sarcastic verses 'Upon *Aglaura* printed in Folio'[1] was only one of his side-swipes at the extravagant amateurs. However, Brome himself was not above exploiting the cult of platonic lovers for the benefit of the general public, in *The Lovesick Court* (1633–4). The uneven tone of the play makes it difficult to decide whether it is intended as imitation or parody of the courtly cult.[2] Like Suckling, Brome links his love theme to a plot of courtly intrigue featuring a king who is sickened by 'th'unquiet commons . . . with their impertinent discontents and strife'. The love action of the play, however, is clearly linked to romance with an appeal to an oracle to decide which of the ideal friends, Philocles and Philargus, should marry the lady Eudyna. The most clearly parodic elements in the play are in the low-life aping of platonic love (II.i), though the tirades on the conflicting claims of love and friendship are no more extreme in setting or expression than in many another Caroline play. Brome gives theatrical weight to his theme by his use of dumb show and elaborate emblematic spectacle, but its resolution emerges from adept plotting rather than the enacted motivation of the characters. There is no necessary connection between the king's political problems and the preoccupations of his courtiers, and the play is another version of the familiar romance form adapted to prevailing fashion.

A more pointed attack on the theory and practice of platonic love is to be found in a curious, anonymous play of disputed date, *The Lady Alimony* (1636–42). Professor Bentley suggests that the play proper is contained in the last four acts, Act I being an induction added at a later date.[3] The play is a straightforward attack on the hypocrisy which masqueraded as platonic love, and the prologue to Act II clearly states its anti-platonic sentiment, denouncing ladies

[1] Preface to *The Weeding of Covent Garden*.
[2] See Alfred Harbage, *Cavalier Drama* (New York, 1936), 158–9, and R. J. Kaufmann, *Richard Brome, Caroline Playwright* (New York, 1961), 109–30.
[3] *Jacobean and Caroline Stage*, V, 1362–3.

Who make free Traffick of their Nuptial Bed
As if they had of Fancy surfeited.

The action of the play, such as it is, concerns the efforts of a number of divorced ladies to get alimony from their husbands and sets the ladies' infatuation with courtiers against the sexual inadequacies of their marriage partners. The issues are presented in a series of dumb shows and set pieces in which the ladies complain about their unhappy marriages and engage in delighted dialogue with their courtly suitors. Some of the complaints about the husbands are pure bawdy, but some, like Lady Tinder's objections to her husband's adultery with prostitutes and the sexual humiliation to which she is subjected, strike a genuinely plaintive note which goes beyond the commonplaces of *risqué* comedy. The broadest comedy, however, comes in the parody of courtly language, which, together with the silliness of the names and the affectation of both courtiers and ladies, produces the most intense mockery of platonic hypocrisy.

The disorganized plot, with a completely irrelevant military expedition and a Puritan campaign against the Turk, prevents the play from making any statement either against the court or for it. Moreover, by the end, the ladies have lost all sympathy; they are parodied by a set of country women insisting on their right to 'ale money' (alimony!) and are eventually sent back to their husbands by the virtuous military Duke. In the absence of information about the play's authorship or the circumstances of performance, it is impossible to say if it was seriously conceived as propaganda against the court, but it does indicate the ability of popular drama to absorb and transform current fashion.

(iv) Thomas Heywood

The tension between old and new in Stuart drama is perhaps best illustrated in the work of Thomas Heywood, a hardy old professional who began his forty-year career under Henslowe and ended it as principal dramatist to the Queen's Men. The two parts of his *Fair Maid of the West* were written twenty years apart and their differences show how prevailing dramatic modes had changed. They were nevertheless both performed at court in 1630, which suggests a fairly catholic range of taste even in the courtly audience.

Part I (1597–1610) is a robust, episodic adventure story, dealing with

Bess's fidelity to her lover Spencer, her successful administration of his pub in Foy, and her heroic voyage against the Turk, ending, predictably, with the lovers' reunion. The dramatic style moves easily from fast blank verse and colloquial exchanges to set speeches of high passion like Bess's farewell to Spencer's picture (III.iv) or the affecting sentimentality of her will in favour of the town poor (IV.ii). Heywood uses dumb show and chorus to move the action along, and Bess's virtue and courage are emphasized throughout. Simple and direct devices ensure the audience's involvement. When Bess's chastity is threatened by Roughman the gallant, she responds with an immediate appeal to law and order, and a similar spirit of community is invoked in her preparations for the voyage:

> First, at my charge Ile feast the towne of Foy;
> Then set the Cellers ope, that these my Mates
> May quaffe unto the health of our boone voyage,
> Our needfull things being once convay'd aboard,
> Then casting up our caps in signe of joy,
> Our purpose is to bid farewell to Foy.
>   *Hoboyes* [*Hautboys*] *long.* (IV.ii.108–13)

If the simplicity and episodic nature of Part I lack intensity, Part II (1630) amply makes up for it. There the action turns on sexual passion and revenge, and the dramatic style with its tirades and its elaboration of suspense is directed to involving the audience's concern for carefully delineated absolutes of love and honour. At the end of Part I, Bess and Spencer were reunited at the court of Mullisheg, the ruler of Morocco; Part II opens with Mullisheg lusting after Bess, and his wife Tato seeking revenge. In the rhetorical questions of Tato's opening tirade, Heywood attempts to dramatize her mental agitation, to enact the passion for its own dramatic ends rather than as a motive for action. Later in the same scene Mullisheg tries to suborn one of Bess's followers to procure her for him. The poetic periphrases and the lengthy crescendos of the soliloquy in which the man considers the proposal are quite different in style from the direct reactions to be found in Part I. In the earlier play there is never any doubt that right will prevail; in Part II the conclusion is held in suspense while the maximum is wrung out of the situation. The emotional reaction is orchestrated through the dramatic structure of each scene, even when the outcome is assured. Scenes like the one in which Bess moralizes on an hourglass (III.ii), or Spencer promises never to make love to Bess again and she in turn that she will be revenged on him, are staples of Fletcherian tragi-comedy.

Heywood's popularity at court and his ability to handle new forms of tragi-comedy show a true professional versatility, but he remained an old-fashioned dramatist in both allegiance and style. In the prologue to *A Challenge for Beauty* (1634) he deplores the new influences on English drama in terms both patriotic and traditionalist:

> For where before great Patriots, Dukes and Kings
> Presented for some hie facinorious things,
> Were the Stage-Subject; now we strive to flie
> In their low pitch, who never could soare hie:
> For now the common argument intreats,
> Of puling Lovers, craftie Bawdes or cheates.

The play itself, despite its Caroline themes of love and honour, is built round that oldest of folk devices, the impossible task imposed on a virtuous lord, and the dramatization is at its liveliest when Heywood uses such well-tried formulae as a dialogue between a clown and a straight man (II.i), a disguise (III.i), and the emotional build-up to the totally expected reversal which concludes the plot.

Heywood's clearest commitment to the forms and ideology of his earlier plays is found in *The English Traveller* (1627), written for the Queen's Men. The prologue to the play attempts to present it as a new kind of drama, rejecting 'Song, Dance, Masque, to bumbaste out a Play', but its opposition of country and city, young and old, is firmly in the traditions of Jacobean citizen comedy. The traditional ideology is established in an early sequence in which the parasitical serving man, Reginald, cruelly expels the worthy country retainer, Robin, asserting:

> If thou be'st borne to Hedge, Ditch, Thrash and Plough
> And I to Revell, Banquet and Carrowse . . .
> > thinke it onely
> Thy ill, my good, our severall lots are cast,
> And both must be contented. (I.ii)

For the purposes of the action, however, Reginald becomes the classic witty servant, and a good deal of the comedy derives from his ingenious efforts to save his drunken young master from the justifiable wrath of his merchant father. Heywood's professional skills are seen in his simple but effective use of the stage, as in the scene where Reginald is comically trapped: '*Enter at one doore an Usurer and his Man, at the other Old Lionell with his servant. In the midst Reginald*' (III.i). Some concession to absolutes of love and honour is made in the subplot of Young Geraldine's adulterous passion for Wincott's wife, but dramatic suspense is much more frequently directed to comic ends and even this plot turns on the more old-fashioned imperatives of filial piety. At the end of the play the young are repentant, the old forgiving and the villain rides away: the comic order which is restored has none of the tense ambiguity of contemporary tragi-comedy.

(v) The open-air theatres

Heywood's continued ease with old-fashioned dramatic form may have been due to the fact that in working for Beeston at the Cockpit he had not moved significantly upmarket from his earlier position as principal dramatist at the Red Bull. Carew links the two theatres in his commendatory verses to Davenant's *The Just Italian* (1629) when he complains that the unreceptive audience 'still slight / All that exceeds Red Bull and Cockpit flight'. This denigration of audience taste was an attempt to claim for Davenant the twin attributes of exclusiveness and modernity, and reflects the continued rivalry between the two traditions in the theatre. This rivalry was more commercial than artistic. T. J. King, in an analysis of 276 plays, has shown that 'there were no significant differences in the staging requirements of the various companies'[1] and Anne Jennalie Cook has concluded that the social composition of all theatre audiences was substantially the same, consisting of the 'privileged' of all classes who had money to spare from basic necessities, together with an exploiting sub-class of prostitutes, vendors and thieves such as might be found at any large social gathering.[2] Nevertheless, the cultural fact remains that differences were perceived and insisted upon. In the Praeludium to a revival of Goffe's *The Careless Shepherdess* (1638),[3] Thrift, a citizen, Spark, an Inns of Court man, and a 'Country Gentleman' discuss the forthcoming play: their comments provide a paradigm of the conflicts within the contemporary audience. Spark dismisses the taste of the other two, who 'did nothing understand but fools and fighting', and adds: 'The Motley Coat was banished with Trunk

---

[1] T.J. King, 'Shakespearean Staging 1599–1642', in *The Elizabethan Theatre*, III, ed. David Galloway (London, 1973), 8.
[2] Anne Jennalie Cook, 'The Audience of Shakespeare's Plays: A Reconsideration', *Shakespeare Studies*, 7 (1974), 283–306.
[3] Reprinted in *The Seventeenth Century Stage*, ed. G. E. Bentley (Chicago, 1968), 28–37.

Hose / And since their wits grew sharp, the Swords are sheathed.' The Country Gentleman 'would have the fool in every act', and Thrift for his part leaves the theatre after the prologue, resolving to go 'to the Bull or Fortune, and there see a Play for two pense with a Jig to boot'. The divisions in the dialogue are too suspiciously tidy for historical evidence but they focus the conflict between chronology and style. The fashion for 'fools and fighting' clearly persisted, but the sophisticated at least *claimed* to prefer wit to weapons.

The private indoor theatres had become associated with sophistication in the early years of the century when the boy players acted there.[1] Their claim to exclusiveness rested on their higher prices and a drama characterized by witty and parodic satire. The audience was thus assured both of its social superiority and of its critical discrimination in appreciating the mockery of older revenge drama in Marston's *Antonio's Revenge* (1599–1601) or Jonson, Chapman and Marston's *Eastward Ho* (1605). Moreover, the smaller stages of the indoor theatres and the closer proximity of the audience worked against the large effects of procession and show which had been used at the Fortune and the Globe, so that even when the indoor theatres were taken over by adult companies a distinction of dramatic style persisted.

Indeed, the principal distinction between open-air and enclosed theatres seems to have been one of dramaturgy rather than ideology. Even such fashionable dramatists as Fletcher and Massinger could, when commercial need arose, turn their hand to the open-air theatre style. *The Prophetess* (1622), written by them for the Globe, presents its formulaic action through a series of grand theatrical effects laid on by the prophetess Delphia. She enters (II.3) on a 'Throne drawn by Dragons' and provides heavenly music as an accompaniment to the Emperor's coronation, as well as thunder and lightning of disapproval when he woos Flavia. By Act IV the plot has become so complicated that explanatory action has to be provided in dumb show, and in Act V the story is further clarified by a Chorus.

However, the artistic consensus was to move away from the drama of dumb show and noise. Bentley writes: 'By 1620 at the latest most of the [King's] company's extant new plays were prepared for Blackfriars, and when there was a slip in the arrangements, prologues and epilogues are sometimes very frank in their statement of the inferiority of the Globe.'[2]

[1] See Michael Shapiro, *Children of the Revels* (New York, 1977), and H. N. Hillebrand, *The Child Actors* (Urbana, Ill., 1926).
[2] *Jacobean and Caroline Stage*, VI, 193.

12 'A Fantastic Umbrageous Lover', 1631

13 'Hog-headed man', 1632

14 'An airy spirit', 1635

Four Antimasquers by Inigo Jones

15 'John of Leyden', 1638

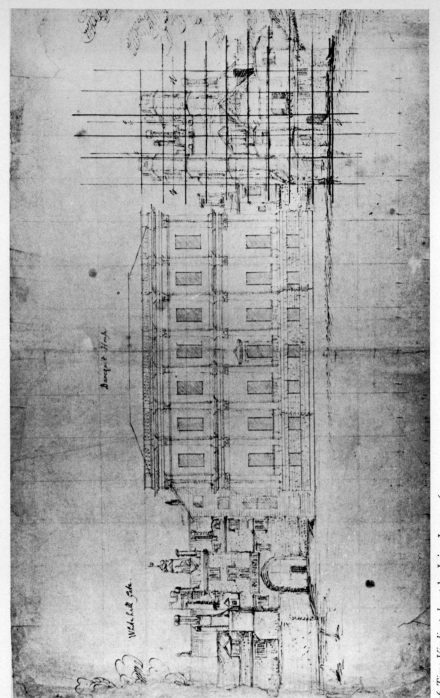

16 *Time Vindicated*, set by Inigo Jones, 1623

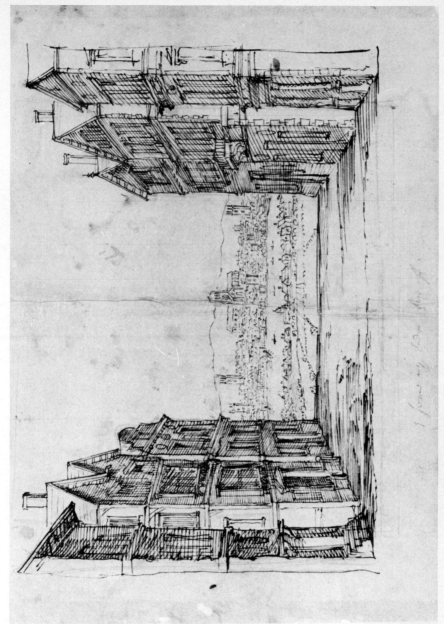

17 *Britannia Triumphans*, set by Inigo Jones, 1638

18 *Albion's Triumph*, masque costume, 1632

19 *Chloridia*, masque costume, 1631

20 Henrietta Maria, *c*. 1632

21 *Arténice*, set by Inigo Jones, 1626

Basilino.

·71·

22 *Shepherd's Paradise*, 1633, costume for Basilino (to be played by a woman)

23 Interior setting for a play, by Inigo Jones

24 *Queen of Aragon*, set by Inigo Jones, 1640

25 John Fletcher

26 James Shirley

A King and no King.

Acted at the *Globe*, by his Maie-
sties Seruants:

Written by *Francis Beamount*, and *Iohn Fletcher.*

AT LONDON
Printed for *Thomas Walkley*, and are to bee sold
at his shoppe at the Eagle and Childe in
Brittans-Burse. 1619.

27 *A King and No King*, 1619

A MAD DESIGNE: OR, A Description of the King of Scots marching in his Disguise, after the Rout at *Worcester*, With the Particulers where He was, and what He and his Company did, every day and night after He fled from *WORCESTER*.

I.

CHARLES STUART sits upon the Globe, in a melancholly posture, between hope and fear, hee fixeth his eyes upon *Brittainy* and *Ireland*, and viewes not onely Europe, but the world in a landskip, and hath both Pope, Cardinall and the Fryers Pouch, tyed to his Girdle by imagination.

II. The Bishop of *Clogher*, Generall to the Scots King in *Ireland*, at *Masse*, with the Marquesse of *Ormond*, and the Lord *Inchequeen* attending with Torches at the Altar upon him, and the Lord *Taaffe* holding up his train.

III. The Scots Army consisting of four parties and Factions. 1. Papists, represented by the Cardinall and his troop in the Van, whereof the Marquesse of *Huntley* is Generall. 2. Prelaticall Malignants, represented by the Bishop and *Callis*, and that fry, the Generall of which was the Duke of *Buckingham*. 3 Presbyterians represented by the two burning Torches, one of English Fugitives, the other of Scottish brethren, that came for our gueds, the two Generalls of which are Major Generall *Massey*, and the Earle of *Leven*. And 4. Old Cavaliers, represented by the fooles head upon a pole in the Rear, whereof the Earle of *Derby* hath been Generall, and the foole upon an Hobby-horse; wherein the Earle of *Cleaveland* hath been his Competitor.

IV. The two ridiculous Anticks one with a Fiddle, and the other with a Torch, set forth the ridiculousnesse of their condition when they marched into *England*, carried up with high thoughts yet altogether in the darke, having onely a fooles bawble to be their light to walke by, mirth of their own whimsies to keep up their spirits, and a sheathed sword to trust in. And a fooles cap was the best peece they had to make them merry with, as appeared by severall intercepted Letters from Duke *Hamilton*, the Earle of *Lauderdale*, and others.

V. Lamenting posture of Ladies, Papists, Children, and Scotch women resemble the rout at *Worcester* on the third of *September* 1651. bemoaning the sad conditions of themselves, and their unhappy Cause, and unfortunate Hesbands, Fathers, and friends.

VI. The Scots Kings flight from Worcester represented by the Foole on Horse-back, riding backward, turning his face every way in feares, ushered by *Duke Hambleton* and the Lord *Wilmot*, the particulers of which perambulation was thus.

1 While he called upon Duke *Hambleton* to stirre up his men, to keep the Royall Fort at Worcester, September 3. himselfe gave the slip to his Lodging, and fetched away the richest Treasure he could presently come at.

2 Whilst Major *Cobbet* was entring on the one side of his House, he escaped out at a back doore on the other, and about seven a clock that night with a party of Horse posted away from Worcester, flying towards Scotland.

3 The next day being September 4th. *Charles Stuart* the Scots King, with the Duke of *Buckingham* and the Lord *Wilmot* came to a Country mans house in Cheshire that stood alone, and asked for Victuals; the man told them he had none fit to entertaine his Majesty, but if they pleased to light, he would get what the Country would afford; but seeing themselves discovered they were afraid, and yet being very hungry and dry, asked for any thing they had, and some cold powthered Beefe was brought to them; the Scots King drunke off a Flaggon of Beere, and with a peece of Bread in one hand, and of Beefe in the other, the others also having got each a slice away they all rid, and that morning marched into the borders of Lancashire, and all that day after lay close in a hollow Tree, turning loose their Horses at a farre distance before they came to the place where they resided.

4 On the fourth of September at night, they came like so many Hermits, or *Diogenes's* out of their Tubs, and went a Pilgrimage all that night on foot,

5 The next day, Septemb. 5. they betooke themselves to hide them in a Wood, and got among Thickets to hide themselves as well as they could, and got some Hips and Hawes, and such things as they could conveniently get (without venturing too farre) in the Wood, where every noyse put them into a feare of being surprized.

6 On the fifth of September at night they went on their journey.

7 On the sixth of September, they came early in the morning to a Shepherds Tent, which they surprised, and called to the Shepherd, who when he had opened the doores, they kept him in the House, and would not let him goe out, nor his Wife, but discoursed about the Gentry thereabouts, by meanes whereof they came to know that a Lady in which they had some confidence lived neare, whither they hasted with all speed; and the Lord *Wilmote* comming to the doore got admittance to the Lady, and prevailed with her to give them all possible assistance; and the Scots King being come to the Lady, and having saluted her, they sate in Counsell to consider how the businesse should be ordered, and it was agreed, and accordingly done.

1 *That they should have their haire cut in the Country fashion, like plaine Country Fellowes, which was done accordingly.*

2 *That they should weare plaine Country fashioned cloathes, which were presently got for them.*

3 *That they should be reputed to be Servants to the said Lady.*

4 *That in this pretence she should goe with them to Bristol, or some other Port, to endeavour the transporting of them beyond the Seas.*

8 On the seaventh and eighth dayes of September they lay there, and waited on the Lady in severall offices, and places, and the Scots King himselfe stood bare before her when he waited on her, as well as the rest.

9 On the ninth of September, they tooke an intended voyage for Bristol, and the Scots King rid before the Lady on one Horse, the Duke of *Buckingham* before her Gentlewoman upon another Horse, and the Lord *Wilmot* as her Groome upon an Horse by himselfe.

10 About the middle of September they got to Bristol, but they heard in their Inne so great talke what search was made after them, that they presently tooke Horse, not daring to stay there, and away they came for London.

11 About the twentyeth of September they got to London, and went abroad sometimes in the mornings, and at evenings, but generally lay very close all day, and the Scots King and *Wilmot* waited upon the Lady at one Lodging, and the Duke of *Buckingham* waited as a Serving-man to the Gentlewoman at another.

12 About the latter end of September, the Scots King with the Lady came to see his Souldiers in the Tuttle Fields at Westminster, and the Lady threw them some monies, but they stayed not.

13 Another day the Scots King came into Westminster Hall, and viewed the States Armes over the places of Judicatory, and viewed the Scots Colours hanging on both sides the Hall, that were taken from his Father, and from him.

14 The Lord *Wilmot* procured a Merchant to hire a ship of forty tuns to transport them, which cost them 120. l.

15. About the middle of October having taken leave of, and thanked the Lady, with many salutations and promises, to Graves-end they went, and from thence on, and a shipboard.

16 As soon as my Lord was entred the Barque, and the King as his Servant; the Master of the Vessell came to my Lord, and told him, that he knew the King, and told him, That in case it should be known he could expect no mercy; which saying troubled them: But at length what with mony and promises, they prevailed, and so set saile for *Havre de Grace*, where they landed; and from thence to *Roven*, where they cloathed themselves, and writ to *Paris*.

17 The late Queen of *England* his Mother receiving an expresse from him, made present supplication to the King of *France* for his reception, in which the Queen Mother was no little active with her, and so he was permitted, and an Expresse sent to the Duke of *Orleans* for instructions therein.

18 Answer was returned back to appoint him *Jesse* by the way of *Rhoane*, and some supplyes of money from his Mother was sent to him; for his better accommodation in the way.

19 The Scots King being upon his march sent an Expresse, giving many thanks for the courtesie, and informing his intentions to be at *Magny* the 28 (*alias* 18) *October*: and hee being advertised that there should bee provisions made for him at the *Louver*, he sent word that he intended the 29 (*alias* 19 present) to goe from *Magny* thither. On the said 28 of *October*, (which was the Saturday) the Scots King had laine the night then past within a dayes journey of *Magny*; from whence came an Expresse to his Royall Highnesse the Duke of *Orleance*, as also Letters from his Mother.

20 The Duke of *Orleance* sent forth some Coaches from *Paris*, to meet him at *Magny*, where he lay that night.

21 And the next day being the Lords Day, the Scots King came to *Paris*, being met a little from the Townes end by the Duke of *Orleance* and some others. His Highnesse the Duke of *Orleance* conducted the Scots King through part of the City to the Louver, but with no small discontent of the Citizens, who are some of them ready to mutiny about it, and yet many flocked to see him, and amongst those divers mocked and jeered; so that the great resort seemed to be rather in derision and scorn, then out of any good will.

His Mother knew so well the dis-affections of the people, that she did not come along at all with him, nor did meet him, untill she heard that he was come to the Louver, and then presently she repaired to him.

She hath spent most part of her time of late about the raising of a Fabrick at *Chaliot*, for the making of a Nunnery, from whence she now came to visit her son.

22 There was then a grave Councell held at the *Louver*, of the Scots King, the Duke of *Orleance*, the late Queene of *England*, and some others, who after some complements, required a Narrative of the English Affaires, the relation whereof produced some laughter, at the rediculousnesse of his condition.

23 The Substance of the Scots Kings Speech.

The Scots King told them what happened at the fight at Worcester, *gave some repraachful words against the* Scots, *put some scurrilous language on the Presbyterian party in* England, *and boasted much of his own valour.*

Told them how hee slipt out of Worcester, *and how near he was taking there, first in the Fort, and after in his Chamber:*

How he disguised himselfe and went from County to County, and what shift he made for victualls and lodging.

Sometimes being driven to beg a peece of bread and meat, and ride with bread in one hand and meat in the other.

And sometimes setting a Guard about a little Cottage while hee rested there untill the morning. That he went up and down London, *in a Gentlewomans habit, where he saith, he never saw handsomer Coaches then they have now; that he met with severall persons that wished him no harme, and that at last he got to the Sea-coast, and there imbarqued himselfe for this Coast, in a Boat that my Lord* Wilmot *had provided and hired beforehand. He said he knew nothing what was become of the Duke of* Buckingham; *and that he had no other Company or Followers but the said* Wilmot, *since he landed. He said further, that he was never in better health having got no harm at all in the fight.*

24 *Ormond* and *Inchequin* are sent for from Caen, my Lord *Taaffe* from Holland, who hath been Treating with *Loraine* to undertake the businesse of Ireland, which is all agreed on, if the King will consent that *Loraine* shall have the Title of Protector, and the Towne of Lymrick, a cautionary Garrison for his Souldiers. Upon these conditions he hath undertaken to land six thousand Horse and Foot before Christmas in Ireland. *Taaffe* hath already received twenty thousand Pistols, and about fourteen dayes since a small Vessel was sent to Lymrick, to assure them of assistance.

25 Some are of opinion that the King shall suddenly make a marriage with *Madamaiselle*, the Queen having treated much about it of late.

VII. The late Queen of England his Mother, with the Dukes of *Orleance*, *Guise*, *Beaufort*, and *Thurenne*, with divers Priests, and Nuns, came to visite him at the *Louver* in *Paris*, where after they had had conference with, and lamented him, they tooke their leave and returned; the Lords to the Court, and his Mother with her Fry to *Chaliot*, where she is erecting a Nunnery.

FINIS.

LONDON
Printed by *Robert Ibbitson*.
1651.
November 6.

28 'A Mad Designe', 1651

Changling

Simpleton

Sr I Falstafe

Hostes

French Dancing Mr.

Clause

29 *The Wits, or Sport upon Sport*, title page, 1662

A new

PLAY

Called

CANTERBURIE

His

Change of Diot.

Which sheweth variety of wit and mirth : privately acted neare
the *Palace-yard* at Westminster.

In th { 1 Act, the Bishop of Canterbury having variety of dainties, is not
satisfied till he be fed with tippets of mens eares.
2 Act, he hath his nose held to the Grinde-stone.
3 Act, he is put into a birdCage with the Confessor.
4 Act, The Jester tells the King the Story.

Printed Anno Domini, 1641.

30 *Canterbury, His Change of Diet*, title page, 1641

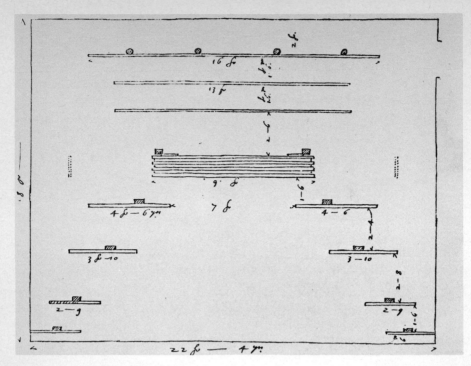

31 Plan of the stage at Rutland house

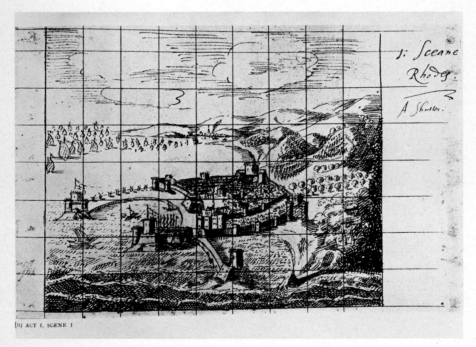

32 Siege of Rhodes, set by Webb, 1656

Shirley's prologue to *The Doubtful Heir*, which the King's Men performed in 1640, warns the audience that there are to be

> No shews, no dance, and what you most delight in,
> Grave understanders, here's no target fighting
> Upon the Stage, all work for Cutlers barr'd,
> No bawdery, nor no Ballets [ballads]; this goes hard; . . .
> Without impossibilities the Plot,
> No clown, no squibs, no Devill in't. . . .

This prologue could be read as a kind of reverse flattery, assuring the audience of the excellence of their taste in attending a play which offered none of these old-fashioned devices. But Shirley's kind of intimate personal drama, with its interior settings and its close psychological effects, was much better suited to the smaller stage of the enclosed theatres.

Even the players at the open-air theatres tried to participate in the latest fashionable style. The prologue to *The Two Merry Milkmaids* (1619), performed at the Red Bull, tells the audience that they are to

> Expect no noyse of Guns, Trumpets nor Drum
> No Sword and Target, but to heare Sense and Words
> Fitting the Matter that the Scene affords.

Professor Bentley has suggested that, since this was the first play to be produced under the new management of the Company of the Revels, the prologue may represent an effort to elevate the taste of the Red Bull audience.[1] It certainly recommends that, as the play contains less noise, the spectators might perform their side of the bargain by calming down a little, but it by no means rejects the most popular elements of traditional drama:

> For we have in't a coniurer, A Deuill,
> And a Clowne too; but I feare the euill
> In which perhaps unwisely we may faile
> Of wanting Squibs and Crackers at their taile.

The Two Merry Milkmaids is unevenly constructed but contains powerful local effects. The clowns are given full scope in such set pieces as a wooing lesson and the opportunities for trickery afforded by a ring which makes one invisible, but there are also passages of fine poetry in the Duke's enraptured acceptance of Dorigene's love and the powerful rhetoric of her defence when

---

[1] *Jacobean and Caroline Stage*, III, 102.

she is tried for adultery. The ideology of this romance action is not significantly different from that of the private theatre plays. The opening scenes of the play derive some comedy from the conflict between court and country, but the merry milkmaids turn out to be gentlewomen and there is no loss of decorum in one of them marrying a Duke.

Other plays from the Red Bull display a similar formulaic handling of available characters and plots. The satiric malcontent appears as Misogenos in *Swetnam the Woman Hater* (1617–18) and a lustful Turk creates the tragic potential for *The Two Noble Ladies* (1619–23), though his stratagems are thwarted by a conjurer. The theatrical effects are certainly very broad. *The Honest Lawyer*, produced by Queen Anne's Men in 1616, achieves its comedy through 'humours' characters like Nice and Thirsty and such well-worn but effective *commedia* turns as the mock doctor who cures his patient's gout by nailing his foot to the stage and making off with his purse. Moreover, the very full stage directions of *The Two Noble Ladies* suggest an acting style which similarly depended on stylized gesture. The conjurer Cyprian intervenes at a number of crucial and dangerous moments so that '*The guard stands fixed, their eyes rowling from the King to Cyprian, and so to and fro*' (l. 480 S.D.), or a potential enemy '*stands fixed in a posture of running at him with his sword*' (l. 490 S.D.).

A good deal of the later public theatre repertory is lost, but in what remains the plots continue to turn on money and sex, and there is little evidence of a coherent counter-culture appealing to a lower-class social group. What is clear is that mockery of the Red Bull and the Fortune provided the élite companies with a means of reinforcing the image of their own superiority, and by implication that of their sophisticated audience. Sophistication meant innovation, but the interaction between old and new, élite and popular, provided much of the variety and energy of Stuart drama.

3 Collaboration

In his introduction to the published text of *Sejanus* (1605), Ben Jonson confesses that 'this book, in all numbers, is not the same with that which was acted on the public stage wherein a second pen had a good share'. In his insistence on the artistic autonomy of the tragic writer, Jonson repudiated the common theatrical practice of his time in which plays were seldom seen as the considered artistic expression of a single gifted individual. Bentley points out that 'as many as half of the plays by professional dramatists in the period [1599–1625] incorporated the writing at some date of more than one man.'[1] The Jacobean dramatists collaborated for the same reason as Hollywood scriptwriters: they were the employees of a booming entertainment industry which demanded a steady output of actable material from which a repertory could be built. The repertories of the acting companies, in turn, established the conventions on which collaborations could be based. The most successful collaborations were thus among dramatists who shared the same theatrical experience and assumptions.

The usual practice was, it seems, to assign different plots or acts for each contributor to work on independently. In evidence at the lawsuit which

[1] G. E. Bentley, *The Profession of Dramatist in Shakespeare's Time, 1590–1642* (Princeton, N.J., 1971), 199.

followed the production of *The Late Murder of the Son upon the Mother, or Keep the Widow Waking* (1624), Dekker claimed: 'Hee wrote two sheetes of paper conteyning the first Act . . . and a speech in the Last Scene of the Last Act.'[1] Presumably his collaborators, Ford, Rowley and Webster, were allotted similar tasks.

The need for speed is most evident in the plays which cashed in on the box-office appeal of a recent scandal, like *The Jeweller of Amsterdam* (1617) by Fletcher, Field and Massinger, or *Sir John van Olden Barnaveldt* (1619), which was written, acted, censored and acted again within six weeks of the Dutch patriot's trial and execution. By 1625 the number of collaborations had dwindled, since the players could draw on a substantial repertory of old plays, but in 1634 the scandal of the Lancashire witch trials brought collaborators together again. Within a year of the trial, Heywood and Brome had written *The Late Lancashire Witches* and the powerful King's Men petitioned the Revel's office 'complayning of intermingleing some passages of witches in old playes to ye pʳiudice of their designed Comedy of the Lancashire witches, & desiring a prohibition of any other till theirs bee allowed & Acted.'[2]

Yet these were no botched jobs. In 1621 a three-way collaboration between Ford, Rowley and Dekker produced a play, *The Witch of Edmonton*, within nine months of the publication of *The Wonderful Discovery of Eliz[abeth] Sawyer a witch late of Edmonton*. Despite the speedy and fragmented conditions of composition, the play achieves a remarkable unity. There are three distinct actions involving different sets of characters, but since each is concerned with the effects of evil forces their juxtaposition creates a cross-current of irony which is no less powerful for being perhaps fortuitous. The Devil appears in each action in the figure of a black dog, but the device is treated in different ways by each dramatist, showing the potential variety inherent in the simplest convention.

Rowley's part in the play deals with Cuddy Banks, the charming if simple-minded hobby-horse of the Edmonton morris team. He asks the witch to make Katherine Carter in love with him and is ducked in the stream by a spirit disguised as his love. This innocuous conjuring was evidently a popular moment in the play and is depicted in the woodcut title page of the first edition. Rowley takes it beyond mere slapstick, stressing the innocence of Cuddy's strightforward friendliness: 'you shall have Jowls and Livers: I

---

[1] *Jacobean and Caroline Stage*, III, 255.
[2] ibid., III, 73.

have Butchers to my Friends that shall bestow 'em: and I will keep Crusts and Bones for you, if you'll be a kinde Dog, *Tom*.' (III.i. 118–20).

Dekker, on the other hand, treats witchcraft with serious psychological attention. Mother Sawyer's opening soliloquy fully expresses the pain and anger of a social outcast:

> why should the envious world
> Throw all their scandalous malice upon me?
> 'Cause I am poor, deform'd and ignorant,
> And like a Bow buckl'd and bent together,
> By some more strong in mischiefs then my self?
> Must I for that be made a common sink,
> For all the filth and rubbish of Men's tongues
> To fall and run into? (II.i. 1–7)

She is then beaten by Old Banks and teased by the youths of the morris team until she seems fully justified in her vow that:

> would some power good or bad
> Instruct me which way I might be reveng'd
> Upon this Churl, I'd go out of my self,
> And give this Fury leave to dwell within. (II.i. 102–5)

For her, the Black Dog is the vengeful analogue to her oppressor:

> this Miser, this black Cur,
> That barks, and bites, and sucks the very blood
> Of me, and of my credit. (II.i. 111–13)

and she uses its power for more serious ends.

In Ford's plot, Frank Thorney carries full moral responsibility for murdering his bigamous wife, Susan, but the Black Dog none the less appears at the crucial moment, seeming to precipitate the almost casual violence of the action itself. By this stage we have seen how evil interacts with the personality of the evil-doer and the contrasts between the different scale of evil actions in the three plots provide a thematic coherence for the play. A further coherence is assured by the details of provincial life which each action provides. The story of Cuddy Banks bewitching the fiddler at Frank and Susan's wedding, and the scene in which Mother Sawyer is blamed for Anne Ratcliffe's madness, have no narrative connection but they combine to build up a picture of a community severely disrupted and disturbed by the evil in its midst. This aspect of the play is most fully developed by Ford. His section deals with the complications which follow Frank's marriage to Winifred without his father's consent. With characteristic dramatic irony, Ford has Frank appeal for support to his employer, Sir Arthur, who is then revealed himself to have seduced Winifred. Ford's interest here seems less in the dramatic conflict than in exploring relationships of class and dependence which both sustain and constrict his characters.

Sir Arthur's deviousness is contrasted in the following scene with the straightforward dealing of self-consciously honest yeomen:

> OLD THORNEY.   You offer Mr *Carter*, like a Gentleman,
>   I cannot finde fault with it, 'tis so fair.
> OLD CARTER.   No Gentleman, I, Mr *Thorney*; spare the Mastership,
>   call me by my name *John Carter*; Master is a title my Father, nor his
>   before him, were acquainted with. Honest *Hertfordshire* Yeomen,
>   such a one am I; my word and my deed shall be proved one at all
>   times. (i.ii.1–8)

The contrast carries no sentimental certainties, for the older men's bargain intensifies Frank's plight, in contracting him to marry Carter's daughter in return for the money which will save Thorney's land. The familiar conflict between money and love transcends mere plot: the loss of money is made dramatically real in Thorney's speech describing his financial situation (i.ii. 124–46) so that the irony of Frank's entry into the festive scene is the more intense because of our awareness of the social and economic expectations which stand behind the welcome he receives.

The potential for complicated plotting in this imbroglio is not developed at all. Further evidence of the community's suspicion of strangers is seen when two visiting gentlemen are blamed for murdering Susan, but Ford otherwise concentrates on creating sympathy for his characters in the beautiful language with which Frank woos Susan (ii.ii) or the poignancy of Carter's reaction to her death:

> I'll not own her now; she's none of mine.
> Bob me off with a dumb shew? No, I'll have life.
> This is my Son too, and while there's life in him,
> 'Tis half mine (iii.iii.100–3)

The final scene of the play takes place in London, where both Mother Sawyer and Frank are taken for trial and execution. Frank is sent to the gallows, though he redeems himself in a moving plea for forgiveness.

Mother Sawyer is condemned too, and Sir Arthur let off with a fine for his part. But the final word rests with Old Carter, who once again asserts the values of country life:

> Come, come, if luck had served, *Sir Arthur*, and every man had his due, somebody might have totter'd ere this, without paying Fines: like it as you list. Come to me *Winnifride*, shalt be welcome: make much of her, *Kate*, I charge you: I do not think but she's a good Wench, and hath had wrong as well as we. So let's every man home to *Edmonton* with heavy hearts, yet as merry as we can, though not as we would. (v.iii.162–8)

The remarkable unity of tone which the play achieves results from the fact that each of the collaborators came from the same old-fashioned theatrical milieu. Dekker was the oldest of the trio and had been successful in the Elizabethan theatre with good-humoured citizen comedies such as *The Shoemakers' Holiday* (1599). Rowley began his career with the Prince Charles's Men who played at the Red Bull, and later collaborated with Middleton for the King's Men.[1] Ford seems to have worked under Dekker's tutelage in the early 1620s.

In *The Virgin Martyr* (1620), the same homogeneity could not be expected: Dekker's collaborator, Massinger, was more closely involved than he with the new dramatic style of psychological confrontation. The fact that the play was written for the Red Bull theatre may account for such large-scale effects as the procession of Jupiter (III.ii) or the appearance of Harpax's ghost '*in a fearfull shape, fire flashing out of the study*' (v.i.123 S.D.). The story of Dorothea the martyr and her Roman persecutor Theophilus is dramatized both as a clash of personalities and as an old-fashioned psychomachia, complete with a guardian angel called Angelo. The first kind of action produces verbal set pieces like the conversion of Theophilus' daughters; the other relies on more old-fashioned staples like the comic vices' clown routines (III.iii) or the appearance of Angelo bearing fruit and flowers from the garden of Eden (v.i.) Though one must bear in mind Bowers's caution about determining the specific contribution of each dramatist,[2] it does seem that the more old-fashioned dramatic effects occur in the scenes generally thought to be by Dekker.

---

[1] Though the Middleton–Rowley collaborations are among the most famous of the period, Middleton dominates them so completely that it seems preferable to consider them separately. See pp. 216–20.

[2] Introduction to *The Virgin Martyr* in *The Dramatic Works of Thomas Dekker*, ed. F. T. Bowers, 4 vols (Cambridge, 1953–61), III, 368.

The difference in styles is not simply one of speech versus action. Massinger is responsible for the striking visual effect of the procession: '*Enter Priest with the Image of Iupiter, Incense and Censors, followed by* Caliste, *and* Christeta, *leading* Dorothea' (III.ii.31 S.D.). He uses it, however, to create suspense, leading up to the volte-face when Theophilus' daughters '*spit at the Image, throw it downe, and spurne it*'. His spectacle produces not only variety but also a visual summary of the preceding action, providing dramatic motivation for the daughters' execution on stage. Massinger also wrote a scene (IV.i) in which first Antoninus, Dorothea's suitor, and then a slave, are urged to rape her on stage. The material is once again used for suspense and moral display rather than mere sensationalism. Antoninus refuses at the crucial moment and even the slave reveals himself too noble to commit such a devilish act. Compared with these, Dekker's effects are in no way more sensational but they follow the pattern of conventional martyrology in presenting cruel actions which shock the audience and also demonstrate the wickedness of Dorothea's persecutors. In Act IV, scene ii, she is whipped on stage and in Act IV, scene iii, beheaded, but the sheer sadism of these stage effects is mitigated by the preceding contest between the good angel, Angelo, and Theophilus, the secular representative of evil.

The clearer religious inspiration of Dekker's part of the play also provides him with the imagery for fine poetic speeches. His presentation of Dorothea owes something to another martyr, the Duchess of Malfi, but her faith springs from something more than firmness of character. Confronting Theophilus she asserts:

> The visage of a hangman frights not me;
> The sight of whips, rackes, gibbets, axes, fires
> Are scaffoldings, by which my soule climbes vp
> To an Eternell habitation. (II.iii.166–9)

Angelo's eleventh hour conversion of Theophilus promises to bring him to:

> a Riuer that shall wash
> Thy bloudy hands cleane, and more white then Snow,
> And to that Garden where these blest things grow,
> And to that martyr'd Virgin, who hath sent
> That heauenly token to thee. (V.i.159–63)

Massinger's Dorothea displays the much more secular virtue of chastity, and her defence of Christianity takes the form of an attack on the lusts of the pagan gods, which owes more to Ovid than to Christian martyrlogy:

> Yet *Venus* whom you worship was a whore,
> *Flora* the Foundresse of the publike Stewes,
> And has for that her sacrifice: your great god,
> Your *Iupiter*, a loose adulterer,
> Incestuous with his sister, reade but those
> That have canoniz'd them, youle find them worse
> Then in chast language I can speake them to you. (III.i.139–45)

The local effects achieved by each dramatist are equally powerful; the differences of emphasis do not create damaging inconsistency since they are linked by a strong narrative line. They do, however, indicate the relative autonomy of each partner within a collaboration to write the kind of drama to which he is most accustomed.

The smoothest and most successful collaborations achieved by the great King's Men team centred on Fletcher. His work with Beaumont before 1613 includes some of Fletcher's most successful plays, *The Maid's Tragedy*, *Philaster* and *A King and No King*, and the unusual intimacy in which Beaumont and Fletcher composed these plays is noted by many of the writers of commendatory verses to the First Folio:

> Both brought Your Ingots, Both toil'd at the Mint,
> Beat, melted, sifted, till no drosse stuck in't,
> Then in each Others scales weigh'd every graine,
> Then smooth'd and burnish'd, then weigh'd all againe,
> Stamp't Both your Names upon't by one bold Hit,
> Then, then 'twas Coyne, as well Bullion-Wit.

Even if we make allowance for poetic licence, Berkenhead's lines suggest a degree of co-operation which went beyond simply dividing the scenes for comedy.

There is no comparable evidence about the closeness of Field and Massinger's working relationship with Fletcher, but they none the less achieved a similar coherence because of a similar commitment to the demands of the new theatrical style. Some of the plays left a plot unresolved – *Love's Pilgrimage* (1616) – or a character differently named in different portions of the play – *The Knight of Malta* (1616–18) – but most of them display a stylish dovetailing of the different plots to create suspense and variety as well as a mechanically even division of labour.

A common feature of the new drama was its organization in space rather than time, together with a minimum of attention given to motivation. Events arise from chance encounters, making it easier to form a plot out of scenes written quite separately. Moreover, simple plot coherence is beside the point. There is often suspense about how – and even whether – the various strands will ever be knotted, as the plays present their dazzling variety of star turns.

Act I of Fletcher and Massinger's *The Custom of the Country* (1619–20) turns on the familiar romance theme of a lustful ruler in pursuit of a maiden's virginity, in this case supported by the custom of *jus primae noctis*. Fletcher wrote the opening act with accustomed verve, involving the audience's sympathies first with a sequence in which Zenocia, after passionately repudiating her lover's accommodating willingness to accept her even without her virginity, wittily rejects the Count's proposal to make an honest woman of her and forgo all future exercise of his rights. The full emotional impact of the dilemma is then exploited in the moving anti-epithalamium, 'no masque but murdered honour', which Zenocia's father prepares for her wedding night. The stage is strewn 'with withered flowers, your Autumn sweets/By the hot Sun ravisht of bud and beauty', and the bridal bed is hung with black. The prepared masque then provides a perfect reversal when the masquers – her lover Arnoldo and his friend Rutilio – abduct the bride and escape by sea, hotly pursued by the thwarted Count.

With all the skill of a Hollywood serial writer, Fletcher then drops this plot. Act II, by Massinger, introduces the entirely different world of the lady Guiomar, whose problems with her braggart son Duarte make up the action of the second plot. The two plots are then joined in space as first Zenocia, and then Arnoldo and Rutilio, arrive separately in the same place, having been attacked by pirates. Arnoldo is led off to attempted seduction by Hippolyta, a nymphomaniac who has also become Zenocia's employer, while Rutilio becomes involved in yet another plot by first killing Duarte in a brawl, then being sheltered by Duarte's mother, finally ending up employed in a male brothel. Acts III and IV are a masterpiece of collaboration in which the action cuts from one set of characters to another in a dazzling series of set pieces displaying their discomfiture. The unabashed contrivance of the plots makes it impossible to be concerned with either the moral or the emotional issues, and the audience can simply enjoy the comic possibilities of Hippolyta's attempt to seduce Arnoldo, or the outrageous star turn in which Rutilio, exhausted by overwork and surfeit in the brothel, encounters the skeletal figures ('*3 with Nightcaps very faintly*') of his predecessors in the job. The initial dilemma, so carefully set up, is completely forgotten, although the Count and Zenocia's father do turn up to increase the suspense in the middle of Act III.

The prologue to the play stresses the appeal of a varied plot, but concedes its complexity:

> the plot neat and new
> Fashion'd like those that are approved by you,
> Only 'twill crave attention in the most;
> Because one point unmark'd, the whole is lost.

Yet its appeal is not restricted to the comic twists. As well as the witty set pieces exploiting a ridiculous situation, there are, particularly from Massinger, speeches of high poetic seriousness such as Duarte's lament (v.i) on the inconstancy of womankind, or his mother's stern rejection of Rutilio's advances (v.i.380–1). This gallimaufry even achieves a kind of thematic coherence: each action demonstrates the potentially disastrous consequences of sexual exploitation and the misuse of different kinds of power. The main consistency, however, lies in the play's dramatic style. Fletcher's set pieces are comic and Massinger's moralizing, but they function within the same range of dramatic decorum. It may seem curious to apply the term decorum to a play which Dryden found to contain 'more Baudry . . . than in all ours together',[1] but as Lovelace observed in his commendatory verses to the First Folio, Fletcher knew

> how to cloathe aright your wanton wit
> Without her nasty Bawd attending it.
> View here a loose thought said with such a grace,
> Minerva might have spoke in Venus face.

The decorum of this dramatic style consists in using inference rather than explicit action, in implying convolutions of plot rather than presenting melodramatic action on stage, in exciting the audience with poetry and wit rather than with physical display.

Both characters and values are drawn from a common stock, as we see in *The Elder Brother* (1624–5), of which Massinger wrote the first and last acts, and Fletcher – in his last work for the stage – the matter in between. The familiar stereotypes include the scholar, Charles; the foolish father, Brisac, who favours his younger son Eustace, a would-be courtier; the humorous uncle, Miramont, in love with learning though he has none; and the lovely

---

[1] Quoted in *Jacobean and Caroline Stage*, III, 328.

heroine, Angellina, who cures Charles of his unworldliness and makes him reclaim both his birthright and her love. The even tenor of the play is entirely undisturbed by special effects, and its easy language perfectly demonstrates Fletcher's ability, so praised by Dryden, to imitate the conversation of gentlemen. The smooth, gentlemanly tone is broken only when Brisac also breaks decorum by attempting to seduce a servant's wife (IV.iv). He is comically exposed by his son and the servant, who use the incident to secure – respectively – a rightful inheritance and an increase in property.

The style of the play does nothing to startle the sensibilities of its audience. There are no melodramatic effects or violent confrontations, and the protagonists, accordingly, end by finding the *juste milieu* between a misanthropic retreat into the world of books and mindless courtly affectation. The opposition between Charles the scholar and Eustace the courtier is summed up in Angellina's statement of their strengths and weaknesses in the opening scene, and the whole action is further projected in her wish for 'A full Estate, and that said, I've said all'. The ideological centre of the play is Miramont, the country gentleman. He loves learning and can distinguish it from the 'quodlibets' of country justices; though he despises Eustace's foppery, he admires the young man when he turns 'an Oliver and a Rowland' by offering to fight a duel. He is also instrumental in satisfactorily resolving the plot. In his new admiration for Eustace, he makes him his heir.

Despite the consistency of their values and styles, these well-made collaborations for the King's Men did not impose a dull homogeneity on the dramatists who produced them. The mechanical tests used to assign authorship are severely complicated by the number of hands which intervene between the author's manuscript and the copy for the printed text, but in the finished plays the preoccupations, skills and styles of the different authors are often discernible. Massinger's principal contribution, for example, was the ability to enunciate serious themes with considerable theatrical style. In *The Fatal Dowry*, in which he collaborated with Field, his opening scene sets a telling stage picture against operatic sweeps of dramatic blank verse. In a device which owes something to the first court scene in *Hamlet*, the hero, Charolais, says nothing for the first fifty lines but dominates the action by his silent, black-clad presence. His stillness is set against the noisy ebb and flow of lawyers, favourites and creditors, and its emblematic significance is made clear in the ensuing dialogue. Charolais' friend Romont asks whether the court will release the body of Charolais' father, a former marshall who has died in a debtors prison. The lawyers

callously weigh the usual penalty for financial debt against the debt of
gratitude which the state owes to 'such a Master in the art of warre', and
their hypocritical sophistry is contrasted with the dignity of Charolais as he
eloquently defends his refusal to oppose the court's decision:

> They are too old to learne, and I too young
> To giue them counsell, since if they partake
> The vnderstanding, and the hearts of men,
> They will preuent my words and teares: if not,
> What can perswasion, though made eloquent
> With griefe, worke vpon such as have chang'd natures
> With the most sauage beast? (1.i.61–7)

Massinger's effects are not original but they exploit the available dramatic
materials to the full. In the final sequence of the scene, Romont has a speech
of comfort for Charolais which once again runs parallel to its physical action:

> The difficulties that you incounter with,
> Will crowne the vndertaking – Heauen! you weepe:
> And I could do so too, but that I know,
> Theres more expected from the sonne and friend
> Of him whose fatall losse now shakes our natures,
> Then sighs, or teares, (in which a village nurse
> Or cunning strumpet, when her knaue is hangd,
> May ouercome vs.) (1.i.180–7)

The speech deals with emotion, places it in perspective and draws the
correct moral distinctions. It provides a gloss on Charolais's dumb show of
passion.

   This opening scene shows Massinger's characteristic dramatic style. He
handles the stage picture with some dexterity, but is also concerned to draw
out its moral and thematic implications. The Senecan *Controversia* which is
the play's source concerns the clash between legal and moral claims. Their
juxtaposition in the opening court scene thus prepares for the further
conflict in the final act, where Charolais's legal right to murder his wife for
adultery must be weighed against his moral debt of gratitude to her father.
Massinger's greatest skill is shown in the way he gives these nice distinctions
a dramatic life. The climax of the play is emblematically theatrical: Rochfort
is blindfolded so that he can act as an impartial judge of his own daughter's
adultery. Having heard her confession, he pronounces his judgement:

> Heauen take mercy
> Vpon your soule then: it must leaue your body.
> Now free mine eyes. (IV.iv.119–21)

Charolais then kills Beaumelle on stage. Justice ceases to be blind. With a characteristic Massingerian volte-face, Rochfort shifts his role, and his emotional range, from judge to father:

> could not one good thought rise up,
> To tell you that she was my ages comfort,
> Begot by a weake man, and borne a woman,
> And could not therefore, but partake of frailety?
> Or wherefore did not thankfulnesse step forth,
> To vrge my many merits, which I may
> Object vnto you, since you proue ungratefull,
> Flinty-hearted *Charaloys?* (IV.iv.168–75)

But Massinger's talents are not restricted to the dramatization of fine points of law and morals. He gives the conflict its emotional basis by the suspense and tension created in the scene where Beaumelle's adultery is discovered. Charolais attends a banquet in a 'music house', where the songs which entertain him speak of the casual immorality of Beaumelle's world. During the first song, he hears her laughter within but puts aside his suspicions. It is only at the end of another song that her voice is unmistakable; Charolais drags her on to the stage and fights her lover to the death.

A fully effective reaction to the moral problems which Massinger presents depends upon the play excluding all sympathy from Beaumelle herself. Her role in the play is left to Massinger's collaborator, Nathan Field, who uses the range of satiric conventions to portray her as the familiar witty and amoral type. Field's part in the play falls more evidently into a series of set pieces and Act II in particular seems designed as a separate whole. It opens with the self-consciously theatrical funeral of Charolais's father in which Charolais explicitly places himself centre stage, rebuking an enthusiastic fellow mourner: 'Peace, O Peace, this scene is wholly mine'. There follows a series of introductions to the characters, in which the role each is to play is clearly indicated. Beaumelle is introduced engaged in an arch conversation about sex with her two maids, one grave and one witty. The contrast between the maids gives a rhythm to the discussion, while the explicitness of the sexual jokes gives an edge to the fast-flowing prose. Field uses a sparse, almost dumb-show method to make his points. When Beaumelle's lover, Young Novall, is introduced the stage is divided; we see 'AYMER *trim* NOVALL, *whilst* BELLAPERT *her Lady*' (II.ii.78 S.D.). In a further demonstration of character, Charolais rejects a display of gold in favour of Beaumelle's hand in marriage, and the act ends as it had begun, with a procession: '*Hoboyes. Here a passage ouer the Stage, while the Act is playing, for the Marriage of* CHAROLAIS *with* BEAUMELLE' (II.ii.359 S.D.).

Field's contribution shows his sense of dramatic pace and his ability to handle witty dialogue, both skills which feature in his independent writing. They are essentially theatrical talents which he may have learned during his career as an actor in the coterie theatre of the Children of the Chapel, and as an adult with the King's Men.

Even Fletcher, while clearly the most original of the King's Men collaborators, creates his variety of comedy by playing on a series of formulae, usually to do with seduction. His comedy depended on the audience knowing the basic model and being further entertained by such variations as the double bed trick of *The Little French Lawyer* (1619). The stylization and self-conscious contrivance of the comedy contributes an aesthetic charm which adds to the more immediate bawdy appeal. In *The Spanish Curate* (1622), where Massinger deals with the serious plot, Fletcher's contribution turns on Leandro's attempts to seduce Amarante, the virtuous wife of a worthless lawyer. In their first scene together (II.iv) he is hiding in the discovery space and attracts her attention with a lute song. She does not turn to him, but without directly conversing each character disingenuously talks about the other. A field of dramatic force is thus created as the audience's attention moves between the discovery space and the main stage. Despite the easy naturalism of the dramatic style, there is a satisfying symmetry about the scene, shared by the culminating sequence of this plot when the pair finally meet over a game of chess.

Not all the King's Men collaborations achieved this deft confidence of dramatic style. Later revisions of Fletcher's work jerk from one conventional set piece to another, though Massinger, the most frequent reviser, attributes this to the loss of Fletcher's controlling influence. In the prologue to his revision of *The Lovers' Progress* (1623, revised 1634) he candidly admits the extent to which the play's success depends upon fitting the available material into scenes:

> though his powers
> Could not as he desired, in three short hours

Contract the Subject, and much less express
The changes, and the various passages
That will be look'd for, you may hear this day
Some scenes that will confirm it is a play,
He being ambitious that it should be known
What's good was Fletcher's, and what ill his own.

The denouement of *Love's Pilgrimage* (1616, revised 1635) goes even further in mocking the very conventions which have sustained the rest of the action. The two heroines have been disguised as men for most of the play, and when each reveals her true identity to her lover, another character comments: 'I am afraid they will all four turn women if we hold longer talk'. The dramatists can pick up or drop a dramatic device as needed, for, as the plot hurries to its conclusion, a character who has deceived her own brother with her disguise for four acts is instantly recognized by her father, who has pursued her through the play and must be reconciled to her before a satisfactory conclusion can ensue.

Dependence on convention, then, was not in itself artistically disabling. It sometimes resulted in dull and repetitive writing but it also provided the dramatic expectations which a writer could either fulfil or deny to create the maximum variety and suspense. It could only emerge in a sophisticated theatre with a regular audience which both knew the forms and enjoyed new variations on them. Collaborations may not have produced works of lasting serious significance, but when the collaborators were congenial and their responses to convention inventive, they provided the staple fare for a successful theatre industry which in its turn sustained creations of individual genius.

4 John Fletcher

Whether as collaborator or in his individual works, the most important single influence on the plays and playwrights of the Stuart theatre was John Fletcher (*plate 25*), whose name is synonymous with the fashionable dramatic style:

> From thence a thousand lesser Poets sprong
> Like petty princes from the fall of Rome.
> When Johnson, Shakespeare, and thy self did sit
> And swayed in the Triumvirate of wit. . . .

When the unpublished 'Beaumont and Fletcher' plays were collected in the Folio of 1647, these lines of Denham were among thirty-four commendatory verses which ended with the publisher Humphrey Moseley's shrewd comment: 'If this Booke faile, 'tis time to quit the Trade.'

The enthusiasm of the commendations is partly due to the fact that many of the writers felt that they were writing the epitaph of the drama itself, but they were also paying tribute to plays which had held the stage for a generation after their authors' deaths. The great achievements of their collaboration, *The Maid's Tragedy*, *A King and No King* and *Philaster*, were completed before 1612, when Beaumont retired from the stage. However,

Fletcher continued as chief dramatist to the King's Men for a further decade, refining the patterns of tragi-comedy and romance which were carried on by Massinger for another decade and then by Shirley until the closing of the theatres.

(i) Tragi-comic dramaturgy

The new mode of tragi-comedy introduced by Beaumont and Fletcher was not the mongrel form, mingling kings and clowns, which had been the bane of neo-classical critics. It had a new sophistication and a firmer philosophical base. This was based largely on Guarini's famous argument in the introduction to *Il Pastor Fido*:

> what need have we today to purge pity and terror with tragic sights, since we have the precepts of our most holy religion, which teaches us with the words of the gospel? Hence these horrible and savage spectacles are superfluous, nor does it seem to me today we should introduce a tragic action for any other reason than to get delight from it. [1]

Drama was thus released from dealing with absolutes of moral truth and could entertain with a new decorum, answering the demands of purely aesthetic pleasure. Lovelace defined the attractions of the genre in his contribution to the Folio verses:

> But ah, when thou thy sorrow didst inspire
> With Passions, blacke as is her darke attire,
> Virgins as Sufferers have wept to see
> So white a Soule, so red a Crueltie;
> That thou hast griev'd, and with unthought redresse,
> Dri'd their wet eyes who now thy mercy blesse;
> Yet loth to lose thy watry jewell, when
> Joy wip't it off, Laughter straight sprung't agen.

There no longer seemed any incongruity in having high drama and farce in the same action. The dramatist's skill lay in controlling the effects, the

---

[1] Tr. A. H. Gilbert, in *Literary Criticism from Plato to Dryden*, ed. A. H. Gilbert (Detroit, Mich., 1962), 523.

audience's in recognizing the emotional claims, of each.

By building the tragi-comedies out of discrete units of emotion, comedy or suspense, Fletcher manages to insulate the separate parts of his plays one from another. In *Monsieur Thomas* (1615) Valentine returns from his travels accompanied by his new friend, Francis; Francis falls in love with Valentine's mistress, Cellide, and the artificial opposition between love and friendship can be acted out. Valentine urges Cellide to love his friend; Cellide first angrily refuses and then agrees in order to prevent Francis from dying of a broken heart. The conflicts and dramatic style of the play are crystallized in Act III, where Cellide visits Francis on his death-bed and offers to love him. He, of course, rejects her noble gesture, to maintain his own noble stance towards his friend, who is observing the scene unnoticed. Cellide, in a histrionic crescendo, insists that he make love to her, since Valentine is 'old and impotent'. Valentine witnesses Francis's continued and increasingly self-righteous refusal, but leaves before Cellide can reveal that she was only testing Francis, thus creating possibilities for further emotional upheaval.

This farrago of high-flown emotions coexists quite successfully with a plot in which dramatic contrivance is directed towards total farce. Monsieur Thomas, also returned from his travels, is anxious to make peace with his mistress, Mary, but he is torn between behaving like a roarer to please his father and revealing his new polished self, which will please his mistress. Out of this dilemma Fletcher creates scenes of wonderful comedy in which Mary and her maid, familiar, comical, witty women, constantly get the better of him. He serenades Mary, is enticed up to the balcony by her maid, and then falls from it terrified by the devil's mask Mary has assumed. He goes to Mary's bed disguised as her sister and makes love to a blackamoor, watched by the giggling women; the final humiliation comes when, still disguised, he is accosted by his lustful friend Hylas. No connection at all is made between the excesses of high-minded love in the one plot and the folly of comic love in the other; as far as the play is concerned they are entirely different emotions. The juxtaposition of tragic and farcical scenes brings just the confluence of tears of joy with tears of laughter which Lovelace had described.

The dangers of this emotional manipulation are that the comedy will undermine the tragedy or that it will not be entirely clear which emotions are to be mocked and which indulged. *Monsieur Thomas*'s contrast between farce and high drama is easy enough, but an audience's sensibilities are more challenged by the balance of tragedy and comedy in *The Mad Lover* (1617).

The opening of the play presents the familiar comic situation of a solider in love. Memnon, having bombastically told the court and the audience that he is unskilled in courtly compliment, is struck completely dumb by the princess's beauty, and when he recovers his voice makes love to her in the most forthright manner. At this stage he is an obvious comic butt, but the court against which he reacts is characterized in an equally stereotyped manner. The ladies show enough sophistication to mock the windy rhetoric of his introduction to the King, but they are also guilty of facile bawdy and cruel teasing which originates in satire rather than comedy.

Fletcher's skill with local effects results in this case in a confusion of sympathies. The comedy of Memnon's reaction to the princess leaves us quite unprepared for the serious afflictions of his love melancholy. The scene where Siphax tries to talk Memnon out of suicide is partly burlesque but also achieves a certain pathos in Fletcher's treatment of the familiar *contemptus mundi*:

> 'Tis but to dye, Dogs do it, Ducks with dabling,
> Birds sing away their Souls, & Babies sleep 'em. . . . (II.i.)

The uneasy comedy of Memnon's attempts to have his heart cut out (III.ii) contrasts with the charming interlude of the revelatory masque in which Orpheus and Charon describe the torments of those who die despairing. This scene is the Fletcherian set piece at its most delightful, but it cannot alter the basic situation of the play, which has further mockery in store. In another scene (IV.v) Memnon is offered a whore disguised as the princess in an attempt to purge his love melancholy by physical consummation. He realizes that he is being fooled, since the whore 'stinks like a poyson'd Rat behind a hanging', whereupon the comedy is turned against her as he threatens to test the invulnerability of her supposed royalty with a Numidian lion.

At every turn the dramatist's eye is on the audience rather than the characters, providing a maximum of dramatic variety even at the expense of other forms of consistency. Such variety, however, also reflects on the importance of style in such a theatrical world. The play partly deals with the commonplace opposition between courtly and soldierly behaviour, but for both types of characters the correct style of self-presentation is all-important. In a central scene of the play, Polydore, Memnon's friend, arrives before the princess, pretending to present Memnon's heart to her. The elaborate ceremonial of the presentation not only distances the grotesque deceit, but also impresses the princess with Polydore's worth. She admires his performance in almost technical terms:

POLYDORE.   Great Lady,
   Excellent beauty –
CALIS.   He speaks handsomely:
   What a rare rhetorician his grief plays!
   That stop was admirable. (III.iv.23–6)

In other circumstances such comments would seem mocking, but in this case they prepare the way for the couple's eventual union. After this pivotal scene, the weight of the action is transferred from Memnon's melancholy to the affair between Polydore and Calis. Decorum forbids a union between a princess and a graceless soldier; instead, Memnon is brought to his senses by the unabashed contrivance of news of a Spartan invasion, leaving the way clear for a more appropriate – but equally theatrical – resolution. Polydore is presented to the princess in his coffin, from which he rises only when assured of her love and Memnon's blessing.

Everything can ultimately be controlled by the benevolent author: the pleasure for the audience derives partly from the variety of aesthetic experiences and partly from guessing at the outcome. Clues are sometimes provided in the narrative, but are often more subtly indicated by dramatic patterns. In that *tour de force* of plotting, *The Chances* (1613–23), each of the first five scenes of Act I introduces a different set of characters and begins a plot. The only clue for the audience is that in Act I, scene iii, one of the men finds himself unexpectedly in charge of a baby, while in Act I, scene vii, an unknown lady flings herself on the mercy of his friend. The ensuing riddles were evidently part of the pleasure. Cartwright's commendatory verses to the 1647 Folio convey something of what must have been the original audience response.

                  all stand wondering how
  The thing will be until it is; which thence
  With fresh delight still cheats, still takes the sence;
  The whole designe, the shadowes, the lights such
  That none can say he shewes or hides too much.

The most elegant of Fletcher's plots have a kind of symmetry, offering the pleasures of expectation fulfilled, even in the surprises. In *Rule a Wife and Have a Wife* (1624) the title implies such a symmetry. Perez boasts how he will tame a wife and is completely outwitted by Estafania; Margarita, seeking only her own pleasure, marries an apparently compliant nonentity, who then proceeds to use all the statutory and traditional powers of a husband to keep her chaste. This decorous resolution, however, comes early in the action – Fletcher has further surprises in store. Estafania continues to tease and cozen Perez until they become comic partners, and Margarita, once she recognizes that her husband Leon is not prepared to be a willing cuckold, joins with him in outwitting her other suitors. The plots rapidly turn to inventive farce when Margarita and Leon lock the braggart Spaniard, Cacafogo, in the cellar, persuading the amorous Duke that the ensuing racket is the work of an avenging devil. The farcical action releases the characters from concern over passion or morals into a comic world where the clever control the dull. The play does have its lustful Duke, its threat to cuckold Leon. However, just as the plot fulfils expectations early in the play, so the overall moral lines are kept perfectly clear by firm statements such as Leon's unexpected insistence on his economic and conjugal rights (III.v). In Fletcherian comedy, decorum is never breached by a direct challenge to conventional sexual views.

(ii) Variations on a theme: the lustful ruler

The theme of sexual oppression provided Fletcher with a wide range of possibilities, comic, satiric and sentimental. The extent of his dramatic variety can perhaps best be seen by looking at one aspect of this theme, the 'lustful ruler' plot, in comedy (*The Humorous Lieutenant*, 1619), tragi-comedy (*A Wife for a Month*, 1624), and tragedy (*Valentinian*, 1614).

In *The Humorous Lieutenant*, the true lovers establish the sentimental and honourable norms in their touching duet of parting (I.ii) and their rousing assertions of the heroic code (II.iv). This framing action, however, surrounds a wittily observed court where sexual corruption is cynically accepted. The lustful king is served by a fat, dynamic entrepreneur who treats her job as court bawd with all the business acumen of any city comedy usurer, setting income from prostitution against expenditure for bribery. She is introduced organizing an international trade with the help of two secretaries and an enormous ledger:

LEUCIPPE.   Where lies old Thisbe now, you are so long now –
2 MAID.   *Thisbe, Thisbe, Thisbe*, agent *Thisbe*, O I have her,
   She lyes now in *Nicopolis*.
LEUCIPPE.   Dispatch a Packet,
   And tell her, her Superiour here commands her

The next month not to fail, but see deliver'd
Here to our use, some twenty young and handsom,
As also able Maids, for the Court service,
As she will answer it: we are out of beauty,
Utterly out, and rub the time away here
With such blown stuff, I am ashamed to send it. (II.iii)

This satiric context makes it easier to sustain Celia, the current object of the King's fancy, in the role of witty woman. When she is first tricked to court she is completely in control of the situation, answering Leucippe's blandishments with rude references to her size. When she finally meets the King, she uses Hamlet's device of making timely comments while pretending to report on a book she is reading:

He says here, that an Old Man's loose desire
Is like the Glow-worm's light, the Apes so wonder'd at:
Which when they gather'd sticks, and laid upon't,
And blew, and blew, turn'd tail, and went out presently:
And in another place he calls their loves,
Faint Smells of dying Flowers, carry no comforts;
They're doting, stinking foggs, so thick and muddy,
Reason with all his beams cannot beat through 'em. (IV.v)

It is hardly surprising that the King is deterred from further pursuit: wit, it would seem, is a more effective protection than virtue.

The King's lust is mocked in the subplot, as indeed is the heroic code which governs the rest of the play. The eponymous lieutenant, who does not wish to go to war until he can marry his pregnant mistress, observes:

It shows as mad a thing to me to see you scuffle
And kill one another foolishly for honour. (III.iii)

He himself becomes a comic butt as a result, especially in the scene where he faints in terror and is mistakenly revived by an aphrodisiac potion which makes him dote on the King. In a very funny dialogue two gentlemen describe how he

Is really in love with the King, most dotingly,
And swears *Adonis* was a devil to him:
A sweet King, a most comely King, and such a King. (IV.v)

Their tale is followed by a comic encounter between the King and his doting subject which tellingly parodies the King's own lust and his claim on the women at his court. Thus, in the context of comedy, he is an utterly unthreatening figure; Fletcher ignores the darker side of the theme.

When sexual morality is complicated by the duties owed to absolute power, as in *A Wife for a Month*, the full potential of the 'lustful ruler' plot is exploited. The sexual theme provides the excitement of the action: the King's tyrannical power both prolongs and intensifies the lovers' frustration. The play's opening leads straight to an attempted seduction of the heroine. At this stage, Evanthe's reaction is witty rather than outraged:

> FRED.   Gentle *Evanthe*.
> EVAN.   The Gracious Queen, Sir,
>   Is well and merry, Heaven be thanked for it,
>   And as I think she waits you in the Garden.
> FRED.   Let her wait there, I talk not of her Garden,
>   I talk of thee sweet Flower.
> EVAN.   Your Grace is pleasant
>   To mistake a Nettle for a Rose.
> FRED.   No Rose, nor Lilly, nor no glorious Hyacinth
>   Are of that sweetness, whiteness, tenderness,
>   Softness, and satisfying blessedness
>   As my *Evanthe*. (I.i.)

The King's lust is offset by Valerio's true and honourable love for Evanthe, expressed in the most extreme, if also the most conventional, terms. He is undismayed at the news that he can enjoy Evanthe only for a month before submitting to execution:

> When I have once enjoy'd my sweet *Evanthe*
> And blest my Youth with her most dear embraces,
> I have done my journey here, my day is out,
> All that the World has else is foolery,
> Labour and loss of time. (I.ii)

Valerio's equanimity and Evanthe's good humour in the face of such tyranny are, however, only the first turns of a screw which is progressively tightened. The revelation of the play's real climax is prepared with all the available theatrical resources. The wedding of Valerio and Evanthe is ironically prolonged by a masque: the Graces unbind Cupid who brings on assorted passions as masquers. This symbolic release of passion is made totally explicit in Valerio's exulting anticipation of his night with Evanthe, the ironic prelude to the cruel prohibitions the King is to impose. When the King's agent arrives to tell Valerio that he is forbidden to consummate the marriage, he does so by teasing hints that Valerio will never enjoy his wife, provoking his excited and lengthy speculation about the cause. The sexual explicitness of this dialogue is nothing to the unremitting coyness of the ensuing encounter with Evanthe herself. Valerio is forbidden to tell Evanthe of the King's command, so the scene can indulge the titillating dramatic reversal of expected behaviour, as Evanthe is eager and Valerio bashful, finally pretending embarrassed impotence. Nor is Fletcher content with this display: the King later tells Evanthe that Valerio's real motive has been cowardice, thus precipitating a further scene of passionate recrimination between the lovers.

These scenes are attentuated and painful, not so much because of their emotionalism or even their sexual explicitness, as because they rigidly exclude any ventilating humour. The witty woman of Act 1 is submerged first by her maudlin sympathy for Valerio's plight and then by her outraged, but coy, disappointment. The parallel scene in *The Maid's Tragedy* (1608), where Evanthe refuses to consummate her marriage of convenience, has an ironic wit which builds up to the show-stopping line: 'A maidenhead, Amintor, at my years?' Moreover, in the earlier play, the scene provides a basis for further action, whereas in *A Wife for a Month* all the dramatic inventiveness has gone into extracting the greatest number of turns out of an essentially simple, if rather recherché, situation.

The tragi-comic genre of the play also contributes its special effect. The main plot is shadowed by a second, stylishly integrated action in which the rightful king recovers his health and his usurped kingdom. The knowledge that a happy ending is assured creates a curious dislocation between the comic essence of the situation and the intense passion which is wrung from it: the true tragi-comic emotion reverberates between the steady ground bass of the comic plotting and the high notes of passion caused by the lovers' plight. The final happy ending is both certain and irrelevant. It can be achieved in a single *coup de théâtre* as Valerio throws off his disguise, the true king enters triumphant, and the lovers are united.

In tragi-comedy disaster is always deflected and a special dramatic reaction invoked; in tragedy the crisis is always real, the danger followed by the death. Fletcher's tragic treatment of the lustful tyrant, *Valentinian* (1614), deals with the Emperor's successful attempt to rape the chaste Lucina and the revenge which follows her inevitable suicide. In the first part of the play, the trajectory of the action is clear enough but it is teased out, the climaxes, in every sense, deferred. Lucina is first unsuccessfully propositioned by court ladies in a scene (i.ii) which provides the double thrill of the women's sexual sophistry and, countering their speeches, Lucina's splendid rhetorical defence of chastity. She is then enticed to court by a trick, and there follows a lengthy sequence which sets the mood for the audience, if not for Lucina herself: she is greeted by songs, a display of jewels and elaborate preparation for the short encounter with Valentinian. At their meeting he announces that he 'did but try your temper'. From this anticlimax the audience is lulled through the entr'acte music before the jolt of the opening words of Act iii: ''Tis done'.

Only after the rape does Fletcher present a confrontation between Valentinian and Lucina. He thus avoids repeating the panders' arguments for seduction, and can make much more of Lucina's impassioned mixture of sorrow and scorn:

> Call in your Lady Bawds and guilded Pander's
> And let them triumph too, and sing to *Caesar*,
> *Lucina*'s faln, the chaste *Lucina*'s conquerd;
> Gods! what a wretched thing has this man made me!
> For I am now no wife for *Maximus*
> No company for women that are vertuous,
> No familie I now can claim, nor Country,
> Nor name but *Caesar*'s whore. (iii.i)

Nowhere is the operatic quality of Fletcher's drama more clearly seen than in such speeches, which are arias without music. The intense feeling is entirely conveyed in the carefully paced rhetoric. It demands an acting style which is both static and – paradoxically – detached, to avoid detracting from the careful orchestration of emotion created by the verse. When Lucina's husband, Maximus, hears of her plight, he advises her 'go silver swan and sing thine own sad requiem'. This image of artifice defines Fletcher's artistry to perfection. It is not designed to extend our understanding of the passions involved or to convince us of their appropriateness. Their theatrical impact depends entirely on their auto-nomous poetic beauty. Such static dramaturgy reflects an equally static acceptance of received moral values. Motives require no exploration, for lust is villainous, chastity heroic, and unlawful sex a correspondingly tragic theme. In the first part of the play such an acceptance presents no dramatic problems because the absolutes involved are easily dramatized and require no special argument.

When the question of revenge against Valentinian arises the moral debates become more attenuated and more abstract. In *The Maid's Tragedy* (1608), Fletcher had already dramatized the debate over whether to kill a tyrant for sexual wrongs; he now experiments with a further twist. When Maximus enters after Lucina's suicide, he announces 'there's no way else to do it; he must dye' (III.iii). However, it gradually emerges that he is referring not to Valentinian but to his friend Aecius, who must die because he stands between Maximus and his revenge on the Emperor. The familiar love and friendship theme is linked to the political loyalty theme for a novel intellectual and dramatic effect.

The remainder of the play consists of a series of demonstrations of abstract moral qualities, as a further plot concerning Valentinian's intrigues against Aecius is introduced into the already complicated structure. As the deaths crowd in, we witness the dramatic problems created by a play of ideas which sacrifices credible causation to novel effects and extreme positions. In the scene of Aecius' death (IV.iv) the dramatic interest lies less in the culmination of the plot than in each character's demonstration of his moral fibre. The bawds, originally charged with the murder, cannot bring themselves to kill, comically demonstrating their cowardice and providing the perfect contrast to Pontius, who engages with Aecius in refined debate about the different degrees of honour to which each is entitled. Having stabbed himself to avoid a dishonourable murder, he invites Aecius to 'die as I do' and then delivers a long speech explaining the particular significance of his action. Aecius' admiration for such refined resolution then exceeds his basic sense of self-preservation as he declares that his mentor has

> fashion'd death
> In such an excellent, and beauteous manner,
> I wonder men can live. (IV.iv)

Dying is more important than being dead; the theatrical act takes over from the desired end. Act V opens with the stage direction, '*Enter* PHIDIAS, *with his dagger in him, and* ARETUS, *poysoned*'. The two courtiers further prolong their agony by discussing how they must remain alive to see the Emperor, already poisoned, die. Valentinian's death-bed scene is fully heightened by music, attendants and an agonizing but uninformative confrontation with his murderer. However, the poetic beauties which gave such power to Lucina's arias are now dissipated in exclamations which lose all contact with the dramatic situation and become exaggerated rant. Moreover the play does not end with Valentinian's confession: his death in turn must be avenged. The balance between heightened set piece and plotting is completely upset. The 'feigned difficulty' and 'happy reversal' move from the flirtatious to the chaotic.

(iii) Fletcherian social satire: *The Wild Goose Chase*

The full range of Fletcher's theatrical virtuosity is evident in the contrast between the operatic artifice of *Valentinian* and the easy appearance of realism created for the comic world of *The Wild Goose Chase* (1621). For the later play Fletcher adapted traditional satiric form, placing it in a recognizable social milieu, neutralizing its misanthropic force. Mirabel, the wild goose of the title, is the dramatic offspring of both Benedick and Bosola. In the plot, he plays the confirmed bachelor who resists all efforts to catch him but is eventually tamed and brought to conjugal harmony. However, in his language and attitudes he displays, not the elegant misogyny of a Benedick, but a gross, exploitative contempt for women closer to the tragic satire of Webster or Marston. He has none of the earlier satirist's moral horror of the world, only a cynical acceptance of human failing. When his former mistress, Oriana, reminds him of a pre-contract to marry her, he replies:

> I must not lose my liberty, dear Lady,
> And like a wanton slave cry for more shackles.
> What should I marry for? Do I want anything?
> Am I an inch the farther from my pleasure?
> Why should I be at charge to keep a wife of mine own,
> When other honest married men will ease me?
> And thank me too, and be beholding to me:
> Thou thinkst I am mad for a Maidenhead, thou art cozen'd;
> Or if I were addicted to that diet
> Can you tell me where I should have one? thou art eighteen now,
> And if thou hast thy Maiden-head yet extant,
> Sure 'tis as big as Cods-head: and those grave dishes
> I never love to deal withal. (II.i)

In the comic world, such pathological sexual vanity is only another form of attitudinizing: it has no influence on the action in which the witty women of the play plot revenge for the gentleman's scorn and vie with Mirabel for comic control. Mirabel acts as a kind of detached master of ceremonies, orchestrating such comic clashes between the men and the women as the farcical scene in which the bashful Belleur, trying to woo his lady, is pushed back and forth between Mirabel's encouragement and the ladies' contemptuous chill.

Mirabel's lack of emotional involvement, and his evident enjoyment of the sport he makes with fools, give him the greatest comic power. He successfully devises a ploy to make Lillia jealous by pretending that Pinac has got a better match in an English lady, and is then triumphant when the ladies try the same trick on him. When he is told that Oriana is about to marry 'a brave Savoyan, Nephew to the Duke', he affects a brave resignation:

> I was a poor servant of hers, I must confess, Sir,
> And in those daies, I thought I might be jovy,
> And make a little bold to call into her:
> But Basto, now; I know my rules and distance;
> Yet if she want an Usher. . . . (III.i)

He is rather taken aback when the 'lord' himself appears, but sexual vanity rather than moral sensibility is at stake: his greatest irritation is 'that this Bilbo-Lord shall reap that Maiden-head/That was my due'.

Fletcher's novelty consists in making such a cynical figure so comically attractive, but doing so enables him to make a more complex satiric point in the resolution of the play, which reveals the connections between sex, money and power. Mirabel remains impervious to all appeals to fulfil his contract with Oriana. When he hears that she is on her death bed he is temporarily chastened but scorns to be caught by a trick. He is, however, willing to be bought. In a final device, Oriana disguises herself as the sister of an Italian merchant, bringing treasure as a reward for Mirabel's having once rescued him. He suddenly finds that

> She has a Spring dwells on her lips: a paradise:
> This is the Legacie. . . . (v.vi)

The scene continues with suitable gestures of renunciation and self-sacrifice, but it is significant that the play's final image shows Mirabel united, not with the Oriana he has rejected throughout the action, but with a new, richer woman more to his taste:

> I'le burn my book, and turn a new leaf over,
> But these fine clothes you shall wear still.

In comedy as in tragi-comedy, the implications of the characters' attitudes and moral statements are seldom carried beyond the local effect they make. Character is conceived entirely in terms of the stereotypes required by particular situations. Consequently the appeal of the plays lies in the 'strange turns and windings' which these characters can be made to follow. Stapylton may have admired the way 'his maine end does drooping Vertue raise . . . While Vice (her paint wash't off) appears so foule', but this banal moralizing seems a commonplace skill compared with the controlled management of a triple plot or the careful pacing of the movement towards a happy ending. It is essentially a comic skill, and it is in Fletcher's comedies that his hothouse concerns with sex and honour are given room to move to the most satisfying theatrical effect. There are fewer 'big scenes', fewer operatic set pieces than elsewhere, but these are replaced by an ease of conversation and an action that entertains.

5 Fletcherian echoes

Philip Massinger

After Fletcher's death in the plague of 1625, his place as principal dramatist for the King's Men was taken by Philip Massinger. It was an appropriate choice, for in his collaborations with Fletcher and his independent plays for both the King's Men and Beeston's companies at the Phoenix, Massinger had shown himself a master of the fashionable dramatic style. The complexities of his tragi-comic plotting outdid Fletcher, and by the end of his career, in *The Bashful Lover* (1636), he could produce the virtuoso combination of rival suitors, a disguised girl following her lover to the wars, and a reunion between father and long-lost daughter, bringing all three actions together in a scene which included a duel, a threatened rape and a conjuring trick. Narrative skill was, however, the least of Massinger's talents: his dramatic style is extremely sensitive to non-verbal theatrical effects and his unusually explicit stage directions show a precise awareness of the actor's craft.[1] However, these aspects of the Fletcherian style have become self-regarding. In Fletcher, the characters' emotions are carefully

[1] See *The Great Duke of Florence* (1627), IV. i. 100; *The Maid of Honour* (1621), III. iii. 200; *The Renegado* (1624), II. iv. 9.

orchestrated; in Massinger, the characters themselves draw attention to the orchestration. At the denouement of *The Emperor of the East* (1631), Athenais fears that she may have caused her supposed lover's death and so prepares for death herself. Dressed in sackcloth, with loosened hair, she recites a lengthy rhyming speech and then comments on it:

> Thus like a dying Swan, to a sad tune
> I sing my owne dirge. (v.iii.15–16)

Fletcher's Lucina had also been compared to a dying swan (see p. 192) – but by her husband, not herself.

The sense that Massinger's characters are distanced from their own emotions is enhanced by his habit of dividing the stage between observers and observed.[1] In *The Renegado* (1623–4), Vitelli allows himself to be seduced by the Tunisian princess Donusa, then remembers his Christian duty and rejects her advances. Though the situation itself is exciting, Vitelli responds to Donusa's passionate pleading by symbolic actions rather than words: he '*Returnes the Casket*' and '*Throwes off his cloke and doublet*'. Meanwhile two unseen observers above the stage provide additional commentary on the mime below:

> ——By *Mahomet* she courts him.
> ——Nay kneeles to him;
> Obserue the scornefull villaine turnes away too,
> As glorying in his conquest. (III.v.71–3)

The resulting separation between motive and action, personality and response, is paralleled by a similar separation between ideas and action in the plays. Where in Fletcher the values behind the plays are implicit and unexceptionable, Massinger makes them explicit and incorporates them into his dramatic style. Character is as often as not fixed by description, and the intellectual issues of the play are stated as such in the opening dialogue. *The Duke of Milan* (1621–2), for example, opens with a lively scene of revelry, establishing the tone of its courtly world, while a careful commentary by two lords reveals the cause of the war, the insecurity of the state, and the dangerous uxuriousness of the ruling Duke. More significantly, these commentators also make clear the moral line by a smooth interpolation of *sententiae*, giving an impression of weighty and considered

[1] See *The Unnatural Combat* (1626), III. iv; *The Roman Actor* (1626), I. iv; *The Great Duke of Florence* (1627), II. iii.

judgement. The intellectual issues are often taken from the irresolvable dilemmas of the Senecan *Controversiae*, debating themes for young lawyers, which as we have seen occasionally touch on political issues.[1] Nevertheless, personal relationships, love, friendship and honour remain central to the plays.

In the court prologue to *The Emperor of the East*, Massinger says that he

> labour'd that no passage might appeare,
> But what the Queene without a blush might heare.

However, despite the conventional moral resolutions of his plays, Massinger directs a good deal of dramatic inventiveness to more prurient taste. Donusa's seduction of Vitelli is only one of a number of such scenes; Massinger provides further diversion by having a woman fight over a man (*The Maid of Honour*, 1621; v.ii), fight with a man (*A Very Woman*, 1634; i.iii) or be stabbed by a man on stage (*The Duke of Milan*, v.iii). Female chastity exists only to be besieged, and an ethic which places death before dishonour results in some morally dubious if dramatically exciting confrontations.

The contradictions of Massinger's sexual politics appear most striking in *The Bondman*. His characters divide into the chaste and the lustful, the honourable and the corrupt. These divisions have some political force when Timoleon, the virtuous general, rehearses Massinger's preoccupation of the 1620s – the degeneracy of a civilian court and the poor rewards for virtuous soldiers (i.iii). But courtly depravity is given a more explicitly sexual tone in the gratuitous double entendres of the court ladies (i.iii.45–81) and the salacious scene (ii.ii) where Asotus, the court fop, makes lustful advances to his own stepmother, who is pretending that she is the chaste Cleora.

The punishment for the court's viciousness is a slave rebellion which Massinger exploits more for its sexual excitement than its political significance. When the noise of the uprising is first heard, Timandra indulges in a long speech anticipating the terrors of 'base lust/And lawlesse rapine', while Cleora '*starts*' and '*wrings her hands*' at the prospect. The main scene of the slaves' triumph shows them humiliating their former owners in a parody of court behaviour which reflects their simple-minded revenge motivation. More attenuated sexual excitement is achieved, however, in the

---

[1] See Eugene Waith, 'John Fletcher and the Art of Declamation', *PMLA*, 66 (1951), 226–34, and *The Pattern of Tragicomedy in Beaumont and Fletcher* (New Haven, Conn., 1952); also p. 179 above.

scene where the slave leader, Pisander, woos Cleora, insisting on the honour and respect of his true devotion. She, perhaps to indicate her virtue, neither moves nor speaks; she simply responds to Pisander's approaches in a series of stylized gestures carefully orchestrated through the stage directions inserted into his speech. The climax of the scene comes when Pisander asks her to 'Reward my temperance with some lawfull fauour' (III.ii), and 'CLEORA *kneeles, then puls off her Gloue, and offers her hand to* PISANDER' (l. 103 S.D.). This theatrical understatement in fact creates a scene of sensational eroticism. The attitude behind Pisander's protestations of respect is exposed by the imagery of his speech:

> (nay, feare not Madam,
> True loue's a servant, brutish lust a Tyrant)
> I dare not touch those viands, that ne're taste well,
> But when they are freely offred. (III.ii.82–5)

The notion that Cleora is merely a commodity for consumption is further revealed by the attitude of her former suitor, Leosthenes, after the slave rebellion has been quelled. He is filled with jealous fears that she has been raped, but his fears are less for her safety than for his honour. There is something pathological about his assertion that if he could believe in her continued chastity he

> should receaue it with a ioy beyond
> Assurance of Elizian shades hereafter. (IV.iii.47–8)

The issue of sexual honour takes over the play completely in the second half, which turns on whether Pisander has raped Cleora. Her continued defence of his honesty serves more to arouse Leosthenes' agonized suspicions than to raise questions about the links between rank and human worth. All these issues are trivialized by the final contrivance of the plot, which ends in characteristic Massingerian style. An affecting duet between Cleora and Pisander in prison is overheard by her lover and brother, who rush in to kill the slave. They are prevented from doing so by the upright judge Archidamus, who insists that he be fairly tried. The legal contest is easily resolved when Pisander proves that he is no rebellious slave but a gentleman in disguise and worthy of Cleora's hand.

Intellectual issues give a weight and seriousness to Massinger's drama and it is possible to extrapolate from them statements of a subversive and startling kind. His romantic dramaturgy, however, enclosed them within a world which was completely unthreatening because so evidently controlled by the author. His best plays exploit the strengths of this dramatic control. In *The Roman Actor* (1626), claimed as 'the most perfit birth of my Minerva', Massinger's fondness for significant gesture and *coups de théâtre* advances the action as well as creating more local effects of tension and suspense. In the first act of the play, Caesar's tyrannical power is dramatized by simple physical effects. When Domitia's husband, Lamia, objects to Caesar's interest in his wife, the arrival of the tyrant's messenger is heralded thus: '*Stampes. Enter a Centurion with Souldiers*' (I.ii. 73 S.D.). When Caesar himself appears, he demonstrates his arrogance with a triumphal entry and compares himself to Julius, Vespasian and Titus. Massinger's common technique of dividing the stage allows the Stoics to indicate their opposition in ironic asides and foreshadow Caesar's eventual downfall. The plot avoids easy contrasts, counterpointing the development of the affair between Domitia and Paris with the accumulation in each act of further motivation for the final onslaught against Caesar. Since Paris is an actor, the play is organized around the four plays within the play which provide both poetic and dramatic images for the action.

In Act II, scene i, Caesar is presented as a theatrical impresario. He first agrees to the presentation of 'The Cure of Avarice' as an attempt to reform Parthenius' father, Philargus, and then in grotesque parody forces Lamia to be the audience of his wife's adulterous performance. When the play is performed, Philargus remains entirely unmoved, wishing only to be left to his own avarice. Caesar makes this philistine reaction an excuse to kill him, thus adding Parthenius to the company of revengers. The second action of the play is also initiated when Domitia falls in love with the actor, giving the scene a further level of powerful, if unspoken, dramatic intensity.

The second of the plays within the play follows on from the unpleasant scene in which Rusticus and Sura are tortured. Massinger thus juxtaposes the revenge plot with the love affair, whilst economically indicating Caesar's hideous ability to move from torture to entertainment. Domitia's growing passion for Paris is revealed in her uncontrolled interruptions of the scene; and when she finally courts Paris directly, she turns to the theatrical metaphor in her suggestion that he must be a true lover to play the lover so well. Paris, loyal to Caesar, denies this with a defence of the actor's artistic detachment, but ironically is trapped in his role by Caesar, who is watching the action from above:

Where in my selfe the *Theater* of the Gods
Are sad spectators. (IV.ii. 115–16)

In the discussion on the player's art, Paris has insisted that,

> my part being ended,
> And all my borrowed ornaments put off,
> I am no more, nor lesse than what I was
> Before I enter'd. (IV.ii. 49–52)

This connection between being and doing is echoed in the action of the play. After the torture and murder of the Stoics, Caesar feels 'By my shaking/I am the guiltie man, and not the Iudge' (III.ii.116–17), and when he finally kills Paris in the last play within the play, he cries:

> O villaine! thankelesse villaine! I shoulde talke now;
> But I have forgot my part. But I can doe,
> Thus, thus and thus.   *Kils* PARIS. (IV.ii.281–3)

After Paris' death, the action is dissipated as the powerful image of acting and role-playing gives way to ghosts and omens, the paraphernalia of revenge. Nevertheless, the coherence of image and action in the first part of the play demonstrates the value of a controlling idea as a focus for Massinger's undoubted theatrical skills. Quite different from the decorous smoothness of his more Fletcherian plays, *The Roman Actor* shows Massinger's debt to the poetic style of the powerful earlier Jacobean tragedy.

(iii) John Ford

A similar tension between Jacobean tragedy and Fletcherian romance animates the work of John Ford. His early plays were written in collaboration, and in this apprenticeship he learned the technique of composition by scenes. His debt to Fletcher is accordingly most evident in his set pieces. Some, like the masque of melancholy in *The Lover's Melancholy* (1628), or the subplot of that play, are direct imitations of Fletcher.[1] However, *Love's Sacrifice* (1625) suggests that Jacobean satire was a more congenial mode to him than Caroline tragi-comedy. The play depicts a court whose corruption – the banishment of the honest Roseilli, the unbalanced uxoriousness of the Duke – is both enacted on stage and

---

[1] Cf. *The Mad Lover* and *Monsieur Thomas*.

commented on in the anxious asides of surrounding courtiers. In the figure of D'Avalos, Ford presents the traditional satiric and politic malcontent, who is rendered a genuinely sinister figure by his continual watching presence, quick to overhear and equally quick to use what he has heard. He provides an active and evil counterpart to the virtuous but passive Roseilli, who wanders through the play disguised as a fool (cf. Marston's *Antonio's Revenge*, 1604) until he takes over the dukedom at the end.

The linking figures of D'Avalos and Roseilli lend coherence to a plot of thwarted and adulterous love. Bianca is married to the Duke, to whom she owes a great debt of gratitude. Fernando falls in love with her; though she rejects him in public, she later goes to his bedchamber, declares her love for him and agrees to consummate it, but insists that she must then kill herself. Their speeches twist between the poles of passion and duty, and, though they have little surface decoration, are given great emotional power by the visual effect – Bianca has '*her haire about her eares, in her night mantle*'. Other powerful set pieces of passion include D'Avalos's attempt to make the Duke mad with jealousy (III.iii) and the revelation of Bianca's passion (v.i) when she taunts the Duke until he is driven to fulfil her wish for death.

In his handling of the subplot, Ford experiments with a darker comedy. It involves Ferentes, a court libertine who has seduced three women and refuses to acknowledge the children they are to bear. The treatment of this action avoids both the moral outrage of the main plot and a conventionally gross 'low-life' tone. Ferentes is totally unrepentant, and his cynical male opportunism has a theatrical force which is close to comedy.[1] When he is confronted by all three ruined women at once, he makes no excuses, calmly insisting that he will marry none of them:

> Nor you, nor you, nor you.
> And to giue you some satisfaction, I'le yeeld you reasons: you, *Colona*, had a pretty art in your dalliance, but your fault was, you were *too suddenly won*; you, *Madam Morona*, could haue pleas'd wel enough some three or foure & thirty years agoe, but you are *too old*; you, *Iulia*, were young enough, but your fault is, you haue a *scurvy face*; now every one knowing her proper defect, thanke me, that I ever vouchsaf'd you the honor of my bed once in your lives. (III.i)

Ford's handling of this plot reverses the usual tragi-comic model: instead of tragical posturing in an essentially comic situation, there is outrageous

---

[1] Cf. Mirabel in *The Wild Goose Chase*, quoted p. 194.

humour in a situation which is inescapably tragic. The ladies contrive a masque in which they each appear '*in odd shapes and dance*'; they make ironic gestures of compliment to Ferentes and then '*fall upon him and stab him*'. By 1625 the device of a 'reversed revel' was part of theatrical stock-in-trade, but Ford's placing of it creates a turning point in the play: the decisive physical action exposes the dangerous potential of the play's passionate entanglements and ensures the ultimate violent outcome. Ferentes' dying speech draws the ironic moral: 'Uncase me; I am slaine in iest, a pox upon your outlandish feminine Antiks: pull off my Visor' (III.iv).

Fletcher's most important legacy to Ford was the poetic style in which characters dramatize themselves and their highly charged moral and emotional dilemmas. In *The Broken Heart* (1627–31), as in *Love's Sacrifice*, he creates an impossibly enclosed situation in which passion can only struggle and suffer with no hope of release. At its turning point, Penthea, the wronged heroine, talks with her brother, who is himself feeling the pangs of unrequited love and regrets that he forced her to marry against her will. The scene she foretells her own death and bequeaths to the Princess Calantha her with a song, and the two figures are 'discovered'. Their speeches blend into a poetic duet which contrasts their sorrows with the happy state of the labourer and 'the handmaid to the wages/Of Country toyle'. Elegiac pathos is Penthea's dramatic mode throughout the action. In another melancholy scene she foretells her own death and bequeaths to the Princess Calantha her three jewels – her youth, her fame and her brother. To the protest, 'You feed too much your melancholy', she replies:

> On the stage
> Of my mortality, my youth hath acted
> Some scenes of vanity, drawne out at length
> By varied pleasures, sweetned in the mixture,
> But Tragicall in issue. (III.v.15–19)

Her language and actions are the self-consciously adopted style of a tragic figure.

As in Fletcher, evocative images and poetic lyricism create a kind of mood music indicating the emotional function of the scene. In Ford's play, however, there is a sense that the dramatic methods have been chosen by the characters rather than by the controlling dramatist. The characters constantly search for appropriate acts, refining their reactions with conscious artistry in which poetry and theatricality combine to meet the requirements of style. In a famous scene, Calantha is dancing her wedding

revels when successive messengers announce that the King, Penthea and
Ithocles are dead. At each announcement she ignores the news, crying out
for more music, to the amazement of those around her. Ford borrowed the
device from Marston's *The Malcontent* (1604), where Aurelia dances on,
ignoring questions about her husband's disappearance. Marston's scene
simply points up Aurelia's callousness with a contrast between revelling and
death; in Ford, Calantha's stoicism is an instructive model, teaching
Bassanes self-control and giving Orgilus the courage to punish himself for
Ithocles' death. At the end of the play, Calantha explains her gesture in a
scene whose staging is the epitome of beautiful contrivance:

> *An altar covered with white. Two lights of Virgin wax, during which
> musicke of Recorders, enter four bearing Ithocles on a hearse, or in a chaire,
> in a rich robe, and a Crowne on his head; place him on one side of the Altar,
> after him enter Calantha in a white robe and crown'd. . . . Calantha goes
> and kneeles before the Altar, the rest stand off, the women kneeling behind;
> cease Recorders during her devotions. Soft musicke. Calantha and the rest
> rise, doing obeysance to the Altar. (*v.iii S.D.)

The use of music and silence during this stunning dumb show are evidence
of Ford's poetic sense of theatre, but the arrangement is credited to
Calantha, who is preparing her own farewell to the world. She ceremonially
marries Nearchus, her father's choice of husband, and prepares to die with
these words:

> I but deceiv'd your eyes with Anticke gesture,
> When one newes straight came hudling on another,
> Of death, and death, and death, still I danc'd forward,
> But it strooke home, and here, and in an instant,
> Be such meere women, who with shreeks and out-cries
> Can vow a present end to all their sorrowes,
> Yet live to vow new pleasures, and outlive them:
> They are the silent griefes which cut the hart-strings;
> Let me dye smiling. (v.iii.68–76)

In *The Lover's Melancholy* (1628), the characters' own attention to style is
made more explicit in the role of Corax, the court physician who uses theatre
as a cure. The three main characters, Menaphon, Meleander and Palador,
all suffer from a disabling melancholy whose causes are located outside the
action of the play. Corax exposes the cause of Palador's melancholy with the
aid of masque and revelation (III.iii) and restores Meleander to sanity by

aversion therapy – he appears to him in a 'frightful mask and headpiece' – together with a soothing acquiescence in his view of the world. Corax's treatment of the melancholy figures is based on models provided by Burton's *Anatomy of Melancholy*, but the theatrical as against the clinical interest of these scenes is due to Fletcherian dramatic models. Palador is cured when he is reunited with his lost mistress, Eroclea, and the scene of their reconciliation has immense emotional and theatrical power. As Palador gradually recognizes his lost love, poetic images of time and the vanity of human suffering counterpoint the slow and solemn movement towards reunion. Meleander's restoration is similarly paced: '*Soft Musicke. Enter Meleander (in a Couch), his hair and beard trimd, habit and gowne chang'd*' (v.i). From this quiet opening, the momentum of the scene increases as Meleander is presented with honour upon honour and finally with his lost daughter, Eroclea. At this point the formality of the scene is broken by the emotional and psychological realism of Meleander's reaction:

> If I should speake as much as I should speake,
> I should talke of a thousand things at once,
> And all of thee, of thee (my child) of thee:
> My teares like ruffling winds lockt up in Caves,
> Do bustle for a vent. (v.i)

The revelations, carefully stage-managed by Rhetias and Corax, lead up to the final entrance of the Prince to set the seal of a happy ending by announcing a triple wedding.

The story that Ford uses has the familiar tragi-comic elements of a long-lost mistress and daughter, past wrongs and present passion, which are presented in detail by Rhetias' explanatory dialogues (I.ii and II.i). For whereas Fletcher more usually makes his plot out of a series of revelations, striving for rapidly alternating emotional effect, Ford includes all the potential for his happy ending in the beginning, leaving himself free to concentrate on poetic and dramatic display.

Despite the self-conscious artistry of his scenes, Ford does not allow dramatic decorum entirely to smooth away their troubling impact. His early collaboration with Dekker and Heywood gave him access to the more robust public theatre traditions, evident in his comic writing,[1] and his Fletcherian style is on occasion animated by satiric echoes from Webster and Middleton. Sometimes it is a matter of a single speech used to place a character. Rhetias'

---

[1] This includes the creation of such comic stereotypes as Cucullus the cuckold in *The Lover's Melancholy* and the *commedia* duel between comic rivals for the hand of the lisping Amoretta in *The Lady's Trials* (1638).

claim to moral integrity is established by his contempt of courtly affectation in a speech (1.ii) whose poetic power derives from the images and rhetoric of Juvenalian satire. When Meleander is introduced, his psychological disorder is indicated by the shift from his lyrical memory of Eroclea to his violent fit of satiric madness:

> range, range on,
> And rowle about the world to gather mosse,
> The mosse of honour, gay reports, gay clothes,
> Gay wives, huge empty buildings, whose proud roofes,
> Shall with their pinacles, even reach the starres. (II.ii)

The impact of these speeches remains isolated. Meleander's views can be dismissed as the product of his madness, and the action does not need them to reflect on the outer world. Satire is another dramatic device, grist to the tragi-comic mill.

In *The Fancies Chaste and Noble* (1631, revised 1635–6), on the other hand, satire unbalances the tragi-comic equilibrium of the play to an extent which suggests an essential antithesis between it and Fletcherian tragi-comedy. In none of Ford's other tragi-comedies is the unexpected quite so emphatically displayed. The libertine turns out to be a courtly uncle, the bawd a kindly chaperone, and the powerfully realized corruption of the courtly world a false image. The dramatic methods employed make it more than usually difficult to suspend judgement until the pleasant surprises of the conclusion. The play opens with a powerful satiric statement on the familiar theme of the corrupted court; furthermore, the satirist himself displays the corruption he denounces by persuading his friend Livio to prostitute his sister to the reigning duke, Octavio. The action, although conventional, is marked off from the tragi-comic mode by the force of the verse:

> Thy beautious sister like a precious Tissue,
> Not shapt into a garment fit for wearing,
> Wants the adornments of the Workemans cunning
> To set the richnesse of the piece at view,
> Though in her selfe all wonder. . . .
> A way there may be (know I love thee *Livio*)
> To fix this Iewell in a Ring of gold,
> Yet lodge it in a Cabanet of Ivory. (I.i.151–8)

The imagery of such speeches is rooted in the traditions of complaint which gave such range to the satiric writing of the turn of the century. They are reminiscent of Vindice's language in *The Revenger's Tragedy* (1606) and that play is again echoed in the force with which Livio persuades his sister to go to court (1.i.48 ff.). Like Tourneur and Webster, Ford transmutes these images into theatrical emblems as in the moment when Livio comes on stage in his new court clothes, showing

> How by a new creation off [of] my Taylors
> I've shooke of old mortality, the rags
> Of home spun Gentry (prethee sister marke it)
> Are cast by. . . . (1.i.409–12)

The sense of a corrupted world extends even into the low comedy of the subplot with Secco's entrance, which, in an image taken from Marston, creates an emblem of corruption: '*Enter* SECCO *with a Castingbottle, sprinckling his Hatte and Face, and a little lookeing glasse at his Girdle, setting his Countenance*' (ll. 234–6; cf. Marston, *Antonio and Mellida*, III.ii). Secco is a barber, imitating and affected by the decadence of the court he serves. His intrigue with his eunuch servant and Morosa, 'an old rotten Codled mungrell, parcell Bawde, parcell midwife', provides a gross and parodic counter-image of the sexual games which make up the main action of the play.

The satiric themes, the attack on human venality, the picture of a court poisoned at the fountainhead, are simply dropped in Act v. It turns out that the Fancies, formerly presented as a courtly brothel, are the Duke's virtuous nieces, and that all the *double entendres* and insinuations have been the result of the audience's corrupted expectations. Some hint of the innocuous end of the play is provided with the information that Duke Octavio is in fact impotent. Morosa tells Castamela what he will expect of her:

> MOROSA.   He will not presse beyond his bounds
>   He will but chat and toy, and feele your
> CASTAMELA.   Guard me,
>   A Powerful *Genius*! feele
> MOROSA.   Your hands to kisse them (11. 924–8)

and so on. Her unfinished sentences create expectations in the pattern of a familiar dirty joke, a model which informs the whole play with the implication that corruption is in the eye of the beholder. It could be seen as a powerful attack on tragi-comic expectations or it could be the logical extension of a dramatic form which turns serious matters into comic, and so unthreatening, games.

Ford's dramaturgy is most telling when he succeeds in establishing a dialectic between action and passion, between theatrical device and poetic imagination. At the sensational finale of '*Tis Pity She's a Whore* (1629–33), Giovanni interrupts a banquet, entering '*with a heart upon his dagger*'. The physical image of the bleeding heart is the culmination of a train of metaphors in which love and the heart have been referred to with both bombast and sentimentality. In declaring his incestuous love, Giovanni passionately asks Annabella to 'Rip up my bosome, there thou shalt behold/A heart, in which is writ the truth I speake'; Annabella mocks her suitor, Soranzo, by saying that if she saw his heart she would swear that he was dead; when he says he is sick at heart, she calls for *aqua vitae*. The physical revelation at the end is the reality which puts all other assertions about love and fidelity to the test. Giovanni cries:

> *Soranzo*, see this heart which was thy wifes,
> Thus I exchange it royally for thine. (V.vi.73–4)

There is a kind of pathetic heroism in his assertion 'in my fists I bear the twists of life', but the gory realities of his hold on the life and death of another are manifest even as he says it.

Gifford's assertion that Ford's poetry 'flings a soft and soothing light over what, in its natural state, would glare with salutary and repulsive horror' is an untheatrical reading of the play.[1] It none the less points to a tension in Ford's work between characters who are capable of poetic insight and those to whom it is denied. We can recognize the sophistry of Giovanni's attempt to justify incest by an analogy with the neo-Platonic love of the beautiful, but we also recognize in his poetic solos an intellectual passion which is his claim to our sympathy. The action of the play does not support his view that '*love* will wipe away that rigour,/Which would in other *Incests* be abhorr'd', but the mutual passion of the incest is dramatically contrasted with the facile cynicism of Putana, the nurse, and the more machiavellian corruption of Soranzo, Annabella's husband. In the scene which follows the consummation of the incest, the lovers act out their passion in poetry whose very lyricism is ironic. Giovanni compares them to Jove and Leda, and the beauty of the image is a reminder of the unnaturalness of that doomed love. At the same time the harmony of their union is expressed by the way their

---

[1] W. Gifford (ed.), *The Dramatic Works of John Ford*, 2 vols (1826), I, xxiv.

speeches never break the blank verse line (II.i.31–5) which is immediately
flattened by Putana's bustling prose:

> Nay, what a Paradise of ioy have you past under? why now I commend
> thee, (Chardge) feare nothing, (sweeteheart) what though hee be your
> Brother; your Brother's a man I hope, and I say still, if a young Wench
> feel the fitt upon her, let her take any body, Father or Brother, all is one.
> (II.i.41–5)

In his careful attention to complexity of image and impression, Ford
resembles his Jacobean mentors Webster and Middleton, and, like many
another play, 'Tis Pity borrows from the earlier drama. The lovers and
Putana owe something to Romeo, Juliet and the Nurse in Shakespeare's
play; and the figure of Bergetto, Annabella's foolish suitor, is modelled on
the Ward in Middleton's Women Beware Women. Despite its derivative
quality, the subplot of Bergetto and Philotis is a remarkably coherent comic
contrast to the main action of the play. Bergetto is clearly not an appropriate
suitor for Annabella, but his comic infatuation for Philotis has an innocent
charm to set against the frantic intrigues of the other lovers. The scene
where he is mistakenly murdered achieves considerable pathos through his
comic incredulity at the physical reality of death:

> I am sure I cannot pisse forward and backward, and yet I am wet before
> and behind. . . . Is all this mine owne blood? nay then good-night with
> me, *Poggio*, commend me to my Unkle, dost heare? bid him for my sake
> make much of this wench, oh – I am going the wrong way sure, my belly
> akes so. oh, farwell, *Poggio*. (III.viii.11–12; 30–3)

Episodes like this, and the muddled violence of the revenge plot involving
Vasques and Hippolita, show Ford's debt to the Jacobean satiric tradition in
which heroic aspiration is set against physical necessity only partially
transcended by the style of the characters' hopeless defiance. Ford has none
of Fletcher's deft control of plot or his essentially comic skills of teasing and
playing with an audience. But it was by blending Fletcherian theatricality –
the self-conscious attention to style, the grand gesture – with satiric and
psychological insight that he created the most powerful of Caroline
tragedies.

(iii) William Davenant

Fletcher himself founded no school, but his mode of tragi-comedy created an easily imitated norm for fashionable Caroline drama. William Davenant, for example, explicitly allied himself with the demands of the new élite. He accordingly wrote masques with Inigo Jones, a masque and a play on platonic love, and, in his commercial work with the King's Men, Fletcherian romance. In his versions of the form, the hallmark is decorum. The emotional volatility of the characters, the rarefied conditions of the action, are conveyed in a language smoothed into courtly circumlocution. In *The Cruel Brother* (1626–7) Lucio's protestation of love renders Lear's terrified 'that way madness lies' blandly as:

> This way to madness leads: teach not my heart
> Such modern Heraldry. Let it dispose
> Of charitable thoughts with natural eyes
> Unlimited by customary form
> Which gain and nicety have made an art. (1.i)

The action includes a 'satirical courtier', Castruchio, whose language and behaviour are modelled on that of Bosola in the *Duchess of Malfi* (1614). Unlike Bosola's, however, his part in the action is restricted to set-piece flytings with other courtiers and the mockery of an obvious satiric butt, the unfortunate Lothario. Davenant's borrowings from Webster's language are similarly isolated and smoothed out. Ferdinand's sinister comparison between the Duchess and 'the irregular crab who though it goes backwards thinks that it goes right because it goes its own way' (1.ii. 275–6) is made simpler in Castruchio's fear that he will never thrive,

> unless I imitate the crab
> And find my way, as he doth his, backwards.
> That is to make petition to the foot
> That he will please t'instruct, and teach the head
> When to commiserate my affair. (1.i)

The emotional impact of the action is orchestrated through careful separation of gesture from the speech which instructs the appropriate response. In the scene where Lucio and Corsa plight their troth, each of the lovers kneels silently while the speech of Corsa's brother invokes 'chaste obedience', 'celestial heat', marriage 'fruitful as the vine', and so on. Davenant also shows his skill at manipulating his audience's response in the tirade of Corsa's confession (IV.i) and the song which creates the mood of Act V, scene i.

In a play constructed by the movement from one emotional high point to another, the plotting is often weak. Act I introduces a series of relationships with little scope for action, and the controlling plot of the lustful Duke's attack on the virtuous women does not emerge until Act III. A good deal of the dramatic capital of the play comes from reactions to the ladies' disgrace, yet the poetic justice of the Duke's death is effected, not by the wronged gentlemen, but by the protagonists of a quite different subplot. Decorum demands that ladies be chaste, gentlemen honourable, and even lustful dukes murdered only by villains. The dialectic arises in the ideological conflict between the insistence on chastity on the one hand and political fidelity on the other, usually at the expense of the unfortunate women on whose bodies the conflict is fought out. Their belief in the vital importance of chastity must remain completely inviolate even when they are powerless to protect it against political might. After Corsa has been raped by the Duke (IV.ii) she herself believes 'I am a strumpet grown', and her brother's reaction to the news displays a deeply misogynist doublethink, rendered plausible only by the abstractions in which the language deals:

> If compulsion doth insist until
> Enforcement breed delight, we cannot say
> The female suffers. Acceptance at the last
> Disparageth the not consenting at the first:
> Calls her denial, her unskilfulness;
> And not a virtuous frost i' th' blood. (V.i)

The separation of action from abstraction is achieved without irony so that the play lacks the dramatic tension which informs earlier Stuart drama. Foreste bleeds Corsa to death on stage in a sacrificial gesture, and, while he watches her bleed, wishes he could 'separate/The blood defil'd from what is pure'. The physical and dramatic fact of her blood on the stage presents no bar to his conceit and the line carries none of the irony of Beatrice Joanna's despairing cry to her father at the end of *The Changeling* (1622):

> O come not near me, sir, I shall defile you
> I am that of your blood was ta'en from you
> For your better health. (V.iii.149–51)

A preoccupation with love provides both the dramatic movement and the theatrical problems of Davenant's tragi-comedy *The Siege* (1629), where the

military action serves only to provide the necessary barriers and complication to the lovers' sentimental impulses. There is a stated conflict between
love and honour: Florello, from the besieging army, is in love with the
governor of Pisa's daughter; when he finally changes sides to be with her,
she makes him go back across the enemy lines and admit his treason. The
values of love, however, transcend all: when Florello confesses his treason to
his commanding officer, the general is entirely sympathetic and the pair
discourse on the power of worthy women. The plot continues in this fashion
through rivalries and despair to a conclusion in which Pisa is destroyed but
all the heroes live happily to dance at the wedding.

It is easy to mock such frivolities in Stuart tragi-comedy. They are not
simply a product of bad writing. On the contrary, individual scenes are
tightly constructed and written to create the maximum of local emotional
and theatrical effects. Such writing is the product of a highly developed
professional theatre whose conventions have been standardized into easily
adaptable formulas which can be exploited by a wide variety of practitioners
of varying talent. It is far from the uneven 'impure art'[1] of the great
Jacobeans, and is less to twentieth-century taste, but it was the staple of the
élite Caroline theatre. Davenant was no innovator in dramatic style. His
success in the Restoration depended as much on his contacts and his
entrepreneurial skills as on his special place in Caroline drama. These skills
were given only limited scope before the Civil War, largely because of the
power and influence of the existing professional managers and companies.
Nor is there any evidence that he would have made great changes in the
Caroline theatrical scene had he been given the chance. In his masque
writing he was happy to follow the lead of Inigo Jones, and his brief period
of control of the King and Queen's Young Company brought no new
departures.[2] The novelty of his operatic entertainments at Rutland House
in the 1650s was a clever ploy to bypass the ban on plays;[3] Davenant, in his
role of theatrical entrepreneur, belongs to the history of Restoration drama.

---

[1] The phrase is T. S. Eliot's. See *Selected Essays* (New York, 1950), 76–7.
[2] For a discussion of Davenant's aspirations to theatrical innovation, see John Freehafer,
'Brome, Suckling and Davenant's Theatre Project of 1639', *Texas Studies in Literature and
Language*, 10 (1968), 367–83.
[3] See pp. 298–300.

6 Satiric drama

(i) Thomas Middleton

Fletcherian tragi-comedy was not the only alternative to the bombast of old-fashioned theatrical styles. The boy players who had mocked the traditions of tragedy in their parodies of revenge plays also acted satires on the London scene. The transmutation of this satiric subject matter, in the adult drama of the 1620s and 1630s, reflects the changing conventions and expectations of Stuart drama.

In Middleton's city comedy, the topographical accuracy of Moll Yellowhammer's flight up the Thames (*A Chaste Maid in Cheapside*, 1611–13; IV.iii), the local colour of the christening scene (III.ii) and the Lenten promoters (II.i), and the physical detail of Quomodo's fantasy about the logs and apples 'from his land in Essex' (*Michaelmas Term*, 1604–6; III.iv) seem to present the lived texture of London life. Moreover, these city comedies turn on imbroglios between ambitious citizens and decayed gentry, underworld sharpers and country innocents, which fit almost too easily into paradigms of social mobility and economic change. However, Middleton does not take sides. Our triumph over the fall of Sir Walter Whorehound (*Chaste Maid*) is no greater for his being an aristocrat, and no sharper than the comic glee brought by the discomfiture of Sir Bounteous Progress or Penitent Brothel (*A Mad World My Masters*, 1605). The plays do deal critically with the social fabric of a particular community: Middleton notes how love, sex and family ties have become commodities and is mercilessly satirical towards the pretensions of *petit bourgeois* characters like Maudlin Yellowhammer or Mrs Quomodo. But he does not follow the divisions of contemporary political conflict. His cheating draper and tight-fisted usurer are parasites on, rather than creators of, the consumer economy; both gullers and gulled form the petty criminal subculture of the city rather than the powers who control it. They have no social links with the great city merchants who controlled royal finances or with the conservative gentry who formed the opposition to Charles and his court some thirty years after these plays were written.

The cultural interest of Middleton's drama lies in the interaction of topical subject matter with traditional dramatic form. Its comic patterns are those of New Comedy and Italian *commedia erudita*, while many of the funniest sequences – Moll and Touchwood Junior rising from their coffins (*Chaste Maid*, v.vi) or the fake doctor episodes in *Mad World* (iii.ii) and *Anything for a Quiet Life* [1621] (ii.iv) – are similar to the *lazzi* of the *commedia dell' arte* which Middleton could have seen when an Italian company visited London in 1604.[1] His rogues and tricksters are drawn both from the traditional witty servant of these comic forms and from direct observation of contemporary London life, while his comic method fuses the infinitely expanding joke with a realistic use of physical gesture and detail. A good deal of the comedy arises from Middleton's keen sense of the ridiculous. The characters' very names place them in a grotesque and fantastic world, and though some of them – Witgood, Savourwit, Hoard – are linked to humours and morality characteristics, there are others such as Onesiphorus Hoard or Penitent Brothel which are funny for their own sake as well as parodying Puritan outlandishness.

This combination of grotesque names and repetitive comic situations demands a style of playing as closely linked to clown traditions as to naturalism. Falselight and Shortyard from *Michaelmas Term*, for example, may have had analogues in the real London underworld but they are also a comic duo like Groucho and Chico Marx. They manipulate the other characters by sheer comic bravado, which may be analogous to, but is not the same as, economic exploitation. In the scene where Allwit, the formerly

[1] Allardyce Nicoll, *The World of Harlequin* (London, 1963), 169.

acquiescent cuckold of *A Chaste Maid*, refuses sanctuary to the desperate Sir Walter Whorehound, he completely controls the comic situation. When he self-righteously observes: 'I tell you truly/I thought you had been familiar with my wife once' (v.i.144–5), it is morally outrageous; it is also hilariously funny. William Gaskill's production of *A Chaste Maid* (Royal Court, 1966) in which the characters were dressed as recognizable modern types and the acting followed *commedia* and music hall techniques,[1] was not simply a factitious attempt to make a Jacobean play palatable for a modern audience: it was a recognition that the plays deal with basic social relationships. Middleton himself acknowledged the same thing. In Act v of *A Mad World My Masters*, Follywit incorporates the constable who comes to arrest him into the action of his play within the play. The constable, of course, cannot play his part and is berated by the stage audience. When Follywit and the players have made off with their spoils, Sir Bounteous asks the constable: 'art not thou the Constable i' th' Comedy?' to which the hapless man replies: 'Ith comedy? why I am the constable i' th commonwealth sir' (v.ii.169–71).

The commonwealth and the comedy are constantly brought together in Middleton's plays, not merely by topicality but by tangible dramatic action which gives life to imagery and theme. His two powerful tragedies, *The Changeling* (1622) and *Women Beware Women* (1621), avoid Fletcherian abstraction in favour of a physical detail which gives urgency and force to his tragic theme. In *The Changeling* de Flores has successfully murdered Beatrice Joanna's betrothed at her request. When he returns to claim her virginity as his reward, the following exchange takes place:

DE FLORES.　　I've a token for you.
BEATRICE.　　For me?
DE FLORES.　　　　　　　But it was sent somwhat unwillingly,
　　I could not get the Ring without the Finger.
BEATRICE.　　Bless me! What has thou done? (III.iv.26–9)

The physical horror of the beringed severed finger, together with its phallic symbolism, reminds the audience of murder's bloody reality, but, more significantly, Beatrice's reaction sums up in a single moment her criminal naïvety and her tragic awakening as de Flores forces her to become 'the deed's creature'. Even such a conventional device as the ghost of Beatrice's

---

[1] For a description of this production, see R. B. Parker (ed.), *A Chaste Maid in Cheapside* (London, 1969), Appendix V.

dead betrothed is introduced at the moment where it will have the most revelatory impact both on characters and audience. The events of the plot, the transfer of Beatrice's betrothal to her lover Vermandero, are economically dispatched in dumb show which ends in an emblematic tableau:

> DE FLORES *after all, smiling at the accident;* ALONZO's *Ghost appears to* DE FLORES *in the midst of his smile, startles him, shewing him the hand whose finger he had cut off. They passe over in great solemnity.* (IV.i S.D.)

The effort to portray the moral issues of the play in physical terms sometimes backfires, as in the silly contrivance of the chastity test (IV.i), but the overall impression of the play's movement is a progression of telling physical images.

The language similarly contains its own dramatic resonance. Sexual double talk, which provided so much of the comedy in *A Chaste Maid*, here provides a grotesquely witty undercurrent. De Flores' continual punning on 'will' and 'service' reveals his private obsessions, but the innocent use of the same words by other characters shows how trapped they are by their sexual desires. Alsemero's summary of the action (V.iii.195–203), with its puns on 'change', becomes more than a pat unification of the plots: it carries with it all the echoes of language and action.

In *Women Beware Women*, metaphors make us aware of the rule of art and pretence, explicitly in Hippolito's outrage at the way Leantio flaunts his conquest of Livia:

> Art, silence, closeness, subtlety, and darkness,
> Art fit for such a business; but there's no pity
> To be bestow'd on an apparent sinner,
> An impudent day-light leacher [lecher]. (IV.ii.7–10)

The image of decorous art masking a deadly reality is finally revealed in the masque at the end of the play. Livia the procuress plays Juno Pronuba, 'that rul'st o'er coupled bodies/Ty'st man to woman'; Isabella is the nymph 'In love with two at once'; and Hippolito is murdered by Cupid's arrows, a dramatization of the familiar emblem of Cupid and Death. The need for multiple murder makes some of the effects preposterous and the scene too drawn out, but one can appreciate in the iconography Middleton's attempt to create a witty decorum which none the less exposes the games and role-playing carried on throughout. Such emblematic moments form the structural pillars of the play. The triple plots of seduction, adultery and incest are contrived in private but demonstrated in public ensemble scenes.

While Bianca is seduced by the Duke on the upper acting level, her mother-in-law and Livia the procuress play a game of chess below in which the white king is checked and the 'pawn cannot come back to relieve itself'. At the centre of the play (III.ii) all the characters meet at a banquet where Bianca sits in state with her lover, and the incestuous couple Hippolito and Isabella dance for the assembled company. Nor does Middleton content himself with summing up past action, for this is also the occasion when the complex interchange of couples is completed as Livia seduces Bianca's husband. The social as well as personal interaction reveals itself with admirable economy in the tension of the scene in which Bianca and Leantio archly admire each other's spoils.

> LEAN.   A bowe i'th' ham to your greatness;
>   You must have now three legs, I take it, must you not?
> BIAN.   Then I must take another, I shall want else
>   The service I should have; you have but two there.
> LEAN.   Y'are richly placed.
> BIAN.   Methinks y'are wond'rous brave Sir.
> LEAN.   A sumptuous lodging.
> BIAN.   Y'ave an excellent Suit there.
> LEAN.   A Chair of Velvet.
> BIAN.   Is your cloak lin'd through Sir?
> LEAN.   Y'are very stately here.
> BIAN.   Faith something proud Sir.
> LEAN.   Stay, stay, let's see your Cloth of silver Slippers. (IV.i)

Here, the sequence is drawn out not only to make the thematic point but, more important, to keep the audience in suspense as to how long this sophisticated neutrality can be sustained before one of the speakers cracks. The scene is very similar in construction to the *lazzo* of *commedia*, where the basic dialogue can be improvised indefinitely before the pivotal line – in this case, Leantio's 'Y'are a whore' – is introduced. Comic technique is adapted to satiric tragedy.

This flexible dramatic style, fusing language and action into dramatic metaphor, did not lend itself to tragi-comedy, where the implications of action must be constantly held suspended for the happy ending. The duelling action of *A Fair Quarrel* (1615) deals with the familiar preoccupations of the genre. It provides scenes of emotional anguish as Lady Ager 'confesses' that her son is a bastard, in order to prevent him from fighting a man who has called him 'son of a whore'. On the duelling ground, however,

he finds a new cause when his opponent denounces him as a coward.
Emotions are further twisted when he falls in love with the sister of the man
he has wounded. A much more adroit dovetailing of plots, however, occurs
in the story of Jane. She is separated from her lover by her ambitious father,
then falls victim to the all too predictable lustful demands of the physician
who delivers her child. Jane's haughty resistance to blackmail is admirably
displayed and there is true tragi-comic wit in the outcome of the plot. The
doctor's revelation that she is no virgin ironically saves her from being
married to the idiotic country suitor, Trimtram, while her lover, Fitzallen, is
happy to accept her, knowing that the child is his.

But the play easily drifts towards comedy. The thwarted duel sequences
(II.i and III.i) hover on the edge of farce, while the finale of the play
contains one of the funniest moments in Jacobean theatre. Trimtram and his
servant Chough, already deprived of any sinister potential by the scene in
which they earnestly pursue their education in a roaring school (IV.i),
promise not to tell Fitzallen that Jane has had a child. Their sympathy for
him makes them compromise and pass the information on in a song by
which a potentially tense dramatic moment is completely exploded:

> CHOUGH.   *sings* Take heed in time oh man unto thy head,
> TRIMTRAM.   *sings* All is not gold that glistereth in bed. . . .
> CHOUGH.   Looke too't, I say, thy Bride's a Bronsterops,[1]
> TRIMTRAM.   And knowes the thing that men weare in their slops. (v.i)

Fitzallen then compounds the comedy by demanding a substantial dowry to
compensate for Jane's misdemeanour, thus ending up, as a comic hero
should, with his beloved and her money.

Middleton's more serious tragi-comedies show a surprising inability to
cope with plot. Suspense and emotional patterning, so essential to tragi-
comedy and so powerfully worked into his tragedies, completely elude him.
Significant conflict is introduced into the opening scenes and then dropped.
There is a wearying inevitability about the pairings off and reconciliations of
these plays, huddled into happy endings by such improbable surprises as the
grasping court lady's revelation that she was only testing her new husband
(*Anything for a Quiet Life*, 1620), or the hired murderers' announcement that
they have not fulfilled their commission (*The Witch*, 1615). The action is
filled out with scenes of jollity or horror; the resolutions are much the same
whether effected by disguised gypsies (*More Dissemblers Besides Women*,

---

[1] This preposterous nonsense word is introduced during the roaring school sequence and is a
running gag for the rest of the action.

1615 and *The Spanish Gypsy*, 1623) or lasciviously intoned witchcraft (*The Witch*). Middleton was unable to handle the poetic abstractions which true tragi-comedy required. His most successful plays remained true to a dramaturgy which tied emblem and metaphor to physical theatrical effect.

(ii) Philip Massinger

Massinger's debt to earlier theatrical tradition is also evident in his best-known play, *A New Way to Pay Old Debts* (1625), though his adaptation of the city comedy mode in that play indicates the shift in sensibility which took place in the satiric comedy of the 1620s. The plot resembles Middleton's city comedy *A Trick to Catch the Old One*, in which a young prodigal attempts to trick his creditors and recoup his lost fortune by pretending to have made an advantageous match. In Middleton's play, Witgood wins the audience's sympathy by his comic ingenuity, which is opposed to the obvious moral and economic baseness of his creditors. The setting is firmly placed in London, and the cast of whores, usurers and tricksters permits few distinctions of moral preference. Massinger, on the other hand, by setting the play in the world of country gentry, can establish a norm quite absent from earlier city comedy. The courtly conversations between Lovell and Lady Alworth would not be out of place in the world of tragi-comedy, and the city financier Sir Giles Overreach is isolated from the rest of the characters by his London origins, which thus seem to be intrinsically related to his villainy. Even his daughter Margaret, since she embraces the aristocratic morality, is ashamed of her father's aspirations for her advancement.

The action can accordingly proceed by a symbolic restatement of accepted values. Welborne has simply to fulfil the moral requirements of his name, silencing Lady Alworth's initial scorn with the reminder that 'The blood that runs in this arme, is as noble/As that which fills your veines' (I.iii.88–9). Lady Alworth's ability to recognize Welborne's nobility through his ragged clothes is in turn a token of her own true nobility, and the importance of their encounter is conveyed through the amazed reactions of the watching servants. With Lady Alworth's help, Welborne succeeds in regaining his property and goes off to prove his nobility still further in the wars; Margaret marries young Alworth in spite of her father's hope for a better match; and Lovell and Lady Alworth are left to comfort one another's declining years.

Despite this romantic plot, the themes of the play were felt to have a striking contemporary relevance. Henry Moody's commendatory verses note that 'thou couldst not/So proper to the time haue found a plot', and there are certain parallels between the career of Sir Giles Overreach and that of Sir Giles Mompesson, whose financial dealings were investigated by the House of Commons in 1621. The historical Sir Giles, however, was a gentleman who took advantage of the confused contemporary financial legislation and the economic expansionism of the Crown. Massinger's villain is a low-born city usurer whose extortion and corruption are more clearly illegal, and thus reflect less directly on the contemporary situation.

Moreover, within the structure of the play, Overreach, for all his machinations, never seriously engages with either characters or action. His tirades about how he will ruin that poor farmer or force this *déclassée* lady to wait on his daughter may have brought a shiver to his audience, but his victims never appear in the action. His plans are carried out by the hilariously incompetent Marall, who is easily outwitted by Welborne. The threat presented by his agent Greedy, the corrupt Justice of the Peace, is neutralized by the comic presentation of his gluttony, which contributes to the realistic texture of the play without undermining its aristocratic ideology. By this means the vitality and justification of the real threat to the *status quo* is left unexamined and Massinger's audience can be reassured by the coincidence of aristocratic, moral and aesthetic values in the guiding force of Lovell and Lady Alworth. The hysterical and apoplectic end of Sir Giles converts him finally into a wicked giant of romance who vanishes in a clap of thunder when the magic words are spoken. His threat to the happy world order is that of a pathological villain rather than an alternative world-view.

Massinger's control over his comic world is much less complete in his later comedy *The City Madam* (1632). The play deals with conflicting aspirations within a wealthy citizen family, and its dramatic energy comes from a poetic style whose fertile use of imagery creates a detailed sense of London life. The inappropriate profligacy of Sir John Frugal's wife and daughters is comically realized in the worthy steward's despairing catalogue of their gastronomic excesses:

HOLDFAST.   Did you not observe it?
There were three sucking piggs serv'd up in a dish,

> Took from the sow as soon as farrowed,
> A fortnight fed with dates, and muskadine,
> That stood my Master in twenty marks a piece,
> Besides the puddings in their bellies made
> Of I know not what. I dare swear the cook that dress'd it
> Was the Devill, disguis'd like a Dutch-man. (II.i.8-15)

The all-important features of class and lineage can similarly be identified. The cultural touchstones are indicated in the flyting between the rival suitors for Frugal's daughters:

> LACIE.   What a fine man
>   Hath your Taylor made you!
> PLENTY.   'Tis quite contrary,
>   I have made my Taylor, for my cloaths are pai'd for
>   Assoon as put on, a sin your man of title
>   Is seldom guiltie of. . . .
> LACIE.   . . . thy great grandfather was a Butcher,
>   And his son a Grasier, thy sire Constable
>   Of the hundred, and thou the first of your dunghill,
>   Created gentleman. (I.ii.43-6; 67-70)

The combination of localized detail with verbal exuberance owes a good deal to earlier city comedy, especially in the low-life scenes. In a scene reminiscent of *The Alchemist*, the prostitute Shave'em laments the decline in trade and then fights with her rough-necked clients, who remember her when she was a 'wastcotier in the garden allies,/And would come to a saylors whistle'. The very comic vitality of these scenes, however, creates tensions between comedy and romance, between the play's asserted values and the dramatic life of the characters. Having established the ideological drift of the play, Massinger then draws the mixture of satire and comedy into the romantic formula of 'the prince in disguise'. In Act III, Sir John first retires to a monastery and then is reported dead, leaving family, debtors and apprentices in the care and power of his brother Luke. Luke, of course, reveals his true colours. With considerable harshness he calls in the apprentices' bonds, consigns the debtors to prison, and reduces the allowance and sartorial style of Sir Frugal's family. Massinger uses the prince-in-disguise plot to restore order through a substitute tyrant. By being more tyrannical than Sir John, Luke can arrange affairs to his taste and Sir John can take over again untainted by harshness, having observed the effects of such control.

The play thus develops from an evocation of London life into a controlled plot focusing on Luke himself. In the earlier part of the play he is the one character to elude easy judgements or categories. Sympathy is directed towards him in the opening dialogue between the apprentices, and reinforced by the high-handed treatment he receives from the ugly sisters, Sir John's daughters. When he persuades Sir John to be merciful to the debtors (I.ii) we see him as the virtuous, put-upon younger brother who has genuinely repented his former wild ways but has learned from them the virtues of mercy.

In his characterization of Luke, Massinger has to deal with the problem of city comedy: that prodigality is more attractive than thrift. When Luke persuades the apprentices to give up their thrifty ways for the 'ravishing lechery' of 'the musical chime of Gold in your cram'd pockets' (II.i), we sympathize with their excited approval. Even the soliloquy that reveals Luke's villainy carries with it an imaginative intensity which makes moral disapproval irrelevant. Massinger solves the problem by firmly imposing the control of the plot and turning Luke into a machiavel and a villain who violates not only the economic but the moral law. In his new character of miser and extortioner, he encourages the parasites Getall and Shave'em so that he can surprise the young men at their most extravagant, and he seizes his debtors' assets just as they are about to redeem their debts. He can now be categorized in the simple emotive terms of his debtors' insults: broker, Jew, imposter, cut-throat, hypocrite (IV.iii.60–1). His assertion that he is merely imitating Sir John, behaving according to citizen values, is allowed no dramatic force.

The action demands a distinction between Luke's cruel extortion and Sir John's thrifty self-interest, but this is extremely difficult to dramatize; moreover, the evil of the Frugal ladies' social aspirations is far from self-evident. By moving to a morality-like action, Massinger avoids the awkward implications of his plot. Luke agrees to sell his sister and nieces to the Indians (Sir John and the girls' suitors in disguise) for human sacrifice. At a banquet he is shown an emblem of his own intransigent cruelty – first the fable of Orpheus, then a procession of his debtors 'heaving up their hands for mercy'. Neither show impresses him; whatever effect Orpheus may have had on his hearers, Luke denies the power of art to move a resolute man. By further 'magic' the suitors reappear and Sir John discovers himself. The extravagant symbolism is used to justify the conclusion, in which the ladies repent their errors and Luke is banished to make what he can in Virginia. Sir John is willing to extend mercy to the debtors, though no further than 'lawfull pity can give way too't'. The safe certainties of romance assert themselves at the end.

(iii) Ben Jonson

Jonson, who had pioneered satiric comedy and achieved dazzling success with adaptations of Old Comedy in *The Alchemist* (1610), *Volpone* (1606) and *Bartholomew Fair* (1614), responded to changes in the theatre with greater flexibility than many of his contemporaries. He was deeply contemptuous of the continuing popularity of 'mouldy tales' from a previous age, and his own later work shows constant experiment in the search for new comic form. In *The Devil is an Ass* (1616), his first play after the great success of *Bartholomew Fair*, he reasserts what is vital in the traditions of English drama but assimilates it to new preoccupations. The framing action deals with Pug, a minor devil, who wishes to test his powers in London, although Satan has contemptuously relegated him to the minor league of Lancashire and Northumberland. He is accompanied by a Vice, Iniquity, who speaks in the rhyming couplets of the old dramatic style. The parody provides a focus for contrasting old and new drama, as well as old and new manners. The satire on contemporary manners, more vicious than the devils themselves, is turned into surreal comedy by the images of the exhausted Vices returning to Hell for a rest. The literary and satiric joke is further extended (1.ii) when Fitzdottrel complains of his failure to conjure a devil and covertly mocks the Faustian tradition in his assurance that he would treat the devil well:

> Not, as the Conjurers doe, when they ha' rais'd him.
> Get him in bonds, and send him post, on errands,
> A thousand miles. (1.ii.37–9)

Within the framework of Pug's apprenticeship are a number of actions of gulling and deceit in which Jonson moves away from the method of humours comedy to more farcical set pieces such as the sequence in which Wittipol first declares his feelings for Fitzdottrel's wife (1.vi). The comedy here emerges partly from Fitzdottrel's naïve folly but principally from the completely mechanical nature of the situation. Wittipol makes a contract with Fitzdottrel by which he is allowed to speak to his wife 'Your quarter of an houre, alwaies keeping/The measur'd distance of your yard, or more'

(I.vi.67–8), but is able to subvert this agreement by having his friend Manly stand in for him while, in the person of the woman, he replies courteously, before the bemused couple's eyes, to his own proposition.

Alongside this plot are the staples of city comedy – the citizen who seeks to make his son a gentleman and Meercraft's plotting with his fraudulent projects. But these simply provide another form of folly quite devoid of serious social or economic analysis.

After *The Devil is an Ass* Jonson, preoccupied with court masques and his scholarly work, withdrew from the stage for nine years, returning in 1626 with *The Staple of News*. Here his mistrust of his audience and his actors, never far from the surface in his earlier work, becomes more explicit. In the prologue he wishes that the audience 'were come to hear, not see, a play' since 'He'd have you wise/Much rather by your ears than by your eyes'. His insistence on the pedagogic function of the drama did not result in dull didacticism. Jonson's new play was both formally experimental and theatrically dynamic. Its title refers to attempts to catalogue and control the activities of the new profession of journalist, but the main action of the play with the Pennyboy family and the Lady Pecunia is an adaptation of the old prodigal son play to the norms of citizen comedy. Its dramatic force once again derives from Jonson's ear for language and his ability to contrive comic scenes. From the verve and inventiveness of Pennyboy Junior's opening speech, to Pennyboy Senior's vehement denunciation of his son's prodigality (IV.iv.150 ff.), the play is carried by language whose concreteness of reference, fascination with slang, and elasticity of verse-form is the antithesis of romance decorum. The comic situations also arise out of such mad Jonsonian inventions as the jeering match, akin to the game of vapours in *Bartholomew Fair* (IV.iv); in the stage business where Pennyboy Senior interrogates his dogs, Jonson revives the old-fashioned clown monologue to richly comic and ironic effect, moving the speech along a series of dramatic rather then merely rhetorical impulses.

The whole style of the play makes it very difficult to place the comic interludes in which the gossips on stage comment – often unfavourably – on the action. From his comments elsewhere it is clear that he had little time for the contemporary vogue for revivals of the old drama. Yet the enthusiasm with which the gossips discuss *The Merry Devil of Edmonton* or *Dr Lambe and the Witches* – as well as his own *The Devil is an Ass* – is most appealing. It is as though Jonson recognized what was living in the older drama and tried to retain some vestige of it in his own later work.

The demands of fashion, however, presented their own challenge and in

1629 Jonson produced his only work apart from the unfinished *Sad Shepherd* dealing with love, *The New Inn, or The Light Heart*. The framing action of the play, including a lost child and myriad disguises and changes of identity, seems a mocking acknowledgement of the convenience of romance motifs for providing a plot. The revelations involved are carefully restricted to the final scene, where they are used to sort out the action, denying the audience any of the suspense, anticipation or even pleasing surprise which animates most romance. Jonson seems unwilling to trivialize his serious concerns with the nature of love by having its consummation depend upon coincidence and turns of fate. The main action of the play turns on the court of love presided over by Prudence, Lady Frampul's maid. Here Lord Lovel, at first mockingly and then with increasing seriousness, is invited to discourse on the nature of love. Lovel's discourses show Jonson at his most didactic, as his own definition of the play's business reveals:

> Lovel . . . having two houres assigned him of free colloquy, and love-making to his Mistresse, one, after Dinner, the other after Supper; the Court being set, is demanded by Lady Frampul, what Love is? . . . To whom, hee first by definition, and after by argument answeres, proving, and describing the effects of Love so vively, as she, who had derided the name of Love before, hearing his discourse, is now so taken both with the Man and his matter, as shee confesseth herselfe enamour'd of him.

Such a device is intrinsically undramatic. It allows no scope for passion, complication and reversal, the staples of love stories. Lovel's analysis of the nature of both melancholy and love is predictably learned and morally serious, and its sermon form renders it dull.

Love, moreover, is seen not as animating passion but in the context of aristocratic virtues. The Host of the New Inn, eventually revealed as the true, reformed aristocrat Lord Frampul, opens the play by urging Lovel to give up his melancholy and tendentiously enquiring whether his name means Love-well or Love-ill – the theme question for the rest of the play. His right to ask such questions and the validity of his point of view is then further asserted by his correct analysis of the decline of courtly virtue. Lovel's second discourse concerns valour, the true coeval to love, and the whole action is meant to return the young aristocrats – Lady Frampul, Lord Beaufort and indeed Lovel himself – to the true road of virtue, which will revive 'these nurseries of nobility' in aristocratic households and the court.

The play is set in the uncourtly milieu of an English country inn, but Jonson unfortunately ignores the possibilities for local colour which this setting might provide. The low-life guests Tipto and Fly, with their drinking bouts and dull jokes, are shadows of their predecessors in the vapours of Bartholomew Fair. The scenes in which they occur are doubly tedious because they so obviously function as foils to the truly 'refined' entertainment of Lovel and the Host. The characters are all placed along a scale of true virtue which considerably restricts their dramatic movement, often with seriously jarring effect. One of the funniest episodes in the play is the arrival of Lady Frampul's tailor, Nick Stuff, with a grand lady dressed in Lady Frampul's long-expected new clothes. It turns out that Nick Stuff's humour is to dress his wife in his customers' clothes, take her to an inn and make love to her as a grand lady. This harmless if curious perversion is treated with the utmost censure, for it involves base imitation of aristocratic style without aristocratic virtue. The court's judgement on the unfortunate pair has its intellectual coherence, but the way it is announced shows these refined persons indulging vicious class hatred:

HOST.   Pillage the Pinnace.
LAD[Y F].   Let his wife be stript.
[LORD] B.   Blow off her upper deck.
[LORD] L.   Teare all her tackle.
LAD[Y F].   Pluck the polluted robes ouer her eares;
   Or cut them all to pieces, make a fire o' them:
PRU.   To rags, and cinders burn th'idolatrous vestures . . .
HOST.   And send her home,
   Divested to her flanell, in a cart.
LORD L.   And let her Footman beat the bason afore her. (IV.iii.90–9)

The nice distinctions of the moral message and the uneasy tone of the dramatization may have contributed to the play's failure in the theatre. Jonson, characteristically, blamed the actors. The title page of the 1631 edition described it as 'neuer acted, but most negligently play'd, by some, the Kings Seruants. And more squeamishly beheld, and censured by others, the Kings Subiects'. However, Jonson evidently expected to be misunderstood, for the prologue defiantly insists:

If any thing be set to a wrong taste,
'Tis not the meat, there, but the mouth's displac'd,
Remoue but that sick palat, all is well.

The disastrous failure of *The New Inn* and his paranoid reaction to it seem to have made Jonson more anxious to explain his purposes to the audience in an unambiguous way. The critical commentators in *The Magnetic Lady* (1632) have none of the theatrical life of the gossips in *The Staple of News* and their comments seem designed to pre-empt criticism of a more specific kind. Probee and Damplay comment on the plotting of the play and the identity of satirized characters, and are read familiar lessons on the unfolding of the action and the neutrality of satire along with the whole vexed question of 'who should teach us the right or wrong at a play'. Yet Jonson's sense of his isolation and the futility of correct writing is none the less evident. Probee and Damplay claim to represent the people. Moreover: 'Not the *Foeces*, or grounds of your people . . . your sinfull sixe-penny Mechanicks – but the better, and braver sort of your people! Plush and Velvet-outsides! that stick your house round like so many eminences' (Induction, 32–7). Jonson, however, no longer seems to believe in the coincidence of good taste with good breeding; the boy asks the critics to undertake that this public 'shall know a good *Play* when they hear it; and will have the conscience, and ingenuity beside, to confesse it' (55–7).

In spite of this firm theoretical defence, *The Magnetic Lady* lacks the sparkle of Jonson's earlier work. As with *The New Inn* its outcome depends on events outside the action and its successful moments draw on Jonson's traditional skills of comic characterization and energetic language. Such figures as Sir Diaphanous Silkworm the courtier or Mistress Polish the religious sister are delightful vignettes, but they belong in humours comedy and fit only fortuitously into the more tightly plotted action of the new style.

With *The Tale of a Tub* (1633), his last complete play,[1] Jonson moved away not only from the complex plotting of his recent work but also from its preoccupation with urban life. He sets the action with a somewhat tongue-in-cheek prologue offering

> antick Proverbs, drawne from Whitson-Lord's
> And their Authorities at Wakes and Ales,
> With countrey precedents, and old Wives Tales;
> . . . to shew what different things
> The Cotes of Clowns, are from the Courts of Kings.

The setting is, in fact, suburban rather than rural, and in giving his country characters thick rural accents Jonson may have been parodying the urban-centred consciousness of his élite audience. In other respects the play is his least satiric. Like *Bartholomew Fair* it is plotted in space rather than by the

---

[1] For a discussion of the date of this play, see *Jacobean and Caroline Stage*, IV, 633–6.

interaction of events, as different sets of characters attempt to secure marriage to Awdrey, the daughter of the high constable of Kentish Town. The setting and spatial organization of the play allow Jonson scope for his acute observation of character along with his skill in building up scenes of crazy farce. But these dramatic skills have become an end in themselves: the humours are no longer obsessive deviations from a moral just balance, and the sharp edge of social satire has entirely disappeared. Jonson also seems to have lost faith in his ability to make the action clear: the entertainment with which the play ends re-enacts its movement in a series of 'motions', and the process of confusion is laid bare. The flatness of the final masque may have been the result of censorship.[1] Jonson's satire on his old enemy Inigo Jones remains in the figure of In and In Medley with his verbal tics and his talk of surveying, but it has nothing of the raging wit of the 'Expostulation' or the other poems directed at his erstwhile collaborator.

(iv) Caroline satirists

Although Jonson's success and power as a playwright rapidly declined after the death of James I, his influence on the younger generation of dramatists was widely acknowledged.[2] Even those whose main theatrical mode was Fletcherian romance used the humours method of characterization and the urban settings which Jonson had pioneered. However, as is often the case with imitative forms, the method took over from the purpose, and later city comedy neglected both the satirical point of Jonson's social observation and the moral force behind his notion of humours. The term was co-opted by Fletcher in 1619 for his *The Humorous Lieutenant*, and it is as a shorthand for characterization that the device is employed by later dramatists as much under Fletcher's as Jonson's influence. Moreover, the satiric malcontents so carefully placed in Macilente in *Every Man Out of His Humour* or Surly in *The Alchemist* became stylized into figures like Shackerley Marmion's Snarl (*Holland's Leaguer*), whose attacks on women are merely one element in a debate, or Bostock, in Shirley's *The Ball*, whose misanthropy has no force within the context or action of the play.

This formulaic tendency in later satire is well illustrated by Shackerley

---

[1] See p. 102.
[2] See Joe Lee Davis, *The Sons of Ben* (Detroit, Mich., 1967).

Marmion's *Holland's Leaguer* (1631). The title refers to a notoriously successful brothel in the suburbs of London, but the action of the play follows a conventional romantic pattern, bringing lovers together and exposing affectation by a series of comic displays. All the satiric attention is turned towards vanity and love. Philautus the misogynist is contrasted with Trimalchio the foolish gallant; Triphoena the silly court lady is set against the more sensible women, Millicent and Faustina, who initiate the gulling which makes up the action of the play. The brothel is used as one of the set scenes of the play; all the men repair there, only to be caught by the tricksters disguised as a constable and a watchman. The scene is wittily based on jokes contrasting love and war, but at no point does it allow contrasts between the finances of prostitution and the free love practised outside. None of the characters is placed socially; the prostitutes are merely prostitutes, the projectors are projectors, and even the constable, the watchman and the justice of the peace are played by gentlemen from the main action of the play. In spite of its reference to the contemporary London scene, this drama is inward-looking and its very satire serves to underpin a moral neutrality which takes no account of economics or political tensions or class. It is the satire of the in-joke, the dominant group against the deviant; it excludes the troubling ambiguity of Jonson's satiric masterpieces.

In the hands of a skilled dramatist, the new satiric formula could nevertheless produce most effective comedy. A good example is Davenant's *The Wits* (1633). When a licence was applied for, it was censored by Sir Henry Herbert, whose inclinations were always conservative and who seems to have been no admirer of the author. However, in a famous judgement, the King himself ruled that 'faith' and 'slight' were 'asservations only, and no oathes'.[1] This decision seems to recognize the importance of verisimilitude in the tense colloquial dialogue, which is remote from the windy abstractions of Davenant's tragi-comic style.

The plot of *The Wits* draws on the familiar comic opposition between youth and age, but Davenant has wittily reversed the convention by making the old men belatedly riotous. Their plan to 'cozen in our age' is given a further comic range by applying the ruthless commercial language of the gulling plot to the sex war:

> They wil immure themselves
> With Diamonds, with all refulgent Stones,
> That merit price: ask 'em who payes? why Ladies!

[1] Adams, *Herbert*, 22; quoted in *Jacobean and Caroline Stage*, III, 222.

> They'll feast with rich Provencal wines; who pays?
> Ladies. They'le shine in various habit, like
> Eternall Bridegromes of the day; aske 'em
> Who payes? Ladies. Lie with those Ladies too,
> And pay 'em but with Issue-Male, that shall
> Inherit nothing but their witt, and doe
> The like to Ladies, when they grow to age. (II.i)

Unfortunately for the men, they have tangled with women who have learned their own shrewdness and resistance to exploitation in an equally hard economic school. The ensuing battle is highly diverting, as well as reflecting a kind of realism by being couched in these hard-nosed financial terms. When Luce complains that her lover, Young Pallatine, is keeping her short of cash, she is all too aware of the alternatives open to her:

> That I must teach Children in a darke Cellar,
> Or worke Coifes in a Garret for crackt Groates,
> And broken meat! (III.ii)

The wit of these characters lies in their ability to survive precariously on the edge of élite London society; despite the satiric exposure of that society's values, the play must have provided amusement to those who felt themselves secure within it. Still more reassuring is the characters' evident contempt for all those who lie outside their own milieu. When the ladies first encounter the gentlemen who thought to exploit them, they secure an immediate advantage by affecting to find them both *petit bourgeois* and, worse still, countrified. Their arch enquiries about country habits are a *tour de force* both of comic writing and of wittily detailed description of the world they affect to despise:

> Pray how doe the Ladies there? poor Villagers
> They churne still, keepe their Daries, and lay up
> For Imbroidered Mantles, against the Heires birth! . . .
>
> > > > penny Gleek I hope's
> In fashion yet, and the treacherous foot
> Not wanting on the Table frame, to jogge
> The Husband, lest he lose the Noble that
> Should pay the Grocer's Man, for Spice and Fruit! (II.i)

The men in their turn are not at a loss; they reply with equally disingenuous enquiries about life at court. The whole scene radiates a comedy born of precise social knowledge. It is the tone which animates the best Restoration comedy, in which the knowing ladies and the sharp-witted gallants play a sexual game whose stakes are entirely financial.

The satire which animates this drama is based partly on the class conflict found in Jacobean city comedy. The victim of the action throughout the play is Sir Tyrant Thrift, a usurer. He is treated with contempt, not because of moral objections to his usury, but because his parsimony violates the ideals of conspicuous consumption and aristocratic contempt for the source of one's income. In the fashionable play world of the 1630s, the point of view was that of the sophisticated gentleman about town, mocking the affectation and simplemindedness of citizen and gallant alike.

Killigrew's *The Parson's Wedding* (1639–40) celebrates the effortless superiority of a group of young men about town who unite to exploit women and the lower classes, untrammelled by moral scruple or financial necessity. The young heroes are not distanced or judged in any way, and their attractive ease and style draws the audience into sharing their commitment to wit, pleasure and the good life. The only division between them is competition for sex, which they wittily recognize as another expensive commodity. Careless, for example, affects to despise the pursuit of women and is disarmingly clear about his own motives:

> I'm so full of that resolution to dislike the sex that I will allow none honest, none handsome. I tell thee, we must beat down the price with ourselves, court none of 'em, but let their maidenheads and their faces lie upon their hands till they're weary of the commodity. Then they'll haunt us to find proper chapmen to deal for their ware. (II.v)

Wanton, the witty whore, shares the gallants' easy cynicism and mocks Puritan attitudes in a comic account of the consequences of making adultery punishable by death:

> None would lose an occasion nor churlishly oppose kind nature nor refuse to listen to her summons when youth and passion calls for those forbidden sweets. When such security as your lives are at stake, who would fear to trust. (IV.i)

But the true opponents in the play are not committed Puritans. They are the dull, the prudish, and the lower class. At the centre of the play is a tavern scene (III.v) in which a tailor and a scrivener are cruelly mocked and insulted for the bad manners of dunning a gentleman. The crowning joke comes when Lady Loveall, the gallants' common mistress, is first insulted and then left to pay the bill: 'they have treated her upsey whore, lain with her, told, and then pawned her' (III.v).

The realism of the setting is insisted upon by such references as the comment on the ordinance against discharged soldiers (I.i) or the good-humoured mockery of courtly amateur playwrights (III.ii). But the tone is comic rather than satiric. The virtuoso denunciation of the country knight's son – 'Hobbinol the second . . . 'tis a very veal, and he licks his nose like one of them' – serves only to display superior city wit, and the whole action would have provided gallant young bachelors with a thoroughly pleasing image of themselves inhabiting an unthreatened world.

The movement from satirizing the city to celebrating it in city comedy is seen even more clearly in the so-called 'place plays' of the 1630s.[1] Though often seen as an imitation of the colourful particularity of *Bartholomew Fair*, they use London as a location for the plot rather than as a microcosm of society. Such spurious topicality had been scorned by Jonson himself in the prologue to *The Staple of News*:

Alas! what is it to his Scene, to know
How many Coaches in *Hide-parke* did show
Last spring, what fare today at *Medleyes* was,
If *Dunstan*, or the *Phoenix* best wine has?
They are things – But yet, the Stage might stand as wel,
If it did neither heare these things, nor tell.

The London setting affected neither the satiric edge nor the comic plotting of these plays. In *Covent Garden* (1633), Nabbes holds together incidental satiric portraits of such figures as Artlove the platonic lover within a plot which deals with the rivalry between suitors for three women. The result is a smoothly conventional work. The suggestion that Lady Worthy may cuckold her husband provides a flutter of dramatic excitement, but accepted morality is left undisturbed when she reveals that the whole stratagem was under her control and her husband's jealousy unfounded. The Epilogue describes

A *Play*, wherein was no *disguise*;
No *Wedding*; no improbable *devise*:
But all an easie *matter*, and contein'd
Within the time of *action*.

[1] See Theodore Miles, 'Place Realism in a Group of Caroline Plays', *RES*, 18 (1942). Brome and Shirley's 'place plays' are discussed below on pp. 241–3, 254–5.

The principles of decorum and unity which brought such comic intensity to Jonson's early work now endorse a dramatic ease which neither threatens nor exposes the *status quo*.

Nabbes's *Tottenham Court* (1634), set in a suburban resort, rejects satire and city comedy completely, offering instead '*a Tale/Drest up of a faire Milke-Maid*'. It is clear that Nabbes is completely at home with this genre. His plot, which skilfully handles three groups of characters, moves from a running race – a lively exit for his characters, but also a borrowing from Shirley's *Hyde Park* – to such *commedia* devices as the episode where a would-be seducer is tricked into hiding in a trunk which turns out to contain a rival suitor. The suburban setting demands a countrified romance, and this is provided in the story of Bellamie and Worthgood, lovers who have fled from a tyrannical uncle. In keeping with decorum, the country-folk who rescue them turn out to be Worthgood's sister and father in disguise. The three neatly turned plots reunite the families, reform the rakes, and demonstrate the resourcefulness of the women who succeed in protecting their much besieged virtue. The play is in every sense wholesome: in his prologue, Nabbes uses the culinary metaphor to reject the 'salt' and 'relish' of fashionable drama; and it is true that, though the plots are similar, the ideology the same, he avoids the sexual titillation and the intense theatrical excitement of the drama he imitated.

(v) Moral masques

Nabbes's unexceptionable moral position also lies behind his *Microcosmos* (1637), which adapts the masque devices of dance and revelation to a more traditional morality play form. Will Cufaude's commendatory verses to the first edition report:

> All was instruction mingled with delight.
> Nor are thine like those Poets looser rimes
> That waite upon the humours of the times:
> But thou dost make by thy Poetick rage
> A *Schoole* of Vertue of a common *Stage*.

Where the court masque was moving to much more pointed political material, Nabbes was content to create a moral work. Physander, his hero, is tempted by Sensuality and saved from her by Bellanima and Temperance; he submits to Fear, the servant of Conscience, and is finally helped by Hope to overcome Despair. This clear morality action is seconded by another plot in which discord among the four elements and the four humours is expressed in dance. The action proceeds by an allegorical psychomachia, expressed in dance and mime, together with the revelation of harmony which characterized the traditional finale of a masque:

> Here the last Scene is discover'd, being a glorious throne: at the top whereof LOVE sits betwixt IUSTICE, TEMPERANCE, PRUDENCE and FORTITUDE, holding two crownes of starres: at the foote upon certain degrees sit divers gloriously habited and alike as Elysii incolae; who whil'st LOVE and the VERTUES lead PHYSANDER and BELLANIMA to the throne, place themselves in a figure for the dance. (v.i)

In the elaboration of these stage directions, Nabbes seems to have had some version of movable scenery in mind, but that was his only innovation in this form. In 1630, Thomas Randolph, the Cambridge playwright, had created a similar moral masque, *The Muses' Looking Glass*. The first act is a kind of prologue in which Roscius attempts to convince two Puritan hawkers that the theatre can serve a moral function by holding up the mirror to 'The native foulnesse, and deformity/Of our dear sin'. The rest of the action, however, takes the form of a series of exemplary dialogues in which moral absolutes are discussed in their social form. Social decorum and moderation are the keynotes as the dialogues seek a mean between such qualities as excessive courtesy and 'peevish and impertinent distaste' or arrogance and modest dissembling. The Puritans are none the less convinced by the display, and the entertainment ends with Flowerdew pronouncing:

> Now verily I find the devout bee
> May suck the honey of good Doctrine thence;
> And bear it to the hive of her pure family
> Whence the prophane and irreligious spider
> Gathers her impious venome! (v.i)

This adaptation of morality form to masque, or moral absolutes to social virtues, seems entirely characteristic of the ideological trend in Stuart drama. In 1624, Dekker and Ford had written a moral play 'in the nature of a masque' called *The Sun's Darling*, which was revived in 1638. In it, Raybright passes through the Seasons, in whose company he encounters various type-characters. However, the cyclical movement of the play requires him to move through Winter to Death, with the reminder that he 'should bid farewell/To a vain world of wearinesse and sorrows' (v.i. 316–17). The note of *memento mori* on which the play concludes jars against the bland topical humour of the rest of the action. It was a note which was rigorously avoided by later writers in this form. Shirley's *Cupid and Death* (1653), for example, takes its story from the legend of Cupid and Death exchanging arrows. The story is rooted in neo-Platonic theory concerning the paradoxical relationships between Eros and Thanatos, but Shirley turns it into a jolly tale with opportunities for scenic display and facile satire at the expense of folly. Even the effects of death are not permanent and at the end of the play Shirley presents the apotheosis of the slain lovers in Elysium.

Such wishful thinking seems far from the fierce moral concern of Jonsonian drama. His belief that the theatre could instruct and improve a whole society was denied by the commercial and also the artistic failure of his later work. The work of his more successful imitators displays the tendency for pattern to harden into formula, and satire to soften into comedy. Their success depended on the recognition that the entertainment provided by a flattering mirror is the most marketable commodity of the theatrical profession.

7 Caroline professionals: Brome and Shirley

(i) Richard Brome

The most explicit Caroline debt to Jonson is in the work of Richard Brome. He had been Jonson's servant, his characters often refer to their Jonsonian lineage, and his comedies evoke the traditions of 'just judgement and the seal of Ben'. Jonson was initially happy to acknowledge his disciple. His patronizing commendation of *The Northern Lass* (1629) praises Brome's

> observation of those Comick Lawes
> Which I, your *Master*, first did teach the Age.
> You learn'd it well, and for it serv'd your time
> A Prentise-ship: which few doe now a dayes.
> Now each Court-Hobby-horse will wince in rime;
> Both learned and unlearned, all write *Playes*.

Brome himself, however, defended the comedy rather than the 'lawes'. The prologue to *The Sparagus Garden* (1635) warns:

> That to expect high Language, or much Cost,
> Were a sure way, now, to make all be lost.

> Pray looke for none: He'le promise such hereafter,
> To take your graver judgments, now your laughter
> Is all he aymes to moove.

Laughter Brome can certainly move, using the Jonsonian skill of characterization exploiting the theory of humours and created through comic language. In the first scene of *The City Wit* (1629–37), Pyannet, the hero's citizen mother-in-law, delivers a diatribe against him. Crasy protests that he has been bankrupted by his kind heart and she retorts:

> Kind heart! What should Citizens do with kind hearts; or trusting in any thing but God, and ready money? . . . Honest man! Who the Devill wish'd thee to be an honest man? Here's my worshipful Husband, Mr *Sneakup*, that from a Grasier is come to be a Justice of the Peace: And, what, as an honest man? Hee grew to be able to give nine hundred pound with my daughter; and, what, by honestie? Mr *Sneakup* and I are come to live i'th City, and here we have lyen these three years; and what? for honesty? Honesty! What should the City do with honesty; when 'tis enough to undoe a whole Corporation? Why are your Wares gumm'd; your Shops dark; your Prizes [Prices] writ in strange Characters? What, for honesty? Honesty? why is hard waxe call'd Merchants waxe; and is said seldome or never to be rip'd off, but it plucks the skin of a Lordship with it? what! for honesty? (1.i)

This list of double-dealing and sharp practice is a staple of Jonsonian satire, but it has become so commonplace that it can be subsumed into the comic *élan* of the speech. Brome piles up the examples as far as they will go, and then deftly twists direction as Pyannet turns her attention from Crasy's commercial to his sexual inadequacies. Social conflict is now simply the framework for comic action. The humour emerges from the scabrous language and comic inventiveness with which all the characters rehearse their known and expected vices. Within these clearly accepted limits, the characters skip through infallible, because familiar, comic routines which owe as much to *commedia* as to specifically Jonsonian traditions.

In an attempt to recoup his fortunes, Crasy disguises himself as a doctor, joining forces with a 'widow' (who says that she is really a whore) and Crack, her singing man. They see their relationship as an 'Indenture Tripartite . . . Like *Subtle*, *Doll*, and *Face*'. The remainder of the comedy, however, has none of *The Alchemist*'s single-mindedness either in satiric impulse or in comic form. Crasy's frenetic activity and protean changes of disguise are

directed to maintaining the *status quo*, to restoring by witty means what he
could not retain by honest ones. In this context, his moralizing over the
ingratitude of his creditors is so intrusive as to appear parodic, the more so in
its change from prose to verse:

> Now they all shall feele
> When honest men revenge, their whips are steele. (v.i)

His antics in the disguises, first of a lame soldier, then of a scheming
physician, are too comic to carry moral conviction.

   Though the foolish are exposed in the end, none of the tricksters is really
criminal. In a volte-face reminiscent of Jonson's *Epicoene*, the 'whore'
reveals that she is Jeremy, Crasy's apprentice, in disguise, and that Crack,
the supposed pimp, is his brother. It is as if Face in *The Alchemist* had
turned out to be Lovewit in disguise. The prevailing values of good humour
are restored in Crasy's final call:

> Let us make this a merry night.
> Think of no losses. Sirs, you shall have none;
> My honest cares being but to keep mine owne.
> What, by my slights, I got more then my due,
> I timely will restore again to you.

Such un-Jonsonian geniality recalls the older public theatre traditions of
Dekker and Heywood.

   Brome used a variety of theatrical models for *The Northern Lass* (1629)
and it may have been the combination of Dekkerian sentimentality with
Jonsonian wit which brought the play its success both at the Globe in 1629
and at its revival for a courtly audience in 1638. The story of the forsaken
Northern Lass is closest to Dekker, but Brome complicates that action with
a wittily exploited mistaken identity situation in which the true Constance is
confused with the whore who takes her name. This comic action is made
even funnier by the unabashed social climbing of the city characters,
comically proud of their good city ancestry. The complexities of
seventeenth-century social mobility are summed up in Widgine's contrasting
images of status and power:

> A good man i' th' City is not call'd after his good deeds, but the known
> weight of his purse. One, whose name any Usurer can read without
> spectacles; one that can take up more with two fingers and a thumb upon
> the Exchange, than the great man at Court can lift with both his hands;

one that is good only in Riches, and wears nothing rich about him, but the Gout, or a thumb-Ring with his Grand-sirs Sheep-mark, or Grannams butter-print on't, to seal Baggs, Acquittances, and Counter-panes. (II.i)

Such comments give an authenticating edge of realism to the romantic action, which works through the permutations of marriageable people in the cast until a satisfactory set of unions is achieved.

The prologue to the play 'thinks it long/Since you were last delighted with a song'. Brome's unusually musical play makes good this deficiency with the Northern Lass's love-songs on the one hand, on the other with the rowdy *charivari* (III.iii) which chastises the Widow Fitchow's scolding. Some of the song sequences achieve a more complex tension between irony and pathos. The misalliance between Luckless and Fitchow is celebrated in a melancholy masque preceded by Constance's song of resignation:

> *Nor Love, nor Fate dare I accuse*
> *For that my Love did me refuse;*
> *But oh mine own unworthiness,*
> *That durst presume so mickle bliss.*
> *It was too much for me to love*
> *A Man, so like the gods above;*
> *An Angels shape, a Saint-like voice,*
> *Are too Divine for Humane choice.* (II.vi)

There is a comic incongruity between Constance's pathetic description of her lost lover and Luckless's actual incompetent efforts to make the most capital out of his marriage. The masque is a variation on the familiar 'reversed revels', but it also affects the plot by making Luckless realize that the true Constance still loves him, and that he must get out of his marriage to Fitchow.

The wittiest turn on the effects of song is played when Constance's uncle takes up with Luckless's cast-off whore, also called Constance, and prepares to marry her off to Widgine, who thinks he is getting the true Northern Lass. Constance the whore acts the part of the true Constance most effectively. The song of forsaken love she sings to her 'wayward Barn' is painfully sad despite the comic situation, while the combination of bawdy double entendre and pastoral charm in the song of the serpent and the flowers has all the pathos of Ophelia's madness. Against these atmospheric effects, Widgine acts out the role of Luckless in a Chinese box of parody and double deception.

This skilful control of dramatic organization is also a feature of Brome's 'place plays' of the 1630s. *The Weeding of Covent Garden* (1632) has a cast of Jonsonian humours but the action turns on the New Comedy formula of conflict between the generations. The deceptions which Crosswill's children practise on him provide Brome with material for beautifully paced comic scenes. His riotous son Mihil, for example, pretends to be engaged in legal disputation with scholars who are, in fact, his creditors in disguise. The simple comic deception is twisted further when Mihil puts the case of his (real) debts as the subject for hypothetical disputation, and further still by Crosswill's irritation that his son should be so scholarly, coming to a comic crescendo at the arrival of Mihil's riotous friends.

The romantic plot similarly turns on deceptions, though of a less mercenary kind. Crosswill's children all recognize that he will never allow them to marry their own choices and try to overcome the problem by offering him a series of wildly unsuitable matches. There is a moment of comic suspense when Crosswill almost agrees to Mihil marrying a bawd, but in the end their perverse stratagems pay off. Brome is aware that the turns of his plot take some following. When Katherine is explaining to her new friend, Luce, how her brother turned precisian, she compares herself with a poet who would entreat an audience

> to mark the Plot, and several points of my play, that they might not say
> when 'tis done, they understood not this or that, or how such a part
> came in or went out, because they did not observe the passages. (III.ii)

She recounts the story of Gabriel and his fallen mistress, Dorcas, the point where the romantic and the comic come together. As in *The Northern Lass*, the past story is pathetic but the means of reconciliation are comic; they include such elements as Dorcas's sudden refusal to ply her prostitute's trade, to the consternation of the bawd, and Mihil's energetic struggle to drink his brother Gabriel out of his precise humour.

The play is held together not merely by the devices of the plot but by the sense of place created by the accumulation of authentic detail. The play opens with Cockbraine admiring Rooksbill's new houses, and in the second scene the wild young men are attracted into a brothel by Dorcas singing on a balcony, an innovation of the building style used in Covent Garden. In the tavern scene, attention is constantly diverted from the main characters with the bustle of service to other rooms, with '*Fidling of rude tunes*', and such commercial mumbo-jumbo as 'Half a dozen of clean pipes and a candle for the *Elephant*. . . . Carry up a *Jordan* for the *Maidenhead* and a quart of white muskadine for the *blew Bore*'. The chaos of the tavern exacerbates Gabriel's religious humour, and his denunciation of 'prophane tinkiling the cymbals of Satan that tickle the eare with vanity' attempts to recreate the effect of Jonson's show-stopping entrance for Zeal of the Land Busy with his cry of 'Down with Dagon' (*Bartholomew Fair*, v.v).

As in Jonson's *Fair*, the energy of London life is shown to be unassailable. Although some of the comedy turns against the excesses of the young gentlemen and their roaring fraternity, Cockbraine, like his 'Reverend Ancestor Justice Adam Overdo', is quite incapable of suppressing their enormities. His efforts provide the finale of the play, in his noisy arrival with the 'blew Gown college' of magistrates and officers. He is completely dismayed, however, when each person he tries to arrest is immediately bailed by the newly reconciled older generation. Brome's play is here significantly different from Jonson's. Jonson's pig woman, horse courser and ladies of pleasure are part of a genuinely anarchic world whose power to overwhelm the forces of order is unnerving as well as comic; in Brome, even the prostitute is a respectable young lady in disguise, and the lines of conflict have been simplified into the comfortable New Comedy opposition between old men and lovers who can easily in the end make common cause without any fundamental reconsideration of 'Adam, flesh and blood'.

In spite of their vivid local colour, these plays do not deviate from the accepted theatrical versions of Caroline social life. The romance plots which move them, the humours which circumscribe their characters, simplify their thematic concerns. In his suit against the Salisbury Court, Brome claimed that *The Sparagus Garden* (1635) had brought the company £1000.[1] Its spectacular popularity may have been due to its synthesis of so many elements of contemporary theatre within easily accepted ideological limits. The romantic main plot of young lovers thwarted by warring parents was a familiar theme and Brome gives it a little more edge by opposing class as well as ancient animosity. One of the fathers is also involved in the other plot, an attempt to cheat a young heir whose country ways and gullible nature provide further comedy. However, even the city comedy turns on romance: the boy aspires to gentility because of his mother's death-bed revelation that he is a gentleman's unacknowledged son.

The ensuing complications are brought together in the eponymous garden sequences. At the level of plot, the garden is a Jonsonian 'centre

---

[1] For details of this lawsuit, see pp. 107–9, and Ann Haaker, 'The Plague, the Theatre and the Poet', *Renaissance Drama*, NS 1 (1968), 283–306.

attractive', bringing all the characters together. However, it is also a *paysage moralisé* which teaches characters and audience a lesson. The aristocrats who frequent the garden act as touchstones for the behaviour of the other characters, models against which to set their jealousy, their longings and their empty aspiration. In a singularly old-fashioned moment, redolent more of late morality than citizen comedy, the 'Courtiers Clinquant' demonstrate their natural superiority in a show of elegant language followed by music and a dance (III.iv). It presents a still centre, a point of reference which focuses the values of the play.

The Antipodes (1638) shows a similar commitment to an idealized aristocratic norm, though in its case the values are aesthetic as well as social. Much of the action takes place in a play within the play, insulated and protected from the outside world by the genial dramaturge Letoy, who self-consciously contrasts his old-fashioned English values with those of 'publique shewes, and braveries' (I.v). His social virtues are echoed in his generous patronage of the players whom he instructs in a speech which is a comic analogue to Hamlet's. He insists most forcibly on the supremacy of the writer in dramatic production, reprimanding Byplay's old-fashioned tendency to 'hold interloquutions with the Audients'. The point of his comments is the artistic inadequacy of the previous age:

> Before the stage was purg'd from barbarisme,
> And brought to the perfection it now shines with. (II.ii)

The players are to be used to cure Peregrine, the son of Letoy's friend Joyless, of the melancholy obsession with Mandeville's *Travels* which has prevented him consummating his marriage to Martha – who has consequently also run mad. The players create the topsy-turvy world of the Antipodes in the hope that this reversal will turn Peregrine's mind back to a true appreciation of reality. The action then proceeds by a series of comic episodes which illustrate the reversals of Antipodean society. These scenes move between simple comic inversion, like the '*three old men with sachells*' (II.ix S.D.) or the drunken granny who is a bear-baiting fan (III.ix), and more extended pieces which reverse the satiric commonplaces of earlier drama: lawyers refuse fees (III.ii) and gentlemen refuse to cuckold citizens (III.vi).

In a note appended to the 1640 quarto of the play, Brome comments: 'You shal find in this Booke more than was presented upon the *Stage*, and left out of the *Presentation*, for superfluous length (as some of the Players pretended).' On this occasion, the players' sense of theatre was more acute than Brome's, for there is no sense of development in the Antipodean scenes. Once the comic point about reversal has been made, the satire which follows has no room for manoeuvre. It implies a static model of society which can be simply reversed and still make sense. Peregrine accordingly does not come to any clearer understanding of his situation. At the crisis of the Antipodean section, we are told that Peregrine has laid waste the tiring house. His quixotic encounter with 'Our Helmets, Shields, and Vizors, Haires and Beards,/Our Pastbord March-paines, and our Wooden Pies' (III.v) does not make him question his previous experience, and the play forgoes any exploration of illusion and reality, delusion and understanding, for the sake of the immediate comic effect of Byplay's descriptive speech. Peregrine merely conquers the tiring house and declares himself King of the Antipodes. The action is further prolonged by having the new king travel about his realm in disguise to find out its evils and come to sensible judgements about the qualities of a healthy society. None of these observations is taken very far, and Peregrine's eventual cure comes not by a return to right reason but by a 'royal marriage' to his real wife, Martha. The marriage is duly consummated; it is sex, rather than any of the action's moral or politic lessons, which effects Peregrine's return to sanity.

The cast of courtiers and carmen, Puritans and projectors, which animates the inner play suggests a plan of social satire and political didacticism, but the resolution of the plots turns on the control of sexual rather than social failings. Alongside the story of Peregrine's humours is the parallel attempt to cure Joyless's jealousy, which is also achieved by Letoy's machinations and his thespian skills. He pretends to encourage Joyless's wife, Diana, in an adulterous affair, and engineers a scene where his attempt at seduction can be observed. The scene is isolated from the rest of the action. In the earlier part of the play Diana is presented as a lively girl, irritated but not oppressed by her husband's jealousy; she now responds to Letoy's suggestions with the outraged rhetoric of a Lucrece, a response to his taking on the role of classical seducer with high-flown language to match. The scene is a witty parody of Fletcherian seduction, but its dramatic potential is strictly limited to providing the happy Joyless with ocular proof of his wife's fidelity.

The static oppositions of the action are further established in the finale, which takes the form of a charming masque-like morality. The reconciled couples enter in procession to '*a solemne lesson upon the Recorders*' and sit to watch the final reversal which restores true order. Discord, attended by her faction of Folly, Jealousy, Melancholy and Madness, is routed by Harmony accompanied by Mercury, Cupid, Bacchus and Apollo. Brome puts his faith in personal virtues not of character but of good living – 'the Gods of health, love, wine and wit' (v.xi).

At a later stage, Brome did embark on more pointed satire and his *Court Beggar* (1640) was banned because 'it had relation to the passages of the King's journey into the Northe'.[1] In Act III, the courtly Sir Ferdinand runs mad and imagines himself taken prisoner in Scotland. He takes the doctor who attends him for a Presbyterian 'That better can *pugnare* than *orare*', and shows most anxiety for the fate of his horse and armour. The episode mocks Suckling's disastrous performance in the Bishops' Wars, whither he had marched with a showy 'Troope of 100 very handsome young proper men . . . clad in white doubletts and scarlett breeches, and scarlett Coates, hatts and feathers, well horsed and armed'.[2] Like the jokes about Sir Ferdinand's verses and womanizing, this episode mocks courtly affectation as much as royal incompetence, for Brome's animosity to Suckling was less political than personal and professional. As a professional dramatist he felt most threatened by the courtly amateurs then in vogue. His prologue warns his audience against those 'who in a way/To purchace fame give money with their Play' – a reference to Suckling sponsoring the Blackfriars production of *Aglaura* (1637) – and distanced his own comedy from the new style.

The satire in the play is far from politically partisan. The courtier is made to look ridiculous, but so too is the country fellow, Swaynwit. The citizen, though he continually blusters about a 'cause', comically refuses (III.i) to fight for Religion, King or Country. The action consists of vignettes in which the wits and fools display their comic humours. Some of these are topical, like the reference to

> A new project
> For buylding a new Theatre or Playhouse
> Upon the Thames on Barges or flat boats (I.i)

which reflects the current professional rivalry between Beeston and Davenant.[3] However, most of the references to contemporary abuses owe as much to theatrical tradition as to any direct observation of London life. Monopolists plague Sir Mendicant, the aspirant courtier, with proposals for a tax on girl babies, new fashions and Cavaliers who cuckold tradesmen, but

[1] Adams, *Herbert*, 66, quoted in *Jacobean and Caroline Stage*, I, 333.
[2] *Aubrey's Brief Lives*, ed. O. L. Dick (London, 1960), 'Sir John Suckling'.
[3] See John Freehafer, 'Brome, Suckling and Davenant's Theatre Project of 1639', *Texas Studies in Literature and Language*, 10 (1968), 367–83.

these projectors are in no way individualized; they echo one another's words in a comic routine. The humour once again resides in verbal ingenuity, which often moves from the satiric to the surreal.

The action is loosely held together by the framing romance plot of Charissa trying to thwart her father's plan to marry her to Sir Ferdinand, but the displays of wit are the real action, creating a movement from chaos to harmony. The most chaotic moment in the play comes when all of the characters gather to rehearse Courtwit's masque and the bewildered Sir Raphael encounters them 'Fidling, Footing, Singing, Acting'. The masque which is to resolve the action begins as anti-revels, supposedly celebrating the unhappy union between Charissa and the lunatic Sir Ferdinand, but it soon dissolves into laughter at the incompetence of the boy Cupid. The true finale comes when Mendicant is danced out of his humour. He enters, '*attir'd all in Patents; A Windmill on his head: They all Dance. In the Dance they pull off his Patents: And the Projectors Clokes, who appeare all ragged. At the end of the Dance the Projectors thrust forth*' (v.ii S.D.).

All the other humours are as easily resolved. The satiric moments do not impinge on the action of the plot and are easily forgotten when it is resolved. Charissa marries her beloved and even Sir Ferdinand is sufficiently forgiven to be allowed to marry the much-sought-after Lady Strangelove. In the epilogue, the comic butts themselves appeal to the sympathies of an audience which includes 'Ladies . . . Cavaliers and Gentry [and] the City friends'; Brome even appeals to 'my Countrey folkes too if here be any o'em'. In the troubled political situation of 1639–40 this seems like a desperate attempt to unite all factions in the approval of a self-consciously old-fashioned and morally healthy form of art. Such positive values as are stated in the play echo Jonson's formulation of forty years before. In the opening scene of the play, Charissa deplores her father's move to court, and her lengthy reminder of what he has lost recalls Jonson's eulogy 'to Penshurst'. The times, however, had changed and so had theatrical styles. There is little scope in Brome's play for the support of such a life. He contented himself with witty barbs at the most extreme examples of courtly folly for the entertainment of his urban and urbane patrons of the stage.

A more consistent evocation of nostalgia is to be found in Brome's final play, *The Jovial Crew* (1641). The stable centre of the action is Squire Oldrents, a figure representing financial stability and generosity which bring him 'all the praises of the Rich/And prayers of the Poor' (1.ii). As if in recognition of the old-fashioned nature of his theme, Brome returns to the form of romance, although his prologue gently mocks plays where 'some impossibility/Concludes all strife and makes a Comedie'. The romantic narrative provides the loosest of frames for the songs and dances, the demonstration of the jovial pastoral life.

The scenes of the play are dramatically enclosed within their conventions. When Strangelove, Oldrents's steward, returns to his beggar crew, he first hears them in a song offstage:

> From hunger and cold who lives more free,
> Or who more richly clad than wee?
> Our bellies are full, our flesh is warm,
> And, against pride, our rags are a charm.
> Enough is our Feast, and for tomorrow
> Let rich men care [,] we feel no sorrow.
> No sorrow, no sorrow, no sorrow, no sorrow;
> Let rich men care, we feel no sorrow. (1.ii)

The stage direction then indicates: '*He opens the scene; the* Beggars *are discovered in their postures; then they issue forth.*' The beggars themselves are constantly performing, not only for the audience in the theatre but for the other characters on stage. Their canting language, their feasts and their customs, enacted with great verve and style, are part of an entertainment staple, first popularized in the coney-catching pamphlets of the sixteenth century and appearing on the stage in a number of plays in the 1620s.[1] Like earlier pastoral, the presentation of these beggars embodies familiar rejections of urban and materialist society. The jovial crew includes a poet, a lawyer, a soldier and a courtier, who tell of their loss of fortune and recount well-known abuses of the time. The overall sense of the play, however, completely endorses a paternalistic version of the *status quo*. When Oldrents's daughters take up begging as a diversion, their natural superiority shines through; and the reconciliations at the end of the play include the restoration of the beggars themselves to their lost lands. The play's charm depends upon that wish-fulfilment of romance which seemed so necessary to the divided society of the 1640s. Dedicating the text ten years later, Brome suggests, 'since the Times conspire to make us all Beggars, let us make our selves merry; which (if I am not mistaken) this drives at'.

Brome's claim to Jonson's mantle as satirist was recognized even after his death, but so too was the palliative power of his mockery. In his

---

[1] E.g. Jonson, *The Gypsies Metamorphosed* (1621); Fletcher, *Beggars' Bush* (1622); Middleton, *The Spanish Gypsy* (1623).

commendatory verses 'Upon the Ingenious Comedies of Mr Richard Brome', Alexander Brome wrote:

> Bishops and Players both suffered in one vote.
> And reason good, for they [the Puritans] had cause to feare 'em,
> One did suppresse their Schismes, and t'other jeere 'em.
> Bishops were guiltiest, for they swelled with Riches [;]
> T'other had nought, but Verses, Songs and Speeches.

In other words, Brome made no particular political capital out of his 'verses, songs and speeches'. As a Caroline dramatist, he subordinated satire to romance and the ideals of humane and gentlemanly behaviour; as a professional, he was chiefly concerned to unite his audience in appreciation of his fine comic skills.

(ii) James Shirley

In the Epilogue to *The Court Beggar*, Brome assured his audience, with a characteristic pun:

> Hee's no dandling on a Courtly lap,
> Yet may obtaine a smile, if not a clap.

His professional contemporary, Shirley (*plate 26*), was happier to present the courtly élite in his audience with an image of themselves. On occasion the mirror reflected a little too accurately – as in the case of *The Ball* (1632), which brought Henry Herbert's reprimand because 'ther were divers personated so naturally, both of lords and others of the court'.[1] But Shirley also drew some uncharacteristic approval from Herbert: he found the rhetorical attitudinizing of *The Young Admiral* (1633) 'a patterne to other poetts, not only for the bettring of maners and language, but for the improvement of the quality'.[2] The satisfaction rather than the improvement of the quality seems to have been Shirley's chief professional aim and his rehearsal of the familiar ideology displays an almost parodic ease. The plot of *The Gentleman of Venice* (1639) turns on the fact that Giovanni, supposed son of the palace gardener, is the true son of the Duke. We are alerted to his

[1] Adams, *Herbert*, 19.
[2] ibid., 5.

innate superiority from his first entrance, when he elegantly describes how he has made the garden his academy and reads a moral lesson from the characters of the flowers. These traits are visually underscored when he returns from the wars 'plumed and brave', and he is contrasted with the usurping son, who not only brawls drunkenly with the lower orders but actually enjoys a bit of digging.

When Shirley was in Ireland in the train of Lord Deputy Strafford, he continued to produce the fashionable forms of drama, reassuring his audience in the prologue to *The Doubtful Heir* (1638) that the play was typical of the London stage. He did, however, make some concession to his audience's particular situation in *St Patrick for Ireland* (1639). Fletcherian conventions of suits proposed and lovers thwarted are overlaid with the magic and spectacle of the pagan court which Patrick must convert, and Shirley can draw an obvious political analogy in the story of a British saint reforming a barbaric people. He was beaten to the post of Poet Laureate by William Davenant in 1638, but after his stay in Ireland he succeeded Massinger in the more congenial post of chief dramatist to the King's Men. For, despite his commitment to the courtly audience, Shirley's artistic affinities were with the professionals. His earliest play, *Love's Tricks, or The School of Compliment* (1625), is very clumsily plotted around an inane love story, but the parodic solos of Orlando Furioso, the roarer, and the scenes depicting the compliment school show the ease with which he could handle the comic material of his predecessors.. In 1652, verses prefixed to *The Cardinal* recognized his place in the great tradition:

> when men have nam'd
> *Ionson* (the Nations Laureat,) the fam'd
> *Beaumont*, and *Fletcher*, he, that wo' not see
> *Shirley*, the fourth, must forfeit his best ey.

Such praise was more than conventional: Shirley often directly imitated earlier dramatic techniques.[1] In 1631 he seems to have been particularly influenced by *The Revenger's Tragedy*, for both his plays that year draw on its plot and language. Vindice's speech tempting Castiza with the pleasures of courtly service is almost irrelevantly adapted in *Love's Cruelty* (1631), and *The Traitor* adapts the main plot in which a Duke lusts after a courtier's sister. The demands of Caroline decorum soften the horror and satire of the

---

[1] See R. S. Forsythe, *The Relations of Shirley's Plays to the Elizabethan Drama* (New York, 1914).

original. The disturbing sequence in which Tourneur's Duke kisses a poisoned skull is muted in Shirley's denouement to the Duke finding the chaste lady dead in bed.

In tragedy, these imitated set pieces seldom impinge on the main action of the plays. Their speeches anatomize court corruption and denounce the effects of lust, and many a malcontent rehearses the satiric clichés of Jacobean tragedy. The carefully stage-managed theatrical effects actually stand in the way of developing plot and character. Lovers come together after much heart-searching only to find, first that they are incestuous, and then that they are not (*The Coronation*, 1635; *The Court Secret*, 1642); and characters take awesome decisions which define their very nature and then find they need not carry them out (*The Young Admiral*, iv.ii and *The Imposture*, 1640, iv.iv). The dramatic technique of witholding essential information from both characters and audience is carried to such absurd lengths that it results not in heightening but attenuating the dramatic interest and often requires a new intrigue to resolve the plot as late as Act v (*The Maid's Revenge*, 1626; *The Coronation*, 1635; *The Imposture*).

The restrictions imposed by Caroline decorum are evident in a comparison of Webster's *Duchess of Malfi* (1614) and Shirley's *The Cardinal* (1641). Bosola and Ferdinand, the most complex and ambiguous characters, are omitted from the action and the Duchess's sin of sexual independence is neutralized into mere disobedience. Her brave bid for freedom is reduced to a choice between a courtier and a scholar, and any hint of moral irregularity is denied, since she wishes for nothing more than 'Two lovers in their chaste embrace to meet'. The Cardinal himself is a far less sinister figure than in Webster, and though the Duchess denounces his corruption in powerful satiric terms she does not suggest that his tyranny is symptomatic of the evil at the centre of their world. All of the events are engineered from outside and presented to both audience and characters as theatrical gestures. When Columbo receives the Duchess's letter releasing him from their engagement, he moves in a short space of acted time from utter rage, threatening to kill the messenger, to the conviction that the letter is a test of his passion which must be reciprocated. In the central scene of the play, Alvarez is abducted in a wedding masque, and the conventional ironic contrast between celebration and death is fully extended when the body is returned as a grotesque wedding gift. However, by the end of Act iii the initial plot has been resolved. A new revenge plot is introduced and the characters dispatched in lurid style: the Cardinal tries to rape the mad Duchess, is murdered by the avenging Hernando, but succeeds in giving her poison. In

Shirley's tragedy and tragi-comedy the moment is everything: As the repentant Duke confidently comments, surveying the carnage which ends *Love's Cruelty* (1631):

> when their funerall rites and teares are done
> New joyes shall rise with the next mornings Sunne.

In comedy, too, Shirley is best at the set scene, often mocking styles which in other contexts he uses quite seriously. The lords' affectation in *The Humorous Courtier* (1630) and the bandit aping a prince at the false court in *The Sisters* (1642) are simply funny turns. Sometimes Shirley's parodic urge takes over a whole plot, causing a troublesome inconsistency of tone. The main plot of *The Wedding* (1629), where Beauford's bride, Gratiana, is slandered on the eve of their marriage, is enacted in high romantic style. The passionate denunciation scene, the stylized slow motion of the lovers' confrontation, and Beauford's preparation for his own funeral, are all clichés of romance: in this play their emotional power is placed more at risk than usual by the comic realism which surrounds their action. Though the details about food and servants, visits to the cobbler, visits to the tailor, are partly an ironic build-up to the foiled wedding (II.iii), the serious action is more completely undermined by the antics of the comic duo Rawbone and Lodam. They are funny on sight, one thin and one fat – 'the lean jade' and 'the barell of Heidelberg' – and they appear at the most incongruous moments: after Gratiana's affecting return of Beauford's vows and jewels, Rawbone enters to woo Jane; similarly, the farcical duel between rival suitors must cast some comic aspersions on the more serious conflict between Beauford and Marwood. The clash of styles between tragi-comedy and farce is too sudden even for comic relief. The dramatic heritages of Jonson and Fletcher cannot be combined in the same play.

In a number of the comedies Shirley experiments with this combination of romance, sentimentality and realism, and the balance between the different elements is crucial to the success of the comic tone. In *The Example* (1634), Sir Solitary Plot, Jacinta and her witless suitors, Vainman and Pumicestone, clearly derive from Jonsonian models and their plot has a Jonsonian comic vitality. The sequence where Jacinta insists that one suitor remain completely silent while the other contradicts everything she says (IV.ii) is a masterpiece of farce. But such comedy cannot coexist with the sentiment of the main plot, in which the virtuous Lady Peregrine is pitted against Lord Fitzavarice, a rake without gallantry and a seducer without charm. Shirley's presentation of this lord at first displays a remarkable understanding of sexual psychology. He proposes that Lady Peregrine pay off her husband's debts by granting sexual favours at £100 a time. Naming the price gives the bargain a kind of rawness; sex is treated as a commodity which will ensure the lady's financial security and contribute to Lord Fitzavarice's status about town. When he is first rejected he comments petulantly:

> The world takes notice I have courted her,
> And if I mount her not, I loose my honour. (I.i)

Even the sexual pleasure to be gained is measured as a reflection on his prowess. He takes most delight in

> A wench that must be purgd, sublimd, calcind,
> By'th chemistrie of Love, till shee become
> A glorified spirit, and acknowledge
> Shee tooke' her exaltation from me! (II.i)

The climax comes when Lord Fitzavarice tries to rape Lady Peregrine at dagger point; she faints and he is terrified that he has killed her. But the requirements of the plot prevent Lord Fitzavarice from being a total villain, and he is given a scene of repentance and reconciliation. The dynamism of the interaction vanishes beneath a static emblem of moral change, as the lady describes her vision:

> LADY P. My [Me] thought, from a steepe precipice as you were falling
>   Into the Sea, an arme chain'd to a Cloud
>   Caught hold, and drew you up to Heaven . . .
> LORD F. I feel a holie flame disperse rich heate,
>   About me, the corruption of my blood
>   Is fallen awaie, and of that virtue, which
>   A divell in mee would have betray'd, I rise
>   A servant, and admirer. (III.i)

The sudden weight of this romantic turn knocks the play completely off balance. The repentant lord must be rewarded with a mistress and the comic subplot must proceed to a romantic conclusion. The witty, independent Jacinta accordingly confesses to an utterly unexpected passion for this libertine, and all the play's dramatic dynamism is surrendered to the technical requirements of symmetry.

In the most successful comedies, Shirley abandons the troublesome fervour of romance and responds more closely to the demands of plot in the tradition of New Comedy. The main plot of *The Constant Maid* (1639), for example, involves Hartwell's desire for his true love, Frances. The barriers to his love are not only his lost fortune but the fact that Frances's mother, Lady Bellamy, is also infatuated with him and that her nurse is pressing the claims of Startup, a foolish country squire. The ladies in the play still conform to sentimental demands and Frances's selfless renunciation of her love in obedience to her mother (IV.ii) would do credit to a romantic heroine. However, the romantic interest is merely a frame for the action; the comic formula demands that Jack shall have Jill, but on the way Shirley entertains the audience with Startup's drunken and gauche attempts to woo Frances (II.i) and the farcical counterplot of Hartwell's servant, Close, who persuades Startup that Hartwell is going to kill him, forcing him out into the street dressed in nothing but a blanket (III.iii and IV.i), while Hartwell, dressed in Startup's clothes, takes up the midnight assignation with Frances which the nurse has arranged for his rival. The farce is pushed even further in the secondary plot, in which Playfair tricks and teases Hornet the usurer so that he can marry his niece. The complications here involve Hornet's niece pretending to be first melancholy and then mad; Hornet's hold on reality is further strained by his being summoned to 'court' (acted out, of course, by Playfair's servants) where he is knighted, dressed in fine clothes and presented with a masque (III.i and IV.iii). This diversion is meant to occupy Hornet while Playfair makes off with his niece, but the comic inventiveness with which it is carried out takes it far beyond a mere plot device and makes it the centre of the play, another opportunity for the witty to triumph over the dull, the urbane over the unsophisticated. It is all too easy to mock Startup who is over-impressed by his small fortune and his short lineage, gets drunk on a little sack, and commits the *faux pas* of trying to take tobacco in a lady's presence. Hornet is a rather more interesting case since he is a most reluctant courtier. He has the canny instincts of the small city businessman who recognizes the financial dangers of being taken up by the court set, and his awareness of how 'a man cannot grow rich, but one state surgeon or other/Must practice on his purse' (II.ii) adds a sense of satiric truth to the scenes in which he is gulled.

The success of these comedies, however, depends less on satiric realism than on treating familiar comic formulae with witty novelty. In *The Gamester* (1633), Shirley brilliantly intertwines his two plots. In one, Wilding forces his wife to solicit his attractive young ward for him. After the statutory moralizing, she hits on the obvious ruse of substituting herself for the ward, using the usual bed-trick conventions of insisting on silence and darkness. Shirley then introduces the witty twist. Before the proposed adultery can take place, Wilding loses heavily to Hazard, the gamester. He agrees to pay his debts by letting Hazard take his place in bed with his ward. Wilding's wife then confesses that she has taken the ward's place, creating in effect a double trick: Wilding is not only thwarted of his lust but also cuckolded himself. Comic decorum demands that nothing should actually have happened, but Shirley wrings two acts of high comedy out of Wilding's contorted attempts to disguise his cuckoldom by forcing his valuable and lovely ward on to Hazard. It is conventional drama at its best, playing games with the comic patterns, demanding from an audience only attention and not factitious involvement.

A similar urbane acceptance is called forth by the lively local colour of the gaming and tavern scenes. In a central sequence (III.iii) Hazard and Wilding observe as some aristocrats and their parasites pass across the stage. Each figure is a type of profligate and decayed gentleman hoping to recoup lost fortunes by gambling, but Hazard and Wilding's point of view invites the audience to share their hold on the city world rather than to lament the passage of a more stable society. The sharks and tricksters of older city comedy are now stylish gallants, and wit is more important than class. Social mobility is now seen as inevitable and wryly summed up by the citizen, Old Barnacle:

> we that had
> Our breeding from a Trade, cits as you call us,
> Though we hate gentlemen our selves, yet are
> Ambitious, to make all our children gentlemen . . .
> There is a whirle in fate, the Courtiers make
> Us cuckolds; marke we wriggle into their
> Estates, poverty makes their children Citizens;
> Our sonnes cuckold them, a circular justice. (1.i)

The witty turn of this speech is typical of the play as a whole: morals are sacrificed to wit and satiric comment has become an acknowledgement of the *status quo*.

A similar detailed portrayal of the leisured urban life is to be found in *Hyde Park* (1632), where Shirley has created a comic style stripped of all trace of romance or melodrama. The plot is built out of a series of illustrative encounters interweaving three plots: the witty shrew, Carol, is outwitted by an intelligent rake, Fairfield; Julia avoids the dishonourable advances of Lord Bonvile and converts him to virtuous service; and Mistress Bonavent is reunited with her husband. The characters move around the London scene from a wedding feast to the fashionable resorts of Hyde Park, as the plot is organized in space rather than progressing to a denouement. Even the arrival home of the long-lost Master Bonavent occurs unobtrusively at the beginning of the play, and the note with which he reveals himself to his wife is itself a parody of romantic plotting:

> I was taken by a *Turkish* Pirate, and detain'd many yeares
> A prisoner in an Island, where I had dyed his Captive,
> Had not a worthy Merchant thence redeemed & furnished me. (IV.iii)

The emphasis is primarily on realism and the accurate portrayal of the leisured classes, but there is also a stylishly contrived series of parallels between the competitions among the suitors and the episodes of racing and gambling, linked by the use of the same language in both.[1] Love, for these financially independent and assured young people, is merely another diversion; Mistress Carol's mockery of 'I, Cicely, take thee John' further suggests that marriage is a strictly *petit bourgeois* preoccupation. Carol does eventually marry, but by a contract of equals with little concession to sentimental ideals.

Much of Shirley's most witty comic writing is lavished on misogamist ladies like Jane in *The Wedding* (1626), Penelope in *The Witty Fair One* (1628), or Jacinta in *The Example* (1634). They derive partly from the dramatic tradition which stretches from the witty heroines of Shakespearean comedy to the sophisticated ladies of Restoration comedy, but their power in Shirley's work indicates the importance of a carefully defined sexual morality in his comic world. The rejection of romance in his comedies of London life is in part a rejection of the sentimental approach to *petit bourgeois* morality. In *The Ball*, the plots are tied to the credible motivations of sexual jealousy and wounded pride, but the style of these amorous encounters is quite antithetical to romantic comedy. In Act III, scene iv, Lady Lucina's suitors realize that she has been teasing them all and come to confront her with this knowledge. The unfortunate Bostock, who has been charged with delivering this denunciation, begins in fine style:

> Thou Basiliske . . .
> Whose eyes shat [shoot] fire, and poyson,
> Malicious as a Witch, and much more cunning,
> Thou that dost ride men. (III.iv)

[1] Albert Wertheim, 'Games and Courtship in James Shirley's *Hyde Park*', *Anglia*, 90 (1972), 71–92.

It is a speech which might have been appropriate in tragi-comedy, but Lady Lucina responds with a mocking literalism which completely destroys its emotional and moral impact.

Significantly Bostock is in other ways the most harshly treated character in the play. He is a false aristocrat whose comic obsession is to claim connection with all the titled of the town. As punishment he is kicked and railed at; he is also denounced by his aristocratic cousin, Lord Rainbow, in one of the most serious speeches of the play. Contrasted with him is Lady Lucina's most acceptable suitor, Colonel Winfield, whose experience is not only military but sexual. Before Lady Lucina will agree to marry him, she asks him to swear that he is honest. He replies with blunt frankness:

> 'Tis out of fashion indeede with gentlemen
> To be honest, and of age together[;] 'tis sufficient,
> We can provide to take our pleasures too,
> Without infection. (IV.iii)

He further insists that, given the ladies' indulgence in such entertainments as going to the ball and tennis, he is not even insisting on a double standard. In fact, as the ladies prove, the entertainment is innocent – in the show which precedes the ball, Diana wins her contention with Venus – but the point is made without either prudery or humbug.

For the comedy is controlled by the values of the *honnête homme* who understands the social milieu and does not allow unseemly passion to jeopardize his control over it and himself. He treads the middle ground between cynicism and sentimentality, between foppery and provincialism. The placing of characters defines this middle ground. A figure like Lady Bornwell in *The Lady of Pleasure* (1635), who aspires to a life of fashionable promiscuity, comes in for as much ridicule as any fop or country bumpkin; and she is firmly controlled by the authoritative figure of Sir Thomas Bornwell. Although Shirley depicts an urban society, the figures who are accorded unreserved respect, more even than the gallant men of wit, are sober and senior figures of the old aristocracy who provide reassurance that, when the game is over, the values of the old world will reassert themselves. In the event, such harmony proved impossible to sustain. When the society which employed him collapsed, Shirley first fought for the King and then retired to schoolteaching. For his pupils he wrote a number of moralities which show flashes of his old comic verve. Abstractions were now all that remained to him.

(iii) Conclusion

What the later Stuart drama reveals above all is the triumph of romance over satire. The traditions of complaint and satire which gave such power to the work of Webster, Marston and the later Shakespeare emerged only occasionally in plays which seemed, in context, old-fashioned. Despite realistic settings in comedy and political themes in tragedy, the cutting edge was blunted by the demands of decorum, both moral and aesthetic. Chaste ladies and honourable gentlemen were sorely tried but the values of honour and chastity were never fundamentally questioned; sex and money remained the rewards of wits, but wit was seldom at odds with morality or power. The aesthetic demands of decorum separated the styles of tragedy and comedy, the grand gesture from realistic action, poetry from prose. Each dramatic genre was, however, constructed out of similar theatrical motifs of set speech, familiar encounter and surprising revelation, a dramatic style seen in a more stylized form in the court masque, where the final reassertion of harmony was explicitly connected to the benevolent King. It was a drama of moral and aesthetic certainty whose polished surface reflected back an idealized version of its audience's aspirations.

The mainstream of Stuart drama has correspondingly little appeal for modern spectators, who prefer psychological ambiguity and moral doubt, and who like their artists to be rebellious. Ben Jonson's irascible denunciation of his commercial audience, Middleton's temerity in writing *A Game at Chess*, the hint of political opposition in Massinger's treatment of tyranny, are accordingly overvalued as solitary examples of true artistic integrity, different in quality and kind from the routine productions of their professional contemporaries. Yet these three artists were equally professional, equally dependent on the commercial theatre not only for their livelihood but for the basic material from which they wrought their complex work. Even the courtier dramatists, who held themselves apart from those 'who doe write for almes',[1] drew on the conventions developed by the professional stage.

There is little point in deploring or mocking the conventional quality of much Stuart drama. To understand its cultural impact one must link that conventionality to the emergence of a fully professional theatrical organiz-

---

[1] William Cartwright, commendatory verses printed in the Beaumont and Fletcher Folio (1647), but written earlier (1638?). See G. B. Evans, *The Plays and Poems of William Cartwright* (Madison, Wisc., 1951), 741–2, n.

ation with a huge turnover of plays catering for a clearly defined audience who might recognize and enjoy varied treatments of familiar formulas. The commercial dominance of the King's Men may, for example, have contributed to the prevalence of romance, since it was the invention and style of their principal dramatist. A systematic analysis of other companies' repertories and personnel could well illuminate other aspects of convention, making more complex connections between actor, audience and play.

IV The plays and the playwrights: 1642–60

Lois Potter

1 Closet drama and royalist politics

(i) Problems of definition

Nearly all histories of English drama stop at 1642 and start again in 1660. This is because of the assumption that the intervening period must have been an age of closet drama, and hence remote from the mainstream of dramatic history. A further assumption is embodied in the title of the only full-length critical study which bridges this gap, Alfred Harbage's *Cavalier Drama*.

Both assumptions are basically right, but they need qualification. It has already been shown that the acting of plays never altogether stopped, despite the closing of the theatres in 1642.[1] The fact remains that attending a public performance meant risking arrest and a fine. Despite occasional optimistic rumours about the resumption of theatrical activity, there was obviously no encouragement for anyone to take up a career as professional actor or playwright. However, this very fact means that we need to re-examine the concept of closet drama, usually regarded as an élitist alternative to the professional stage. At a time when there was no authorized

[1] See above, pp. 65–7, 120–4.

professional stage, the question 'Was it acted?' ceases to be an adequate way of distinguishing among the many different works written in dramatic form: the historian of mid-seventeenth-century drama cannot legitimately ignore any of them.

The relation of the drama to such concepts as 'cavalier' and 'Puritan' is likewise a complex one. Royalists liked to accuse their opponents of hostility to all forms of culture, but much recent scholarship has been devoted to correcting this one-sided view. It has been shown that in the period before the war some people on both sides had objections to the theatre, for a variety of reasons. Some admired classical drama but not the modern stage; some liked plays but not the expensive and exclusive court masques; some objected not to plays but to the rowdy spectators who attended them; some wished only for the banning of performances on Sundays.[1] Theatrical imagery and allusions can also be found in works by writers of all parties. Royalists accuse Parliament of acting a *Comedy of Errors* or *A King and No King*.[2] The editor of Charles I's private correspondence, which was captured and published by parliamentary order after the Battle of Naseby, introduced it as a dramatic 'discovery': 'now by Gods good providence the traverse Curtain is drawn, and the King writing to *Ormond* and the Queen, what they must not disclose, is presented upon the stage.'[3] A royalist news-sheet paraphrases *Hamlet*; a Leveller news-sheet paraphrases *Julius Caesar*.[4] Examples of this kind are so abundant as to be confusing. References to performances may well be metaphorical rather than real: writers who claim that a play was 'acted' often mean that the events it describes really happened. Thus when Edmund Gayton, an important source of information on this period, describes an audience intimidated into applauding a bad play by the presence of 'Whifflers' round the hall, he is probably referring to the most famous spectacle of the age: the trial and execution of Charles I, called by Marvell 'the royal actor'.[5]

[1] See E. N. S. Thompson, *The Controversy Between the Puritans and the Stage* (New York, 1903), esp. 181–4, and Margot Heinemann, *Puritanism and Theatre* (Cambridge, 1980), 18–47.

[2] E.g. in *Mercurius Vapulans* (27 November 1647), quoted, with many similar examples, in Leslie Hotson, *The Commonwealth and Restoration Stage* (Cambridge, Mass., 1928), 29. See the prophetic title-page of *A King and No King* (plate 27).

[3] [Henry Parker], *The King's Cabinet Opened: or, Certain Packets of Secret Letters & Papers, written with the King's own hand, and taken in his Cabinet at Naseby-Field June 14 1645* (1645), 4.

[4] Respectively, in *Mercurius Melancholicus*, No 5 (25 September–2 October 1647), and *The True-Informer or Monthly Mercury* (7 October–8 November 1648), also quoted in Heinemann, *Puritanism and Theatre*, 253.

[5] *Pleasant Notes upon Don Quixote* (1654), 263.

But, as Milton pointed out, in answer to someone who had noticed the theatrical imagery in one of his pamphlets, the mere presence of such language does not necessarily imply sympathy with the theatre.[1] Prynne himself wrote *Histrio-Mastix* in the form of two 'tragedies', divided into acts and scenes, and a Presbyterian preacher gave the title *Tragi-Comaedia* to a sermon in which he gloated over the fate of spectators under whom the floor collapsed at an illegal performance.[2] In any case, it is pointless to try to identify a particular attitude to the theatre with one side or another; much of the time, in fact, there were three sides rather than two. In an understandable desire to get rid of the conventional 'Puritan' stereotype, some recent writers have stretched the term so far as to leave almost no one of any importance who could be described as a cavalier. It would be fairer to recognize that all parties contained a strange mixture of characters and attitudes, at least during the 1640s. Allegiances constantly changed, or were changed from without. What happened in the theatre is much like what happened in the larger sphere of political and religious thought. The sometimes eccentric and fragmentary works of the 1640s (part of the 'flowery crop of knowledge' which Milton celebrated in *Areopagitica*) give way in the 1650s to the search for a government – and a theatre – of compromise and consensus.

(ii) Publication and translation

In 1653, shortly after a raid on an illegal Red Bull performance, the preface to a newly published play suggested mockingly that it was safer 'To make the press act', and thus save the ladies from fainting 'At the red coates intrusion'.[3] On the whole, this was what happened. The publication of plays became an important substitute for theatre-going as well as a political act in its own right. Some pre-war works may have got into print on the strength of their titles alone, since readers could be trusted to find a topical meaning in anything referring to a 'king' or 'rebellion'.

---

[1] *An Apology Against a Pamphlet* (1642), in *Complete Prose Works*, ed. Don M. Wolfe, 8 vols (New Haven, Conn., 1953–73), I, 886–8.
[2] John Rowe, *Tragi-Comaedia* (1654), quoted in Thornton S. Graves, 'Notes on Puritanism and the Stage', *SP*, 18 (1921), 150–6.
[3] 'R.C.', Preface to *The Queen, or, the Excellency of Her Sex* (1653).

It was rare for anyone to tamper with the text of an earlier play.[1] But the transformation of play text into published book, complete with dedication, preface, commendatory verses and a special prologue to the reader, provided ample opportunity for the expression of personal opinion. The best-known dramatic publisher of the period, Humphrey Moseley, was a strongly committed royalist. His most spectacular gesture was the publication early in 1647 of a folio of hitherto unprinted plays by Beaumont and Fletcher. The actors of the King's Men provided the texts and dedicated the volume to Philip, Earl of Pembroke, a former Lord Chamberlain who was now a supporter of Parliament. He had been, with his brother, the dedicatee of the Shakespeare First Folio as well; the actors probably meant their action to be conciliatory, a plea for support in their attempts to have the theatres reopened. The enormous number of poems which followed this dedication had the effect of signatures on a petition. But the uncompromisingly royalist tone of this 'morale-boosting gesture of defiance'[2] may well have had the opposite effect from that intended: Pembroke took a hard line towards the stage when the subject was debated in the House of Lords later that year. Undeterred, Moseley went on to publish William Cartwright's *Plays and Poems* in 1651, the year of Worcester, with so many prefatory verses that the book became a joke even among fellow royalists.

The translation, like the publication, of earlier works was a means by which indirect comment could be made. Fanshawe's version of *Il Pastor Fido* (published in 1647, but probably written while he was with the King at Oxford in 1643–4) is prefaced by a dedication to Prince Charles which suggests that the play's pastoral scene can be regarded as 'a *Lant-skip* [landscape] of these Kingdoms, (your Royall Patrimony) as well in the former flourishing, as in the present distractions thereof'. In 1649, Christopher Wase produced a less graceful, but certainly remarkable, translation, dedicated to Charles's sister: '*The Electra of Sophocles, presented to her highness the Lady Elizabeth, with an Epilogue Shewing the Parallel in two poems, the Return and the Restauration.*' The translation makes its point partly through notes and partly through loaded phrases like 'root and

---

[1] An exception is 'F.J.', who adapted Thomas Randolph's pre-war *Hey for Honesty* (a topical satire based on Aristophanes' *Plutus*) to make it still more topical in the year of publication, 1651. See Cyrus L. Day, 'Thomas Randolph's Part in the Authorship of *Hey for Honesty*', *PMLA*, 41 (1926), 325–34.

[2] See P. W. Thomas, *Sir John Berkenhead* (Oxford, 1969), 134.

branch'; at one point it borrows a phrase from a letter of Charles I, 'the best author of English'. A dedicatory poem succinctly makes the 'parallel':

> Our *Agamemnon's* dead, *Electra* grieves,
> The onely hope is that *Orestes* lives.

In case anyone is wondering about Clytemnestra, Wase explains in a note that she represents 'the queen politick, which hath trull'd it in the lewd embraces of the soldiery'. James Compton, Earl of Northampton, translated Seneca's *Agamemnon*, perhaps for the same reason that drew Wase to the Electra story; he also adapted Machiavelli's *Mandragola*, setting it in Commonwealth London and transforming the Roman Catholic friar, Fra Timoteo, into a Puritan called Renchtext.[1] In 1659–60 another translator made a similar gesture simply by rendering William Drury's *Aluredus sive Alfredus* (1619) as *Alfred, or Right Re-enthroned*. Thus, the contemporary context allowed these translators to find, or create, extra levels of meaning in existing works.

(iii) Royalist modes: masque and romance

Much of the subject-matter of pre-war drama was at least potentially political in its implications. After 1642, it became impossible to see it in any other way. This was particularly true of the two forms that had been most in fashion at court, masque and romance. Charles I's fondness for masques was still being held against him in the 1650s, when he was remembered as having 'spent immense treasure . . . in Playes and Maskes, more transitory then a Winter's night';[2] a 'Pasquil Dialogue' of 1659 represented his ghost complaining of the way in which 'Masks or Theatral presentments' had been used as an excuse for rebellion.[3] A pro-parliamentary pamphlet of 1643 parodied Shirley's famous pre-war masque *The Triumph of Peace*,

---

[1] See William D. Wolf, 'The Authorship of *The Mandrake* and *Leontius, King of Cyprus*', *The Library*, 6th series, II, 4 (1980), 456–60, and Hilton Kelliher, 'A Hitherto Unrecognized Cavalier Dramatist: James Compton, third Earl of Northampton', *British Library Journal*, VI (1980), pp. 158–87.

[2] [F. Osborne?], *A Seasonable Expostulation with the Netherlands* (Oxford, 1652), 15.

[3] *The Court Career* (1659), 10.

turning it into an indictment of the cavaliers.[1] In a broadsheet published two months after the Battle of Worcester (*plate 28*) Charles II's attempted invasion is depicted as a procession of fools such as had formed part of Shirley's *Triumph*: the King is 'marching in his disguise' – that is, theatrical costume – and a hobby-horse represents the cavaliers.

Milton – his own masque at Ludlow Castle now far behind him – referred contemptuously to the emblematic frontispiece of *Eikon Basilike* (Charles I kneeling in prayer, spurning an earthly crown for a crown of thorns, and casting his eyes upwards to a crown of glory) as a 'Masking Scene' with 'devices begg'd from the old Pageantry of some Twelf-Nights entertainment at *Whitehall*'.[2] This sarcastic comparison was relevant in so far as it recognized the strongly visual character of court culture, where both religion and entertainment drew on complex symbolism and ritual. The masque was an organism made up of soul (the moral) and body (the expensive and elaborate technical means by which it was presented). The arcane nature of its symbolism was often lost even on the courtiers, who tended to take it simply as spectacle. Thus, to defend the masque was not only to defend the hierarchical social order which it celebrated, but also to make some claims for oneself as an intellectual. In 1646, the Presbyterian Samuel Sheppard replied to Lilburne's attack on the House of Lords, which accused them among other things of having been chiefly concerned with such frivolities as masques:

> and what though they beheld Masques, do not all wise men know, that a Morall Masque is profitable to see? and though to the unlearned, who may refraine the sight of them, they seem Riddles, and Nulls, yet to the knowing, who are able to explain the sense and meaning, and to cracke the shell, they finde a sweet and pleasant kernal.[3]

Sheppard, who had been a supporter of Parliament only in the hope of seeing the King restored at the head of a Presbyterian state church, was one of many writers who moved into the royalist camp when they became alarmed at the growing influence of social and religious democrats on the other side. Some of the 'dramatic' pamphlets in which he seems to have had a hand make use of so many songs and descriptions of visual action as to suggest that they are meant to evoke memories of masques as well as plays. A

[1] See J. Jacquot, 'Une Parodie du *Triumph of Peace*, Masque de James Shirley', *Cahiers Élisabéthains*, 15 (April 1979), 77–80.
[2] Preface to *Eikonoklastes* (1649), in *Complete Prose Works*, II, 342, 343.
[3] *The Famers Famed* (1646), 13.

'Pageant' in *The Scottish Politick Presbyter* (1647) depicts Scots elders running away from soldiers (the Independents). In another short piece, Mrs Parliament makes a spectacular entrance 'in a Scarlet coloured Robe, riding on a beast of many heads, and a Cup of Red Wine in her hand'.[1] *The Famous Tragedy of Charles I* (1649) includes a scene where Cromwell and his mistress are the chief spectators of a masque which reverses all the usual conventions: the performers are apparently Members of Parliament, dressed to represent not the virtues normally embodied by courtly masquers but the vices which are really theirs.

Masque and pastoral had become virtually synonymous before the war, because many masques had pastoral settings and many pastorals had been produced in the same lavish style as the masques. Thus, two pastorals of 1651, Leonard Willan's adaptation of D'Urfé's *Astrée* and William Denny's allegorical *Shepherd's Holiday*, end with a general dance which seems to be envisaged as involving the spectators. Denny, indeed, notes in the dedication that his work 'might heretofore have passed as a masque had it not been for vizards'. Neither pastoral seems to have been performed, and neither contains any overt reference to contemporary events (though Denny's platonic treatment of marriage and chastity, prefaced by a 'key' to the allegory, sometimes recalls *Comus*). But the form itself was meaningful. Even before the war, the pastoral setting – Eden or Arcadia – had been a symbol of the precarious peace of England. In Mildmay Fane's *Raguaillo d'Oceano* (1640) the character representing England has a Virgilian tag as his scutcheon: 'a Shepheard Swaine asleepe whilest his flocks are feeding about him representing Security with this word – ffoelices Nimium, Bona si sua Norint.'[2] An untitled masque of 1643 links the disruption of Arcadia to the usual pastoral cause, Love, but depicts its effects on Time in terms of contemporary events.[3]

The subject matter of romantic tragi-comedy, a closely related form, was still more topical. The chief character of these plays, after all, was the ruler – sometimes banished, sometimes wandering in disguise among his subjects, sometimes surrounded by designing favourites, or confronting rebellion, or sacrificing his kingdom for his love. The Civil War provided many opportunities for the Stuarts to play these roles. Charles II's escape after

---

[1] 'Mercurius Melancholicus', *Mistress Parliament, Her Gossiping* (1648).

[2] Ed. Clifford Leech, Materials for the Study of the Old English Drama, xv (Louvain, 1938; repr. 1963), ll. 155–9.

[3] This masque has been known under several titles. R. C. Elsely, in an unpublished thesis edition for the University of Birmingham (1950), calls it *Time's Triumph*; it has also been edited, as *Time's Distractions*, by Diane W. Strommer (College Station, Texas, 1976).

Worcester was obviously the stuff of which legends are made – even while trying to play it down, the official Commonwealth newspaper agreed that the story 'would suffice to make a very pretty *Romance*'.[1] The figure of Henrietta Maria was equally important. In selling her jewels to finance the royalist cause, for example, she was behaving like the typical romantic queen. She is depicted as *The Banished Shepherdess* in the play which Cosmo Manuche presented to her at the Restoration. Charles I's devotion to the Queen – 'though she be of the weaker sexe, borne an Alien, bred up in a contrary Religion'[2] – was so often used against him by parliamentary writers that royalists felt obliged to go to the opposite extreme in identifying themselves with the romantic couple. Their best-known propagandist, Sir John Berkenhead, was known to his friends as Cratander, the hero of one of Charles I's favourite plays.[3] Even John Tatham, by no means a courtier-dramatist, refers in *The Rump* (1660) to 'heroicks' when he means cavaliers.

Romance, like masque and pastoral, was thought of as a particularly aristocratic form, but it was capable of appealing to a wider audience. The plays given at two illegal performances of 1653, known to historians only because both ended disastrously for the spectators, were Killigrew's *Claracilla* and the old play *Mucedorus*. The first of these was done by professionals at the Red Bull, the most popular of pre-war theatres, though it may have had a more exclusive atmosphere on this occasion. *Mucedorus*, based on a story from the *Arcadia*, was given by amateurs in Oxfordshire, who took the production on a tour of several villages (the floor finally collapsed beneath the spectators at an inn in Witney). The demand for plays like these may have been pure escapism. But the tragi-comedies written at this period show some attempt to assimilate and discuss current events within the romance framework. Since these plays were mostly written by amateurs, the level of their analysis can be somewhat disappointing:

> Shoo'd they reform things, with too strict a course,
> Instead of mending, they woo'd make things worse.

This is from Act I of George Cartwright's *The Heroic Lover, or The Infanta of Spain* (1661, but, he claims, written much earlier). The play is dedicated to Charles I and full of extreme royalist sentiments, but its encapsulation of the political debate between the King and his advisers, though perhaps

---

[1] *Mercurius Politicus* (30 October–6 November 1651).
[2] *The King's Cabinet Opened*, 43; cf. Milton, *Eikonoklastes*, in *Complete Prose Works*, III, 420–1.
[3] P. W. Thomas, *Sir John Berkenhead*, 101 and 137.

designed to lay the blame on the latter, is not ultimately flattering to Charles
I either:

> KING.   What can we do against a multitude?
> CARD[INAL].   Do as you've done, use them extremely rude.
> KING.   But that will but provoke them more and more.
> CARD.   The Way to keep them down, 's to keep them poor.
>
> (III.iii)

The portrayal of such ruler-adviser relationships may be part of an attempt
to justify Charles's autocratic behaviour before the war. In answer to a
pamphleteer who had tried to show that the execution of Charles I was the
culmination of a hereditary curse on the house of Stuart, Balthazar Gerbier
wrote a pamphlet tracing the role of false favourites in English history.[1]
One of Gerbier's relations later dramatized the same concept in *The False
Favourite Disgraced, and the Reward of Loyalty* (1657). In Cosmo
Manuche's *The Just General* (1652), on the other hand, a young king is
brought to realize that he has been unjustly suspicious of the title character.
The play may well refer to some episode in the royal army, in which both
Manuche and his patron Northampton served.

Perhaps out of caution, few dramatists built their plays around the once-
popular figure of the evil usurper. One exception is Leonard Willan's
Orgula, or the Fatal Error (1658), in which he even has the title of Lord
Protector. The authors of other tyrant plays are careful to point to a
historical source for their plots. 'T. B.''s *Rebellion of Naples* (1649) was
based on the recent career of Massaniello, and the various 'Andronicus'
plays which appeared immediately after the Restoration, though obviously
intended as attacks on Cromwell, had a common source in Thomas Fuller's
life of the Byzantine usurper, Andronicus Commenius. One of these plays,
though published anonymously in 1661, appears to have been written in the
1640s by Fuller himself, at a time when Cromwell could not have seemed a
likely ruler.[2] In fact, much of the interest of *Andronicus* lies not only in the
depiction of the villainous central character but also in its analysis of the
lesser mortals caught up in a time of violent political conflict. The play is
written in the form of Senecan tragedy, with the usual mixture of horrific

---

[1] Sir Edward Peyton, *The Divine Catastrophe of the Kingly Family of the House of Stuarts*
(1652), reprinted in Sir Walter Scott (ed.), *Secret History of the Court of James the First*, 2
vols (Edinburgh, 1811), II; Gerbier, *Les Effects Pernicieux de Meschants Favoris* (Hague,
1653).

[2] See James O. Wood, 'Thomas Fuller's Oxford Interlude', *HLQ*, 17 (1954).

actions and sententious speeches, but it gets far closer to contemporary
events than do the romantic tragi-comedies. The Chorus discusses such
problems as whether to stay in the country or emigrate, the difficulty of
knowing what to believe when bombarded with so many conflicting news
reports, the dangers of relying on foreign aid, and the relation of moral
decadence to civil unrest. A courtier defends his decision to temporize:

> If any whisper but the lowest word
> Of Loyalty, there's one to cut his throat.
> Hence houses rifled, goods pillag'd, lands forfeited,
> Our selves disabled from all further service.
> Had we not better for a time comply;
> Spend what we please in thoughts, but speak nothing,
> Bow to our foes, that they may not break us?
> Storms will not always last, when this is over,
> In season due we will discover our selves. . . . (III.v)

This thoughtful if unheroic speech sounds like the result of Fuller's own
deliberations, but it is not clear from the play whether it is meant to be
endorsed. Probably Fuller himself did not know.

John Tatham's *The Distracted State* was published in 1651 but claims on
the title-page to have been written ten years earlier. It has convincingly been
shown, however, that this claim was meant as a blind.[1] Read with the
earlier date in mind, the play seems to be a meaningless bloodbath set in a
particularly awful royal court. But once it is seen in the context of the debate
as to whether royalists could justifiably swear loyalty to the new Commonwealth, the play becomes a satire on the history of the rebellion. The
action moves from an initial usurpation by the rightful king's brother,
through another usurpation by a courtier, to a popular uprising, then a
jostling for power by rival generals and finally a duel in which they kill each
other just as the rightful king, previously believed dead, arrives home to
reassume his throne. The breathtaking succession of usurpations is comic –
one character comments:

> These are fine turning times. I wonder when
> 'Twill come to my turn to be King! (IV.i)

– but it also demonstrates the logical consequences of the 'might is right'
principle, invoked by some writers to justify taking the oath of allegiance to

---

[1] See J. M. Wallace, 'The Case for Internal Evidence (10): The Date of John Tatham's *The
Distracted State*', *Bulletin of the New York Public Library*, 64 (1960).

the Commonwealth. Tatham's moral is not that either Charles I or Charles II is necessarily superior to the leaders of the new government, but that any disruption of the political order is bound to lead to anarchy.

This curious double view of *The Distracted State* – tragedy from the one side, satire from the other – illustrates the difficulty of interpreting political drama. This is particularly true when, as seems often to be the case, the author was himself divided in his response to events. The love and honour conflicts of heroic tragi-comedy inevitably took on new meaning at a time when there were so many pressures on one's honour. Throughout the period – first with the Solemn League and Covenant (the price demanded by Scotland for entering the war on the side of Parliament in 1643), then with the Engagement to the Commonwealth in 1650, and finally with the Clarendon Code of 1661 – men were compelled either to swear allegiance to things in which they did not believe or to suffer personal hardship and be ridiculed as fanatics. The result is exemplified by one of the characters in Manuche's *Faithful Shepherdess* (1660), who explains that he has complied with the Commonwealth in his way:

> I serv'd them: as many did
> Layed by my Consience, And tooke their mony. (1.i)

The loss of self-respect implied in such behaviour perhaps explains the curiously cynical tone of much tragi-comedy, which contrasts oddly with its apparent commitment to heroic ideals. This cynicism is by no means confined to the usual comic subplot of gulling scenes set in a tavern. It is in the heroic plot that it is more striking: in the constant stress on the hypocrisy of religious leaders, the corruption of courtiers and the fickleness of crowds. Even the soldier, who had traditionally been regarded as a simple, honest man, a touchstone for the other characters, is often portrayed as dangerous, lawless and ambitious. Paradoxically, cynicism and royalism reinforce each other. In a society consisting of so many untrustworthy elements, the king seems the one symbol capable of creating order and inspiring loyalty. It is hardly surprising that this loyalty sometimes seems to be of a peculiarly blind and desperate sort.

(iv) Killigrew and Manuche

The two most prolific royalist writers of tragi-comedy were closet dramatists against their will. Killigrew had had plays performed before the war and may have had them acted by a company of English actors who are known to have been in Paris during the 1640s; as we have seen, at least one of them was also given illegally in England. However, the preface to the Restoration edition of his comedies and tragedies seems to place the ones written after 1642 in the category of closet fantasies: 'If you have as much leasure to Read as I had to Write these Plays, you may, as I did, find a diversion, though I wish it you upon better terms than Twenty Years Banishment.' He was, of course, in very different circumstances when he wrote this preface: along with Davenant, he had been granted the lease of a licensed playhouse, and his essentially practical intentions are clear from the fact that he set about cutting and revising his Commonwealth plays with a view to performance. Manuche was less fortunate, to judge by the introductory verses to *The Loyal Lovers* (1652), where he asks to be judged by 'Such as hath liv'd high, and know miserie'. His dramatic career continued after the Restoration, as did his complaints of poverty, although he was also awarded twenty pounds as royal bounty, in compensation for his earlier sufferings. However, it appears that his loyalty was not as absolute as Killigrew's, since he had also tried to get compensation from Cromwell in 1656 for his services 'in making discoveries of the disturbers of our present happy Government'.[1] The prologue to *The Just General*, which he says is his first play, was 'Intended for the Stage', as was that of the unpublished *Love in Travel*; both could have been acted at Castle Ashby, the home of the Earl of Northampton. Northampton, to whom Manuche dedicated several of his plays, was himself a playwright and translator, and the large collection of manuscripts recently discovered at Castle Ashby suggests that he was the centre of a good deal of mid-century dramatic activity.[2]

Killigrew's plays have many of the qualities of closet drama: self-indulgence, length, elaborately described settings. This is probably because he was thinking in terms of the court theatre before the war, and of the audiences which had sat through the seven hours of Montague's *Shepherd's Paradise* in 1633. His stage directions are practical on the whole, though it would have been expensive to construct the prison scene of *Bellamira Her Dream* (c. 1652), with its secret passage to the seashore. He tends, however, to mention essential props only as afterthoughts, thus giving the impression

[1] Wayne H. Phelps, 'Cosmo Manuche, Royalist Playwright of the Commonwealth', *English Language Notes*, 16 (March 1979), 209.
[2] See W. P. Williams, 'The Castle Ashby Manuscripts', *The Library*, 6th series, II, 4 (December 1980), 391–412.

tha' he is making the story up as he goes along. Tragi-comedy at its most romantic is often juxtaposed with surprisingly down-to-earth sentiments. Killigrew's fights, for example, may display superhuman endurance on the part of the combatants, but the stage-directions show that he wanted the effect to be realistic, even brutal. In *Bellamira*, one of the heroes is robbed by soldiers who throw him down while '*he kicks and bites all the while*' (V.v). With a rather naïve pleasure, he explains how such effects can be achieved: '*They cuff and struggle upon the floore, and are both bloody, occasion'd by little spunges ty'd of purpose to the middle fingers in the palmes of their hands*' (*Thomaso*, pt I, V.ix). On the other hand, he sometimes seems totally lacking in visual sense. The villain of *Cicilia and Clorinda* (*c.* 1650) is described as wearing what must have been the standard costume for such characters: 'ORONTE *is clothed in black, with black Feathers, black Perriwig, his person is crooked and ugly, with a Dagger by his side*' (pt. I, I.i.). So unmistakable a physique naturally creates difficulties when Oronte wants to disguise himself; he finally decides to dress as an old beggar woman, and Killigrew leaves him in this costume for the rest of the play without seeming to realize what a ludicrous effect it is bound to have on the near-tragic ending. It may be pathetic when Aspatia in *The Maid's Tragedy* dies in her disguise as a youth, but it is unlikely that any actor would have agreed to play Oronte's death scene disguised as an old woman.

The semi-autobiographical *Thomaso, or the Wanderer* (*c.* 1654) is Killigrew's most complex mixture of realism and fantasy. Its central characters are the author himself and his friends – 'Remnants of the broken Regiments; Royal and Loyal Fugitives, highly guilty all of the Royal Crime' (pt I, I. ii). This is how they see themselves; another character describes them as 'a race of men who have left praying, or hoping for daily bread; and only relye upon nightly drink' (pt I, II.iv). The setting, Madrid, is as vividly evoked as it might have been in a letter home; the characters comment with fascination on the recognized and respectable status of local prostitutes, and joke about the dryness of the river: 'two and twenty Arches, over a Kennel of snow water! . . . 'tis the first River I ever saw Coaches take the Air in' (pt I, I.ii). Yet the subplot, in which two of Thomaso's sillier companions marry a pair of wealthy monsters in expectation of seeing them restored to normality by a Jonsonian mountebank, is far-fetched even for a period which had recently known a revival of interest in magic and astrology. The sexual mores of the characters at times seem astonishingly liberal: in the presence of both her lovers, the courtesan Angelica gives one the money she has just received from the other, saying, 'buy thy pleasure;

follow thy *Capricha* with any woman in Madrid' (pt 2, I.v). And when the hero finally decides to settle down with a suitably rich and beautiful wife, her attitude to his former mistresses is sympathetic and helpful. But Killigrew is too completely part of the world he depicts. When one of the Englishmen is cheated of his money by a Spanish courtesan, he hires bravos to slash her face. His friends consider this a mistake, but not for the reasons one might expect. The action, they decide, is the sort of thing one can get away with in England, but not in Spain, where the courtesan has been provoked to take revenge. When Aphra Behn adapted *Thomaso* in 1677, as *The Rover, or The Banished Cavaliers*, she eliminated all the episodes just mentioned. The cavalier mentality was too shocking to be acceptable to a Restoration audience.

Manuche's plays, likewise, are most memorable for their uncritical portrayal of the dashing cavalier. Those of *The Loyal Lovers* and *The Banished Shepherdess* are very similar: they spend a good deal of their time in taverns (in a room called the King's Head), and the sort of oath which comes automatically to their lips is:

> And if I fail to serve Thee, to my last drop of blood,
> May miserie enforce mee take up arms against
> My naturall Prince. (*Loyal Lovers*, 1.i)

Their main object in life, apart from drinking, is the cheating and ridiculing of rich Puritans. In the subplot of *The Just General*, the hero Sunklow swindles Goldcalf out of the lands which the latter's father had acquired through 'unjust dealing', and warns that if his victim attempts to retaliate:

> I'll nail your ears to the wall; a punishment
> Your honourable father (long before his death) wisely
> Prevented, by leaving them behind him on the Pillory,
> For Cozening such honest Gentlemen as my self. (v.i)

In *The Banished Shepherdess* it is government money that the royalist comrades steal, but it is made clear that the Roundheads were in any case planning to embezzle it themselves. However, it does not seem to occur to the royalists to hand the money over to the treasury of their banished ruler; instead, they spend it on clothes and drink. In *The Loyal Lovers*, it is with the theft of a rich citizen's daughter that the young men are involved. To the usual problems of the penniless lover in comedy, Manuche adds the fact that the girl's father intends her to marry only 'one [who] dares lift his hand/Against his sacred Prince . . . And by sinister waies hoard up unlawfull Wealth' (II.i). Manuche's moral line is nothing if not consistent: the rich are rich through treachery and the poor are poor because of their loyalty, so it is positively virtuous for the latter to rob the former. His characters may behave like the Hobbesian sensualists of Restoration comedy, but they justify themselves in the language of an earlier moral code.

(v) The Duchess of Newcastle

Margaret Cavendish, better known as the Duchess of Newcastle,[1] was even more prolific than Manuche and Killigrew, but seems to have neither expected nor desired to see her works performed. Her choice of the dramatic form can be explained by her admiration for the works of Shakespeare and for her husband, who had a hand in several comedies produced both before and after the war. In *Annals of English Drama*, the Duchess's works are classified as 'anomalous', a description which would fit so many plays of the period as to be almost a category in its own right. She herself was aware that her writings might be difficult to fit into a conventional definition of drama:

> having pleased my Fancy in writing many Dialogues upon several Subjects, and having afterwards order'd them into *Acts* and *Scenes*, I will venture, in spight of the Criticks, to call them *Plays*; and if you like them so, well and good; if not, there is no harm done.[2]

Shy, under-occupied and a compulsive scribbler, Margaret Cavendish inevitably created the most transparent fantasies of self-aggrandizement. In both her autobiography and her life of her husband, she depicts herself as living in a dreamworld of uncritical admiration for the dashing soldier, writer and politician of twice her age, and many of her plays reflect a desire to play a more significant part in his life; hence her favourite fantasy roles: the spell-binding orator and the heroic woman warrior. The reality of their life on the continent before the Restoration, which consisted largely of trying to keep the creditors at bay, is probably reflected more closely in plays dealing with the difficulties of housekeeping, the agonies of social embarrassment, and the plight of a wife whose husband keeps having affairs with the servants. Newcastle seems to have understood something of what

[1] For the sake of simplicity, I shall refer to her by this title, though in fact Newcastle did not become a duke until 1665.
[2] 'To the Reader', *Plays Never Before Printed*, etc. (1668).

she was trying to tell him; at least, he was a consistently enthusiastic supporter of her literary ambitions. He wrote songs and scenes for some of her plays, all of which she (and sometimes her characters) scrupulously acknowledged. In *Youth's Glory and Death's Banquet*,[1] for example, the heroine decides that the best use to which she can put her talents is to give a series of public lectures. The lectures, which occupy much of the play, are by the Duchess herself, but they are followed by scenes written by Newcastle in which the listeners, who had at first been sceptical about women lecturing, now extol the wit and beauty of the prodigy.

The Duchess's fantasies, like those of Killigrew and Manuche, have a definite basis in contemporary events. She must have heard of other women who had played an important part in rescuing men: Anne Murray (later Lady Halkett) helped the future James II to escape from Hampton Court; Ann, Lady Fanshawe, altered the name of a government pass to enable her husband to accompany her out of the country; Jane Lane was the key figure in Charles II's escape after the Battle of Worcester. Her obsession with public orations was equally topical. Academies at which general lectures were given had existed for some time in France and Italy, and Charles I had sponsored one before the war; in 1649, Sir Balthazar Gerbier opened one in London and his orations, which he published, are very similar to those in the Duchess's plays. Moreover, Newcastle himself, in *The Varietie* (1649, but apparently acted before the war), had included a series of lectures by a Mrs Voluble.

It might be possible to relate the fragmentary nature of the Duchess's plays, and their oscillations between violent action and static dialogue, to the sense of frustration among the exiled royalists who, after 1651, were largely restricted to a life of talking, plotting and waiting. But there are enough similarities between the Duchess's plays and *The Concealed Fancies* (1646), written by two daughters of Newcastle's first marriage, to suggest the source of this curious dramaturgy. All three women appear to have learned from Newcastle both an admiration for the Jonsonian comedy of humours and a sense that the ability to construct a plot was somehow not to be expected of them. A prologue to *The Concealed Fancies*, apologizing for its faults, announces:

> 'tis woman all ye way
> For you'll not see a Plot in any Act.[2]

---

[1] *Plays Written by the Thrice Noble, Illustrious and Excellent Princess, the Lady Marchioness of Newcastle* (1662).
[2] Ed. Nathan C. Starr, *PMLA*, 46 (1931), 806.

Newcastle's own plays are essentially a series of humours, or comic turns, which generally required the collaboration of a professional playwright to unify them. This is probably where the Duchess got the idea that 'Poets that write Playes, seldom or never join or sow [sic] the several Scenes together; they are two several Professions.'[1]

Thus her plays, like all her other works, are spun entirely out of her own mind; unlike Killigrew, she despised romances, which might have supplied a structure of sorts for her often entertaining dialogues. She was clearly fascinated by the apparently unending fertility of the imagination. But she was also aware, more than is sometimes supposed, of its ridiculous side. The title character of *The Lady Contemplation* is entirely given over to elaborate daydreams with which she regales a long-suffering friend. Naturally she is annoyed when the latter interrupts her while she is describing her career as general, the oration she delivered to her troops, and the dress she wore for the occasion:

> You have put me out as you always do, and therefore I will tell you no more . . . but I could have told you how I kill'd the General of the Enemy with my own hand, and how I releas'd my Husband, and of such gallant Acts as you never heard the like of.[2]

One sometimes wishes that Killigrew and Manuche were equally conscious of the relation of heroism to fantasy.

---

[1] *Plays . . . by the . . . Marchioness of Newcastle*, sig. A 10–v.
[2] ibid., pt 2, II. x.

2 Short plays: drolls and pamphlets

(i) Popular forms

John Arden has regretted the absence of a popular voice in professional
English theatre of the period: 'If it had been possible, say, for John Bunyan
to have written plays and had them produced, our theatre would have found
for itself a very different history'.[1] In fact, many of the shorter plays of the
time do draw on precisely the forms which Bunyan so memorably combined
in *Pilgrim's Progress*: the trial scene, the fair, the mountebank speech, the
dialogue of scoundrels lamenting their detection, the crossing of the river,
the reading of the will. It is difficult to know whether to describe these as
genuinely popular forms, since many of them derive from the work of
Lucian and a long literary tradition of polemic dialogue, but there are many
points at which they merge with mummers' plays, jigs, moralities, and the
repertoire of the professional fool, whose mocking function may be taken
over, in the more sophisticated pamphlets, by Charon or a comic servant.

   Though these devices could be used for the purpose of political satire, no
one class or party had a monopoly on them. The 'drolls' that were published

[1] Author's note to *Pearl* (1979).

in the 1650s and after the Restoration (*plate 29*) represent a development from the song-and-dance dialogue, or jig, which concluded the performances of the pre-war popular theatre. Some were cut down from longer plays. None appears to have any political content.[1] An interest in short plays was already present before the war – in works like *Four Plays in One* and in the increasing tendency for antimasques to become self-contained interludes – and farce was not necessarily a popular genre. Newcastle's *Varietie* provided the source for one of the drolls, and his *Pleasant and Merry Humour of a Rogue*, as its title indicates, is little more than a series of drolls linked by the figure of the rogue himself. A curious piece of uncertain date, *The London Chanticleers*, has a cast consisting of cockney street-criers, a ballad-singer and a tavern-keeper, and seems a cross between jig and ballad opera. The prologue says that the play is bringing London to spectators unable to go there themselves. This has been variously explained as a reference to royalists during the Interregnum, to a university audience, and to a time of plague.[2] Whichever of these hypotheses may be the most likely, they do suggest that a taste for 'low' comic opera, like that for the romantic play, was more widespread than might be supposed.

On the other hand, the brevity of these pieces made them relatively easy to perform surreptitiously. There appears to have been some tradition of tavern performances. If Edmund Gayton is to be believed, spectators in pre-war years 'so courted the Players to re-act the same matters in the Tavernes, that they came home, as able Actors as themselves'.[3] He may be referring to the public rooms, but it was also possible to hire a private one. In Newcastle's *Varietie*, one of the characters has equipped his tavern room with a descending throne which he uses for acting out private fantasies. Such elaboration is admittedly exceptional, but there is probably some degree of authenticity in Manuche's *Loyal Lovers*, where a small group of royalists in a private room at a tavern put on a short farce, involving only two characters, which satirizes the supposed amours of the Independent preacher Hugh Peters.

We have already seen (pp. 165–6) that a taste for fools, fights and jigs was regarded as low long before 1642. Because of the semi-privileged status of fools, and their tendency to ad-lib, plays in which they appeared were particularly likely to be subversive. In 1621, a play performed at Kendal

---

[1] See J. J. Elson's introduction to his edition of *The Wits, or Sport upon Sport* (Ithaca, N.Y., and London, 1932), 21–2.
[2] *Jacobean and Caroline Stage*, v, 1364–5.
[3] *Pleasant Notes upon Don Quixote* (1654), 140.

Castle made use of a dialogue between two fools and a boy to explain the spectacle of ravens feeding on sheep in terms of an allegory of encroaching landlords and their tenants. We know of it only through the Star Chamber proceedings to which its performance led.[1] After the abolition of Star Chamber it became easier for such protests to find their way into print. The first pamphlet to use an obvious dramatic form seems to have been *Canterbury His Change of Diet* (1641), one of many pamphlets that rejoiced in Laud's imprisonment and recalled his former tyrannies. The scenes are emblematic (*see plate 30*) and the characters' names symbolic: the punishment of Prynne and other opponents is represented by the serving of a dish of ears to 'Canterbury', whose finicky appetite cannot be placated by more ordinary dishes. The language is a mixture of prose, blank verse and rhythmic doggerel, and the final scene is a jig. Immediately before it, a jester gleefully tells a 'King' of his delight at seeing Laud and his 'confessor' singing in a cage like two birds. The birdcage image is an appropriate one for imprisonment; it probably derives from a pun on the names of Bishop Matthew Wren, and a ship-money judge called Finch who had recently 'flown' to Holland; it may also refer to Shirley's ironic dedication of his *Bird in a Cage* (1633) to Prynne, who was then in prison by order of Laud.[2] Reluctance to kick those who were already down was uncommon on either side at this time. The death of every well-known politician was sure to be followed (if not preceded) by the appearance of a mock will and last speech purporting to be his, a dialogue describing his crossing of the Styx and an account of his reception in the other world. Another favourite device, which can be traced both to mummers' plays and to classical comedy, is the quack doctor offering a mock diagnosis of society's ills. Mountebanks must have been a common sight in London, since one dialogue (*News out of the West*, 1647) is a plea for better control over the practice of medicine by someone who thinks that quacks do more harm than civil war. A dialogue of 1649 uses the comic cross-talk of a French mountebank and his servant, John Capon, to attack the Rump Parliament. The 'doctor' sends Capon for his universal remedy; the latter returns with a halter. Sent off a second time, Capon returns late, because, as he explains, he ran into a man with news from Westminster:

[1] Mildred Campbell, *The English Yeoman under Elizabeth and the Early Stuarts* (1942), 152, from Star Chamber 8, 34/4; quoted in *Jacobean and Caroline Stage*, IV, 472–3.
[2] See Margot Heinemann's account of this play in *Puritanism and Theatre* (London, 1980), 245–7.

MOUNTEBANK.   Wat did he say?

CAPON.   Why a said they were all knaves; nay worse, I dare not speak the words I heard him say, for fear of Reason.

MOUNTEB.   *Treason* thou wouldst say.

CAPON.   I say *Reason* Master; What is Reason with other men, is Treason with them.

In an effective change of tone at the end, the mountebank decides to give up and return to France, because 'this be dying Nation, lost, lost begar utterly lost, lie in a deep Lethargy, be uncapable of her own good or recovery'.[1]

Real satiric drama does not reappear until after the abdication of Richard Cromwell. An interesting variation on the 'Dialogue of the Dead' form was the dialogue between the living and the dead. *The World in a Maze, or Oliver's Ghost* (1659) makes Richard and Oliver Cromwell talk, not like figures in a Menippean satire, but in the semi-doggerel of the Fool and Old Man of a mummers' play:

RICH[ARD].   The complaints of the Commons is great and who shall stay their cryes.

O[LIVER].   The man that hath no deceit, and when will he arise.

RICH.   If you be my fathers Ghost answer me this,
Who cut the man off that did not amiss.

O.   That Riddle if I be not mistaken is concerning the *Jews*, putting Christ to death who had no sin, or guile found in him.

RICH.   Sure thou art not my Fathers Ghost that cannot unfold this riddle.

In the spate of pamphlets gloating over the imprisonment of the Commonwealth leaders early in 1660, there is one which is interesting because it uses against them precisely the same 'popular' style which had formerly been directed against prelatry. *A Phanatick Play* (1660) opens with a dialogue between a jester and a Jack Pudding, who look forward to seeing 'a new Play after the old fashion', with the fanatical Sir Arthur Haslerig as the Devil. Watched by these two ironic commentators, the Rump politicians frantically try to think of ways to save themselves. Their game of cards, with the English crown as the stake, is interrupted by the noise of the north wind (Monk's march from Scotland) and finally by the entrance of 'a King' and 'a General'. The jester then announces: 'Gaffer King, Gaffer King, hear, here

[1] *The Disease of the House* (1649).

they have put *Lambert* and *Haslrig* into a great Bird-Cage; did you ever see the like to this that they have now done?' The song of the two prisoners echoes that of Laud and his confessor in *Canterbury His Change of Diet*, and there are other resemblances which cannot be mere coincidence. Perhaps an opportunistic printer adapted this play from an earlier pamphlet. But it is not impossible that the same writer was responsible for both. It has been suggested that he was the Leveller Richard Overton;[1] certainly, this reversal of political allegiances would not be out of keeping with what is known of his later career and that of his party.

(ii) Drama as journalism

What is striking about the plays which employ popular modes is their tendency to abstraction. The 'King' in *Canterbury His Change of Diet* and *A Phanatick Play* is only a symbol, resembling neither Charles I nor Charles II; *The World in a Maze* hints at the royalist identification of Charles I with Christ, but offers no political analysis. The majority of the pamphlet-plays of the period 1647–9 are quite different. Their authors were royalist journalists with a keen interest in current events. They are not shy about using proper names, and in many cases their plays simply rework newspaper material in dramatic form. Their choice of this form was a protest against the increasingly severe anti-theatre legislation passed by Parliament in 1647 and 1648.

Three of the best-known royalist journals were associated with pamphlet-plays. The first, *Mercurius Melancholicus*, was started in August 1647 by a Presbyterian minister but soon taken over by a team of former ballad-writers – Martin Parker, John Taylor and John Crouch – who, like others of their profession, had found newspapers a better way of reaching a large audience.[2] Traces of the original connection between ballads and journalism can be seen in the format of this and other news-sheets: an introductory summary of the week's news, in ballad metre; a prose diatribe (sometimes resembling a dramatic monologue); a heavily slanted account of the news;

[1] See D. M. Wolfe, 'Unsigned Pamphlets of Richard Overton', *HLQ*, 21 (1958), 167–201; and Heinemann, *Puritanism and Theatre*, 243 ff.

[2] For information about ballad-writers and journalists in this period, see Hyder E. Rollins, *Cavalier and Puritan* (New York, 1923), and Joseph Frank, *The Beginnings of the English Newspaper 1620–1660* (Cambridge, Mass., 1961), esp. 116–98.

and one or two final stanzas to round things off. This form is also reminiscent of drama, with its prologue, play and epilogue. *Mercurius Pragmaticus* was founded a few weeks later, probably by Samuel Sheppard, who rapidly enlisted the services of the leading royalist poet, Cleveland, and the former parliamentary journalist Marchamont Nedham. Sheppard has already been mentioned: he was not only a Presbyterian but apparently a minister as well, though his real interest was clearly writing. He had a hand in an exceptionally large number of journals in this period, where he can often be spotted by his habit of quoting or plagiarizing from Webster.[1] Even the motto of *Mercurius Pragmaticus* – '*Nemo me impune lacessit*' – may well be derived from its use as an exit line in *The White Devil*. The third of these royalist journals, *The Man in the Moon*, was started by John Crouch after the demise of *Mercurius Melancholicus*.

Mercury had been the traditional name for journals ever since the founding of the original *Mercurius Gallo-Belgicus* in Cologne in 1594. Before 1641, English newspapers had been carefully controlled and allowed to report only foreign news, but after that date there were 'men *Mercury*'s, and women *Mercury*'s, and boy *Mercury*'s; *Mercury*'s of all sexes, sorts and sizes'.[2] There was even an early forerunner of the pamphlet-play: *Mercurius Britannicus, or The English Intelligencer* (1641), by the satirist Richard Braithwait; this is a learned piece, originally written in Latin, with Heraclitus and Democritus as commentators, and a chorus of parliamentarians, who attack the ship-money judges but tell a 'conventicle' of plebeians to go home and leave government to their betters.

Some journalists aimed for an impersonal and apparently impartial tone, but others endowed Mercury with a personality of his own; Mercurius Melancholicus, at least in some numbers, models his style on that of the stage malcontent. The Mercuries tended to live up to their name not only in speed but also in unreliability, which is why 'Diurnalls' were commonly nicknamed 'Ly-urnalls'. The royalist ones, for example, frequently report non-existent uprisings and victories for their side, as well as the deaths of their most prominent enemies. A pro-Parliament dialogue of May 1648 depicted them as quacks attempting to cure the 'Malignant' cause with their false rumours.[3]

Both the Government and the Stationers' Company, which was supposed to hold a monopoly on printing in London, were constantly on the lookout

[1] See Hyder E. Rollins, 'Samuel Sheppard and His Praise of Poets', *SP*, 24 (1927).
[2] *A Description of the Passage of Thomas, late Earl of Strafford, over the* River Styx (1641).
[3] *Mercurius Honestus, or News from Westminster* (1648).

for illegal publications. Thus there was a high turnover both of journals and of journalists, one writer often filling in for another during the latter's imprisonment. Nevertheless it is possible to identify some of the pamphlet-plays with particular authors. Sheppard, who appears to have inaugurated the series of pamphlet-plays, brought out Part I of *The Committee Man Curried* on the very day – 16 July 1647 – that the House of Commons drew up a new order for the suppression of stage-plays. Part II, published a month later, is prefaced by a prologue praising the pre-war theatre

> Which once a Hackney coach convey'd you to,
> Where you sate scorning all the raine could doe.

The two plays, which appear to have been conceived separately, offer in miniature most of the standard situations of pre-war drama, with its hard-up cavalier, hypocritical Puritan and rowdy soldier, further enlivened by borrowings from Suckling and Webster. It is the names (the cavalier is Loyalty, his rich uncle Rebellion) which give the material its significance. The same subject-matter was worked into a more coherent political allegory in *The Scottish Politick Presbyter* (17 September 1647), which represents Anarchy (an Independent) as a friend to the royalist Moneyless, and ends with Anarchy's murder of the Presbyterian who has been cuckolding him.

Nedham's *The Levellers Levelled* (3 December 1647) is a more sophisticated piece. It was published under the name of Mercurius Pragmaticus, who also speaks the prologue and acts as chorus. Most of the characters have abstract allegorical names, apart from the astrologer Lilly; Lilburne, the main object of Nedham's satire, appears as 'John O'London' and talks in the manner of Shakespeare's Jack Cade. Like Sheppard's play, *The Levellers Levelled* aludes to other pre-war plays, particularly Jonson's *Catiline*,[1] but it also follows contemporary events more closely than Sheppard and ends with a piece of news only two weeks old, Charles I's escape to the Isle of Wight.

The two-part structure of *Crafty Cromwell* (February 1648) probably reflects the authors' claim to be writing a history play. The two parts are ascribed to *Mercurius Melancholicus* and *Pragmaticus* respectively, and were published to coincide with a new ordinance of 9 February 'for the utter suppression and abolishing of all Stage-Playes and Interludes'. A pro-Parliament newspaper, *Mercurius Anti-Pragmaticus*, had already expressed its approval of the silencing of 'those proud parroting Players'.[2] The prologue to *Crafty Cromwell*, 1, takes up the challenge:

---

[1] As G. E. Bentley has shown, this play is more frequently mentioned than any other in the seventeenth century. See *Shakespeare and Jonson*, 2 vols (Chicago, Ill., 1945), 1, 109–12.
[2] No. 18 (20–7 January 1648).

An Ordinance from our pretended state,
Sowes up the Players mouths, they must not prate
Like Parrats what they're taught upon the Stage,
Yet we may print the Errors of the Age.

As if to reinforce their defiance, the authors draw on familiar dramatic situations: the Ghost of Pym, like Sylla in *Catiline*, draws a curtain to reveal his true heir, Cromwell; the Leveller Rainsborough is drawn in a triumphal chariot; two Jesuits conjure up Behemoth; and Fairfax is danced round by three Furies. Behind all the melodrama is a close record of contemporary events, as reported in newspapers and pamphlets.[1]

The works of *Mercurius Melancholicus* and the *Man in the Moon*, perhaps because of their authors' ballad-writing experience, tend to be more fantastic. In the 'Mrs Parliament' plays published in spring and early summer of 1648, Melancholicus, like Pragmaticus, hides behind a curtain to act as commentator. Mrs Parliament vomits up seditious ordinances, gives birth to a monstrous child called Reformation, and engages in sanctimonious dialogues with her friends, Mrs London and Mrs Synod. The Devil, in another pamphlet, carries Mr Parliament to hell on his back. *The Cuckoo's Nest at Westminster* (1648), a slanging-match between the wives of Cromwell and Fairfax, ends with a messenger bringing news that both men have been killed in a popular uprising in favour of King Charles.

What this scurrility and fantasy actually shows is the increasing hopelessness of the royalist position. This perhaps explains the popularity of the two-part *Newmarket Fair* (June and July 1649), by the Man in the Moon (probably Crouch). Both the bitterest and the funniest of the royalist plays, it went through several editions in 1649; at the Restoration, Part I was reprinted 'at the request of some young Gentlemen, to Act in *Christmas Holydayes*'. Commendatory verses to Part II assure the author that 'True hearts are now reviv'd' by reading this play. It is hard to see why, in a work so dominated by wishful thinking. At the end of Part I, a messenger arrives with the usual news of royalist uprisings, and Cromwell and Fairfax promptly commit suicide. When these villains were needed again for Part II, Crouch solved his problem with characteristic impudence. One royalist commentator simply says to another: ''Tis strange Fidelius that they should recover!' The most effective scene is the one which gives the play its title. The fair was a familiar satiric theme (there had already been a *Lambeth Fair*,

---

[1] As has been shown by John Singleton in his edition of the plays (unpublished MA thesis, University of Birmingham, 1976), 9.

Westminster Fair, Kentish Fair and so on), but the recent selling-off of the dead king's property, which had been particularly shocking to royalists, lends a haunting tone to the speeches of the crier:

> O yes, O yes, O yes, Here is a Golden Crowne, Worth many a hundred Pound; 'twill fit the head of a Fool, Knave, or Clowne; 'twas lately tane from the Royall Head, of a King martyred; who bids most? Here is a *Scepter* for to sway a Kingdom a new *reformed* way: 'twas usurp'd from *one* we did lately Betray; pray Customers come away. (Part I)

A Bartholomew Fairing (30 August 1649) is a rather subtler treatment of the same idea. Three profiteering Puritans, their silly wives, their servants and three smug divines gather for a picnic in the new public park at Richmond, which had once been a royal property. Young Roger Trusty, who has been expelled from Oxford for his royalism, contemplates cuckolding his Puritan master for revenge. But the scheme, like much else in the play, remains on a purely verbal level. The treatment of the parliamentarians is less shrilly antagonistic than in most royalist plays, and the general level of both the verse and the prose is much higher than usual. As the title suggests, the inspiration is pre-war city comedy, and the style often recalls Jonson or Middleton – for instance, in Roger's comment on Puritan appetites:

> There's a weezle will passe a widows house, and nere strain for't. How the dish dances! The Surloyn nere mov'd so fast when 'twas alive.

The Famous Tragedy of King Charles I stands somewhat apart from the other pamphlet-plays by virtue (or vice) of its greater length. But it is still a short work, and gives every sign of being by one of the journalist-playwrights.[1] Its title is misleading. It is primarily a dramatization of events late in 1648, particularly the murder of the Leveller Rainsborough and the siege of Colchester, whose royalist generals, shot after their surrender by Fairfax's orders, are the play's real heroes. The dramatist was obviously overtaken by events, and he eventually added both the title and the final scene in an effort to bring the story up to date. The King never appears; his execution is undramatically recounted in a letter which Cromwell receives after having spent the night with Mrs Lambert. The chorus then draws a curtain to reveal the bodies of the King and three lords

---

[1] Its final chorus borrows from another work attributed to Nedham, *Digitus Dei* (1649), but the rhymes are altered in a manner characteristic of Sheppard's plagiarisms.

who were executed in April 1649. Harbage's comment on this play – 'every slain Cavalier wings instantly to Heaven, and every slain Roundhead dives instantly to Hell' – is not quite fair.[1] The chorus in fact pronounces harshly on the executed nobles, and there are other attempts to achieve historical perspective. For the most part, however, the author seems to have been caught between the demands of journalism and drama.

Despite the constant threat of imprisonment, which few of them escaped, the journalist-playwrights give the impression of enjoying their dangerous lives. They attack each other as well as the government, ride private hobby-horses, and indulge in joke title-pages ('Printed at Cuckoo-time, in a Hollow Tree', 'Printed at You May Go Look', etc.) which do not encourage one to take them seriously. But they clearly saw their work as important. *Newmarket Fair*, II shows Lady Fairfax nervously commenting on those who 'are apt to scandal us, and bring us on their *Stages*', and the prologue gloats that such a prospect 'cannot chuse but make proud *rebels* rage'. The result was that Parliament introduced a new and more powerful ordinance for the suppression of all unlicensed printing. When it came into force, on 20 September 1649, the royalist newspapers either disappeared or altered their contents. Crouch managed to carry on as a journalist by excluding news in favour of gossip, whimsy and bawdy stories. Nedham, after another spell of imprisonment, agreed to edit the official Commonwealth journal, *Mercurius Politicus*. Sheppard wrote at least one more pamphlet-play, *The Jovial Crew, or the Devil Turned Ranter* (1651), but this time he was attacking a sect for which neither the government nor the royalists had a good word. In his last years, he published epigrams, paradoxes and mock almanacs in which days are dedicated to such saints as Aglaura, Arden of Faversham and the Moor of Venice.[2]

(iii) John Tatham and Commonwealth pamphleteering

Between 1649 and the abdication of Richard Cromwell, satire was not much in demand. The drolls published by Robert Cox were tales of cuckolding and knockabout farce; two other pamphlets, *The New Brawl* and *The Gossips' Brawl* (1654 and 1655), are misogynistic dramatizations of alehouse

---

[1] *Cavalier Drama* (New York and London, 1936; repr. New York, 1964), 180.
[2] See Rollins, 'Samuel Sheppard', 535–8.

quarrels. It was not, perhaps, simply the fear of censorship that turned writers away from political subjects. The defeat at Worcester resulted not only in loss of morale among royalists, but also, among the uncommitted majority of the population, in a willingness to settle for the established government. In so far as any political comment appears in the pamphlets, it is indirect; the favourite form is that of the droll, or series of drolls.

Thus *The Prince of Prigs' Revels* (1651), by 'J.S.', one of a number of pamphlets inspired by the highwayman James Hind, devotes each of its short acts to an anecdote from the hero's life. The author is presumably tongue-in-cheek in his opening address to the reader, which insists that he despises mere pamphlets and aims at virtue as did 'incomparable *Johnson* [from whom he borrows a song], excellent *Shakespear*, and elegant *Fletcher*'. But there are occasional moral reflections, when Hind feels 'a civil war within me', suggesting that his criminality is a product of the evil times in which he lives. In the final scene, based on a rumour which was current for some months after the Battle of Worcester, he is shown helping in the escape of 'the Scots King', as Charles II is tactfully called. The epilogue breaks off, with a touch of stop-press journalism, as 'J.S.' declares that he has just heard news of Hind's capture and is going out to find whether it is true. (It was.) It is easy to see how glorification of the romantic outlaw could become a substitute for the more dangerous practice of attacking society directly. The play's title links him with the traditional lord of misrule.

Probably the most successful dramatist of the period, when it came to dealing with politics and getting away with it, was John Tatham. He was a thoroughly professional writer, ready to try anything from pastoral (a school production before the war) to the Lord Mayor's Shows for which he was responsible between 1657 and 1664. We have already seen how he covered his tracks in the full-length play *The Distracted State*, partly by misleading the reader as to exactly when the play was written. He followed much the same method in his shorter piece, *The Scots Figgaries* (1652). The one thing that is clear about this play is that it is anti-Scots. The Scots beggars who come south to prey on the English offer a universal remedy for the country's problems, which turns out to be the pill of sedition. In a trial scene at the end, this remedy is shown to be lethal; the Scots' ally, the soldier Scarefool, is shown to be a coward, and they are all sent packing. There is no attempt to suggest that the country had been in perfect health before the Scots arrived, and a subplot on the usual comic theme of gulling in taverns, although it is totally unconnected with the main satiric plot, helps to reinforce the author's picture of a society where both cheaters and cheated deserve all they get. Moreover, by remaining vague about the date of his action, Tatham lets his readers choose whether to take the play as a satire on the Scots invasion of the early 1640s on behalf of Parliament, their subsequent invasion on behalf of Charles I, or their most recent one on behalf of Charles II. No doubt the fact that the Scots were such an easy target at this period was one reason for the play's success. It may even have been performed. It is difficult to imagine a writer like Tatham spending much time on something so comparatively unprofitable as closet drama.

The Rump, his vivid evocation of the last days of the Commonwealth, certainly *was* performed, and with great success, in 1660–1. Tatham was indebted to the journalists for such devices as his female parliament and the quarrels between the wives of the Commonwealth leaders. But he was essentially a city poet rather than a courtier, and his play differs from Aphra Behn's later adaptation of it as *The Roundheads, or the Good Old Cause* (1681) in the total absence of heroic royalists from its cast of characters. What it offers instead is a remarkable picture of the approaching Restoration as seen through the eyes of the Londoners themselves. Recent controversy about the precise date of this play shows how skilfully Tatham worked.[1] Unlike the journalist-playwrights, he was able to impose a coherent structure on his material rather than simply following the order of events as he had lived them. Thus the latest historical event of which the play takes notice is the imprisonment of General Lambert (4 March 1660), but this is mentioned before the last scene, which depicts the events of 10 February 1660, when Monk declared himself for a free Parliament and the streets of London were full of rejoicing. This crowd scene is carefully balanced against the first one of the play, which depicts Lambert's soldiers just after their general has forcibly dissolved Parliament (in October 1659). As usual in Tatham, the soldiers are shown to be riotous and irreligious; in a later scene, they look forward to looting the shops. They are contrasted with the London apprentices, equally jolly and unruly, but capable of self-discipline. Tempted to set fire to the house of the pro-Commonwealth astrologer Lilly, they decide that they had better not, because 'there's a statute against it. Better once wise than never.' So the end of the play, with its roasting of rumps, hallooing, singing and dancing – and the fantasy sequence where the last remnants of the Good Old Cause find themselves hawking their

[1] See V. J. Scott, 'A Reinterpretation of John Tatham's *The Rump, or the Mirrour of the late Times*', *PQ*, 24 (1945); John Freehafer, 'The Formation of the London Patent Companies in 1660', *Theatre Notebook*, 20 (1965), 9–12; and Gunnar Sorelius, 'The Early History of the Restoration Theatre: Some Problems Reconsidered', *Theatre Notebook*, 33 (1979), 54–6.

wares on the street – is not simply an evocation of what must have been an exhilarating memory for many of its first spectators; it also celebrates, by implication, the return of law and order. At whatever date Tatham actually wrote the play, he chose the right point at which to end it: while people felt that they were 'beginning the world again' and the Restoration was still an exciting prospect rather than a disappointing reality.

Though 1660 saw a resurgence of political pamphlets in dialogue, most of them were simply imitations, even plagiarisms, of their predecessors. Printers took advantage of the political climate to reissue unsold copies of *The Famous Tragedy* and *Newmarket Fair*, with 'Printed in the year 1649', on the title page, proudly proclaiming their courage. Some of the 'Mrs Parliament' plays became *The Life and Death of Mrs Rump* (1660). *Cromwell's Conspiracy* (1660), advertised as by 'a Person of Quality', borrows a good deal of *The Famous Tragedy*, with the Colchester siege replaced by royalist martyrdoms of 1658, a death-scene for Cromwell and a tribute to General Monk. Unlike the dramatist of 1649, this writer felt no hesitation about portraying Charles I on the scaffold:

> Adieu dear friends, adieu to all the World;
> Thus from a Throne to Death a King is hurl'd.
>   *Executioner cuts off his head*. (II.iv)

By now Martin Parker, John Cleveland, John Taylor and (probably) Samuel Sheppard were dead. Crouch wrote an enthusiastic poem welcoming Charles II. Marchamont Nedham went on defending the Commonwealth in print, then escaped to Holland. Characteristically, however, he is next heard of back in England, writing on behalf of the restored monarchy. But then, even Robin Hood, in a short piece performed at Nottingham Castle on Coronation Day (1661), was converted from his talk of liberty to 'a chearfull and ready submission to his Majesties Laws'.[1]

In verses prefixed to the Beaumont and Fletcher folio of 1647, James Howell wondered what the great Jacobean dramatists would have made of so bloody and desperate an age. Those who actually did choose the events of that age for their subject matter were both too deeply involved in them, and in too much of a hurry, to produce anything like the tragedies of their predecessors. The pamphlet-plays are probably at their most successful as parodies. In *The Famous Tragedy*, Hugh Peters addresses Cromwell in high

---

[1] 'Robin Hood and His Crew of Soldiers', in *Rymes of Robin Hood*, ed. R. B. Dobson and J. Taylor (London, 1976), 239.

astounding terms, on the grounds that 'our language should be like those Lawes we meane to give, awfull and to be wonder'd at by mortals'. The result sometimes is mildly amusing bombast: 'thy Nose, like a bright Beacon, sparkling still (the Aetna that doth fame our English world) hangs like a Comet o're thy dreadfull face, denouncing death & vengeance' (I.i). The sources of this style are clear from Peters's comparisons of his leader to Tamburlaine, Talbot and Richard III. But when the author wants to move from the mock-heroic to the genuinely heroic, all he can do is change the imitation Marlowe of the Roundheads for the imitation Webster of the royalists:

> Oh! you have put Balls of wild-fire in my Bowels, I am but all one *Aetna*, Farewell, base gloomie world, in which deluded Man, ravish'd with toyes, hunts after bubbles. . . . (III.i)

It is in this second-hand form that we get our last glimpse of the style of the great age of poetic drama. Already by 1660 it must have seemed obsolete. The 'author' of *Cromwell's Conspiracy*, though he evidently began with the intention of simply copying from *The Famous Tragedy*, ended up jettisoning image after image of 'Asses milke, commixt with Almond flower' and 'Tyrian Silks and Ermins skins'. Ironically, the royalist attempt to revive the cause of a sacred king in the language of a forbidden drama succeeded only in showing that both had ceased to be relevant. What was restored would have to be a different sort of monarchy and a different sort of stage.

3 Towards a 'reformed' stage

(i) Versions of reform

For the closet dramatists and journalist-playwrights, drama was essentially a nostalgic medium: they turned to the past for their models as they would have preferred to return to it in other ways. But for those whose relationship with the theatre was a professional one, it was more important to find a way of re-establishing it on a commercial footing. It was not enough to show that the theatre might be a 'safe', even a positive, social influence. It had to look recognizably new as well. Reforming and re-forming thus went together.

The notion of a morally reformed stage had been raised early in the 1640s. Milton wanted the Long Parliament to sponsor plays on religious and patriotic themes as an alternative to the hated *Book of Sports*. He also hinted that he would be prepared to present a list of possible subjects for such plays.[1] Such a list, in Milton's handwriting, still exists. It consists of titles drawn from the Bible and from British history (British, because at this time Parliament was still grateful for Scottish support), with occasional notes of moral points that could be incorporated in their treatment. For instance,

[1] *Reason of Church Government Urged* (1642), in *Complete Prose Works*, ed. Don M. Wolfe, 8 vols (New Haven, Conn., 1953–73), I, 819–20.

Herod's readiness to grant Salome's request for the head of John the Baptist could be attributed to his having 'well bedew'd himself with wine'; Edward the Confessor would be condemned for his foreign favourites, 'his slackness to redresse the corrupt clergie and superstitious praetence of chastity'; the story of Phineas, who kills a foreign noblewoman, would be used to justify 'reformation & punishment illegal & as it were by tumult'.[1] Many of these themes were later to find their way into *Samson Agonistes*.

Though Milton appears to have intended these plays for public performance – and was not above suggesting such crowd-pulling titles as *Cupid's Funeral Pyre, or Sodom Burning* – the form in which he planned them was that of classical tragedy. In turning to the public festivals of democratic Athens for his models, he was doing much the same thing that he and other parliamentary political theorists and religious reformers were doing when they rejected the 'Norman gibberish' of the laws and the traditional language of the liturgy in favour of a supposedly purer past. Though the closing of the theatres put an end to his project for the time being, the House of Commons did authorize a translation of *Baptistes*, a sixteenth-century pro-Reformation tragedy by the Scottish humanist George Buchanan. Published in 1643 under the inflammatory title *Tyrannical-Government Anatomized: or, a Discourse Concerning Evil Counsellors*, it underlines the relevance of John the Baptist's story through the use of loaded words such as 'malignant' and 'prelate'. The occurrence of lines like 'Profit with bad works joyned I nought account' has led some scholars to ascribe the translation to Milton himself.[2] But the poor quality of the printed text, with verse printed as prose, and the misleading statements on the title page, which gives neither author's nor translator's name, make this view difficult to accept.

There is, however, one other tragedy in classical form which clearly supports the Commonwealth. *The Tragedy of the Famous Roman Orator Marcus Tullius Cicero* (1651) was probably written for school performance: it contains a large number of roles for children and gives detailed stage directions for achieving the illusion of violence. The tone is essentially conciliatory; the chorus praises republican Rome and figures like Brutus and Cassius, but takes care to repudiate Catiline, who had been used as a symbol

---

[1] John Milton, *Poems, Reproduced in Facsimile from the Manuscript in Trinity College, Cambridge* (London, Scolar Press, 1970), 33–40.

[2] E.g. J. T. T. Brown, 'An English Translation of Buchanan's *Baptistes* Attributed to John Milton', *George Buchanan: Glasgow Quatercentenary Studies* (Glasgow, 1907). This edition prints the text as blank verse.

of revolution by many royalists. It also warns against allowing the stern
virtues of the republic to sink into luxury and degeneracy, and above all
expresses the longing for peace after so many years of war. In the year of
Charles II's attempted invasion, it is clear what we are meant to think of the
comment on young Octavius and his claim to be Caesar's avenger:

> O what a golden age w'enjoy'd
> Under the *Reverend Saturnes* of the State!
>   But now an upstart scarce unboyd,
> Unto an age of iron gives new date. (III: Chorus)

It was to this desire for peace and stability that other supporters of the
theatre were to appeal. An anonymous pamphlet of 1647 had suggested,
perhaps ironically, that 'it were a good way to mollifie peoples minds to
suffer Play-houses againe, and . . . a considerable addition to the education
of the Gentry'.[1] Such hopes turned out to be premature in 1647, but in 1653
they can be found again: the stage is described as 'a means to divert
tumultuary and turbulent spirits',[2] and Richard Flecknoe claims that the
gentry 'were as much civiliz'd by the *Stage*, as either by *Travail*, or the
University, in beholding the abridgement there of the best Fashions,
Language, and Behaviour of the Time'.[3] The argument is clear. Far from
being a potentially disruptive force, the theatre is seen as a means of
encouraging the return to a stable, hierarchically based society.

This explains the ironic fact that the establishment of the Protectorate
should have permitted the performance only of the most aristocratic, even
courtly, kind of spectacle. Cromwell's court, though smaller and more
economically run than that of Charles I, was nevertheless like other courts in
its need for display and entertainment, particularly the kind of entertainment which could be counted on to offend no one and which could be
enjoyed by visiting dignitaries who spoke no English.[4] The masque was an
international art form, and music had never fallen under the same
disapproval as the theatre in any case. Shirley's *Cupid and Death*, one of
several 'moral masques' which he wrote for private performance in this
period, was presented, apparently by official command, before the Por-
tuguese ambassador at Whitehall in March 1653. Another private masque –

[1] *A True Account and Character of the Times* (9 August 1647), 8.
[2] Stationer's Preface to Robert Mead, *The Combat of Love and Friendship* (1653).
[3] 'Discourse of Languages', in *Miscellania, or Poems of All Sorts* (1653), 104.
[4] See Roy Sherwood, *The Court of Oliver Cromwell* (London and Totowa, N.J., 1977), for
further evidence of its regal nature.

Cupid's Coronation, by Thomas Jordan, which was acted at a girls' school in 1654 – was adapted by the author for public performance (as *Fancy's Festivals*) in 1657. Jordan, like Shirley, had written for the stage before 1642; he was also a composer, and he was eventually to be Tatham's successor as a writer of Lord Mayor's Shows. He obviously conceived of the masque as a work of popular appeal. The prologue assures the audience that they will hear nothing against 'Religion, Government, or Modestie' and also promises not to be over-intellectual. There was no longer to be any hidden meaning for the élite, as in the works of Jonson and Milton (or, for that matter, William Denny).

Richard Flecknoe – like Jordan, a composer – was the most theoretical of the campaigners for a new theatre, and in fact never seems to have had his works produced in England. Encouraged by Cromwell's assumption of power, he dedicated to the Protector's favourite daughter a work half-way between masque and play, *Love's Dominion* (1654), which had already been performed, in an earlier version, before a court audience in Flanders. Now that the country was rid of 'our sullen Masters', he suggested, the stage might be restored as 'an humble coadjutor of the Pulpit, to teach *Morality*, in order to the others *Divinity*'. He described his piece as 'a Pattern for the Reformed Stage', and the rulers of Love's Kingdom do in fact offer a model of enlightened patronage of the arts when they call for a song in praise of true love as part of their scheme to reform the country. They certainly get what they asked for:

> O fly then far
> Kisses, that are
> Incentives of foul Lust, which no
> Virgin lips shou'd ever know. . . .

The play's (and Flecknoe's) argument is that men's hearts must be touched by music and poetry before they can respond to political and religious exhortations. There is no question of bringing politics and religion into the work itself. In his *Marriage of Oceanus and Britannia* (1659) he goes so far as to lament the troubles of the past and praise the British navy, but music and dancing are offered as a means of diverting Britannia's mind.

Edmund Gayton could not resist a comment on Flecknoe's moral pretensions:

> The stage reform'd (as they say 'tis thought on)
> Time may be spent there well, as reading Broughton.

No fooles with *Harry Codpieces* appeare,
Nor Souldiers suffered in their parts to sweare:
No Lady vitiated o' th' stage before us,
But let *Susanna*'s bathing be by *Chorus*.[1]

Gayton's notion of reform picks up the standard complaints against the theatre – profanity, debauchery, bawdy – and implies the standard defence in terms of realism (soldiers swear 'in their parts' because it is decorum). But there are social implications as well: a reformed stage would get rid of the fool and might introduce the classical chorus. Flecknoe's concept of reform was clearly social as well as moral. The vapidity of his lyrics, so memorably ridiculed later by Dryden, was intentional: he had observed that in Italian opera a single 'Ah' or 'Alas' might be far more moving than a purely verbal conceit. His ambition was to make the English masque into something more like opera, unified throughout by the use of recitative. In defending this new technique, he pointed out that it was intended for the nobility: 'as their Persons, so their Musick, should be elevated above the vulgar'.[2] It is the same argument that was to be advanced for the use of rhymed verse in the Restoration heroic play.

It seems, then, that 'reform' had more than one meaning. On the one hand it implied *moral* reform: an uplifting spectacle free from profanity and bawdy. On another, it meant the inculcation of essentially aristocratic attitudes, the re-establishing of social distinctions and the encouragement of a harmonious, stable society. It also included the idea of *theatrical* reform: the development of techniques allowing the musical and spectacular element to dominate the verbal. As Newcastle's French dancing-master put it in *The Varietie*, 'ven dey are so bissey to learne a de dance, dey vil never tinke of de Rebellion' (III.i).

(ii) Davenant

Sir William Davenant was willing to make use of the same arguments as Flecknoe and Jordan. He described his first venture, *The First Day's Entertainment at Rutland House* (1656), as 'after the manner of the

---

[1] *Pleasant Notes Upon Don Quixote* (1651), 270.
[2] Preface to *Ariadne Deserted by Theseus* (1654). It is printed and discussed in Eugene Haun, *But Hark! More Harmony* (Ypsilanti, Mich., 1971), 35–41.

ancients', and his prologue anticipates that the declamations will have an ennobling effect,

> Quickning by influence of their Noble deeds
> Glory in others, till it Vertue breeds.

It sounds almost like Milton's plans for a classically inspired, state-sponsored moral entertainment. And if Davenant did not actually submit a list of subjects to the government, he did write in 1656 to Thurloe, the Secretary of State, with a proposal for an anti-Spanish spectacle, highly appropriate at a time when the country had just gone to war with Spain. This idea, which became *The Cruelty of the Spaniards in Peru* (1658), may have been inspired by *The Tears of the Indians* (1656), which had just been published by Milton's nephew, John Phillips.[1] Davenant also pointed out the usefulness of the theatre as a stabilizing influence and added a further argument – that the provision of suitably refined entertainments would be an encouragement to the wealthy to stay in London and spend their money there.[2]

It was this willingness to compromise with the Protectorate, and this apparent support for Cromwell's military aims, that made the former Master of the Revels, Sir Henry Herbert, try to discredit Davenant after the Restoration by describing him as Master of the Revels to 'Oliver'.[3] Davenant was admittedly in a difficult situation. He had given long service to the royalist cause, was captured in 1650, and spent two years in prison under sentence of death; after his release, he had soon found himself back in prison for debt. The theatre, for him, represented a badly needed source of income. Not surprisingly he was prepared to offer himself as a reformer, although it seems clear that the 'reform' in which he was really most interested was that of stage technique. As early as 1639 he had received a patent for a new theatre (never built) which would have been used for the public production of plays and operas with the 'scenes' that had hitherto been used only for court performances.[4] It was essentially this scheme that he was trying to revive in the 1650s.

[1] This work, a translation from Bartholomew de las Casas, includes a frontispiece of Indians being tortured, which may well have been the source for one of the 'scenes' painted for *The Cruelty of the Spaniards in Peru*.
[2] Memorandum to Thurloe, 1656, quoted in Arthur H. Nethercot, *Sir William Davenant* (New York, 1938; rev. ed. 1967), 321–2.
[3] See Herbert's petition to Charles II, 4 August 1660, reprinted in Adams, *Herbert*, 85.
[4] Nethercot, *Sir William Davenant*, 168–73.

Part 1 of *The Siege of Rhodes* (1656) probably deserves its usual title of 'the first English opera', at least the first one to achieve production. Its connection with the court masque is clear: its sets, though adapted to the tiny dimensions of the Rutland House stage, were the work of John Webb, a pupil of Inigo Jones, who had worked on some of the pre-war court masques (*see plates 31 and 32*). It differs from the masque in being sung throughout, in uniting the functions of actors and singers, and in being constructed like a play. But it also differs from the works of Jordon and Flecknoe in its greater emphasis on the poetic and dramatic. The text of *The Siege of Rhodes* could be read for its own sake (and was, with great pleasure, by Pepys). On the printed page, indeed, its action seems almost too dramatic for the resources of the singers. But most of the violence may well have been painted on the set. There is little real enthusiasm for war, except in so far as it supplied an opportunity for music and spectacle. In Part 1 of *The Siege*, the breathtaking heroism of the central characters is contrasted with the cynicism of the chorus. In Part 2 – probably written after Cromwell's death – the Turkish leader Soliman admits that he is obliged to seek foreign wars in order to keep his rebellious subjects quiet. The opera, however, shows some sympathy for Soliman, balanced nicely against the romantic appeal of the amorous Alphonso and Ianthe, who, it has been plausibly suggested, were meant to recall Charles I and Henrietta Maria.[1] The statesmanship of the Turk, the passionate recklessness of the lovers, culminate in the classic question of the love-and-honour play:

> Can half the world be govern'd by a Mind
> That shews Domestick pity, and grows kind? (pt 2, v.iii)

Whatever Davenant's own sympathies may have been, he was also aware of the ambivalent response to Charles's character as 'a better man than a king'. *The Siege of Rhodes*, altered to make it more dramatic and to give greater scope to the actresses, went on to enjoy great success after the Restoration.

'Reform' was still the key word when Charles II, shortly after his return, granted Davenant and Killigrew their monopoly on theatrical performances in London. The patent begins with an expression of regret at what the King has been 'given to understand' (one would think he had never been to the theatre in his life): that plays and interludes of a scurrilous nature are currently being performed. However, it adds:

[1] Introduction to *The Siege of Rhodes*, ed. Ann-Mari Hedback (Uppsala, 1973), li–lv.

wee are assured, that, if the Evill & Scandall in the Playes that now are or
have bin acted were taken away, the same might serve as Innocent and
Harmlesse diuertisements for many of our Subiects.[1]

The two managers were then ordered to 'reform' the theatre in both senses –
to introduce actresses in order to avoid the scandal of boy actors, to revise
and clean up the old plays in their repertory, and to introduce to the public
stage the scenic and musical refinements previously associated only with
pastoral, masque and opera.

  In Davenant's *Playhouse to Be Let* (1663) the result can be seen. It is the
long vacation; the theatre has been offered to anyone who cares to use it, and
various performers apply for the privilege. A player sends away a couple of
fencers who want to use the place for a school, suggesting that they try the
once-popular Red Bull instead, since 'There are no Tenents in it but old
Spiders'. He also dismisses a collection of fairground tumblers and clowns,
but reluctantly agrees that

>   till the nation be more civilis'd,
> Your Fool and Devil may be entertain'd;
> They'l get money; none now but very choice
> Spectators will vouchsafe to see a Play
> Without'm.

As an example of the more 'civilized' new drama, he then allows a medley of
short pieces, some of them refurbished from Davenant's Commonwealth
period, others newly written: a translation of a Molière farce, performed in
broken English; a musical mime; a short operatic piece; and a travesty of
Corneille's *Mort de Pompée*. The reference to the Red Bull is particularly
interesting. Davenant was gloating, of course: thanks to his and Killigrew's
monopoly, the actors of that company had been obliged either to join the
new theatres or to be forced out of work.[2] They had managed to keep
performing throughout the 1640s and 1650s, despite Acts of Parliament,
scuffles and arrests; what finally destroyed them was the Restoration.

(iii) Restoration postscript

The indebtedness of the Restoration rake hero to the cavalier hero has

[1] Adams, *Herbert*, 87.
[2] See W. Van Lennep, 'The Death of the Red Bull', *Theatre Notebook*, 16 (1962).

become obvious by this time. Aphra Behn's adaptations of Tatham and Killigrew show that the mythical figures of Roundhead cuckold and rakish loyalist were powerfully attractive. Yet both Tatham and Killigrew required a good deal of simplification to make them acceptable to audiences after 1660. Abraham Cowley found this when he adapted his youthful comedy *The Guardian* (1641) for performance in 1661. His plot was really the same as that of *The Puritan* (1606): hard-up scholar and soldier join forces to cheat rich, hypocritical Puritan citizens. But when his play was performed under its new title, *Cutter of Coleman Street*, Cowley had to defend himself against charges of insulting the royalist army.[1] The Roarers, Hectors, Huffs and so on, whose behaviour had provided so much amusement in the plays of Jonson and Middleton, were uncomfortably like the image of the cavalier in enemy propaganda.

The anonymous author of *The Hectors* (1656) was clearly aware of this problem, in a way that Manuche and Killigrew were not. The central characters of the play are polite and sober – as Harbage notes, it looks forward to the world of comedy of manners[2] – and they reject the excesses of Cavalier and Puritan alike. One reason for the comparative good humour with which the cheaters and victims of the subplot are finally reconciled is that they are tacitly agreed on one thing: opposition to the present government. One of the main victims, a Justice, is being gulled into marriage with a supposedly rich widow. He has a brief Jonsonian fantasy about what he will do with her money: 'I may found Hospitals, Colledges, or build Churches.' His maid interrupts: 'Sir, and have them turned into stables.' He decides on second thoughts that he will invest in causeways and bridges instead (II.iv). Hadland, the impoverished schemer, seems at first sight nothing more than the usual royalist tavern intriguer. However, he attempts to dissociate himself from the shady morality of the Hectors: 'Hast thou not lived by thy profane debauchnesse, and base cowardlinesse to help to sink a cause in which we all do suffer?' (II.i). The pressure of the play is toward conformity and compromise; the hero even approves of following changes of fashion rather than 'with ones single whimseys to oppose what is received by the generality' (III.ii).

Willingness to let bygones be bygones often seems the result of pure cynicism. A pamphlet dialogue of 1652 – *The Cavaliers' Jubilee, or Long Looked for Come at Last* – depicts two former royalists in a tavern. They

---

[1] See his preface to *Cutter of Coleman Street*, in *Essays, Plays and Sundry Verses*, ed. A. R. Waller (Cambridge, 1906).
[2] *Cavalier Drama*, 81–4.

agree that their sufferings for the King have been a waste of time and money: 'they shall not find me at *Dunbar* or *Worcester* for their young bonny Scotch King; if he be so mad after a Crown, let him take heed of a crack'd crown'. Though the dialogue was obviously written as Commonwealth propaganda, the mood it dramatizes can also be found in the works of royalist writers (for instance, in the attitude of Colonel Jolly, in *Cutter of Coleman Street*, which offended some post-Restoration sensibilities). It is present even in Newcastle's *Pleasant and Merry Humour of a Rogue*, which appears to have been written in the last years of the Commonwealth. Newcastle had given vast sums to the King's cause and fought for it until the defeat of Marston Moor, after which he lived on the continent (and on credit) until the Restoration. His royalism appears to have been of the most intransigent variety. Yet in his farce he is idealistic about neither side in the war. The Rogue, pretending to be an ex-soldier, begs money from some unsympathetic gentlemen:

I GENT.   Why, thou mightst have been a soldier, this many years in thy own Country.

ROGUE.   Sir, I do not love to thrive by Rebellion, I have more honour in me.

I GENT.   Why then, thou mightst have been of the Loyal side.

ROGUE.   That was but often very various & transitory, I should many times have been a reformado, without pay.[1]   (1.vi)

It would seem that, in the immediate euphoria of the Restoration, audiences were more eager to laugh at the dramatic caricatures of their political enemies – in Tatham's *The Rump* and Howard's *The Committee* – than to indulge in sentimentality over heroic royalists. Idealization and sentimentality were confined to the panegyrics which greeted the King's return, and Manuche's *Banished Shepherdess*, which depicts members of the royal family and their entourage, never reached the stage. Indeed, the Civil War and Commonwealth were too recent to be dramatized without the danger of unwanted topical applications. But in the early 1680s, when Roundhead and Cavalier became Whig and Tory, several dramatists of the court party wrote plays on the Civil War, perhaps with a sense of nostalgia for a time when to support the King's cause was a matter of heroism, not self-interest. Aphra Behn's *The Roundheads*, which draws on *The Rump* and possibly *Newmarket*

---

[1] Published in Francis Welbeck (ed.), *Welbeck Miscellany*, No. 1 (1933). I have, exceptionally, modernized spelling and punctuation here, as the edition is a faithful transcript of Newcastle's MS., very eccentric in both respects.

Fair as well, is less satiric than either. But the loyalism of her play pales beside that of D'Urfey's *The Royalist* (1682). The hero, Kinglove, insists that all his tenants should join him three times a week in drinking the King's health in front of the Royal Oak, which is on his property. His unshakable loyalty otherwise shows itself chiefly in the cuckolding of villainous Roundheads. The only character to have any scruples about this behaviour is his page – hardly surprisingly, since this is a girl in disguise, longing to prove that she is worthy of Kinglove despite the fact that her father is a Roundhead. At last the opportunity comes: word is brought that Cromwell is on his death-bed and that Charles II desperately needs money to ensure his restoration. When Kinglove discovers, not only the true identity of the page, but also that she has sent the necessary money to the King, he falls into her arms. 'Who loves the King', he declares, 'must love his Honour, Grandeur and Prerogative: His Regal State, which Money must support' (v.i). The blank verse rhythms which are often present in Restoration dramatic prose at its most emotional ring out as impressively as they can, to conceal the depressing truth of the play's message. What Charles II most needed, indeed, was not his subjects' loyalty but their money.

Shadwell's last play, posthumously produced, offers a Whig interpretation of the same period, now seen from the perspective of a nation at war with France and needing to unite in the face of a common enemy. *The Volunteers* (1692) takes its title from the departure of a motley assortment of young men for the wars. The older generation are inspired to relive the past. Major-General Blunt, an old cavalier, good-humouredly tolerates the behaviour of his former soldiers who come to dinner, get drunk, and fight their battles over again:

> 1 CAVAL.   This fellow said, He was nearer being hang'd for Plots for the King than I was.
>
> 2 CAVAL.   Yes, and more, and better Plots, I'll justifie it; the Major-General knows it.
>
> M.G. BL.   Know, —adod, all the Plots that I knew ended in being damnable drunk; and I believe you drank and spew'd in the King's Service as much as most. (v.ii).[1]

On this note of laughter, and with the marriage of the cavalier's daughter to a Roundhead's son, the Civil War passes from memory into history.

[1] Ed. Montague Summers, *The Complete Works of Thomas Shadwell*, 5 vols (1927), v. For a fuller account of Restoration plays on this theme – which, however, does not include *The Volunteers* – see Allardyce Nicoll, 'Political Plays of the Restoration', *MLR*, 16 (1921), 224–42.

Bibliography

Abbreviations

Adams, *Herbert*	*The Dramatic Records of Sir Henry Herbert*, ed. J. Q. Adams (New Haven, Conn., and London, 1917)
Jacobean and Caroline Stage	G. E. Bentley, *The Jacobean and Caroline Stage*, 7 vols (Oxford, 1941–68)
Herford and Simpson	*Ben Jonson*, ed. C. H. Herford, Percy and Evelyn Simpson, 11 vols (Oxford, 1925–52)
MSC	Malone Society Collections

Periodical abbreviations

ELH	*Journal of English Literary History*
ELR	*The English Literary Renaissance*

ES   *English Studies*
HLQ   *Huntington Library Quarterly*
MLR   *Modern Language Review*
MP   *Modern Philology*
PMLA   *Publications of the Modern Language Association of America*
RES   *Review of English Studies*
SEL   *Studies in English Literature, 1500–1900*
SP   *Studies in Philology*
TLS   *The Times Literary Supplement*

I Society and the theatre

GENERAL

The major histories of the theatre are: (a) for the period up to 1616 (though often useful up to 1642) E. K. Chambers, *The Elizabethan Stage*, 4 vols (Oxford, 1923); (b) for the period 1616–42, G. E. Bentley, *The Jacobean and Caroline Stage*, 7 vols (Oxford, 1941–68); (c) for 1642–60, L. Hotson, *The Commonwealth and Restoration Stage* (Cambridge, Mass., 1928). Bentley's work is an outstanding source-book on all matters relating to the London theatres and companies, the dramatists who wrote for them and the plays which they wrote. Glynne Wickham, *Early English Stages 1300–1660* (1959–   ), vol. II, *1576–1660*, pt 1 (London, 1963), supplements Bentley on such matters as state control of the theatres, pageants at court and in the city, the provincial theatre, the status of the playwright. In spite of the untrustworthiness of its detail, one should not forget J. P. Collier, *History of English Dramatic Poetry to the Time of Shakespeare and Annals of the Stage to the Restoration*, 3 vols (London, 1831; second edition 1879), especially vol. III, *Details connected with the Performance of Plays*.

Andrew Gurr, *The Shakespearean Stage 1574–1642* (Cambridge, 1970) is an admirable, succinct account of the world of the theatre. E. M. Albright, *Dramatic Publication in England, 1580–1640* (New York and London, 1927) is still valuable for its wide view of the publication of plays, including the attitudes of government, theatre companies, dramatists and the public. The results of much useful research on the theatre of the period can also be found in the various volumes of *Elizabethan Theatre* (1970–   ) and the annual publication, *Research Opportunities in Renaissance Drama* (1957–   ).

Essential records of the theatre are assembled in the Collections of the Malone Society. A useful collection of documents and pamphlets is W. C. Hazlitt, *The English Drama and Stage under the Tudor and Stuart Princes, 1543–1664*, (London, 1869). *Annals of English Drama 975–1700* by A. Harbage, rev. S. Schoenbaum (London, 1964) brings together in a single, clear chronological table professional and amateur plays at court, in the city, at universities and elsewhere. A companion volume, giving sources of the plays and a bibliography, is currently being prepared by Jill Levenson.

The best working bibliography is in the *Cambridge Bibliography of English Literature*, 1 (Cambridge, 1940), esp. pp. 487–513, and the Supplement of 1957. Bentley's bibliography for *The Jacobean and Caroline Stage* is included in his general index. More recent work is listed in *A Survey and Bibliography of Recent Studies in English Renaissance Drama*, ed. T. P. Logan and D. S. Smith (Lincoln, Nebraska, and London, 1973–8), especially *The New Intellectuals* (1977), which deals primarily with dramatists writing for the private theatres, and *The Later Jacobean and Caroline Dramatists* (1978).

The quarterly *Studies in English Literature* devotes one issue each year to this period, including a survey of the year's publications. The standard and indispensable history of the entire period is S. R. Gardiner, *History of England from the Accession of James I to the Outbreak of the Civil War, 1603–1642*, revised edition, 10 vols (London, 1883–4), and its continuations, *History of the Great Civil War, 1652–9*, 4 vols (London, 1893), and *History of the Commonwealth and Protectorate*, 4 vols (London, 1903). Useful one-volume histories are G. Davies, *The Early Stuarts 1603–1660* (Oxford, 1937; and later editions) and C. Hill, *The Century of Revolution 1603–1714* (Edinburgh, 1961). The early volumes of J. Rushworth, *Historical Collections*, 8 vols (London, 1659–1701) give contemporary accounts and some first-hand reports.

THE COURT

L. Stone, *The Crisis of the Aristocracy, 1558–1641* (Oxford, 1965; abridged edition, 1967), equally valuable in its generalizations and in its detail, amply demonstrates the quality of life of the drama's patrons, and teaches the reader to use with care such terms as gentry, nobility and courtier. D. Mathew, *The Social Structure in Caroline England* (Oxford, 1945) is helpful on bureaucracy, taste and acquisitiveness at court.

Graphic contemporary detail of theatrical life at court is given by letter-writers, especially J. Chamberlain, *Letters*, ed. N. E. McClure, 2 vols (Philadelphia, 1939). Consult also J. P. Feil, 'Dramatic References from the Scudamore Papers', *Shakespeare Survey*, XI (1958).

Imaginative and scholarly essays by Miss C. V. Wedgwood on drama and the monarchy are printed in *Truth and Opinion* (London, 1960) and *Poetry and Politics under the Stuarts* (Cambridge, 1961). M. B. Pickel, *Charles I as Patron of Poetry and Drama* (London, 1936) is a useful general survey of literature and the court. Marion Jones, 'The Court and the Dramatists', *The Elizabethan Theatre*, ed. J. R. Brown and B. Harris (London, 1966), though relating mainly to an earlier period, makes important points. Drama at the viceregal court in Ireland is discussed by W. S. Clark, *The Early Irish Stage* (Oxford, 1955).

A calendar of the seasonal round of entertainment at court is given in M. S. Steele, *Plays and Masques at Court during the Reigns of Elizabeth, James and Charles* (New Haven, Conn., 1926). Entertainments during the progresses of James I are fully documented in J. Nichols, *The Progresses, Processions and Magnificent Festivities of King James I*, 4 vols (London, 1828).

There are studies of the masque by P. Reyher, *Les Masques anglais* (Paris, 1909); E. Welsford, *The Court Masque* (Cambridge, 1927); and A. Nicoll, *Stuart Masques and the Renaissance Stage* (London, 1937). The philosophy of the masque and its function in the Stuart court is fully discussed by Stephen Orgel and Roy Strong in *Inigo Jones: The Theatre of the Stuart Court*, 2 vols (London and Berkeley, 1973) and by Stephen Orgel in *The Illusion of Power* (Berkeley, Los Angeles, London, 1975). *A Book of Masques in Honour of Allardyce Nicoll*, ed. T. B. J. Spencer and S. Wells (Cambridge, 1967), gives texts and descriptions of selected masques.

Much information about the place of drama in the life of the aristocracy is in Herford and Simpson's edition of *Ben Jonson*, 11 vols (Oxford, 1925–52), as will appear when that monumental work is properly indexed. Valuable among contemporary writings is *The Life of William Cavendish, Duke of Newcastle*, by Margaret, Duchess of Newcastle, ed. C. H. Firth (London, 1886), and interesting evidence of the importance of the theatre and theatrical imagination for royalists can be found in *The Memoirs of Anne, Lady Halkett*, which have been edited, together with those of Ann, Lady Fanshawe, by John Loftis (Oxford, 1979).

Henrietta Maria's theatrical ventures are recorded in many biographies. Concerning the court dramatists whom she inspired and encouraged, there is one very good book, A. Harbage, *Cavalier Drama* (New York and London, 1936; repr. New York, 1964).

OPPOSITION TO THE THEATRE

This hostility of the Puritans in the latter end of the great period of English drama is discussed in Russell Fraser, *The War Against Poetry* (Princeton, N. J., 1970). There is valuable material in two articles by Jonas Barish: 'The Anti-theatrical Prejudice', *Critical Quarterly*, 8 (1966), 329–48; and 'Exhibitionism and the Anti-theatrical Prejudice', *ELH*, 36 (1969), 1–29. Evidence that the anti-theatrical prejudice was not a specifically 'puritan' one is presented in Margot Heinemann, *Puritanism and Theatre* (Cambridge, 1980). E. N. S. Thompson, *The Controversy between the Puritans and the Stage*, Yale Studies in English, 20 (New York, 1903), may also be mentioned, along with H. J. C. Grierson, *Cross-Currents in English Literature in the Seventeenth Century* (London, 1929). Charles Kingsley's *Plays and Puritans* (London, 1873) is an important Victorian view on the moral balance of cavalier and Puritan. There are several studies of Prynne, but they have little to say about his attack on the stage. The entire corpus of anti-theatre writing has been reprinted, under the general editorship of Arthur Freeman, under the title *The English Stage, Attack and Defence 1577–1730* (New York and London, 1974).

THE DRAMATISTS

The standard work is G. E. Bentley's *The Profession of Dramatist in Shakespeare's Time, 1590–1642* (Princeton, N. J., 1971), which should be read in conjunction with Bentley's biographical accounts and lists of previous studies in vols III, IV and V of his *Jacobean and Caroline Stage*. The most important single work on the economics of playwriting is W. W. Greg (ed.), *Henslowe Papers* (London, 1907). J. F. Danby considers relations between the social position of the Jacobean dramatists and the art they created in the latter part of *Poets on Fortune's Hill* (London, 1952). L. C. Knights, *Drama and Society in the Age of Jonson* (London, 1937) is not a work of sociology but has much to say on the social and economic opinions of the dramatists. The dramatist's view of his proper place in society is touched on by Leah Jones in *The Divine Science* (New York, 1940).

Two short but excellent accounts of patronage are F. P. Wilson, 'Some Notes on Authors and Patrons in Tudor and Stuart Times', *Joseph Quincy Adams Memorial Studies* (Washington, D.C., 1948), 553–61; and D. Nichol Smith, 'Authors and Patrons', *Shakespeare's England: An Account of the Life and Manners of his Age*, 2 vols (Oxford, 1916; repr. 1950), II, 182–211. Phoebe Sheavyn, *The Literary Profession in the Elizabethan Age* (Manchester, 1909) was republished with revisions by J. W. Saunders in 1967. F. B. Williams, *Index of Dedications and Commendatory Verses in English Books before 1641* (London, 1962) is uncommunicative but could serve as the basis of ' important work on patrons. An earlier article by the same author, 'Special Presentation Epistles before 1641', *The Library*, 5th series, 7 (March 1952), 15–20, has helpful information on the methods of a client in an age of print.

CITY PAGEANTS

The standard study of city pageants and Lord Mayors' Shows is D. M. Bergeron, *English Civic Pageantry* (London, 1971). See also F. W. Fairholt, *Lord Mayors' Pageants*, 2 parts (London, 1834, 1844) and R. T. D. Sayle, *Lord Mayors' Pageants of the Merchant Taylors Company in the 15th, 16th and 17th Centuries* ([London], 1931). Glynne Wickham's *Early English Stages*, vol. II, pt 1, pp. 209–28, 236–44, is important. The essential material has been collected and edited by D. J. Gordon and J. Robertson in *A Calendar of Dramatic Records in the Books of the Livery Companies of London*, MSC, III (1954).

THE AUDIENCE

A. Harbage, *Shakespeare's Audience* (New York, 1941) continues into the post-Shakespearian period. The same author's *Shakespeare and the Rival Traditions* (New York, 1952) should also be consulted. C. Leech's short study 'The Caroline Audience' in *Shakespeare's Tragedies* (London, 1950) is a useful account of the changing composition and tastes of the audience, drawing on prologues and epilogues. L. B. Wright's chapter on 'The Stage and Drama' in *Middle-Class Culture in Elizabethan England* (Chapel Hill, North Carolina, 1935) makes inferences about the social class and attitudes of the audience over a wide period.

A work which would bring together and analyse the many scattered contemporary references to theatre-going would be very valuable. Many will be found in the various volumes of Bentley, including Sir Humphrey Mildmay's diary. Edmund Gayton, *Pleasant Notes Upon Don Quixote* (1654) is an entertaining rag-bag of information. Some contemporary accounts will be found in A. M. Nagler, *A Source Book in Theatrical History* (New York, 1959), originally *Sources in Theatrical History* (New York, 1952), which also gives excerpts from James Wright's *Historia Histrionica* (1699), reprinted in Hazlitt's *Dodsley's Old Plays* (see p. 316) and in

Jacobean and Caroline Stage, II. See also H. Berry, 'The Stage and Boxes at Blackfriars', *SP*, 63 (April 1966), 163–86.

PROVINCIAL THEATRE

Some of the gaps in J. T. Murray, *English Dramatic Companies 1558–1642*, 2 vols (New York, 1910) are revealed by G. E. Dawson's collections of records of acting in Kent in the Malone Society Collections, VII (1965). There are analyses and tables in a pioneer work by L. G. Salingar (assisted by G. Harrison and B. Cochrane), 'Les Comédiens et leur public en Angleterre de 1520 à 1640', a paper given at a colloquium at Nancy, April 1967, and published in *Dramaturgie et Société aux XVIᵉ et XVIIᵉ Siècles*, ed. J. Jacquot, 2 vols (Paris, 1968). Some uncollected Essex records are given by W. Mepham in *Essex Review*, LVII (1948). *Records of Early English Drama* (*REED*) will eventually publish transcripts and translations of dramatic records from all parts of England, up to the year 1642. The volumes published so far are those for York, ed. A. F. Johnston and M. Rogerson, 2 vols (Toronto and Buffalo, 1979) and Chester, ed. L. M. Clopper, 2 vols (Toronto and Buffalo, 1979).

CENSORSHIP AND CONTROL

The one indispensable work on censorship is *The Dramatic Records of Sir Henry Herbert*, ed. J. Q. Adams (New Haven, Conn., and London, 1917). Discussions will be found in E. K. Chambers, *Elizabethan Stage*, I and IV; and Glynne Wickham, *Early English Stages* (1959–   ), vol. II, pt 1 bk 1.

II The theatres and the actors

The first source for information about every aspect of Stuart drama is G. E. Bentley's monumental seven-volume *The Jacobean and Caroline Stage* (Oxford, 1941–68), whose full documentation on companies, staging, theatres and actors, as well as authors and their texts, subsumes all earlier work on the subject. New evidence and documentation, particularly on theatre outside London, which has become available since Bentley's work is being noted in the *Records of Early English Drama*, general editor Alexandra Johnston. Bentley's work includes a full account of the theatre buildings for the period but the staging of plays and the repertory of particular theatres is usefully analysed by G. F. Reynolds, *The Staging of Elizabethan Plays at the Red Bull Theatre, 1605–1625* (New York and London, 1940); T. J. King, *Shakespearian Staging 1599–1642* (Cambridge, Mass., 1971), 1–13; and Gael W. Hammer, 'The Staging of Elizabethan Plays in the Private Theatres 1632–1642' (unpublished Ph.D. dissertation, University of Iowa, 1973). The principal controversy over staging in the Caroline era is the extent to which the movable scenery used in court masques was adopted in the commercial theatres; it is discussed without fully satisfactory resolution in several articles: T. J. King, 'The Staging of Plays at the Phoenix in Drury Lane, 1617–42', *Theatre Notebook*, 19 (1965), 146–66; Kenneth B. Richards, 'Changeable Scenery for Plays on the Caroline Stage', *Theatre Notebook*, 23 (1968), 6–21; L. R. Starr, 'A Note on the Use of Scenery at the Cockpit at Court', *Theatre Notebook*, 26 (1972), 89; John Freehafer, 'Perspective Scenery and the Caroline Playhouse', *Theatre Notebook*, 27 (1973), 98–113; Gael W. Hammer, 'The Staging of Elizabethan Plays in the Private Theatres 1632–42' (unpublished Ph.D. dissertation, University of Iowa, 1973).

The technical aspects of masque staging are probably best studied from the full documentation of Inigo Jones's designs found in *Designs by Inigo Jones for Masques and Plays at Court*, ed. P. Simpson and C. F. Bell (Oxford, 1924), though valuable interpretation and commentary is added in L. B. Campbell, *Scenes and Machines on the English Stage during the Renaissance* (Cambridge, 1923); *The King's Arcadia: Inigo Jones and the Stuart Court, Catalogue of the Quatercentenary Exhibition*, ed. J. Harris, S. Orgel and R. Strong (London, 1973); and S. Orgel and R. Strong, *Inigo Jones: The Theatre of the Stuart Court* (London, 1973). In the court masque, staging and meaning are closely intertwined and the emblematic significance of Jonson's masques has been fully discussed in the pioneering work of D. J. Gordon, 'Poet and Architect: The Intellectual Setting of the Quarrel between Ben Jonson and Inigo Jones', *Journal of the Warburg and Courtauld Institutes*, 12 (1949) and 'Le "Masque mémorable" de Chapman' in J. Jacquot (ed.), *Les Fêtes de la Renaissance*, 2 vols (Paris, 1956). Study of this field has been further expanded by J. Meagher, *Method and Meaning in Jonson's Masques* (South Bend, Indiana, 1966) and S. Orgel, *The Jonsonian Masque* (Cambridge, Mass., 1965). The European context of Stuart court masques is usefully indicated by the range of material covered by the essays in J. Jacquot (ed.), *Les Fêtes de la Renaissance*, and explicit connections are drawn between European absolutism and courtly entertainment by S. Orgel and R.

Strong in *Splendour at Court, Renaissance Spectacle and Illusion* (London, 1973). Rather less attention has been given to the design and staging at Inigo Jones's court theatre, the Cockpit at court, which is described by Glynne Wickham, 'The Cockpit Reconstructed', *New Theatre Magazine*, 7 (1967), 26–36, and discussed by D. C. Rowan, 'The Cockpit in Court', in *The Elizabethan Theatre*, 1, ed. David Galloway (London and Toronto, 1969), and John Freehafer, 'Inigo Jones' Scenery for *The Cid*', *Theatre Notebook*, 25 (1971).

III The plays and the playwrights: 1613–42

BIBLIOGRAPHY

The basic bibliographical tools for the drama of this period are the same as for Tudor and Elizabethan drama. W. W. Greg, *A Bibliography of English Printed Drama to the Restoration* (Oxford, 1939–59; repr. 1962) is invaluable for work on the texts of plays, though it is superseded for more general critical purposes by A. Harbage, *Annals of English Drama 975–1700*, revised S. Schoenbaum (London, 1964). Bibliographies of critical material similarly make little distinction between Elizabethan and Stuart drama, which are dealt with together in the annual bibliographical essays of *The Year's Work in English Studies* (The English Association, London) and *Studies in English Literature 1500–1900* (Rice University, Houston, Texas). An exception is Rachel Fordyce, *Caroline Drama: A Bibliographic History of Criticism* (London, 1978), which provides an up-to-date and full account of monographs and articles on many aspects of Caroline drama, with an excellent index and cross-reference by subject as well as author and play. Other useful guides to critical material are Freda Elaine Penninger, *English Drama to 1660 (excluding Shakespeare)* (Detroit, 1976), which is usefully descriptive, though the range of her work limits her discussion to full-length books alone; and the relevant sections of *English Drama (excluding Shakespeare)*, ed. Stanley Wells (London, 1975).

TEXTS

The texts of plays from this period are usually easily available thanks to the assiduous labours of nineteenth-century editors who produced complete works of all but the most obscure authors. These have been reissued by American reprint companies in readable library editions, together with such invaluable collections as W. Carew Hazlitt (ed.), *A Select Collection of Old English Plays . . . Originally published by Robert Dodsley . . . 1744, 4th ed. Now First Chronologically Arranged, Revised and Enlarged with the Notes of all the Commentators and New Notes*, 15 vols (London 1874–6; repr. New York, 1964); and A. H. Bullen, *A Collection of Old English Plays*, 4 vols (London, 1882–5; repr. New York, 1964). All these early editions suffer from lack of bibliographical sophistication and are unreliable for serious textual work. Modern textual scholars have been rather circumspect in their choice of plays, and excellent single texts of the critically reclaimed plays are repeated in the Revels editions (Methuen and Manchester University Press), the Regents Renaissance Drama Series (Edward Arnold), and the New Mermaids (Ernest Benn). The Nottingham Drama Texts and Renaissance Drama Texts (Garland Press) are making an interesting effort to provide properly edited, photographically reproduced texts of less well-known plays. The Malone Society Reprints, produced to the highest standards of textual scholarship, have full textual apparatus but no critical commentary.

Listed below are the texts which have been used for Part III of this volume, together with the most readily available complete works and scholarly editions. In accordance with the policy of this series, works have consistently been quoted either from old-spelling editions or from the original seventeenth-century text. Many of these have neither scene nor line numbers; for greater ease of reference, therefore, these have been supplied, where possible, from more recent editions. This list is not meant to be a comprehensive guide to *all* available texts. Where several editions of the same work are named, the one used for quotation and consultation is listed first.

ANONYMOUS

The Lady Alimony, or the Alimony Lady, ed. W. Carew Hazlitt, *Dodsley's Old Plays*, vol. xiv.

Swetnam the Woman-Hater Arraigned by Women, ed. A. B. Grosart, London, 1880.

The Two Noble Ladies, and the Converted Conjurer, ed. Rebecca G. Rhoads, Malone Society Reprints, Oxford, 1930.

BEAUMONT AND FLETCHER (*see* Fletcher)

RICHARD BROME

The Dramatic Works of Richard Brome [ed. R. H. Shepherd], 3 vols, London, 1873.

The Antipodes, ed. Ann Haaker, Lincoln, Nebraska, 1966.

A Jovial Crew, ed. Ann Haaker, Lincoln, Nebraska, 1968.

The Antipodes and *A Mad Couple Well Matched*, in *Six Caroline Plays*, ed. A. S. Knowland, Oxford, 1962.

'I.C.'

The Two Merry Milkmaids, London, 1620.

THOMAS CAREW

Coelum Britannicum, in *The Poems of Thomas Carew*, ed. Rhodes Dunlap, Oxford, 1949, 151–85.

LODOWICK CARLELL

Arvirargus and Philicia, pts 1 and 2 (1639), ed. J. E. Ruoff, unpublished Ph.D. dissertation, University of Pennsylvania, 1954.

WILLIAM CARTWRIGHT

The Plays and Poems of William Cartwright, ed. G. Blakemore Evans, Madison, Wisc., 1951.

GEORGE CHAPMAN

The Masque of the Middle Temple and Lincoln's Inn, ed. G. Blakemore Evans, in Allan Holaday (gen. ed.), *The Plays of George Chapman*, 3 vols, London, 1970.

WILLIAM DAVENANT

The Works of Sr William D'Avenant Kt, London, 1673; reissued New York, 1968.

The Dramatic Works of Sir William Davenant, ed. James Maidment and W. H. Logan, London, 1872–4; reissued New York, 1964.

The Wits, in A. S. Knowland (ed.), *Six Caroline Plays*, Oxford, 1962.

ROBERT DAVENPORT

The Works of Robert Davenport, ed. A. H. Bullen, London, 1890.

King John and Matilda, in W. A. Armstrong (ed.), *Elizabethan History Plays*, Oxford, 1965.

THOMAS DEKKER
The Dramatic Works of Thomas Dekker, ed. F. T. Bowers, 4 vols, Cambridge, 1953–61.

THOMAS DRUE
The Duchess of Suffolk, London, 1631.

JOHN FLETCHER (and his collaborators)
The Dramatic Works in the Beaumont and Fletcher Canon, gen. ed. F. T. Bowers, in progress, London, 1966–
The Works of Francis Beaumont and John Fletcher, ed. Arnold Glover and A. R. Waller, 10 vols, London, 1905–12.
Fletcher and Massinger, *Sir John Van Olden Barnavelt*, ed. T. H. Howard-Hill, Malone Society Reprints, 1979 [1980].

JOHN FORD
John Ford's Dramatic Works, ed. W. Bang and H. de Vocht, *Materialen zur Kunde des älteren englischen Dramas*, Louvain, 1908 and 1927; repr. Vaduz, 1963.
The Dramatic Works of John Ford, ed. W. Gifford and A. Dyce, 3 vols, London, 1869; rev. edn A. H. Bullen, London, 1895.
The Broken Heart, ed. D. K. Anderson, Lincoln, Nebraska, 1966.
The Chronicle History of Perkin Warbeck, ed. Peter Ure, London, 1968.
'Tis Pity She's a Whore, ed. Derek Roper, London, 1975.

PETER HAUSTED
The Rival Friends, ed. Laurens J. Mills, Bloomington, Indiana, 1951.

THOMAS HEYWOOD
The Dramatic Works of Thomas Heywood [ed. R. H. Shepherd], 6 vols, London, 1874; reissued New York, 1964.
The Fair Maid of the West, pts 1 and 2, ed. Robert K. Turner, Jr, London, 1968.

BEN JONSON
Works, ed. C. H. Herford, and Percy and Evelyn Simpson, 11 vols, Oxford, 1925–52.

THOMAS KILLIGREW

Comedies and Tragedies Written by Thomas Killigrew, London, 1664; reissued New York, 1967.

The Parson's Wedding, in A. S. Knowland (ed.), *Six Caroline Plays*, Oxford, 1962.

SHACKERLY (ALSO SHAKERLY OR SHACKERLEY) MARMION

The Dramatic Works of Shackerly Marmion, ed. J. Maidment and W. H. Logan, London, 1875.

PHILIP MASSINGER

The Plays and Poems of Philip Massinger, ed. Philip Edwards and Colin Gibson, 5 vols, Oxford, 1976.

THOMAS MIDDLETON

A Chaste Maid in Cheapside, ed. R. B. Parker, London, 1969.

A Game at Chesse, ed. R. C. Bald, Cambridge, 1929.

A Game at Chess, ed. J. W. Harper, London, 1966.

Women Beware Women, ed. J. R. Mulryne, London, 1975.

The Works of Thomas Middleton, ed. A. H. Bullen, London, 1885.

THOMAS MIDDLETON AND WILLIAM ROWLEY

The Changeling, ed. N. W. Bawcutt, London, 1958.

A Fair Quarrel, ed. R. V. Holdsworth, London, 1974.

JOHN MILTON

Comus, in J. T. Shawcross (ed.), *The Complete Poetry of John Milton*, New York, 1963; rev. edn 1971.

WALTER MONTAGUE

The Shepherd's Paradise, London, 1629, and MS.

THOMAS NABBES

The Works of Thomas Nabbes, ed. A. W. Bullen, 2 vols, London, 1882–9; reissued New York, 1964.

THOMAS RANDOLPH

Poetical and Dramatic Works of Thomas Randolph, ed. W. Carew Hazlitt, 2 vols, London, 1875.

GEORGE RUGGLE

Ignoramus, first published 1630, translated by R. C[odrington], London, 1662.

JOSEPH RUTTER

The Shepherd's Holiday, ed. W. Carew Hazlitt, *Dodsley's Old Plays*, vol. XII.

'S.S.'

The Honest Lawyer, ed. W. Carew Hazlitt, *Dodsley's Old Plays*, vol. II.

JAMES SHIRLEY

The Dramatic Works and Poems of James Shirley, ed. W. Gifford and A. Dyce, 6 vols, London, 1833.

The Wedding and *The Lady of Pleasure*, in A. S. Knowland (ed.), *Six Caroline Plays*, Oxford, 1962.

The Triumph of Peace, in T. B. J. Spencer and Stanley Wells (ed.), *A Book of Masques in Honour of Allardyce Nicoll*, Cambridge, 1967.

WENTWORTH SMITH

The Hector of Germany, or The Palsgrave Prime Elector, ed. L. W. Payne, Jr, University of Pennsylvania Publications in Philology and Literature, vol. XI, 1906.

WILLIAM STRODE

The Poetical Works of William Strode, ed. B. Dobell, London, 1907.

JOHN SUCKLING

The Works of Sir John Suckling: The Plays, ed. L. A. Beaurline, Oxford, 1971.

THOMAS TOMKIS

Albumazar, a Comedy, ed. Hugh G. Dick, University of California Publications in English, no. 13, 1944.

AURELIAN TOWNSHEND

Tempe Restored, in *Poems and Masks*, ed. E. K. Chambers, Oxford, 1912.

THE THEATRE PUBLIC

Theatre practice and court patronage overlap in the story of Davenant's proposal to build a new theatre in Fleet Street, told by John Freehafer in 'Brome, Suckling and Davenant's Theatre Project of 1639', *Texas Studies in Literature and Language*, 10 (1968), 367–83, but there is no full account of the court's role in fostering or for that matter hindering the development of Stuart drama. A useful documentary account is provided in J. Q. Adams, *The Dramatic Records of Sir Henry Herbert, Master of the Revels, 1623–1673* (London, 1917), and particular cases are discussed by W. R. Gair, 'The Politics of Scholarship: A Dramatic Comment on the Autocracy of Charles I', *The Elizabethan Theatre*, III, ed. David Galloway (London and Toronto, 1973), 100–18; Marvin Morillo, 'Shirley's Preferment and the Court of Charles I', *SEL*, 1 (1961), 101–17; Margot Heinemann, 'Middleton's *Game at Chess*: Parliamentary Puritans and Opposition Drama', *ELR*, 5 (1975), 232–50. However, the fullest account of censorship and control of drama remains V. C. Gildersleeve, *Government Regulation of the Elizabethan Drama* (New York, 1908), which gives a comprehensive account of available evidence but little analysis of its critical or cultural significance.

The commercial relations between professional playwrights and the employing companies of patrons are fully analysed by G. E. Bentley, *The Profession of Dramatist in Shakespeare's Time* (Princeton, N. J., 1971), while the particularly well-documented case of Richard Brome is given special attention by Ann Haaker in 'The Plague, the Theatre and the Poet', *Renaissance Drama*, NS 1 (1968), 283–306. Commercial relations are only one aspect of the cultural relationships between playwright, audience and theatrical company which are the area of another major controversy in discussions of Stuart drama. The assumptions of cultural history rather than literary criticism lie behind discussions of the nature and role of the audience for Stuart drama. These range from hard evidence about prices and particularities – G. E. Bentley, 'The Diary of a Caroline Theatregoer', *MP*, 35 (1938), 61–72; A. J. Cook, 'The Audience of Shakespeare's Plays: A Reconsideration', *Shakespeare Studies*, 7 (1974), 283–306; and L. G. Salingar, Gerald Harrison and Bruce Cochrane, 'Les Comédiens et leur public en Angleterre de 1520 à 1640', in *Dramaturgie et Société*, ed. J. Jacquot, 2 vols (Paris, 1968), II, 525–77 – to judgements about the connections between taste, class and theatrical production: Clifford Leech, 'The Caroline Audience', *MLR*, 36 (1942), 304–19; William A. Armstrong, 'The Audience of the Elizabethan Private Theatres', *RES*, NS 10 (1959), 234–49; and Michael Neill, '"Wit's Most Accomplished Senate"', The

Audience of the Caroline Private Theatres', *SEL*, 18 (1978), 341–60. The ideology and politics of direct opposition to the theatre are analysed in Jonas Barish, 'Anti-Theatrical Prejudice', *Critical Quarterly*, 8 (1966), 329–48.

A provocative recent work, Margot Heinemann, *Puritanism and Theatre* (London, 1980), has suggested that at least in the Jacobean period Puritans were not universally hostile to the theatre and this is further borne out by P. W. Thomas's complex account of the background to the Prynne affair, 'Two Cultures? Court and Country under Charles I', in Conrad Russell (ed.), *The Origins of the English Civil War* (London, 1973).

CULTURAL RELATIONS

Cultural relations are more explicitly the subject of the collection of essays edited by J. Jacquot, *Dramaturgie et Société*, 2 vols (Paris, 1968), vol. II of which includes an illuminating account of the attitudes behind the critical notion of 'decadence' in S. Schoenbaum, 'Peut-on parler d'une "décadence" du théâtre au temps des premiers Stuarts?'. Critical work which analyses plays in terms of their themes is particularly apt to spill over into cultural history since it often involves consideration of contemporary attitudes. The danger is that independent evidence of such attitudes is extremely hard to ascertain and arguments about topicality or pervasiveness of an idea can become caught in a circular trap. Such work often builds on the pioneering studies by Louis B. Wright, *Middle Class Culture in Elizabethan England* (New York, 1935) and L. C. Knights, *Drama and Society in the Age of Jonson* (London, 1937). It includes J. B. Fletcher, 'Précieuses at the Court of Charles I', *Journal of Comparative Literature*, 1 (1903), 120–53, and his *The Religion of Beauty in Women and Other Essays on Platonic Love in Poetry and Society* (New York, 1911); and Kathleen M. Lynch, *The Social Mode of Restoration Comedy* (Michigan, 1926), which, despite its title, traces the modes of Restoration Comedy back through Stuart Drama to Lyly. A bridge between cultural history and criticism is also provided by R. H. Parkinson, 'Topographical Comedy in the Seventeenth Century', *ELH*, 3 (1936), 270–90; G. F. Sensebaugh, 'Platonic Love and the Puritan Rebellion', *SP*, 37 (1940), 457–81; Theodore Miles, 'Place Realism in a Group of Caroline Plays', *RES*, 18 (1942), 428–40; Marco Mincoff, 'The Social Background of Beaumont and Fletcher', *English Miscellany*, 1–2 (1950–1), 1–30; C. Leech, 'Love as a Dramatic Theme' in *Shakespeare's Tragedies, and Other Studies in Seventeenth Century Drama* (London, 1950), 182–203; P. Ure, 'Marriage and Domestic Drama in Heywood and Ford', *ES*, 32 (1951), 300–16; A. Gross, 'Contemporary Politics in Massinger',

SEL, 6 (1960), 279–90; Roma Gill, '"Necessitie of State": Massinger's *Believe as You List*', *ES*, 46 (1965), 407–16; J. A. Barish, 'Perkin Warbeck as Anti-History', *Essays in Criticism*, 20 (1970), 151–71; Philip Edwards, 'The Royal Pretenders in Massinger and Ford', *Essays and Studies*, 27 (1974), 18–36; Judith Doolin Spikes, 'The Elect Nation and the English History Play', *Renaissance Drama*, NS9 (1977), 117–48; Anne Barton, 'He that Plays the King, Ford's *Perkin Warbeck* and the Stuart History Play', in *English Drama: Forms and Development*, ed. M. Axton and R. Williams (London, 1977).

Cultural history is perhaps best left to historians, though their mistrust of literary and theatrical material omits an important dimension. Christopher Hill in the first chapter of *The Century of Revolution* (Edinburgh, 1961) provides a useful summary of the social and political issues of the pre-revolutionary period, and, in *The Intellectual Origins of the English Revolution* (Oxford, 1965), an interesting insight into some aspects of the contemporary intellectual consciousness. In *The English Civil War* (London, 1978) Robert Ashton extends his thesis about the interplay between conservatism and revolution, the opposition between an innovative court and a cautious country, to artistic as well as political considerations, providing a useful basis from which critical work on form as well as theme can be conducted. These studies inevitably focus on the cataclysm of the 1640s. More general works which bear on the preoccupations of drama are: F. J. Fisher, 'The Development of London as a Centre of Conspicuous Consumption in the 16th and 17th centuries', *Transactions of the Royal Historical Society*, 4th series (1948), 38–49; J. Hurstfield, 'Political Corruption in Early Modern England', *History*, 5 (1967), 16–34; Mervyn James, 'English Politics and the Concept of Honour, 1485–1642', *Past and Present*, supplement 3 (London, 1978); Lawrence Stone, *The Family, Sex and Marriage in England 1500–1800* (London, 1977).

CRITICISM

Purely critical writing in the sense of interpretation of individual plays and playwrights abounds and proliferates, and can be located in the bibliographies listed above. The main outline of critical opinion about this drama was laid down in late nineteenth- and early twentieth-century criticism, in particular in essays by T. S. Eliot on Massinger, Middleton, Beaumont and Fletcher, and Ford in *Elizabethan Essays* (London, 1934). A good deal of more recent evaluative criticism is simply an expansion of or a reaction to the judgements laid down there. Early criticism tended to discuss together, under the heading 'Elizabethan drama', the multifarious drama from Marlowe to Shirley. The modern trend towards chronological division was established by Una Ellis Fermor, *The Jacobean Drama* (London, 1936), and by F. S. Boas, who divided his history of the drama into separate volumes on the Tudor and Stuart drama, beginning his *Introduction to Stuart Drama* (Oxford, 1946) with 1613. Little separate general attention has been paid to Caroline drama with the exception of Alfred Harbage's important study of amateur playwrights and their works, *Cavalier Drama* (New York, 1936), which he subtitled 'An Historical and Critical Supplement to the Study of the Elizabethan and Restoration Stage'. Critical surveys which focus on a particular theatrical mode are W. W. Greg, *Pastoral Poetry and Pastoral Drama* (London, 1906) and, more recently, A. C. Kirsch, *Jacobean Dramatic Perspectives* (Charlottesville, Va., 1972). Kirsch presents tragi-comedy as the characteristic genre of Stuart drama, an approach shared by critics who place Fletcher at the centre of the period: Baldwin Maxwell, *Studies in Beaumont, Fletcher and Massinger* (New York, 1939); L. B. Wallis, *Fletcher, Beaumont and Company, Entertainers to the Jacobean Gentry* (New York, 1947); E. M. W. Waith, *The Patterns of Tragicomedy in Beaumont and Fletcher*, Yale Studies in English, 120 (New Haven, Conn., 1952); P. Edwards, 'The Danger Not the Death: The Art of John Fletcher', in *Jacobean Theatre*, Stratford-upon-Avon Studies, 1, ed. J. R. Brown and B. Harris (London, 1961), 159–77; and Clifford Leech, *The John Fletcher Plays* (London, 1962). A slight difference of emphasis occurs when the central dramatist and genre are differently identified, as in Clifford Leech, *John Ford and the Drama of His Time* (London, 1957); Joe Lee Davis, *The Sons of Ben* (Detroit, 1967); or Dorothy M. Farr, *Thomas Middleton and the Drama of Realism* (Edinburgh, 1973).

The principal dramatists of the period have been surveyed in single-volume critical biographies which are a useful starting point for a study of their works: R. J. Kaufmann, *Richard Brome: Caroline Playwright* (London, 1961); A. Harbage, *Sir William Davenant: Poet Venturer 1606–1668* (Philadelphia, 1935); Joan M. Sargeaunt, *John Ford* (London, 1935); A. M. Clark, *Thomas Heywood, Playwright and Miscellanist* (Oxford, 1931); L. J. Mills, *Peter Hausted, Playwright, Poet and Preacher*, Indiana University Publications, Humanities Series, 12 (1944); C. H. Herford and Percy Simpson, *Ben Jonson* (Oxford, 1925), I; Alfred Harbage, *Thomas Killigrew, Cavalier Dramatist, 1612–83* (Philadelphia, 1930); T. A. Dunn, *Philip Massinger, The Man and the Playwright* (London, 1957); R. H. Barker,

Thomas Middleton (New York, 1958); R. W. Vince, 'Thomas Nabbes and the Professional Drama 1630–1642' (unpublished Ph.D. dissertation, Northwestern University, 1968); A. H. Nason, *James Shirley, Dramatist: A Biographical and Critical Study* (New York, 1915).

IV The plays and the playwrights: 1642–60

GENERAL

Everyone studying this period has reason to be grateful to the seventeenth-century bookseller George Thomason. From the opening of the Long Parliament (3 November 1640) until the Coronation of Charles II (23 April 1661), he systematically tried to obtain a copy of every book, pamphlet or newspaper that appeared. Now in the British Library, his enormous collection, made still more valuable by his habit of dating each item as he acquired it, is the indispensable starting-point for all work on the literary history of the Civil War and Commonwealth. It contains most of the plays and pamphlets discussed in this chapter; most have not been reprinted and some exist in no other copy.

The first studies of mid-century drama to draw on the Thomason collection date from 1921. Both appeared in *SP*, 18 (1921): Thornton S. Graves, 'Notes on Puritanism and the Stage', 141–69, and Hyder S. Rollins, 'A Contribution to the History of English Commonwealth Drama', 267–333. See also Rollins's 'The Commonwealth Drama: Miscellaneous Notes' in *SP*, 20 (1923), 52–62. Allardyce Nicoll's 'Political Plays of the Restoration', *MLR*, 16 (1921), 224–42, is a survey rather than a critical study, but it draws attention to the existence of both pamphlet-plays and longer works like *The Rump*. Much useful information is also to be found in W. J. Lawrence, *Pre-Restoration Stage Studies* (Cambridge, Mass., 1927). Leslie Hotson's *The Commonwealth and Restoration Stage* (Cambridge, Mass., 1928), though sometimes queried in points of detail, has never been superseded. The political implications of much dramatic writing and publication in the period were first noted by Louis B. Wright in an important article, 'The Reading of Plays During the Puritan Revolution', *Huntington Library Bulletin*, 6 (1934), 73–108. Alfred Harbage's *Cavalier Drama* (New York and London, 1936, repr. New York, 1964) is still the only full-length critical study of the entire dramatic output of the Caroline and Commonwealth era. However, it can be supplemented and to some extent corrected by Clifford Leech, 'Private Performances and Amateur Theatricals

(Excluding the Academic Stage) from 1580 to 1660' (unpublished Ph.D. thesis, University of London, 1935), portions of which have appeared as separate articles.

Much recent research has concentrated on the end of the period and the events leading to the re-establishment of the professional stage. The useful studies are W. Van Lennep, 'The Death of the Red Bull', *Theatre Notebook*, 16 (1962), 126–34; John Freehafer, 'The Formation of the London Patent Companies in 1660', *Theatre Notebook*, 20 (1965), 6–30; and Gunnar Sorelius's answer to Freehafer, 'The Early History of the Restoration Theatre: Some Problems Reconsidered', *Theatre Notebook*, 33 (1979), 52–61. Margot Heinemann's *Puritanism and Theatre* (Cambridge, etc., 1980), though primarily concerned, as its subtitle indicates, with *Thomas Middleton and Opposition Drama under the Early Stuarts*, contains some discussion of post-1640 drama in its last two chapters; one of these is a revised version of her article, 'Popular Drama and Leveller Style – Richard Overton and John Harris', in *Rebels and Their Causes, Essays in Honour of A. L. Morton* (London, 1978), 69–92.

Special topics
The political journalism of this period, relevant to a study of the pamphlet-plays, is well covered in Joseph Frank, *The Beginnings of the English Newspaper, 1620–1660* (Cambridge, Mass., 1961). P. W. Thomas's study of the best-known of these journalists, *Sir John Berkenhead, 1617–1679, a Royalist Career in Politics and Polemics* (Oxford, 1969), provides valuable insight into the mentality of the royalist propagandists. The ballad-writers, some of whom were also involved in quasi-dramatic productions, are discussed in the introduction to Hyder S. Rollins's *Cavalier and Puritan, Ballads and Broadsides Illustrating the Period of the Great Rebellion 1640–1660* (New York, 1923); see also his 'Martin Parker, Ballad Monger', *MP*, 16 (1919), 449–74. The early operas are put into context in Edward J. Dent, *Foundations of English Opera* (Cambridge, 1928; repr. New York 1965); Eugene Haun, *But Hark! More Harmony, The Libretti of Restoration Opera in English* (Ypsilanti, Mich., 1971), has a useful opening chapter on Flecknoe, Jordan and Davenant, which examines their works in terms of their viability as texts for singing.

TEXTS AND CRITICISM

Most plays of this period can be found, if at all, only in expensive reprints and unpublished thesis editions. Davenant and Tatham have been edited by J. Maidment and W. H. Logan in the series Dramatists of the Restoration –

Davenant in five volumes (Edinburgh, 1872–4; reissued New York, 1964), Tatham in one volume (Edinburgh, 1879). Davenant's *Siege of Rhodes*, however, is available in several separate editions, of which the most recent is that of Ann-Mari Hedback (Uppsala, 1973). Mildmay Fane's *Raguaillo d'Oceano* and *Candy Restored* have been edited by Clifford Leech in Materials for Study of the Old English Drama, XV (Louvain, 1938; repr. Vaduz, 1963). The works of Cosmo Manuche are being edited by W. P. Williams, who rediscovered a number of seventeenth-century manuscripts, first mentioned by Bishop Percy in the eighteenth century, at Castle Ashby in 1977. Professor Williams is also co-editing the major pamphlet-plays of 1641–52, which are appearing in alternate issues of the journal *AEB* (*Analytical and Enumerative Bibliography*). Among the Castle Ashby manuscripts are a number which have been identified by Hilton Kelliher as the work of James Compton, third Earl of Northampton. Kelliher's account of these manuscripts – 'A Hitherto Unrecognized Cavalier Dramatist: James Compton, Third Earl of Northampton' – can be found in the *British Library Journal*, VI (1980), 158–87. The collection of drolls published by Francis Kirkman as *The Wits, or Sport upon Sport* (pt 1, 1662; pt 2, 1673) has been edited by J. J. Elson (Ithaca, N.Y., and London, 1932). Plays and fragments by Sir Thomas Salisbury of Lleweni are being edited by W. Reavley Gair and P. W. Thomas from manuscripts in the National Library of Wales.

There are a few post-seventeenth-century editions of individual dramatic texts. *A Pleasant and Merry Humour of a Rogue*, by William Cavendish, is transcribed by Francis Welbeck in the *Welbeck Miscellany*, I (1933). *The Concealed Fancies*, by Lady Jane Cavendish and Lady Elizabeth Brackley, Cavendish's daughters, was edited by N. C. Starr in *PMLA*, 46 (1931), 802–38. W. B. Gates reprints *The Enchanted Lovers* in his study of *The Dramatic Works of Sir William Lower* (Philadelphia, Pa., 1932). *A True Tragicomedy Lately Acted at Court* (1655–8) has been transcribed from the British Library MS by John Pitcher and Lois Potter, ascribed to Francis Osborne, and edited by Lois Potter in the series Renaissance Drama Texts, general editor Stephen Orgel (New York, 1981).

Among the anonymous plays, *The London Chanticleers* can be found in *Dodsley's Old Plays*, XII, ed. W. C. Hazlitt. *Tyrannical Government Anatomized* was edited by J. T. T. Brown in *George Buchanan: Glasgow Quatercentenary Studies* (Glasgow, 1907). An untitled masque of 1643, known under various editorial descriptions, has been published in an edition by Diane W. Strommer as *Time's Distractions* (College Station, Texas, 1976), but is best read, if possible, in the unpublished thesis edition

(University of Birmingham, 1950) by R. C. Elsely, under the title *Time's Triumph* (though he suggests that *Juno in Arcadia* would be preferable). Another anonymous piece of the same date, which used to be known only by its title, *The Cruel War*, was discovered and published by Jean Fuzier in *Cahiers Élisabéthains*, 14 (1978); it was identified as a parody of Shirley's *Triumph of Peace* by Jean Jacquot in the same journal, 15 (1979).

Apart from Davenant, Shirley and Killigrew (see above, pp. 324–5), the only dramatists from this period to receive book-length treatment are the picturesque Duke and Duchess of Newcastle, in the biography by H. T. E. Perry, *The First Duchess of Newcastle and Her Husband as Figures in Literary History* (Boston, Mass., and London, 1918; repr. 1968) and Douglas Grant's *Margaret the First* (London, 1957). Most of what has been written about other mid-century dramatists is biographical or bibliographical rather than critical. Three useful studies of the context and circumstances of authorship are: Cyrus L. Day, 'Thomas Randolph's Part in the Authorship of *Hey for Honesty*', *PMLA*, 41 (1926), 325–34; James O. Wood, 'Thomas Fuller's Oxford Interlude', *HLQ*, 17 (1954), 185–208; and John M. Wallace, 'The Case for Internal Evidence (10): The Date of John Tatham's *The Distracted State*', *Bulletin of the New York Public Library*, 64 (1960), 29–40. All available information about two interesting minor figures is summed up in H. E. Rollins, 'Samuel Sheppard and His Praise of Poets', *SP*, 24 (1927), 509–55, and Wayne H. Phelps, 'Cosmo Manuche, Royalist Playwright of the Commonwealth', *English Language Notes*, 16 (3) (1979), 207–11.

An intriguing side-issue of this period is the extent of quotation, allusion and plagiarism of the earlier drama in the works of later writers. Identification of these borrowings began as early as Gerard Langbaine's *Account of the English Dramatick Poets* (1691); Rollins's article on Sheppard and Charles R. Forker, 'Robert Baron's Use of Webster, Shakespeare, and Other Elizabethans', *Anglia*, 83 (1965), 176–98, study two of the most notorious practitioners of this art. A collection of passages from earlier dramatists, which appeared in 1655, is analysed in G. E. Bentley, 'John Cotgrave's *English Treasury of Wit and Language* and the Elizabethan Drama', *SP*, 40 (1943), 186–203. Bentley's *Shakespeare and Jonson*, 2 vols (Chicago, Ill., 1945) collects allusions to and imitations of these two writers in the seventeenth century, showing that they reached their peak in the 1650s. His account has been supplemented by that of Ernest Sirluck, 'Shakespeare and Jonson among the Pamphleteers of the First Civil War: Some Unreported Seventeenth-Century Allusions', *MP*, 52 (1955–6), 88–99.

Index